N.H. TECHNICAL INSTITUTE
LIBRARY
CONCORD, NH 03301

The Provincetown Players and the Culture of Modernity

The Provincetown Players was a major cultural institution in Greenwich Village from 1916 to 1922, when American Modernism was being conceived and developed. This study considers the group's vital role and its wider significance in twentieth-century American culture. Describing the varied and often contentious response to modernity among the Players, Murphy reveals the central contribution of the group of poets around Alfred Kreymborg's *Others* magazine, including William Carlos Williams, Wallace Stevens, Mina Loy, and Djuna Barnes, and such modernist artists as Marguerite and William Zorach, Charles Demuth, and Brör Nordfeldt, to the Players' developing modernist aesthetics. The impact of their modernist art and ideas on such central Provincetown figures as Eugene O'Neill, Susan Glaspell, and Edna St. Vincent Millay, and a second generation of artists, such as e. e. cummings and Edmund Wilson, who wrote plays for the Provincetown Playhouse, is evident in Murphy's close analysis of over thirty plays.

BRENDA MURPHY is Board of Trustees Distinguished Professor of English at the University of Connecticut. She is the author of *O'Neill: Long Day's Journey into Night* (2001), *Congressional Theatre: Dramatizing McCarthyism on Stage, Film and Television* (1999), *Miller: Death of a Salesman* (1995), *Tennessee Williams and Elia Kazan: A Collaboration in the Theatre* (1992), and *American Realism and American Drama, 1880–1940* (1987), all published by Cambridge University Press. She has edited *Understanding Death of a Salesman* (with Susan Abbotson, 1999), *The Cambridge Companion to American Women Playwrights* (1999), and *A Realist in the American Theatre: Selected Drama Criticism of William Dean Howells* (1992). She is the author of many articles and reviews on drama and American literature, which have appeared in such journals as *Modern Drama*, *Theatre Journal*, and *American Literature*, and she has contributed chapters to many titles in the *Cambridge Companions* series.

CAMBRIDGE STUDIES IN AMERICAN THEATRE AND DRAMA

General editor
DON B. WILMETH, *Brown University*

Advisory board
C. W. E. BIGSBY, *University of East Anglia*
C. LEE JENNER, *Independent critic and dramaturge*
BRUCE A. McCONACHIE, *University of Pittsburgh*
BRENDA MURPHY, *University of Connecticut*
LAURENCE SENELICK, *Tufts University*

The American theatre and its literature are attracting, after long neglect, the crucial attention of historians, theoreticians, and critics of the arts. Long a field for isolated research yet too frequently marginalized in the academy, the American theatre has always been a sensitive gauge of social pressures and public issues. Investigations into its myriad of shapes and manifestations are relevant to students of drama, theatre, literature, cultural experience, and political development.

The primary intent of this series is to set up a forum of important and original scholarship in and criticism of American theatre and drama in a cultural and social context. Inclusive by design, the series accommodates leading work in areas ranging from the study of drama as literature to theatre histories, theoretical explorations, production histories, and readings of more popular or para-theatrical forms. While maintaining a specific emphasis on theatre in the United States, the series welcomes work grounded broadly in cultural studies and narratives with interdisciplinary reach. Cambridge Studies in American Theatre and Drama thus provides a crossroads where historical, theoretical, literary, and biographical approaches meet and combine, promoting imaginative research in theatre and drama from a variety of new perspectives.

Books in the Series

1. SAMUEL HAY, *African American Theatre*
2. MARC ROBINSON, *The Other American Drama*
3. AMY GREEN, *The Revisionist Stage: American Directors Re-Invent the Classics*
4. JARED BROWN, *The Theatre in America during the Revolution*
5. SUSAN HARRIS SMITH, *American Drama: The Bastard Art*
6. MARK FEARNOW, *The American Stage and the Great Depression*
7. ROSEMARIE K. BANK, *Theatre Culture in America, 1825–1860*
8. DALE COCKRELL, *Demons of Disorder: Early Blackface Minstrels and Their World*
9. STEPHEN J. BOTTOMS, *The Theatre of Sam Shepard*
10. MICHAEL A. MORRISON, *John Barrymore: Shakespearean Actor*

11. BRENDA MURPHY, *Congressional Theatre: Dramatizing McCarthyism on Stage, Film, and Television*
12. JORGE HUERTA, *Chicano Drama: Performance, Society and Myth*
13. ROGER A. HALL, *Performing the American Frontier, 1870–1906*
14. BROOKS McNAMARA, *The New York Concert Saloon: The Devil's Own Nights*
15. S. E. WILMER, *Theatre, Society and the Nation: Staging American Identities*
16. JOHN H. HOUCHIN, *Censorship of the American Theatre in the Twentieth Century*
17. JOHN W. FRICK, *Theatre, Culture and Temperance Reform in Nineteenth-Century America*
18. ERROL G. HILL and JAMES V. HATCH, *A History of African American Theatre*
19. HEATHER S. NATHANS, *Early American Theatre from the Revolution to Thomas Jefferson*
20. BARRY B. WITHAM, *The Federal Theatre Project: A Case Study*
21. JULIA A. WALKER, *Expressionism and Modernism in the American Theatre: Bodies, Voices, Words*
22. JEFFREY H. RICHARDS, *Drama, Theatre, and Identity in the American New Republic*
23. BRENDA MURPHY, *The Provincetown Players and the Culture of Modernity*

The Provincetown Players and the Culture of Modernity

BRENDA MURPHY

CAMBRIDGE UNIVERSITY PRESS
Cambridge, New York, Melbourne, Madrid, Cape Town, Singapore, São Paulo

CAMBRIDGE UNIVERSITY PRESS
The Edinburgh Building, Cambridge CB2 2RU, UK

Published in the United States of America by Cambridge University Press, New York

www.cambridge.org
Information on this title: www.cambridge.org/9780521838528

© Brenda Murphy 2005

This book is in copyright. Subject to statutory exception
and to the provisions of relevant collective licensing agreements,
no reproduction of any part may take place without
the written permission of Cambridge University Press.

First published 2005

Printed in the United Kingdom at the University Press, Cambridge

A catalogue record for this book is available from the British Library

ISBN-13 978-0-521-83852-8 hardback
ISBN-10 0-521-83852-5 hardback

Cambridge University Press has no responsibility for
the persistence or accuracy of URLs for external or
third-party internet websites referred to in this book,
and does not guarantee that any content on such
websites is, or will remain, accurate or appropriate.

*For my favorite performers,
Aldo, Dante, Elaine, Katie, Kevin, Courtney, Andy, Janet, Jen,
and Mike*

Contents

	List of illustrations	*page* x
	Preface	xiii
	Acknowledgments	xviii
1	The founding: myth and history	1
2	The first plays	55
3	*Others* and the Other Players	101
4	Glaspell and O'Neill	160
5	The legacy	217
	Notes	238
	Bibliography	260
	Index	273

Illustrations

1. Hutchins Hapgood and Neith Boyce in *Enemies* (Yale Collection of American Literature, Beinecke Rare Book and Manuscript Library) — *page* 68
2. A scene from *Bound East for Cardiff* (Yale Collection of American Literature, Beinecke Rare Book and Manuscript Library) — 80
3. Marguerite Zorach's linoleum block rendering of *The Game* (Smithsonian American Art Museum, Washington DC/Art Resource, NY) — 98
4. A scene from *The Slave with Two Faces* (Billy Rose Theatre Collection, the New York Public Library for the Performing Arts, Astor, Lenox, and Tilden Foundations) — 127
5. Norma Millay and Harrison Dowd in a rehearsal for *Aria da Capo* (Billy Rose Theatre Collection, the New York Public Library for the Performing Arts, Astor, Lenox, and Tilden Foundations) — 150
6. The middle-passage scene from *The Emperor Jones* (Billy Rose Theatre Collection, the New York Public Library for the Performing Arts, Astor, Lenox, and Tilden Foundations) — 180
7. The auction scene from *The Emperor Jones* (Yale Collection of American Literature, Beinecke Rare Book and Manuscript Library) — 186
8. The expressionist set of *The Verge* (Billy Rose Theatre Collection, the New York Public Library for the Performing Arts, Astor, Lenox, and Tilden Foundations) — 197
9. The Fifth Avenue scene from *The Hairy Ape* (Billy Rose Theatre Collection, the New York Public Library for the Performing Arts, Astor, Lenox, and Tilden Foundations) — 209

10 Cleon Throckmorton's drawing for *The Crime in the Whistler Room* (Author's Collection) 227

The publisher would like to apologize for the poor quality of some of these early theatre photographs – every effort was made to make the reproduction as clear as possible.

Preface

ALONG WITH *THE MASSES* MAGAZINE, ALFRED STIEGLITZ'S Photo-Secession Gallery, known as 291, Mabel Dodge's famous salon, and the Armory Show of 1913, the Provincetown Players was one of the central cultural phenomena in New York's Greenwich Village during the period between 1912 and 1919 that is known as the Little Renaissance. To list the Provincetown's founding members is to chronicle the swiftly changing currents of American avant-garde thought during this period. Central among them were George Cram Cook, a professor of literature, sometime socialist, and philosophical monist who was devoted to the ideal of Dionysian primitivism and hoped to build a Utopian art collective in the Provincetown; John Reed, a Harvard graduate who was to be one of the founders of the Communist Party of the United States and to write a well-known eyewitness account of the Bolshevik Revolution in *Ten Days That Shook the World*; socialists Max Eastman and Floyd Dell, editors of *The Masses*; feminist journalist and labor activist, Mary Heaton Vorse; journalist and "philosophical anarchist" Hutchins Hapgood; fiction writers Susan Glaspell, Neith Boyce, and Wilbur Daniel Steele; feminist lawyer Ida Rauh; painters Charles Demuth, Brör Norfeldt, and Marguerite and William Zorach. Although the founding members shared an ideal of collective creation and a commitment to experimentation, originality, and the "New," they agreed about little else, and the spirit of freewheeling debate pervaded the Provincetown from its inception.

Despite its relatively short life, from 1916 to 1922, the Provincetown Players was the most significant and the most influential American theatre group of the early twentieth century. It was the first theatre group in the United States with a serious artistic agenda, which included the production of new plays by American playwrights and the employment of innovative and experimental production methods. The Provincetown's accomplishments in the theatre are many and varied, and they have been well documented. Major studies include Helen Deutsch and Stella Hanau's descriptive overview of the theatre's history, *The Provincetown: A Story of the Theatre* (1931); Robert K. Sarlós's study of George Cram Cook's shaping influence on the theatre from 1915 to 1922, *Jig Cook and the Provincetown Players: Theatre in Ferment* (1982), Cheryl Black's study of the women participants and the influence of first-wave feminism on the Players, *The Women of Provincetown, 1915–1922* (2002), and Barbara Ozieblo's *Susan Glaspell: A Critical Biography* (2000), which deals extensively with the Provincetown Players. This book builds gratefully on their work, but differs from it in that its focus is not on the Provincetown's role in theatre history, but on its wider significance in twentieth-century American culture, specifically the links between the theatre practitioners and the artists, writers, and thinkers who are associated with the development of the self-consciously modern American culture during the Little Renaissance that preceded a full-blown American Modernism in the arts.

Among writers, the Little Renaissance was characterized by a number of little magazines, ephemeral in nature, but important for the opportunity they gave to poets who were experimenting with what they called the "new verse." Among them were *The Glebe* and *Others*, which were edited by Alfred Kreymborg, who was to become, along with the painters and poets William and Marguerite Zorach, a key figure connecting the Provincetown with the new work that was being done in poetry and the other arts. Although it existed for only four years, *Others* published some of the most important work by many of the most significant American poets who are associated with modernism. It was Kreymborg who contributed the first modernist play to the Provincetown in 1916, *Lima Beans*, which featured *Others* poets William Carlos Williams and Mina Loy as actors. Besides Kreymborg himself, a number of the poets in the *Others* group would participate in the Provincetown Players, including Wallace Stevens, Maxwell Bodenheim, Djuna Barnes, William and Marguerite Zorach, Kathleen ("Kitty") Cannell, and Evelyn Scott. Once the *Others* group began producing plays, Edna St. Vincent Millay, already famous as both poet and actor, became part of the group, writing the most significant play to emerge from it, the anti-war fantasy *Aria da Capo* (1919).

The Provincetown Players lived a short, explosive, and very productive life. By 1922, when the group disbanded, it had produced 93 plays by 47 different American playwrights, and had nurtured the careers of Eugene O'Neill and Susan Glaspell as well as opening up the American theatre to theatrical idioms beyond the limits of realism. The original group was succeeded in Greenwich Village's Provincetown Playhouse by the Experimental Theatre, Inc., a group that included many of the Players and was run by what is known as the Triumvirate, Eugene O'Neill, designer Robert Edmond Jones, and producer Kenneth Macgowan. Under the new aegis, another wave of experimentation took place in what was now a fully formed and self-conscious modernist aesthetic. This included plays by O'Neill that he considered too experimental or too daring for Broadway, such as *All God's Chillun Got Wings*, *The Ancient Mariner*, *The Fountain*, and *Desire Under the Elms*, and plays by modernist writers such as Edmund Wilson and e. e. cummings. In the hands of its founders and subsequent members, the Provincetown Players became a cultural crucible in which the disparate and seemingly random ideas, aesthetics, and cultural values swirling around Greenwich Village in the teens and twenties were annealed into a practical aesthetics for the theatre. The effect of this process is evident not only in the group's own plays, but in the subsequent work of the many artists and thinkers who were members of the Provincetown, or who simply spent time at its theatre, its café, and its legendary parties, participating in the continuous discussion of political, social, and aesthetic ideas and values that was central to its identity. Young artists and intellectuals as disparate as Waldo and Florence Kiper Frank, Edmund Wilson, Sophie Treadwell, S. Foster Damon, Agnes De Mille, Mike Gold, Ann Sutherland, and John Huston gravitated to the Provincetown as naturally as they had gravitated to Greenwich Village, participating in a diverse, vociferous, contradictory, and productive community. This book records the process of creating an important element of cultural modernity that occurred at the Provincetown in the teens and twenties as these artists and intellectuals interacted and worked together, and suggests the impact that the aesthetic ideas formed within the Provincetown movement had on American culture, not only in drama and theatre, but in the fiction, poetry, criticism, and intellectual history of the twentieth century.

It should be emphasized that, while all of the members of the Provincetown Players were enthusiastic participants in the culture of modernity, or what they tended to refer to as the "New," whether in the arts, in philosophical, social, and political ideas, or in the living of their daily lives, they were not all committed to what was already being called "modernism" in 1915, particularly in the visual arts and poetry. Adele Heller and Lois Rudnick's *1915: The Cultural Moment* (1991) eloquently demonstrates the broad cultural context for modernity that existed when the Provincetown Players was being formed. Building on this foundation, the first chapter of this book lays out specific cultural influences on the group's founding members, from the ideas of William James, John Dewey, Sigmund Freud, and Friedrich Nietzsche, to their contemporary versions of anarchism and socialism, to the first-wave feminism in which many of the Players participated, to the aesthetic ideas ranging from the Ashcan School social realism of Robert Henri, John Sloan, and George Bellows to the Fauve and Cubist aesthetics that several of the members had brought back with them from Paris. This account is meant to show the extraordinary range of the founding Players within the culture of modernity, from extreme libertarianism to socialism in politics, and from social realism to pure formalism in art.

In the drama of the Players, this range of aesthetics tended to come down to a split between realist or representational drama and non-representational, or what they preferred to call "presentational," drama, that is, drama that did not pretend to represent anything but itself. In addition to its resistance to the mimetic, this non-representational drama had a number of characteristics that have come to be associated with modernism in the US: the use of myth, literature, or history as setting; fragmentation of the narrative trajectory; the abstraction of some characters into types or symbolic figures; the representation of a character's subjectivity on the stage, the theatrical equivalent of "stream of consciousness" in fiction; abstract, often symbolic set designs and costumes in which color and design were paramount; dialogue that was intended to be poetic, symbolic, and suggestive, rather than to approximate normal speech. As in the visual arts, the most noticeable characteristics of this drama were its abstraction from "the real" and the playwrights' and theatre artists' intention to synthesize all of the elements of the theatre into the creation of an organic, fully authentic and autonomous work of art.

While this study is focused mainly on the self-consciously modernist non-representational plays produced at the Provincetown Playhouse, one of its basic working assumptions is the importance of considering these plays in the context of the broader sense of modernity that prevailed among the Provincetown Players. The second chapter of this book considers all of the plays the Players produced in the important founding year of 1916. Chapter 3 details the important interrelationship between the Players and the group of poets around *Others* magazine, who were responsible for most of the modernist plays that were produced by the Provincetown Players, plays that helped propel Eugene O'Neill and

Susan Glaspell, the subject of chapter 4, in the modernist direction they took after 1916. Finally, chapter 5 suggests some of the ways in which the work of the Players influenced the development of modernism, both in the theatre and beyond it.

Acknowledgments

As always, my primary debt is to my husband, George Monteiro, who not only read every word of this manuscript and gave me the benefit of his wisdom and support throughout the project, but traveled with me to many libraries and archives, and on occasion even took notes. Don Wilmeth and Rebecca Jones have been exemplary editors, and I am grateful for their help. I am pleasantly indebted to my colleague, Glen MacLeod, for his excellent advice and to my gifted research assistant, Laurie Cella, for her unfailing good work and good humor. For providing the funds that made her help possible and for the funds that allowed me to travel to the libraries whose archives were indispensable to this study, I am grateful to the University of Connecticut Foundation. For the fellowship year that gave me the time to write the book, I am equally grateful to the National Endowment for the Humanities and to the University of Connecticut.

The research collections of a number of libraries have been indispensable to this project, in particular, the Billy Rose Theatre Collection, New York Public Library for the Performing Arts, and the Berg Collection, New York Public Library; the Harris Collection of the John Hay Library, Brown University; the Library of Congress; the Beinecke Rare Book and Manuscript Library, Yale University; the Harvard Theatre Collection; the Houghton Library, Harvard University; the Fales Library and Special Collections, New York University; the Charles E. Shain Library, Connecticut College; the University of Maryland Library; and most importantly, the libraries of my home institution, the University of Connecticut, particularly the Homer Babbidge Library and its Inter-Library Loan Division, and the Thomas R. Dodd Research Center. I am especially grateful to the many librarians and curators who have given me the benefit of their experience and expertise in the course of this project.

For permission to reprint photographs from their collections, I am grateful to the Billy Rose Theatre Collection, the New York Public Library, Astor, Lenox, and Tilden Foundations; the Smithsonian Institution; and the Beinecke Rare Book and Manuscript Library, Yale University.

I

The founding: myth and history

THE FOUNDING OF THE PROVINCETOWN PLAYERS IS AN EVENT that has grown beyond legend to assume the status of myth in the annals of the American theatre. Its significance is paramount because, as theatre historians have recognized, the Provincetown, with its nurturance of self-consciously literary American playwrights like Susan Glaspell, Edna St. Vincent Millay, and Eugene O'Neill, has come to represent a new conception of the theatre in the United States. The Provincetown is now seen as the major progenitor of experimental non-commercial theatre in America, the pioneering group that taught theatre practitioners how to develop, nurture, and practice theatre as an art in a country where theatre had always been almost exclusively a business. The growth of the Provincetown myth has been helped by the fact that, as Robert Sarlós has noted, "the group's first stirrings remain a mystery, about which many myths but few facts survive. Accounts, even by participants, are contradictory."[1] As early as 1931, the first published full-length history of the Provincetown, by Helen Deutsch and Stella Hanau, noted that the story of the founding in the summer of 1915 had been told so often that it was already assuming the form of legend:

> Magazines, newspapers, personal biographies, and histories of the theater have carried accounts of the picturesque beginnings until even the phraseology of the tale has become traditional; one always tells of Robert Edmond Jones' improvised settings by saying that "Bobby Jones made scenery from sofa cushions," and of the very first performance by saying, always in the inverted form, "two plays they had." Eugene O'Neill, at his first appearance, is always a "shy, dark boy."[2]

The myth-making actually began with the group's first publicity efforts, as it was moving toward becoming an organized entity and opening its theatre in New York, at the end of the summer of 1916. George Cram Cook, not yet the group's elected president, claimed the centrality that he would later insist on. "It was George Cram Cook's idea," the article reported:

> "Why shouldn't we have a little theatre and try out our new plays?" said [Cook] one day as they were all sunning on the beach after a swim. "Just the thing!" cried Jack Reed. "I've got two that I'd like to try next week." "Where shall we have the theatre?" said they. "Why not out there on the wharf?" suggested someone. An old sea captain was looked up and told they wanted to rent his old shed on the pier for a theatre. "That ain't no theatre," said he. "You wait and see!" said Freddie Burt.[3]

Even making allowances for the prevailing broad journalistic license to depart from the facts in the interest of a good story, it is evident from this account that Cook had ignored reality in order to create his own founding myth in speaking to the reporter. Jack Reed's plays were not submitted until the second summer. The first two plays staged by the group were *Suppressed Desires*, by Cook and his wife, the well-known novelist and short-story writer Susan Glaspell, and *Constancy*, by Neith Boyce, also a successful writer of fiction. They were put on at the home of Boyce and her husband, the journalist and philosophical anarchist Hutchins Hapgood. The idea of using the fish house at the end of a wharf, belonging not to an old sea captain, but to the writer and labor activist Mary Heaton Vorse and her husband Joe O'Brien, emerged only after the first performance at the Hapgoods' cottage. A letter from Boyce to her father-in-law, written two days after the performance on July 15, 1915, sheds a different light on the origin of the theatre group: "You will be amused to hear that I made my first appearance on the stage Thursday night!! I have been stirring up the people here to write and act some short plays – We began the season with one of mine. Bobby J[ones]. staged it on our verandah – The colors were orange and yellow against the sea … I have been highly complimented on my acting!!!"[4]

Probably because of Cook's later centrality to the group and the relatively early departure of Boyce and Hapgood, it is the Cook version that has become the master narrative. Robert Sarlós's standard history, *Jig Cook and the Provincetown Players*, reinforced the centrality of Cook, treating the Provincetown Players as "the theatrical experiment engendered by Cook."[5] Although his account acknowledges that the "first stirrings remain a mystery," it also suggests that "three factors in the group's birth are beyond dispute: the plays were first thought of as a profoundly therapeutic party-game for a small, close-knit group; the idea no sooner emerged than it materialized in the form of scripts; Jig Cook was *spiritus rector* before it all began."[6] This narrative suggests that, in the spirit of George "Jig" Cook's "infectious enthusiasm and dedication to spontaneous group creativity," the Greenwich Village artists and thinkers vacationing in Provincetown that summer "yielded as a group to a spontaneous urge to dramatize issues directly affecting their own lives."[7] This is an important part of the Cook founding myth because of his dedication to the Nietzschean idea of theatre as a Dionysian expression of the group spirit, brought into existence through the mediation of an artistic genius, Cook himself.

The emphasis on spontaneity and on the plays as a "profoundly therapeutic" party game for a group of friends may be slighting some other important factors. As Sarlós notes, there was a growing Little Theatre movement in the United States in 1915, and the people who so enthusiastically entered into the activity of the new theatre group in Provincetown were well aware of it, as well as the work of the European Art Theatres, several of which had brought productions to the US in the previous five years. To situate the contribution of the Provincetown in the context of the cultural moment, and to fully understand the cultural work its members intended to perform, it is important to take note of this performance history.

One of the most significant theatrical events in the second decade of the twentieth century was the American tour of Dublin's Abbey Players in 1911. The "Irish Players," which began their life as the Irish Literary Theatre, a company organized by William Butler Yeats, George Moore, and Edward Martyn to produce original plays by native playwrights, had grown into the Irish National Theatre, a company that not only served native playwrights, but was dedicated to some of the new impulses in the European Art Theatre, particularly those inspired by Edward Gordon Craig's call for a unifying synthesis of the theatrical elements in the production. Craig's desire to, as Sheldon Cheney described it in 1925, "substitute suggestion in place of imitation, simplicity in place of elaboration, expressiveness in place of showiness" and create "a definite spiritual or emotional relationship between the background and the action"[8] supplied an aesthetic basis for the simplified staging methods and naturalistic acting style that had developed by necessity within a company of dedicated amateurs with little producing capital.

Eugene O'Neill saw every one of the Irish Players' productions during their six weeks' residence at the Maxine Elliott Theatre in New York in 1911, and he later acknowledged that "it was seeing the Irish players for the first time that gave me a glimpse of my opportunity . . . I thought then and I still think that they demonstrated the possibilities of naturalistic acting better than any other company."[9] John Reed, at that time a young editor for *American* magazine, also saw the Abbey Players in New York.[10] The Midwesterners among the future Provincetown Players, including Cook and Floyd Dell, then his boss on the literary supplement of the Chicago *Evening News* and later to become assistant editor of *The Masses* under Max Eastman, saw the Irish Players in Chicago. Susan Glaspell wrote in her memoir of Cook that "quite possibly there would have been no Provincetown Players had there not been Irish Players. What [Cook] saw done for Irish life he wanted for American life – no stage conventions in the way of projecting with the humility of true feeling."[11] Dell wrote that it was "a wonderful experience" to "sit in the gallery night after night and see the rich world of [J. M.] Synge and Lady Gregory."[12] The Irish Players, with their amateur origins, their dedication to the drama as a literary art form, their cultural nationalism, their refusal to embrace theatrical convention, and their determination to break new ground in a broad spectrum of drama from the folk plays of Synge, Lady Gregory, and T. C. Murray to the modern, symbolic "Noh" theatre of Yeats, provided a strong precursor and direct model for the Provincetown Players. In their dedication to encouraging "the writing of American plays of real artistic, literary, and dramatic – as opposed to Broadway – merit,"[13] the Provincetown Players were carrying out an American version of the Abbey Players' mission.

A second manifestation of the Art Theatre movement in the experience of many future Provincetown Players was the Chicago Little Theatre, founded in 1912 by Maurice Browne and his wife Ellen Van Volkenburg. Several of the future founders of the Provincetown Players were in Chicago at the time, including the artist Brör Nordfeldt, who designed and built the set for the Little Theatre's production of *The Trojan Women* and acted in some productions, as well as Cook, Dell, and the Provincetown Players' chief play-reader Edna Kenton. They were all caught up in the enthusiasm surrounding the Little Theatre's productions. Browne was deeply influenced by Craig, and Dell's vivid memory twenty years later of the productions of plays by Shaw, Strindberg, Schnitzler, and Euripides testifies to the imaginative power of the theatre

Browne created in his tiny space in the Fine Arts Building across from Chicago's Art Institute. The awareness of the Chicago theatre's successful work and its impact on the city's cultural community was an important impetus in the direction that was taken very early in the career of the Provincetown Players, as were the Craig-influenced production ideas of Maurice Browne.

A more immediate influence on the Provincetown Players was the Paterson Pageant, which had been staged in 1913 in support of the silk workers' strike in Paterson, New Jersey. The moving force behind the pageant was John Reed, known to all of Greenwich Village as "Jack," who had been jailed along with a number of labor activists while he was in Paterson reporting on the strike for *The Masses* magazine. As Linda Nochlin has noted, Reed's Paterson Strike Pageant assumes its full importance only in the context of the more general pageant movement of its time in the US. Nineteen thirteen was something of a year of the pageant, when "the whole country was in the throes of a vigorous pageant renaissance, often referred to as the 'New Pageant Movement.'"[14] It was spearheaded by George Pierce Baker – whose teaching of modern drama and theatre had influenced Reed, Hutchins Hapgood, Robert Edmond Jones, and Eugene O'Neill at Harvard – and Percy MacKaye, "Harvard '97, leader of the 'civic theater' movement and pageant-master extraordinary."[15] The pageants of MacKaye and the civic theatre movement were largely patriotic and celebratory. Nochlin has noted that, in staging a pageant under the aegis of the International Workers of the World (IWW), whose actors were 1,200 striking workers, mainly immigrants, acting out the conditions that had prompted their strike, "Reed may be said to have turned the patriotic rhetoric, the well-meaning 'melting-pot' psychology of the do-gooder civic-theater leaders, back upon itself, revealing its idealistic vision of the immigrant workers' place in their new land for the sentimental cant that it was."[16]

The aesthetic principles of the pageant also foreshadow those of the Provincetown Players. As Martin Green has noted, "the historical ideal behind MacKaye's work was Greek theater, which exerted a guiding influence on both society and the state in ancient Greece. It reconciled the traditions of art with those of democracy."[17] This idea meshed with George Cram Cook's "Greek" ideal for the Provincetown Players, as a theatre that did the sacred work of ritual within a democratic community, by bringing it together through shared creative experience. Reed's biographer notes that Cook had sat "enthralled at the Paterson Pageant" long before he produced his "credo" for the Provincetown Players that "one man cannot produce drama. True drama is born only of one feeling animating all the members of a clan – a spirit shared by all and expressed by the few for the all."[18] Susan Glaspell wrote in her memoir that Reed infused the workers with "the energy of a great desire, and in their feeling of his oneness with them they forgot they were on a stage. That too was a night when we sat late and talked of what the theater might be."[19]

Others who were central to the Paterson Pageant were Robert Edmond Jones and the artist John Sloan, who designed and supervised the painting of the scenery, and Hutchins Hapgood, who chaired the panel of citizen advisors. They relied on their slight theatrical experience, mainly in shows at Harvard, and Reed's experience at working with crowds as a cheerleader, rather than seeking the help of professionals in putting on the pageant. The aim was the kind of authenticity, simplicity, and unity of effect that Gordon Craig and the practitioners of the New Stagecraft were calling for in Europe. A review in the *Survey Midmonthly* testifies to the fact that they were successful in these aims:

> The pageant was without staginess or apparent striving for theatrical effect. In fact, the offer of theatrical producers to help in "putting it on" was declined by those who wanted the workers' own simple action to impress the crowd. There was no complicated detail. The "episodes" – all with the same scenery, a great painted canvas mill building – showed: the workers dully going to work, entering the mill, and then rushing out a little later when the strike was called; picketing and police clubbing in front of the mill; the funeral of Modestino; the strikers giving their children for temporary keeping to "strike mothers" from other cities; and a typical strike meeting addressed by I. W. W. leaders.[20]

Mabel Dodge, who fell in love with Reed while working on the pageant, wrote that Jones "insisted on making it a Gordon Craig affair," noting that he staged the funeral procession and a street scene within the auditorium so that "for a few electric moments there was a terrible unity between all those people. They were one: the workers who had come to show their comrades what was happening across the river, and the workers who had come to see it. I have never felt such a high pulsing vibration in any gathering before or since."[21] The reviewer for the New York *Tribune* understood the connection between this pageant and the New Stagecraft, noting that "there was a startling touch of ultra-modernity – or rather of Futurism – in the Paterson strike pageant."[22]

The most immediate organizational precursors of the Provincetown Players were located in Greenwich Village, and were characterized by the direct participation of key figures among the founders of the Provincetown Players. The Liberal Club, "A Meeting Place for Those Interested in New Ideas," was an old New York institution which, shaken up by the new generation of Greenwich Village leftists in 1912, split apart over the issue of allowing "Negro" members and, under the leadership of Henrietta Rodman, located itself in a new headquarters at 137 Macdougal Street, off Washington Square. The new Club was "the center of much of the resurgence and renaissance associated with Greenwich Village during the flamboyant but fertile years between 1912 and 1918 ... in the five years of its turbulent existence [it] attracted most of the movers and shakers of the pre-war Village to its plays, parties, poetry readings, debates, demonstrations, dances, and art exhibitions."[23] The Liberal Club would come to function as the chief meeting place for the artists, writers, and leftist thinkers who were part of what has been characterized as the New York Little Renaissance, particularly those associated with *The Masses*, Alfred Stieglitz's Photo-Secession Gallery, known as 291, and the Provincetown Players. Among its members were future Provincetown Players Cook, Glaspell, Reed, Dell, Hapgood, Boyce, Eastman, Vorse, Ida Rauh, Alfred Kreymborg, Charles Demuth, Harry Kemp, Edna St. Vincent Millay, Frank Shay, and E. J. ("Teddy") and Stella Ballantine.

The dramatic wing of the Liberal Club was informally known as "The Dell Players" beause it featured plays written by Dell and staged under his direction. Dell, who had been "enraptured" by the work of the Chicago Little Theatre, had begun a play with the poet Arthur Davidson Ficke in Chicago, just before he left for New York. This play, invented over lunch and "called 'St. George of the Minute,' a satire upon 'modern' ideas," reemerged when Dell was asked "to write a play to produce at the housewarming of the Liberal Club" when it moved to Greenwich Village in 1913.[24] Renamed "St. George in Greenwich Village" and produced, as Dell said, "'in the Chinese manner', without scenery – also without a stage, curtains or footlights," the play was produced at the Liberal Club in November. Dell wrote that "the Village enjoyed being satirized, and this was a satire upon everything in which the Village believed."[25] Historian Steven Watson has suggested that the play "set the tone for the new Liberal Club. Presenting the Village through the eyes of a newcomer, Dell's play satirized modern ideas and

Constancy and Susan Glaspell and George Cram Cook's *Suppressed Desires*. Robert Edmond Jones created a simple set for the plays, staging *Constancy* on the verandah, and then having the audience turn their chairs around to view *Suppressed Desires*. Boyce and Joe O'Brien, the husband of Mary Heaton Vorse, played Moira and Rex in *Constancy*, a Shavian discussion play about the male–female dynamics within marriage. Cook and Glaspell played Stephen and Henrietta Brewser in *Suppressed Desires*, a satirical comedy about the new fad of Freudian psychoanalysis. The actors and the audience were so pleased with the experience that they decided to repeat the performance, adding two additional one-act plays to make a bill for which they could charge admission. O'Brien and Vorse owned a wharf with three buildings, one of which was emptied out, and its current tenant, the artist Margaret Steele, who was using it as a studio, was persuaded to vacate it in order to convert the building into a rude theatre, with a capacity of about 100.[33] The performance of *Constancy* and *Suppressed Desires* was repeated in August, and a second bill was produced on September 9. It included George Cram Cook's *Change Your Style*, a satirical comedy based on the running battle between the old-fashioned art schools in Provincetown and the young Post-Impressionist artists who had established their own summer colony there, and Wilbur Daniel Steele's *Contemporaries*, the dramatization of an incident in the previous winter when an IWW organizer, Frank Tannenbaum, had led a group of homeless men to take shelter in a Catholic church, only to be driven out by police at the request of the priests.

With Joe O'Brien's death in October, 1915, it was Cook who took over the plans to refurbish the theatre on the wharf. In the following summer, electricity was installed, an ingenious stage was built in sections that could be moved by hand, circus-style seating was installed, and the theatre was painted. A fire that charred two of the walls nearly delayed the opening, but artists Brör Nordfeldt and Charles Demuth quickly painted the other two walls a smoky shade of grey to match, and the theatre opened on July 13th. The bill included three one-act plays: a revival of *Suppressed Desires*; a new realistic play by Neith Boyce, *Winter's Night*, in which a woman refuses her brother-in-law's marriage proposal on the day of her husband's funeral, leading to his suicide; and John Reed's send-up of Tom Sawyeresque romanticism, *Freedom*. The second bill of the summer is a good indication of what the Provincetown Players was about to become. It included three one-act plays: Lousie Bryant's *The Game*, Wilbur Daniel Steele's *"Not Smart"*, and Eugene O'Neill's *Bound East for Cardiff*. Bryant's play, the subject of Stella Ballantine's notorious comment, "just because someone is sleeping with somebody is no reason we should do her play,"³⁴ is a fairly weak text. What made it interesting was the production, designed and executed by Marguerite and William Zorach as a Post-Impressionist theatre piece, integrating scenery, acting, and dialogue into a performance that showed the influence of Léon Bakst, and embodied the principles of the New Stagecraft as well as their own modernist aesthetics. Wilbur Steele's *"Not Smart"* proved to be one of the strongest of the more traditional plays the Provincetown Players did. A slight dramatic situation revolving around class and regional misunderstanding, it combines elements of the folk play with a sardonic comedy of manners that satisfied the Greenwich Village need to laugh at its own pretensions to liberal values. *Bound East for Cardiff* was recognized by the Provincetown Players and their audience as something truly original in 1916, a play that captured a new authenticity in its rejection of the theatrical conventions of what was currently considered realism. It called for just the artless simplicity they had all admired in the Irish Players and called on the unique assets of the Wharf Theatre. As Glaspell has described it: "The tide was in, and it washed under us and around, spraying through the holes in the floor, giving us the rhythm and the flavor of the sea while the big dying sailor talked to his friend Drisc of the life he had always wanted deep in the land, where you'd never see a ship or smell the sea."³⁵

The third bill, on August 8th, included a revival of *Constancy* and two new plays, Susan Glaspell's *Trifles* and John Reed's *The Eternal Quadrangle*. Glaspell's play has become part of the world repertory, and is widely recognized as a classic of the one-act play genre. Like *Bound East*, it capitalized on the theatre's simplicity and the artlessness of the amateur actors to achieve a realist aesthetic of directness and authenticity in exposing the life of Minnie Wright. These two plays together are a revealing index of the Provincetown Players' contribution to realism in the American theatre. Reed's play is a Shavian comedy on the subject of free love and open marriage. At one level it was assumed to be a response to the open secret in Provincetown of Louise Bryant's simultaneous sexual relationships with Reed and O'Neill. *Enemies*, a Strindbergian discussion play by Neith Boyce and Hutchins Hapgood about the incompatibility of the male and female principles in marriage, was also produced in the summer of 1916, as was Eugene O'Neill's symbolic play *Thirst*, in which he acted with Louise Bryant.

The plays of the summer were so well received that the group decided to try its fortunes as a Little Theatre in New York. A Constitution was drawn up by a committee of Reed, Cook, Eastman, and actor Frederick Burt, and ratified on September 5, 1916.[36] Cook was elected president with a salary of $25.00 per week and Margaret Nordfeldt secretary, at a salary of $18.00. The Executive Committee consisted of them and Floyd Dell, Louise Bryant, and John Reed. Among the other charter members were the writers Max Eastman, Susan Glaspell, Neith Boyce, Hutchins Hapgood, Lucy Huffaker, Mary Heaton Vorse, Wilbur Daniel Steele, and Eugene O'Neill; the actors Ida Rauh, E. J. Ballantine and Frederick Burt; and the painters Charles Demuth, Brör Nordfeldt, Margaret Steele, Marguerite Zorach, and William Zorach. The group was organized as a democratic collective, modeled on two institutions well known to the members, *The Masses* and the Washington Square Players. Article V stated that "the active members as a body" would determine what plays were to be produced and that "all other important questions" would be submitted to them by the Executive Committee.[37] In a series of "Resolutions" authored in lieu of by-laws by Reed, the group resolved that "it is the primary object of the Provincetown Players to encourage the writing of American plays of real artistic, literary and dramatic – as opposed to Broadway – merit" and "that such plays be considered without reference to their commercial value, since this theater is not to be run for pecuniary profit"; that "no play shall be considered unless the author will personally superintend the production at the theater in New York"; and "the President shall cooperate with the author in producing the play under the author's direction ... the author shall produce the play without hindrance, according to his own ideas." As in *Masses* editorial meetings, plays that were submitted were to be read aloud to all the active members, and a vote was to be taken on acceptance or rejection. The "Resolutions" provided that "a majority of active members shall at any time have the power to determine the method of reading and judging plays, whether by mass meeting as at present, or by the appointment of a play-reading committee or otherwise, always providing that no plan is introduced which shall take away the essential democratic control of the active members upon the material submitted."[38]

In his autobiography, Floyd Dell wrote of the enormity of the problem the *Masses* group was trying to solve in its open and democratic editorial meetings: "co-operation between artists, men of genius, egoists inevitably and rightfully, proud, sensitive, hurt by the world, each of them the head and center of some group, large or small, of admirers or devotees; now it seems to me an extraordinary triumph that so much good-humored and effective co-operation was possible between them." He ascribed the success of the *Masses* organization to "Max Eastman's tact and eloquence; he could talk anybody into doing anything."[39] By contrast, the attempt at a democratic organization in the Washington Square Players had been a failure. "After weeks of arguing, democracy got the worst of it, and a committee was set up which limited the decisions to a group of five persons who were thick-skinned enough to disagree continuously without losing their respect for one another."[40] This experience was prophetic for the Provincetown Players. Lucy Huffaker commented on "internal troubles already seething" within the group at the end of the summer, and there would be an escalating power struggle throughout their first New York season, ending with what came to be known as "the massacre" in March of 1917.

We are dependent on the reporting of Edna Kenton, an ardent Cook supporter, for an eyewitness account of that defining year in the group's organization, but even she gives a sense of the concerted drive to consolidate power in the hands of Cook and his allies. Noting that, by the 1921–1922 season, the Provincetown Players was run entirely by the executive committee of five, and that "three of these directors – yes, we were directors then! – could carry any question," she acknowledged that "the same three [Cook, Glaspell, and Kenton] voted together that year – they had to; it was the end of the great experiment." In her account, Kenton tended to gloss over the very real struggle that took place between Cook, Glaspell, and their allies, Ida Rauh and Don Corely, and the more radical group favoring a collective organization: Reed, Hapgood, Dell, Louise Bryant, Brör Nordfeldt and his wife Margaret, who was the group's first secretary–treasurer. O'Neill, with his personal reserve and his special status as the playwright the group had "discovered," managed to stay out of most of the battles, and to remain friendly with both sides. But it is clear that Cook moved very quickly with the help of Glaspell, Rauh, and Kenton to consolidate power within the group and become its "Director," rather than its President.

The first democratic process to go was group play selection in meetings resembling the editorial meetings at *The Masses*. After the second New York bill in November of 1916, this was put in the hands of a committee. Kenton was to become the committee chair, her only official role in the Provincetown Players, a role which was eventually made a paid position at Cook's urging. She wrote:

It was plain by now that our whole scheme of play-reading must be put on another basis than a 'democratic' one. We had tried to read plays aloud to the group twice a week. But the group had already rebelled against that boredom by staying away. So the selection of plays for the rest of that season went automatically into the hands of a small group of the faithful who read Sunday afternoons and decided in camera. The play files were open of course to all members, but as manuscripts tumbled in on us, we had to set up rules for reading and returning the plays to the files. And before rules, the group interest waned further. Susan Glaspell and I were the only members of the group who really read every play that came into us during those six years ... once established before a comfortable fire with a great stack of unread plays between us and with the door firmly locked to intruders, it was fun.[41]

The consolidation of power over the selection of plays was not quite as "automatic" as Kenton suggested. Hutchins Hapgood protested against the "usurping of the selection of plays by any person or 'committee' within the group."[42] Alfred Kreymborg, who became a member after the success of his play *Lima Beans* in 1916, wrote that, while he was allowed to read manuscripts and vote on them, he realized he "did not belong to the inner circle which guided their destinies," and that the play-reading committee's choice of the next bill of plays was "usually an arbitrary selection seconded or revised by the two or three most powerful members."[43]

During the first year, those most committed to the collective ideal resigned: Dell, who left in October of 1916, was replaced on the Executive Committee by Lucian Cary, an old friend of Cook's and Kenton's from Chicago, who had served along with Cook as an assistant to Dell on the literary supplement of the Chicago *Evening News*. Reed and Bryant, who resigned in February, 1917, because of their plans to go to China to cover World War I, were replaced on the Executive Committee by Cook partisans Edna Kenton and Ida Rauh. Brör Nordfeldt, the best known of the modernist artists in the group and the only one of the founders with real theatrical experience, had naturally been designated the head of the design committee. He was forced out of the Players because of his opposition to Cook and Ida Rauh, who had become fast friends, and probably lovers, in the fall of 1916. Like Cook, Nordfeldt had given countless hours and considerable labor to the new theatre in 1916. Besides contributing his design expertise, he had worked side by side with Cook in renovating both the Wharf Theatre and the new space the group rented at 139 Macdougal Street.[44] In New York, besides his own play, *Joined Together*, which unfortunately has not survived, Nordfeldt had designed Boyce and Hapgood's *Enemies* and David Pinsky's *The Dollar*, and co-designed O'Neill's *Fog*. He had acted in *Joined Together*, O'Neill's *Bound East for Cardiff*, John Reed's *Freedom*, and John Mosher's *Bored*. As the season went on, however, Nordfeldt made no secret of his complaints that "Jig and Ida were running things."[45] In February, he was replaced as head of the design committee by Don Corley, a new member who was devoted to Cook. What's more, as historian Cheryl Black puts it, Secretary–Treasurer "[Margaret] Nordfeldt's 'competent grasp of affairs,' ... conflicted with Cook's 'rapt idealism,' and she aroused his resentment by insisting that all receipts and expenditures pass through her hands. Tension between Nordfeldt and Cook escalated when her husband openly challenged the prominence of Cook and Rauh. Thus, when the Players demanded Brör Nordfeldt's resignation in March, 1917, Margaret Nordfeldt resigned as well."[46]

Nina Moise, who had joined the players as a much-needed professional director in early 1917, referred to the March meeting at which the Nordfeldt resignations occurred as "the massacre."[47] Kenton referred to the meeting at Ida Rauh's apartment as the end to the "sad struggles of months," at which the group "amended our constitution until it bore little resemblance to the document we had so trustingly adopted a few months before." As well as demanding Nordfeldt's resignation, the group accepted the resignations of Dell, Eastman, and Hapgood, and in Kenton's words, "descended on delinquents – the drones in the hive. We cleared away trees that had kept us from seeing the forest. Quorums were reduced to a drastic seven. Jig was elected 'President' again and the final word on the selection, casting and production of plays lay in the executive committee of five, two of these the officers and the others elected by the sadly reduced group."[48]

After the departure of the radicals Reed, Bryant, Dell, Eastman, and Hapgood, all that was needed at the March meeting was to consolidate the power of Cook's group. In March the executive committee consisted of Cook, Kenton, Rauh, Cary, and playwright David Carb. In the course of eight months, the Provincetown Players had become Cook's theatre, and few of the founders remained. The process of consolidation continued throughout the next year, so that by March, 1918, the active membership had fallen from twenty-nine to fourteen, and of the original members, only Cook, Glaspell, O'Neill, and Ida Rauh remained.[49] After the second New York season, even the committees were done away with, with the exception of the Executive Committee. There are no records of membership meetings after April, 1918. There is an irony in the legend, carefully cultivated by Susan Glaspell, that Cook was committed to amateurism. She wrote in *The Road to the Temple*: "He believed that the gifted amateur had possibilities which the professional may have lost. It was with an amateur group he worked in those early years; with no money, the only hold he had on them was through making them want to do it. It was his intensity that held the thing together."[50] In fact, he was the first "professional" in the theatre, as the first, along with secretary–treasurer Margaret Nordfeldt, to be paid, and he quickly consolidated the decision-making power in his hands. The amateurs who were not willing to devote themselves completely to his vision of the theatre were quickly dispatched, and the only founders who continued after the second year were the four people who were working very hard to build professional careers in the theatre, Cook among them. After feeling that Kenton had failed to give him enough credit in a publicity article, Cook saw that his title was changed from "president" to "director," and "Under the Direction of George Cram Cook" began to appear on the program under the title, "The Provincetown Players."[51] As Glaspell wrote of Cook, "his instinct as artist was for having its own way ... Sometimes Jig was about as true as a hurricane to the group ideal."[52] By the fall of 1918, the active membership of the Provincetown Players was down to twelve. The organization was moving toward further professionalism, with several paid positions. The character of the theatre had changed radically from the one envisioned by the vacationing Greenwich Village artists and writers in Provincetown in the summer of 1916.

Ideas and politics

The founders of the Provincetown Players were something of a *Who's Who* of the movement that has come to be known as the New York Little Renaissance, a group of writers, painters, and political intellectuals and activists who, as Arthur Wertheim wrote, "were linked together in a common cause to create a new American culture by overthrowing the genteel tradition." Viewing the culture of the nineteenth century as irrelevant and outdated, they "called for new writing and painting expressing the indigenous aspects of American life" and shared a spirit of "iconoclasm, modernism, and cultural nationalism."[53] Most of them knew each other from their interactions at such central Little Renaissance institutions as the Liberal Club and the adjacent Washington Square Bookshop owned by the Boni brothers,

The Masses, Alfred Stieglitz's 291 gallery, and Mabel Dodge's "evenings," where, aided by Hutchins Hapgood, she brought together the key figures in the disparate groups of New Yorkers who were seeking the "new," from intellectuals and writers like Hapgood, Eastman, and Dell to such artists as Marsden Hartley, John Marin, and Francis Picabia to political activists like Emma Goldman and Big Bill Heywood, in order to discuss art, politics, psychology, and every idea or movement that was certifiably "new."[54]

Located at 139, and later 133 Macdougal Street, next to the Liberal Club, the Provincetown Players became one of the central cultural institutions of the Little Renaissance, or the "Insurgence," as most of the participants called the early stirrings of modern culture in Greenwich Village. Its clubroom and restaurant were central gathering places, not only for active members, but for their friends, and, importantly, newcomers to the Village who came hoping to joining the Insurgence that they had been observing eagerly from the small towns and small cities to the West, South, and North of New York. The collective nature of the early Provincetown Players, in which all members were invited to attend rehearsals and offer suggestions about the productions, made for many discussions, often passionate ones, airing the aesthetic, ideological, and philosophical differences among the players. In order to fully appreciate the participation of the Provincetown Players in the Insurgent culture that was to be the basis of American cultural modernity, it is important to consider the cultural background the members brought with them to New York. It is typical of the Insurgent culture that almost none of the founding Provincetown Players were native New Yorkers. Although he was born in New York, the closest thing O'Neill had to a family home was in New London, Connecticut. Mary Heaton Vorse, from Amherst, Massachusetts, and Max Eastman, from Canandaigua, New York, were products of the rural village. Midwesterners Cook, Glaspell, and Dell had come from Davenport, Iowa, by way of Chicago. Hapgood grew up in Illinois and Boyce in Indiana and Los Angeles. Several members came from the far West: Marguerite Thompson Zorach from Fresno; John Reed and Louise Bryant from Portland, Oregon; Wilbur Steele from Denver. Brör Nordfeldt and William Zorach were both immigrants, from Sweden and Lithuania respectively, who had had impoverished boyhoods in Chicago and Cleveland, but managed to get to Paris to study art in their early twenties before moving to New York. In Greenwich Village, and more particularly in the Provincetown Players, these displaced outlanders who came to New York seeking a new, vibrant, and insurgent culture, found what they were looking for, and came together to create something new and uniquely theirs.

William James and John Dewey

Among the important cultural influences of the founding Players were several philosophers. Despite their disparate geographical beginnings, one key American institution that was shared by many of the Players, including Cook, Hapgood, Reed, O'Neill, and Robert Edmond Jones, was Harvard, and the most important thinker at Harvard for two generations of students was William James. Daniel Singal has suggested that "the two key figures in the process of importing the new culture to this country and giving it American roots were William James and John Dewey ... Embracing pluralism as a positive good, and grounding his own system of thought on the experiential basis of 'radical empiricism,' James became the first important American Modernist intellectual."[55] Historian Henry F. May called James "the greatest of the American relativists, and perhaps the central figure of American intellectual history in the early twentieth century."[56] James was unique, May thought, in that he "was at home in Europe and a part of European thought ... yet nobody could possibly be more uniquely American." James moved in both of the main directions that May identified in the culture of American modernity, "toward skeptical practicality and even materialism, and also toward an acceptance of the promptings of intuition and faith." In James, "all these contradictions were held together by an optimism only possible in this place and time – a rare and genuine enthusiasm for variety, change, and freedom, a faith that this was the proper and healthy condition of man."[57]

James had a powerful and direct influence on John Reed, who recorded his personal response to the philosopher in an early article reminiscing about a day spent with him in Cambridge.[58] Hapgood listed James among his most admired Harvard professors, and he wrote that

> the most valuable thing in William James's psychology was his conception of the stream of thought. The old conceptual psychology, the old idea of the faculties of the mind, as if they were fixed things rather than momentary aspects of a living flood, ceased to play a part. And those who knew Williams James felt the extraordinary unconventionality of his mind. Fixtures were not a part of his philosophy; he flowed.[59]

From James, Hapgood drew the principles on which much of his life was based, his devotion to philosophical anarchism in society and his pursuit of unlimited human experience in private life. His wife Neith Boyce wrote in her *Autobiography* of the youthful Hapgood: "Hutch's idea was that one should not resist life but meet all its calls, abandon one's self to it, that all experience was good, the more the better, that even pain was good. He quoted William James, that to refuse any call upon you was to limit your own life. He had made a philosophy out of his temperament and this to him was truth. He said often, 'I am right! I am telling you the truth!' And this with such utter conviction and insistence!"[60] The fundamental conflict between Boyce and Hapgood over this approach to life was to be dramatized in her play *Constancy*, and more emphatically, in *Enemies*, which they wrote and acted in together. It is also the leitmotif in Hapgood's well-known autobiography, *A Victorian in the Modern World*, which defines the fundamental conflict between the traditional values of the culture in which his generation was raised and the modern values of the early twentieth-century culture that he was helping to form. In his study of the relationship between anarchism and modernism, Allan Antliff has pointed out that "Hapgood's support for modernism as a 'dawning force' for individualism, diversity, and innovation" was an anarchist reading "rooted in the pragmatist philosophy of William James," who had linked pragmatism to anarchism in his first published essay on the subject. "When Hapgood declared himself an anarchist 'revolutionist' who questioned 'prevailing standards in art, politics, industry, literature and morality [because] they stand in the way of true progress and of intenser [sic] and fuller life for all of us,' he was, after a fashion, taking pragmatism to its logical political conclusion."[61]

Of the two predominant streams of American Modernist culture that Singal sees proceeding from James and Dewey, the Jamesian stream centers on "the individual consciousness, celebrates spontaneity, authenticity, and the probing of new realms of personal experience, and flows mainly through the arts and humanities." By contrast, the Deweyan stream tends to focus on "society as a whole, emphasizes the elimination of social barriers (geographic, economic, ethnic, racial, and gender), and tries to weld together reason and emotion in the service of programmatic social aims." Singal contends that, with each passing decade of the twentieth century, "these two streams have increasingly diverged, ultimately creating an important internal tension within American Modernism, but that fact should not be allowed to obscure their many close resemblances, particularly at the beginning."⁶² Hapgood was clearly allied with the Jamesian stream, as were most of the other Harvard graduates. John Reed graduated from Harvard in 1910 an enthusiastic devotee of Jamesian experience. The poet and radical Louis Untermeyer called Reed a composite of "Peck's bad boy, Don Giovanni, Don Quixote, Jack London, and the Playboy of the Western World.'"⁶³ In a sense, however, his short life was an embodiment of Jamesian experience. He threw himself into the Provincetown Players as he had into the Paterson pageant and many other activities. As a reporter, he not only observed but participated in the Mexican Revolution, the Paterson silk strike, World War I, and, most importantly, the Russian Revolution, the subject of his most important work, *Ten Days That Shook the World*. Reed's approach to experience led him to a life of activism with seeming inevitability.

Max Eastman and his feminist activist wife Ida Rauh are good examples of John Dewey's direct influence. Eastman had taken Dewey's course in logical theory and modern philosophy at Columbia, and had taught logic under his supervision. His own ideas were based on Dewey's. Arthur Wertheim noted that "Eastman preached a doctrine called scientific socialism, a political philosophy stressing applied logic and experimentalism, which was a radical version of Dewey's program of social engineering." Eastman admired pragmatism, he wrote, "'because it gave a biological foundation to my instinctive scepticism,' and could be applied to solving social problems. My socialism, 'was not a mystical cure-all, but merely a plan which I considered practical for solving the one specific problem of making freedom more general and democracy more democratic.'"⁶⁴ It is not surprising that Eastman found editing *The Masses* a more suitable activity than participating in the productions of the Provincetown Players. Although he did act in at least three plays, Cook's *Change Your Style*, Dell's *King Arthur's Socks*, and Steele's *Contemporaries*, he claims in his autobiography that his contribution to the Provincetown Players was "wilfully slight," and that in Provincetown he did little but pay his dues and "stroll around the wharf sometimes at rehearsals."⁶⁵ His disengagement may have had a more personal source as well. His marriage to Ida Rauh was ending in the summer of 1916, and she began an "intimate, probably sexual," relationship with Cook in the fall as they worked together in the theatre.⁶⁶ Early in their marriage, however, she was a committed radical engaged in socialist and feminist activities. Hutchins Hapgood thought that "Eastman's first interest in the social, political, and labor slant on things was due to Ida and her associations."⁶⁷

Cheryl Black notes that, although she was educated as a lawyer, "Rauh did not settle on a single career, but used her private income to finance various social causes, including the Women's Trade Union League, the National Labor Defense Fund, Heterodoxy, the Lucy Stone League, and the 'Women's Freedom Congress' of the Women's International League."[68]

Friedrich Nietzsche

As important as the Americans James and Dewey were to the founding Players, they were not the most pervasive philosophical influence on the group. This distinction goes to Friedrich Nietzsche. May has noted that "Of all the Europeans who repudiated the nineteenth-century world of scientific progress and moral advance, Nietzsche enjoyed the greatest popularity in prewar America." With the authorized translation of his complete works, 1909–1913, came a "burst of Nietzsche interpretation, praise and denunciation which continued until the war."[69] David Weir has pointed out the irony that "a philosopher who stresses the need for authoritarian politics should be embraced by a group of libertarians,"[70] but so it was. Floyd Dell, who, as a committed socialist, had no use for the Nietzschean vogue, found the deepest irony in what he saw as a reversal of the expected class response to the philosopher: "The aristocracy has betrayed the magnificent confidence he reposed in it; it has never even read its own philosopher. And the mob, instead of remaining content, as he wished it to do, with its doctrines of renunciation, has embraced to a large extent what is a Nietzschean creed: the revolutionary proletariat everywhere regards itself as an aristocracy, and arrogates to itself instinctively every defiant characteristic of the 'master morality'!"[71] In Dell's view, Nietzsche

> sought to provide the European aristocracy with a goal – the Superman; and with a code – adventurous and intense living. But on account of his obscurity this gospel has fallen into the hands of a class of self-appointed interpreters who are, in the main, inferior, dull, and base. So we have the spectacle of the splendid writings of Nietzsche – having the splendors of both great prose and great thought – being championed by heavy-handed oafs whose best feat is to imitate Nietzsche's mob-baiting in a kind of greasy Billingsgate.[72]

Unlike Dell, many self-professed socialists embraced the ideas of Nietzsche, often engaging in intellectual contortions to reconcile the two.

Max Eastman, for example, perhaps showed the colors of his later conservatism in his statement that Nietzsche "advocated the creation of a *genuine* aristocracy. And we may as well agree with him, I think, that that is what we want – not a morass of mediocrity, but an eminence, and also a lively dominance through sheer natural force and influence of the people of real ability and value."[73]

It was not so easy for George Cram Cook, who, back in Davenport, Iowa, had had to deal with Dell's critique of Nietzsche. Dell reported that "in our discussions [Cook] was converted from his Nietzschean–aristocratic–anarchist philosophy to Socialism, and brought by me in triumph to the local."[74] The conversion was not a complete one, however. Susan Glaspell remembered the relationship in a somewhat different light:

> The cock-sure young Socialist [Dell], for whom Herbert Spencer had synthetized [sic] knowledge, kept biting at this Nietzschean, anarchist, profound and lazy man of God, the way a terrier would worry a St. Bernard, who, having risked his life in being a noble dog, after the thrills and sorrows of the world, now, though in the hey-day of his strength, would like to lie for hours in the sun.[75]

Cook's novel *The Chasm* dramatizes the conflict between what Glaspell characterized as "the Socialist and the Nietzschean feeling about life."[76] It was not a conflict that he resolved in any definitive sense, but it is clear that he was much more attracted to Nietzsche than to socialism. Nietzsche's books had a very personal meaning for Cook. It was in reading *Ecce Homo* after a "nervous breakdown," probably an episode of clinical depression, in Iowa that Cook was deeply affected by Nietzsche. " 'In the slow pull back from the abyss, Friend Nietzsche held out a helping hand,' " he wrote. "One morning: 'Behold the sun! Cool sweet fragrant morning in my mind.' "[77] At another point he remarked that Nietzsche had saved his soul " 'from Tolstoi, Jesus, and Mr. and Mrs. Browning.' "[78] Fred Matthews has offered a revealing analysis of the particular appeal that the Nietzsche of *Ecce Homo* had for Cook:

> Its strident aphorisms champion triumphant, guilt-free selfhood against the suppression, conformism, and resulting intolerance of the Christian middle classes. Nietzsche's ideal of the liberated personality testing the limits of possibility anticipated Cook's love for classical Greece. For both men, the aristocracy of Homeric times was a model of masterful, 'truth-telling' transcendence, which Christianity had subordinated to a slave morality of caution, subservience, and hypocrisy.[79]

Nietzsche's philosophy had the effect of loosing Cook from the small-town constrictions he felt in Davenport, particularly after he returned home to run the family farm when he lost his teaching job at Stanford. Floyd Dell, his closest friend in this period, observed that Cook "had accepted the rôle of 'man of genius'" from his mother, who doted on her son and believed him supremely talented. But, Dell noted, "the 'man of genius' must accomplish something to prove his right to that title; and while awaiting the advent of powers mature enough to accomplish his masterpiece, he sinks insensibly to the fretful estate of an aesthete, who feels that his true home is in the Athens of Pericles or the Florence of the Medici. George Cook had gone through all that." It is "a miserable fate to be a non-producing 'man of genius' anywhere," Dell observed, "but it is perhaps worst of all in one's home town."[80]

With the discovery of Nietzsche, Cook found a philosophical basis for his own belief in his genius and a rationale for what he believed was his mission in life. He read through a German edition of Nietzsche's work while managing the farm, and held an ongoing discussion of his philosophy with his friend Rabbi Fineschreiber.[81] His intense identification with the Nietzschean concept of the Superman is evident from a journal entry he wrote on Memorial Day, 1912:

> My own mind has been enough like Nietzsche's for him to be one of the few writers with whom I imaginatively identify myself. My artistic passion is just now excited by the idea of showing as vital, as creative a temperament as this of Nietzsche, environed by American society in 1912 ... An American Renaissance of the Twentieth Century is not the task of ninety million people, but of one hundred. Does that not stir the blood of those who know they may be of that hundred?[82]

Later, after Cook and Glaspell had left the Provincetown Players and New York to live in Greece, Cook confessed to "a mean release just now reading 'Zarathustra.' I am glad to find that the great Nietzsche is in some respects my inferior ... I am truer than Nietzsche – not having quite that strain of irreconcilable elements and beliefs in myself."[83] In Davenport, however, Cook was avidly looking for a way to reconcile the attractions of Nietzsche with the socialist principles he was hearing from Dell. He wrote that those of the intellectual elite should "feel like reaching out to find each other – for strengthening of heart, for the generation of intercommunicating power, the kindling of communal intellectual passion."[84] He identified the mission of developing an American socialist society with the German national spirit of Wagner, the Latin spirit of d'Annunzio, the English Imperialist spirit of Kipling, the American democratic spirit of Whitman, the aristocratic culture spirit of Nietzsche. Isn't the Socialist spirit as deep as any of these? Isn't its spiritual significance even deeper? Isn't it there waiting for vital expression in art – subtle expression, so true, so beautiful, so *un*-antagonistic that it will *compel* – love?[85]

Although Nietzsche provided a rationale for, and a language to express, Cook's identification with the likes of Wagner, d'Annunzio, Kipling, and Whitman, he knew that his role was not that of the great artist or intellectual. Instead he saw himself as the leader of a movement, a group that would work together to realize his vision for society.

In the idea of a theatre, constituted as a modern version of the primitive Dionysian cult that Nietzsche describes in *The Birth of Tragedy*, Cook found the instrument he had been looking for. "To write alone will not content me," he realized. "The blood of backwoods statesmen is in my veins. I must act, organize, accomplish, embody my ideal in stubborn material things which must be shaped to it with energy, toil."[86] The awareness of his temperament combined well with the principle derived from Nietzsche that "'one man cannot produce drama. True drama is born only of one feeling animating all the members of a clan – a spirit shared by all and expressed by the few for the all. If there is nothing to take the place of the common religious purpose and passion of the primitive group, out of which the Dionysian dance was born, no new vital drama can arise in any people.'"[87] Robert Sarlós has formulated the conception of the kind of theatre Cook wanted the Provincetown Players to be:

> Jig's fusion of scholarship and life style rendered palpable to him the triple province of Dionysus – intoxication, sexual rites, and theatre: different forms of release from routine and mortality – which he saw not as a social safety valve, but rather as the basic building material of a creative community. Hence his agreement with Nietzsche that the supreme human achievement was tragedy, i.e., serious theatre capable of redeeming society, and that without untrammeled Dionysian ecstasy, sublime Apollinian [sic] order was unattainable.[88]

Sarlós contends that Cook's "heart was set on the realization of a beautiful paradox, a remote reflection of the glory that was Greece: if enough selfless people with manifold talents and aspirations can be forged into a cohesive group, not only will their pooled energies enhance each other, but … they will, by rotating artistic functions, stretch all their expressive abilities and create a total work of art while increasingly tightening their bonds." The result will be "creative ecstasy: a true community."[89] Cook's Nietzschean aspirations are evident in the leap that Sarlós sees him taking from the creative community of the little theatre to the culture as a whole: "their dreams and intoxication will mingle in the harmonious union of the Dionysian and Apollinian [sic]. And the healing creative ferment will spread forth its power from the group, giving release to 'our unrealized nation,' and through it, to all civilization."[90] Thus, the theatre Cook envisioned himself leading would be the American equivalent of Wagner's Bayreuth, a seminal cultural institution that would define a new civilization in the twentieth century.

Susan Glaspell's devotion to Nietzsche took a different form, but it had a similar origin to her husband's. Like Cook, Glaspell was frustrated and stifled by the small-town atmosphere of Davenport, and, unlike Cook, she did not have an adoring parent to encourage her aspirations for escape. In *The Road to the Temple*, she reports a girlish rebellion against her family's traditional values with some pride: "Declining to go to church with my parents in the morning, I would ostentatiously set out for the Monist society in the afternoon, down an obscure street which it seemed a little improper to be walking on, as everything was closed for Sunday, upstairs through a sort of side entrance over a saloon."[91] In 1907, when Dell and Cook founded the Monist Society, the thirty-year-old Glaspell had long been a self-supporting journalist and writer. Her biographer Barbara Ozieblo reports that "Glaspell's experiences in Des Moines and Chicago had led her to Darwin and Nietzsche, away from the Christian Church in which she had been raised."[92] According to Ozieblo, Glaspell's personal philosophy at this time was a combination of socialism with "a purely American idealism garnered from an amalgam of Emerson's transcendentalism, Nietzsche's overcoming, and [Ernst] Haeckel's oneness."[93] By the time Glaspell wrote her play *Inheritors* in 1920, she was, like Cook, deeply influenced by Nietzsche, particularly the "concepts of eternal recurrence and the will to overcome the self."[94] Glaspell's play *The Verge* (1921), a dramatization of the consequences of Nietzsche's concepts related to the Superman as they are lived out in the life of a woman of genius, is the most Nietzschean play the Provincetown Players produced, and, along with O'Neill's *Lazarus Laughed* (1928), the most Nietzschean of American plays. When Cook and Glaspell went to Greece, the one book Glaspell asked her friend Edna Kenton to send to her was *Thus Spake Zarathustra*.[95] Unlike Cook's, however, Glaspell's Nietzschean aspirations did not require that she be the visionary leader of a group. Her chief interest was in the artist as creative genius, and the heady danger of living on the edge between genius and madness.

Eugene O'Neill discovered Nietzsche when he was in his teens, frequenting the Unique Book Shop owned by the anarchist thinker Benjamin Tucker. At that time, he was equally interested in the anarchism of Kropotkin, Emma Goldman, and Tucker himself, the socialism of Shaw, and the Christianity of Tolstoy as in the writings of Nietzsche. As he grew older, his youthful radicalism died away, and his devotion to Nietzsche became more intense. In 1928, when O'Neill was asked by an interviewer who his literary idol was, he replied, "the answer to that is in one word – Nietzsche."[96] The most important of Nietzsche's books for O'Neill was *Thus Spake Zarathustra*. In 1927, he wrote to fellow Nietzschean Benjamin De Casseres that the book had "influenced me more than any book I've ever read. I ran into it, through the bookshop of Benjamin Tucker, the old philosophical anarchist, when I was eighteen and I've always possessed a copy since then and every year or so I reread it and am never disappointed." He noted that in 1927 there were "aspects of its teaching I no longer concede."[97] But this was by no means the only one of Nietzsche's works O'Neill studied carefully. His second wife Agnes Boulton said that he read and made copious notations in several of Nietzsche's works during the Provincetown Players years, and he had a "worn copy" of *The Birth of Tragedy* in his pocket during an interview with Barrett Clark in 1926.[98]

Nietzsche's influence on Eugene O'Neill was probably greater than on any other English-speaking playwright. Beyond the simple provision of ideas and motifs, Gerhard Hoffman has pointed out that Nietzsche furnished O'Neill with the thematic framework for many of his plays, with general patterns of contrast and polarity among his characters, with the recurrent plot of suffering and redemption, and even with specific formal elements like the use of masks and laughter as expressive dramatic means. Critics have noted the influence of Nietzsche in *Desire Under the Elms* (1924), *Strange Interlude* (1928), *Mourning Becomes Electra* (1931), *The Fountain* (1925), and other plays,[99] but it is more evident in two tragedies written during O'Neill's most intense period of modernist experimentation: *The Great God Brown* (1926) and *Lazarus Laughed* (1928).

Monism and mysticism

Hutchins Hapgood was fond of quoting William James's observation on the popular philosophical phenomenon of monism at the turn of the century: "Criticizing the usual metaphysical conception of monism, or the reduction of all things to one principle or substance, he said emotionally: 'I cannot understand this wild swooning desire to wallow in unbridled unity.'"[100] A wild, swooning desire seems to be just what was behind this popular phenomenon, and it had its effect on the highly tuned emotions of the Provincetown Players, particularly the Davenport, Iowa, group. Henry May wrote that prewar Midwestern rebels who came to New York during the Little Renaissance brought with them two seemingly contradictory cultural legacies: "One was the emotional inheritance of mystical, evangelical small-town religion. The other, apparently opposite, was the region's widespread, untheoretical radicalism."[101] Floyd Dell wrote of a "native American mysticism" in Davenport, "a curious religious expression of romantic libertarian ideas," which George Cook had absorbed from his mother.[102] Dell did not know how much of a mystic his friend was. Glaspell includes in her memoir of Cook his description of a mystical experience at the age of sixteen, in which "the Macrocosm was of one stuff with his own conscious self. He, the microcosm, was not different in kind from the great self of which earth and stars were but the multiform shadow. It was no mere algebraic perception of an abstraction this – it was vision. As truly as Plotinus, as truly as Jesus, this modern boy saw God – saw and loved and felt himself beloved."[103]

The immediate source for this mystical monistic view of the universe, of course, was American Transcendentalism. If the members of the Provincetown Players shared the experience of one philosophical text, it was the essays of Ralph Waldo Emerson. At the turn of the century, Emerson served many ideologies and world views. The philosophical anarchists claimed Emerson and Thoreau "as their ideological kin."[104] Their writings were included in the literature classes at the anarchist Ferrer Center. According to Dell, the *Masses* radicals found "a mass of libertarian eloquence" in the poetry of Whitman, the "burning advice of Emerson to be uncompromising, the invective of Thoreau upon the spirit of social conformity – a veritable arsenal of swordlike thoughts with which to fit youth out for its first struggles with whatever tyrannies of traditional society it might meet."[105] The young artists William Zorach and Marguerite Thompson, writing to each other while they were painting in different regions of France during the summer of 1911, exchanged passionate views on a long passage of Emerson that Zorach had copied out, and the failure of most people to "enjoy an original relation to the universe."[106] As a teenager in Davenport, Cook read Emerson between baseball games. Dell adopted as his maxim "a sentence from Emerson to the effect that whatever one was afraid to do was the thing for him to do."[107] Glaspell expressed an "Emersonian idealism" in much of her early fiction, as well as "an Emersonian need to be at one with nature" in her first novel, *The Glory of the Conquered* (1909).[108]

As pervasive as transcendentalism was, it was pretty much taken for granted by the prewar generation, and its capacity for generating excitement had been taken over by the newest form of monist thought, that of Ernst Haeckel. A great popularizer of a monist conception of the universe, in 1899 Haeckel published a bestselling book that was to be translated and often reprinted, called *The Riddle of the Universe*. Haeckel's popular philosophy "drew together energy and matter, life and nonlife, man and animals into a great, mysterious unity. Man, the earth, and the sun were surely mortal, but to Haeckel the great sum of things was not; worlds would go on indefinitely dying and being born." Yet Haeckel's creed was a secular one. He was an uncompromising iconoclast, who "delighted to repudiate purpose, freedom, personal immortality, and especially that 'gaseous vertebrate' god."[109] Monism's popularity as a secular religion grew quickly. May notes that in 1913 thousands of people were leaving German churches to support Haeckel's doctrines in monist societies. In the United States, monism was spread largely though the efforts of Paul Carrus, a German immigrant who, subsidized by a Chicago manufacturer, published scientific and philosophical texts supporting the monist view as well as the magazine *Open Court* and the journal *Philosophical Monist*. Monism came to Davenport, Iowa, when Floyd Dell proposed that the "society of freethinkers" being formed in 1907 be called the Monist Society, "for the propagation," Cook wrote a friend, "of our philosophy in the guise of religion, or religion in the guise of philosophy."[110] Dell and Cook first became friends over their shared enthusiasm for Haeckel's philosophy, and it was at the Monist Society meetings that they came to know Susan Glaspell.[111] In her memoir of Cook, Glaspell printed some of the laws of monism, as interpreted by the Davenport Society. One of them was to be a thematic principle behind her and Cook's play, *Tickless Time*: "From the last tick of the clock to that moment millions of years ago when the first particle of the oldest stratified rock sank through the sea to its place, the laws of the world have not changed. And this is Monism."[112] Others of the monist principles read like transcendentalism with the divinity removed:

> The mind of man is not distinct from the rest of the universe. It is one form of the one nature.

God did not create the one nature. It is eternal. No particle of it has ever perished or ever will. And this is Monism.
God did not create man. Man rose in nature as one form of nature – even as sun and earth. And this is Monism!
He arose as rain falls, as light travels, as systems revolve, as atoms link.[113]

As Henry May has noted, "readers of Emerson could swallow Haeckel's conclusions without much trouble."[114]

One other monistic thinker whose influence should be mentioned is the gay anarchist Edward Carpenter, whose *Love's Coming of Age, a Series of Papers on the Relations Between the Sexes* (1911) was as much of interest to many of the founding Players as his *The Art of Creation* (1904). Carpenter wrote of "cosmic consciousness" as "a state of mind akin to Buddhist enlightenment in which the distinction between 'the ego and the external world, and the distinction between subject and object, fall away,' and the self achieved unity with the infinite. This consciousness was emotional rather than intellectual; the rationalizing intellect maintained the illusionary separation of subject and object that blinded individuals to a hidden monist reality that needed to be *felt*." In Carpenter's words, "'There is a consciousness in which the subject and the object are felt, are *known*, to be united and one – in which the Self is felt to *be* the object perceived [...] or at least in which the subject and object are felt to be parts of the same being, of the same including Self of all.'"[115]

Psychology

Sigmund Freud's famous lectures at Clark University in September, 1909, and the translation and publication of some of his work by A. A. Brill in 1909 and 1910 set off an explosion of interest in the new theories of psychoanalysis, particularly among the devotees of the "New" in Greenwich Village. As Sanford Gifford has noted, "for psychoanalysis, Freud's Clark lectures were the equivalent of the 1913 Armory Show for the history of modern painting in the United States."[116] Floyd Dell and Max Eastman were among the earliest, most enthusiastic and most knowledgeable proponents of Freudian psychology. Both were psychoanalyzed, Eastman by Smith Jelliffe in 1914 and Dell by Samuel A. Tannenbaum in 1917.[117] Dell, who had first encountered Freud in Chicago through Sherwood Anderson, found that psychoanalysis was already a fad when he came to Greenwich Village in 1913. He wrote several articles for a popular audience about Freud's ideas and their vogue among intellectuals. The tone of his treatment is evident from an article he wrote for *Vanity Fair*:

> Psycho-analysis is the greatest discovery made by intellectual conversationalists since Bergson and the I. W. W. Nothing quite so provocative of argument has happened since Nietzsche. As a science it has been going on quietly this score of years or more. But as a topic of polite conversation, it first saw the light of day a short while ago in the throbbing studios of Washington Square, where it immediately implanted [sic] Cubism, Imagism, and Havelock Ellis.[118]

Eastman also wrote articles explaining Freud to a popular audience, in both *The Masses*, and the mass magazine, *Everybody's*, where he published two articles in 1915 that focused on case studies to show how Freud's theories could be applied to everyday life.[119] Intrigued by Freud's ideas, but not enough to commit themselves to psychoanalysis, were Eugene O'Neill and Hutchins Hapgood. On advice from Robert Edmond Jones, who was under Jelliffe's treatment for depression, O'Neill consulted him for help with his alcoholism and his relationship with his wife Agnes, but saw him only a few times.[120] Hapgood wrote that he had been "busily engaged all my life in confessing to my friends, especially my wife, and, as far as I could, the world, so I had no need either of the confessional or the psychoanalyst" and claimed to have "performed a psychoanalysis" on himself at one point.[121] Hapgood gave a good sense of the extent to which the popular formulation of Freud's ideas by writers like Dell and Eastman had permeated Greenwich village in the teens:

> Psychoanalysis had been overdone to such an extent that nobody could say anything about a dream, no matter how colorless it was, without his friends' winking at one another and wondering how he could have been so indiscreet. Freud's scientific imagination certainly enriched the field of psychology and was a great moment in our knowledge of the unconscious. But every Tom, Dick, and Harry in those days was misinterpreting and misapplying the general ideas underlying analysis. It was a typical case of the natural exaggeration of a new set of thoughts, making them often ridiculous.[122]

Susan Glaspell remarked that, in the Village of the early teens, "you could not go out to buy a bun without hearing of some one's complex."[123]

Glaspell and Cook's resistance to the Freudian vogue is expressed in the mockery of their first play for the Provincetown Players, *Suppressed Desires*.

Fred Matthews has noted that, "when we apply the phrase New Psychology to Cook, it refers to Nietzsche rather than to Freud, Jung, the behaviorists, or the later Americanized psychoanalysis which stressed adjustment to an environment taken as given. There were important continuities between Nietzsche and Freud; the latter acknowledged the philosopher as his great anticipator. But Cook's and Glaspell's mocking attitude toward popular psychoanalysis reflects the difference between Nietzschean transcendence and the more analytic and therapeutic stance of the Freudians."[124] Floyd Dell took a less theoretical view of what he called Cook's fear of "intimate talk." He suggested that Cook was feeling a great deal of guilt over leaving his children in Iowa in order to begin his new life with Glaspell in New York, as well as being faced with the fact that he had not accomplished the great things he had expected to by then, and was essentially living on his wife's earnings in the Village. In Dell's view, "he wished to romanticise and glorify and justify himself; that was his best escape from the dark avenue of thought, at the end of which he would sit, in black and silent gloom, twisting his forelock, facing Failure." In *Suppressed Desires*, he thought, Cook and Glaspell "collaborated upon a little comedy … in which they attacked psychoanalysis as the enemy of marital happiness."[125]

Social and political thought

Anarchism and socialism

Several of the founding Provincetown Players, including George Cram Cook, Eugene O'Neill, and Hutchins Hapgood, considered themselves anarchists at some time during their lives, and a number of the Players were attracted by aspects of anarchist thought. This was particularly true during the first two decades of the twentieth century, when anarchism enjoyed a considerable vogue among intellectuals, who found in its principles a reasonable philosophical and political alternative to the progressive ideology, which they did not think was radical enough to make the necessary changes in the United States' social and political organization, and the socialist ideology, for which their intense iconoclasm and individualism made most of them unfit. Because the post-World War I campaign to depict all anarchists as wild-eyed, bomb-throwing terrorists was so successful, it is important to remember that before the war, anarchism was important as a philosophy and social theory for many people who had no thought of taking up arms to bring down the government, but worked for a gradual change that would free the individual from what they thought were the oppressive laws and social constraints of the modern state and allow all individuals to become "self-determining and value-creating."[126]

The philosophical anarchists anchored their political thought in an Enlightenment belief in the ultimate perfectibility of society. Believing that the modern state, in its insistence on assuming dominion over its citizens, was a corruption of the natural state of harmony among free and equal human beings, the anarchist sought political and social change that would serve the two ends of individual freedom and collective harmony. To the most radical, this meant doing away with the state completely through violent means. To the anarchist syndicalist, it meant replacing the current government with a great labor union, in which all members wielded equal power. As Richard Sonn has put it, "'anarchists were *revolutionaries* in the original sense of the term … they wished to "revolve" back to a more harmonious society. The anarchist rejection of contemporary society was nearly total; their proposed alternative fused elements of a remembered past with a vision of a utopian future.'" Thus, writes David Weir, "the anarchist idea of liberal progress includes a component of romantic regress."[127] By the end of the nineteenth century, Weir notes, "the combination of enlightenment and romantic values that marks the origins of anarchist thought yield two distinct strains of anarchism, one communistic, the other individualistic."[128] Hutchins Hapgood, the chief mainstream spokesperson for philosophical anarchism, placed it squarely in the tradition of American libertarian thought:

> From a political point of view my anarchism was identical with the philosophy of Thomas Jefferson – that that government is best which governs the least; or with that of Goethe, who said that government is best which gets rid of itself. From a moral point of view, my anarchism was that of Tolstoy's non-resistance to evil, the psychological force of which is the most powerful of all in the field. Socially, it meant a willingness to receive hospitably whatever dawning forces there may be in the submerged; a refusal to deny their possible validity in a more complex society. It denies, since it doesn't depend upon force, the philosophy of that anarchism which is politically revolutionary. It is deeply sympathetic with the psychology of the underdog, but it doesn't desire that the underdog should be an upper dog.[129]

Of particular interest where the founding Players are concerned are recent analyses by David Weir and Allan Antliff of the significant connections between anarchist thought and modernist art. Antliff goes so far as to suggest that "anarchism was *the* formative force lending coherence and direction to modernism in the United States between 1908 and 1920,"[130] while Weir contends that "anarchist ideology and modernist culture have something in common that keeps them apart ... radical politics and radical art usually proceed along different lines in the modernist period, a certain shared sensibility notwithstanding."[131] Noting the enthusiasm with which anarchists like Hapgood praised the modernist art in the Armory Show, Antliff suggests that their support "was unequivocally tied to individualism, freedom of expression, and formal experimentation, all of which were pitted against the academic system, its 'dead' aesthetics of beauty, and insistence on the imitation of nature."[132] Weir notes that "anarchist theory allows absolute freedom to artists to paint as they please, without regard for political content, notwithstanding the fact that most anarchists preferred their art to be transparently propagandistic." Taking anarchist philosophy to its logical end, he finds little difference between political principles and aesthetic ones:

> Modernist art, especially in America, is anarchist by association only. That is, people who called themselves anarchists liked it, and they liked it not only because it was new, but also because the bourgeoisie did not. As a result, one minute the lively, documentary realism of the Ashcan School was anarchist art, the next minute the abstract compositions of the fauvists and cubists were. The only aesthetic principle that can accommodate such an extreme shift of taste is radical newness compounded by bourgeois aversion: to be anarchistic, then, culture need only be "advanced."[133]

Weir suggests that anarchist thought was ultimately merged into modernist aesthetics:

> In one sense, anarchy and culture diverged early in the twentieth century, with politics and art separated into their respective areas of social and aesthetic concerns. In another sense, however, these concerns converged, especially among those artists who found in the individualist tradition of anarchism a political cognate for their aesthetic tendencies. As the politics of anarchism declined and were eclipsed by nationalism and socialism, the heterogenous, fragmented culture that emerged at the same time looked a lot like anarchism. Anarchism succeeded, not as politics, but as aesthetics.[134]

Hapgood was an enthusiastic supporter of the modern art movement. The art criticism in his columns in the *New York Globe* register his excitement, beginning with the first exhibit of Rodin drawings at Stieglitz's 291 and building through the Armory Show.[135] The merging of the philosophical and political ideals of anarchism with what he saw as the aesthetics of modern art are evident in what he wrote of the Armory Show: "It makes us live more abundantly . . . will help us all to understand more deeply what happens to us in life – to understand better our love and our work, our ambitions and our antipathies, and our ideals in politics and society."[136] Casting an inclusive net, he claimed as anarchists Rodin, Picasso, Max Weber, and Arthur Dove. He "deftly linked anarchism, antiacademism, and formalist experimentation, drawing the modernists associated with 291 into the same matrix of revolt as [Robert] Henri."[137]

Cook's anarchism was very much of the Romantic primitive school, which sought a Utopian social organization in a return to Nature. Its best expression is probably in "The Needle and the North," a piece of fiction he wrote while he was still in Iowa. The heroine of this book says to the philosophical hero, "'I am afraid you are an anarchist,'" and he reflects, "possibly, but he does not like the word – a negative word suggesting chaos, and we want to come into the beautiful cosmos that is life." Calling attention to a moonlit apple tree, he says:

> "I believe in naturocracy . . . There is no chaos in that city of blossoms. You know of those tiny golden lovers, the grains of pollen, lovers who are also love-letters. They are Argonauts who sail on their airships, the bees, to wed the maiden pistils. They have no law but the law of their own nature, and – Behold the tree! There shall be a humanity like that! There shall be people who discover and obey the fine sure laws that lie within, knowing themselves as from one great law in which all is formed. Panarchy! Or shall we say pantheocracy – the power of Nature, untrammeled by the little laws that malform our lives."[138]

While the libertarian end of the anarchist spectrum was the most congenial to many of the Provincetown Players, there was a collective spirit in anarchism that appealed to Cook as well, fueling his dream of founding an ideal Dionysian community. There actually were several committed socialists among the founding Players, including Eastman, Dell, Reed, and Cook, in some moods. Eastman's "scientific socialism," discussed earlier, was probably the most fully considered version of socialism among the group. Ida Rauh shared her husband's socialist views at this time. Floyd Dell, who had been converted to socialism at the age of sixteen when he was working in a factory in Quincy, Illinois, probably came by his convictions most honestly. By the time he came to Greenwich Village, however, he had spent time in Chicago divided between the bohemia of the art colony where he lived and the bourgeois atmosphere of the arts weekly he edited for the Chicago *Evening News*. He had taken to the decadent pose of wearing a high collar and carrying a walking stick, which he quickly dropped in favor of flannel shirts and corduroy jackets when he got to Greenwich Village, but the intensity of his early socialist convictions had been somewhat dissipated. As noted earlier, it was Dell who claimed to have converted the Nietzschean Cook to socialism after he had come to Davenport and was working as a newspaper reporter. Although the collective socialist ideal met a good deal of resistance in Cook's devotion to Nietzsche and his temperament, there is evidence that he entertained it seriously. In 1912, he wrote an article for *The Masses* entitled "Socialism the Issue in 1912," in which he said, "in spite of its apparent concern with material well being only, the Socialist demand springs out of one of the deepest spiritual needs of man – the need to work creatively in freedom."[139]

Under Eastman and Dell's editorship, socialism was the official political stance of *The Masses*. According to John Reed's biographer, it was seeing their editorial statement, "promising a magazine devoted both to 'free and spirited expressions of every kind' and to the cause of socialism" that convinced him to throw in his lot with the magazine in December of 1912, for he had been looking for a publication that "would attempt to answer unformulated questions about the relationship between radicalism and art."[140] At this time, Susan Glaspell was also interested in radical politics. Her major commitment was to feminism, but in 1914, "she declared in print her allegiance to socialism" as well as woman suffrage.[141]

Unlike the anarchists, the socialists did not take well to the new modernist art. The major conflict over the direction of the arts in the US at the time of the Armory Show was between the European-influenced moderns associated with Stieglitz's gallery, such as Arthur Dove, Marsden Hartley, John Marin, and Max Weber, and the realist school associated with Robert Henri, John Sloan, George Bellows, and their colleagues of the Ashcan School, who sought to break the grip of bourgeois taste on the conception of beauty and art at the same time that they called attention to the aspects of American life that had been willfully ignored by the genteel tradition by introducing a gritty new subject matter and painting it with disturbing honesty. The Ashcan School was the art of

The Masses, and its aesthetic was realistic. As Arthur Wertheim has noted, most socialists did not approve of modernist art:

> Many radical writers felt that the modernists lacked social awareness and were too interested in technique. Although certain socialists like Dell and [James] Oppenheim defended the new poetry, others such as Eastman had conservative literary tastes and condemned the modern verse as sloppy formless writing ... Except for a shared feeling of revolt from the genteel tradition, the era's two movements of socialism and modernism remained aesthetically at odds.[142]

This tension between realism and modernism was to emerge in the Provincetown Players in several forms.

Feminism

As Cheryl Black has noted in her study *The Women of Provincetown*, "the modern feminist movement was born in Greenwich Village in the 1910s, and a considerable number of Provincetown's members, male and female, were at the forefront of the movement."[143] According to historian Nancy Cott, "the very rapid and intense gravitation toward the term Feminism about 1913" signaled a "new phase in thinking about women's emancipation" that distinguished it both from the suffragist movement and from the older Woman Movement of the nineteenth century. The use of the term feminism, notes Cott, "was an explicit and semantic effort to exceed the bound of – to insist on goals more profound than – the rising advocacy of woman suffrage. 'All feminists are suffragists, but not all suffragists are feminists,' explained a participant."[144] Edna Kenton, who joined the Provincetown Players in 1916 soon after its founding, was one of the enthusiastic spokeswomen for the new movement. "Feminism," she wrote, designated "a troop of departures from the established order of women's lives."[145] Winifred Harper Cooley wrote in the popular *Harper's Weekly* that the goal of the new movement was a "'complete social revolution': freedom for all forms of women's active expression, elimination of all structural and psychological handicaps to women's economic independence, an end to the double standard of sexual morality, release from constraining sexual stereotypes, and opportunity to shine in every civic and professional capacity."[146] The Feminist Alliance, a Greenwich Village organization to which many of the founding Players belonged, declared in its 1914 platform: "Feminism is a movement, which demands the removal of all social, political, economic, and other discriminations which are based upon sex, and the award of all rights and duties in all fields on the basis of individual capacity alone."[147]

Cheryl Black has documented the centrality of women in the Provincetown Players, in all capacities from the creative to the managerial:

> More than 120 women were associated with the Provincetown Players. Of those, approximately 40 were important, regularly active members who performed a multiplicity of functions. Thirteen of the company's 29 founders were women; 16 of its 51 playwrights were women; 7 of its 19 executive committee members were women; 6 of its 28 scenic designers were women; its leading costume designer was a woman; its leading actor was a woman; and its leading director was a woman. The company's best-known female member, playwright Susan Glaspell, was second only to Eugene O'Neill in productivity and critical reputation.[148]

The thirteen women among the founding Players were an extraordinary self-selected group. As Black notes, they were "the first generation of American women to reap the benefits of greater educational and professional opportunities." Mostly middle-class in origin, they had rejected their traditional privileged backgrounds and were "far to the left of the 'progressive' political continuum and overwhelmingly committed to feminism." Almost all of them were well-educated, independent professionals "working as writers, painters, poets, doctors, journalists, actors, and restaurant and shop owners. They were extraordinary women, widely talented, rich in experience, and intellectually, artistically, and personally adventurous."[149] As active members of the new feminist movement, the women of the Provincetown "were pursuing a formidable objective: to revolutionize all human relationships – to create a new world. Their every aspiration, including their desire to create an experimental theatre company, can best be understood as part of that objective."[150]

What made the Provincetown Players such a unique cultural formation, however, was that the new feminism was not restricted to the women members. Floyd Dell's feminist credentials went back to his days in Chicago, when he wrote a series of newspaper articles on important feminists and woman reformers. This became his book, *Women as World Builders: Studies in Modern Feminism* (1913). According to Arthur Wertheim, "Dell was among the most dedicated feminists on *The Masses* ... the influential works of Edward Carpenter, Ellen Key, and Havelock Ellis arguing for women's independence and a freer morality stimulated his desire to support the feminist movement."[151] As Wertheim has noted, however, "Dell might admire the new woman, but he basically feared the consequences of her independence." Many of his novels with feminist characters "end with the heroine adjusting to society through marriage and domesticity. Their conclusions show the effects of Dell's psychoanalysis and his postwar conservatism."[152] The pattern was similar for many of the male Players, who affirmed the prevailing feminist ideology while they never overcame a deep psychological resistance to the perceived threat of the new, emancipated woman. Hutchins Hapgood wrote of Neith Boyce and her fellow female newspaper reporters in the early years of the twentieth century: "These and many other young women of the day enjoyed the same spirit as the young men; they suggested the French Bohemia of Mürger, and yet were the equals of their men-friends."[153] Betraying an underlying conflict that would be explored in much of his wife's work, however, Hapgood wrote with approval that, unlike their daughters of the 1920s, "these young women in New York, with the sense of economic liberty, were still deeply held by the traditions of womanly restraint and by the unconscious belief that the ceremony was a necessary condition to love-affairs."[154] Both Hapgood and Dell believed in exploring a new freedom in sexual relationships between men and women, but the freedom was to be largely restricted to the men. Both men, like Max Eastman and George Cram Cook, were well known for the extent of their experiments with sexual intimacy outside of their marriages, but none were willing to grant the same range of experience to their wives. Although he claimed in his sexual autobiography that he desired to have his wife "know other men intimately" in the interest of "greater social relations between her and me, of a richer material for conversation and for a common life together," Hapgood became "very jealous, even violent" when his wife revealed her attractions to other men to him, although he habitually had love affairs with women that he discussed with her.[155] Cook was widely believed to be sexually involved with Ida Rauh, Louise Bryant, and Edna St. Vincent Millay at various times, often encouraging Glaspell to stay in Provincetown and write while he was in New York. Barbara Ozieblo has suggested that "Cook even accepted Nietzsche's perception of woman as the toy of man, although he camouflaged it with current (male) feminist convictions."[156]

One aspect of their lives where the Provincetown men did have a feminist outlook that was very advanced for their time was in child-rearing and domestic duties. Hapgood was a devoted parent, and was much more involved in the daily rearing of his children than was typical at the time.[157] William Zorach has described his somewhat reluctant coming around to Marguerite's feminist ideas about parenting and other domestic duties:

> There is a tendency among men to transform the loved one into a mother image, or at least to seek to identify the two. I had that tendency but Marguerite would have none of it. She was not going to be any man's mother. To her, marriage was partnership; share and share alike, the good, the bad, the difficult, the joys – all of life and living. If one partner possessed a particular quality or ability he should use it for the common good. Work ideas, accomplishments were to be shared ... she felt that the care of the house and children was the responsibility of both of us. I evidently had sewed on buttons and darned my own socks when I was a boy at home. These jobs she never took over nor did she ever look after my personal belongings ... since we both worked at home in the same studio with two children under our feet, we both took care of the house and children.[158]

Few couples were as collaborative as the Zorachs, in art or in life, but the sense that it was appropriate and "modern" for men to be involved in the domestic sphere, particularly in the raising of the children, was a prevailing attitude among the Players. There were exceptions, of course. O'Neill, for example, had no interest in the domestic, and paid little attention to his children when they were young, except to complain about the bother they caused. Cook, who was very enthusiastic about having his children join him and Glaspell for the summers, tended to leave the day-to-day care of them to their stepmother.

Finally, it must be remembered that most of these people had upper-middle-class origins. They expected to have servants to take care of the drudgery of running a house, and almost all of them were provided with at least a cook or a maid-of-all-work, even when they were on vacation in Provincetown. Wilbur Steele's *"Not Smart"* dramatizes the ironic disconnect between some of their leftist values and the traditional attitudes and expectations that were part of the middle-class cultural baggage they brought with them to bohemia. With the exception, perhaps, of the Zorachs', their households were run in a fairly traditional middle-class way. The difference was that the women in them were all professionals who carved the time and space from domestic duties to do their outside work as well as raising children and carrying on what seems to have been a non-stop social life revolving around organizations like Heterodoxy, the Liberal Club, and the Provincetown Players.

Aesthetic ideas

In terms of cultural and aesthetic resources, the two summer seasons that began the Provincetown Players were the richest the group was ever to have. Besides many of the advanced intellectuals of the day, well-known writers like John Reed and Wilbur Daniel Steele, and the budding playwrights Susan Glaspell and Eugene O'Neill, the Players also included significant avant-garde artists in Charles Demuth, B. J. O. Nordfeldt, and Marguerite and William Zorach. The interaction and collaboration of this eclectic and independent group produced some interesting productions, but it is perhaps more interesting as a working model for the production of art in the context of the "Insurgence" of the Little Renaissance.

Gerhard Bach's 1978 description of "three phases of dramatic development" in the Provincetown Players' existence has established the paradigm for the standard historical narrative of the company's aesthetics. Bach described an "initial phase of social realism, leading to the phase of realism vs. symbolism (or the realistic prose play vs. the symbolistic verse play), leading again into the last phase of renewed social realism interspersed with experiments in expressionism."[159] Bach wrote of a "group of playwrights," including Cook, Glaspell, and John Reed, that was characterized by "socio-historical awareness" and "attempted almost unanimously to depict, criticize, and satirize contemporary social ills and to propagate liberalism and a moderate radicalism."[160] The fact that Bach included John Reed's fanciful allegory "Freedom" as an example of "kitchen-sink realism intermingled with traditional idealism"[161] indicates that he had not based his generalizations completely on close analysis of the plays. His characterization of the second phase has been challenged by Barbara Ozieblo. Bach wrote of "an internal war of experimentation between the forces favoring an idealism based on socio-realistic outlook and the forces favoring an idealism completely devoid of contemporary concerns and tending to symbolic representations of more timeless concerns such as 'love and despair,' 'beauty,' death', etc." and contended that "the more pragmatic idealism (again probably due to Cook's influence) survived the battle – which in retrospect is deplorable, since Edna St. Vincent Millay had as much potential for dramatic symbolism as Susan Glaspell had for realism."[162] Ozieblo has taken issue with this reading of the Players' history, contending that "Bach's charge that the Provincetown Players stifled the poetic drama emerging among its members is unfounded."

She noted that "Cook, O'Neill, and Glaspell gradually turned away from realism," and "even in their own work, they were ready to experiment with new forms and styles."[163] While Bach's attempt to fit the aesthetic development of the Provincetown Players neatly into three historical phases does not hold up when the plays and productions are examined closely, he does identify one significant tension within the Provincetown Players' aesthetics, between, broadly speaking, realist or representational art and non-realist or presentational art. I would differ from Bach, however, in suggesting that this tension was not generational, that it was present from the very beginning of the Players, and that it was seminal to the development both of the drama and theatre produced by the Provincetown Players and of modernist art in the US. In order to understand the dynamics of these two impulses in the Provincetown Players, it is important to look more closely at the aesthetic currents in the theatre and the arts in the US of 1915.

One unique circumstance that divided the American theatre from that of Western Europe in the early twentieth century was that literary and aesthetic realism had appeared later on the scene in the US than in Europe. A major publicity campaign by such solidly respectable literary figures as Hamlin Garland and Willliam Dean Howells was necessary to make the realism of James A. Herne's *Margaret Fleming* acceptable to a Boston audience in 1891. American audiences were still being shocked by Ibsen when Alla Nazimova brought her *Hedda Gabler* to New York in 1907. The cast of Shaw's *Mrs Warren's Profession* was jailed for indecency in 1905. Literary and theatrical realism was far from the norm in the American theatre of the early twentieth century, which was for the most part dependent on the conventional dramaturgy of the "well-made play" and the formula melodrama, the spectacular staging effects epitomized in the productions of David Belasco, and the highly artificial acting techniques that had been established in the nineteenth century. For the most part, the founding Players were rather contemptuous of the Broadway theatre. Hapgood, who was full of enthusiasm for the Yiddish theatre, would write of "the meaningless theatricalism of the Broadway theatres" of the time.[164] And Susan Glaspell, who attended the theatre a good deal in 1913 and 1914 because Cook often reviewed plays in the "Letter from New York" he did for the Chicago *Evening News*, wrote:

> We went to the theater, and for the most part we came away wishing we had gone somewhere else. Those were the days when Broadway

flourished almost unchallenged. Plays, like magazine stories, were patterned. They might be pretty good within themselves, seldom did they open out to – where it surprised or thrilled your spirit to follow. They didn't ask much of *you*, those plays. Having paid for your seat, the thing was all done for you, and your mind came out where it went in, only tireder. An audience, Jig said, had imagination. What was this 'Broadway,' which could make a thing as interesting as life into a thing as dull as a Broadway play?[165]

When the founding Players began putting on their own one-act plays in 1915, realistic dramas that reflected the aesthetics of Shaw's *Quintessence of Ibsenism* (1891), of Howells's drama criticism in popular middle-brow periodicals such as *Atlantic Monthly*, *Harper's Monthly*, and *Harper's Weekly*, and of the more leftist realism of Hamlin Garland and *The Arena* magazine, were still new enough to be controversial. But they were not absent from the New York commercial theatre. The previous decade had seen Edward Sheldon's *Salvation Nell* (1908), Eugene Walter's *The Easiest Way* (1908), and Rachel Crothers's *Ourselves* (1913), plays that attempted to relinquish the current sensationalism of plays about the "white slave trade" to dramatize the lives of young impoverished urban women in realistic terms. An American "drama of discussion" analogous to Shaw's could be seen in plays like Crothers's *A Man's World* (1908) and *The Three of Us* (1906), and Augustus Thomas's *As a Man Thinks* (1911). Although it was a small part of the theatrical scene, a context for aesthetic realism existed on the New York stage, both in the native drama and in European touring companies.

Among the plays that were produced by the Provincetown Players during their first two summer seasons in 1915 and 1916, a wide range of current realist aesthetics was reflected. The more old-fashioned of the realistic plays were comedies like Cook and Glaspell's *Suppressed Desires* and *Change Your Style*. These plays in the comedy-of-manners tradition are reminiscent of the popular literary one-act comedies by William Dean Howells that were published in magazines like *Harper's Monthly* during the 1890s and had become the staples of amateur theatricals in the years since. They were a species of coterie drama, more aesthetically ambitious and further reaching in scope than Floyd Dell's *St. George in Greenwich Village*, but still drawing much of their impact from ridiculing the current intellectual and artistic enthusiasms of their friends in Greenwich Village and Provincetown. It was this quality that led to the rejection of *Suppressed Desires* by the Washington Square Players as "too special" for their repertory. Wilbur Steele's *Contemporaries* has many of the qualities of the best urban realism of the time, which was meant to expose the inequities of contemporary society by representing the lives of those who were most victimized by it with unblinking authenticity, but the play's trick ending betrays its origins in Steele's and O. Henry's sentimental magazine fiction. Similarly, Steele's *"Not Smart"*, which goes beyond local color to dramatize the gulf of misunderstanding between the liberal summer people and the local people they employed as servants, depends ultimately on a pun. Reed's *The Eternal Quadrangle* is an example of the American version of Shaw. It combines witty and entertaining dialogue with what is meant to be a shockingly practical proposal for alleviating the sexual double standard. Plays that were more in line with the most sophisticated contemporary writing about dramatic realism by Howells and others, in that they eschewed the artificiality and conventionality of the typical Broadway plot and sought new and authentic dialogue for characters who represented ordinary people with psychological depth, were those like O'Neill's *Bound East for Cardiff*, Boyce's *Winter's Night*, and Glaspell's *Trifles*. Others, like Boyce's *Constancy* and her collaboration with her husband, *Enemies*, drew on the aesthetics of Shaw's drama of discussion and on Strindberg's naturalism to produce what are essentially staged dialogues or monologues revealing the dynamics of contemporary relationships by using the slightest of dramatic situations to provide a realistic framework.

Related to the complicated state of realistic aesthetics in the theatre and other aspects of American art and culture was the relationship between representational and what the artists themselves called presentational aesthetics in the development of modernism within the visual, plastic, and theatrical arts. The early connection between anarchist politics and modernist aesthetics within such groups as that around Stieglitz's 291, as well as the influence of *The Masses* on American avant-garde thinking, meant that early modern art in the US was more political than that in Europe, and therefore tended more toward the representational than the formalist. The conventional historical narrative of the Little Renaissance is that the realistic art of painters like Robert Henri, John Sloan, and George Bellows, associated with the Ashcan School, *The Masses* and the Group of Eight, which, in 1908, mounted the most important avant-garde art show prior to the Armory Show of 1913, was displaced as the reigning avant garde by the discovery of European trends such as Fauvism and Cubism and the rise of American "Post-Impressionism," a term that was used by the artists themselves to mean any form of presentational aesthetics in American art between about 1912 and the end of World War I. Arthur Wertheim notes that two events in 1908 were "crucial to the development of twentieth-century art":

> One was the famous Eight Show held at the Macbeth Gallery. Another was the first exhibition of modern art in America at Stieglitz's Gallery 291 when he displayed fifty-eight drawings by Auguste Rodin. Both the 291 modern artists and The Eight rebelled against the outdated traditions of the National Academy of Design and wanted to broaden the base of American painting. Compared to The Eight, the Stieglitz group was much more revolutionary, and went beyond representational painting to experiment in color, form, and design.[166]

According to this narrative, the impact of the European Cubists, Fauvists, and other Post-Impressionists in the Armory Show was so great that the realist painters simply dropped out of sight on the cultural landscape. The explanation is that the Ashcan realists sought to change the public's conception of the nature of art and the beautiful by offending the bourgeoisie's sense of propriety, introducing a new assertive style and a "vulgar" subject matter to their painting. Remaining within the bounds of realism, however, they failed to grasp the more radical aesthetic ideas the Parisian modernists were bringing to the US, which changed the public's very way of seeing art. In this view, the Armory show had an ironic effect on the realists, who had expected it to propel them to the forefront of American art. Instead it was their undoing, as the European modernists sped past them, and they became part of the rear guard.

The effect of Post-Impressionism on American art and culture in 1913 is hard to overstate. Floyd Dell wrote that "Post-Impressionism exploded like a bombshell within the minds of everybody who could be said to have minds. For Americans it could not be merely an aesthetic experience; it was an emotional experience which led to a philosophical and moral revaluation of life."[167] Hapgood wrote that "the thing that stood out boldly was the vitality of the exhibition as a whole. Life was there rather than art." Hapgood placed the Armory Show in the wider cultural context: "much of the expression of those explosive days was the same, whether in art, literature, labor expansion, or sexual experience, a moving, a shaking time. Post-Impressionist art, experimental literature sprang from the same impulse – the impulse of the day."[168]

Historically speaking, realism was a creation of the nineteenth century, Post-Impressionism of the twentieth, but one did not succeed the other in a neat historical progression in American art. Identifying Stieglitz's magazine *Camera Work* with non-representational art and *The Masses* with realism, Rebecca Zurier has noted that "few artists published in both *Camera Work* and *The Masses*. Yet members of both groups did interact in other situations – at the anarchist Ferrer Center, at Mabel Dodge's salon, at political fund-raising events, and, of course, at Provincetown."[169] Within the Provincetown Players itself, the permeability of the barrier between representational and non-representational artists is easily seen. Both Marguerite and William Zorach had studied with the Ashcan School's leader Robert Henri at the Modern School, and Henri often sent his students to the exhibitions at Stieglitz's gallery 291.[170] Among Eugene O'Neill's close friends during this period were the Ashcan realist George Bellows, with whom he had spent a few weeks in a New Jersey farmhouse in the winter of 1909 while Bellows painted and O'Neill wrote, and the committed Post-Impressionists Brör Nordfeldt, William Zorach, and especially Charles Demuth, with whom he spent a good deal of time in Provincetown.

Mary Heaton Vorse wrote about the battles between the competing schools of artists who gathered in Provincetown during the summer. The Cape Cod School of Art was founded in 1899 by Charles Webster Hawthorne, who had been a student of William Merrit Chase and taught academic painting *en plein air*. The younger, more recent arrivals taught Post-Impressionist painting and other arts, but they were not completely intolerant of older ideas. On September 17, 1914, for example, the *Provincetown Advocate* reported:

> Under the watchful eye of Marguerite Zorach, high priestess of the ultra-modernists, a class of some 30 women artists are sitting day after day close by the sea, with stout wooden frames and balls of many colored yarns, embroidering away at samplers of their own design. The designs vary from conventional to the most excruciating cubist and vorticist designs.[171]

The two groups came together to found the Provincetown Art Association in 1914 and exhibited together in what would become significant shows at the Town Hall beginning in 1915. Vorse reported a lively interaction between the two groups of artists, based on their aesthetic disagreements: "The respective members fight freely together, pound tables, and even heads. Enormous vocabularies of so great a magnitude were developed during this warfare that a philologist should find here a rich store for observation."[172] This lively battle over aesthetics naturally found its way into the Provincetown Players. George Cram Cook's ridicule of the Post-Impressionists in *Change Your Style*, in which Brör Nordfeldt, the head of the Modern Art School on Vorse's wharf, played "Bordfelt, *Head of a Post-Impressionist Art-School*" who comes into conflict with "Kenyon Crabtree, *Head of an Academic Art-School*,"[173] was an overt, although good-natured, representation of the aesthetic battles within the Provincetown. William Zorach recalled his arguments with O'Neill in his autobiography:

> Gene insisted everything had to be factual. If the play called for a stove, it couldn't be a painted box. It had to be an honest-to-goodness stove. If there was a sink, it had to be a real sink. I used to try to make him understand that a stage is a work of art like a painting. It is a world in itself or at least an illusion of a world. You cannot, for instance, have a real tree or a real ocean. There, at least, you have to accept the illusion. I could make no impression on him ... I used to gripe at his literal realism, but whatever he did was true theater.[174]

Despite Zorach's immediate lack of success in converting O'Neill to his Post-Impressionist vision, there is no doubt that his contribution, and those of his wife and Nordfeldt, to the creation of non-representational theatre by the Provincetown, beginning with the production of Louise Bryant's *The Game* in the summer of 1916, were enormously important and influential. O'Neill may have been a realistic playwright in 1916, but by the time he wrote *The Emperor Jones* in 1920, he was already leading the way in American modernist playwriting. Similarly, Susan Glaspell's 1916 play *Trifles* exemplifies the realization of the kind of dramatic realism envisioned by the American realist critics in the 1890s, but by the time she wrote *The Verge* in 1921, she was deeply involved in modernist experiments with dialogue, character, and staging. The Post-Impressionist artists were their immediate contact with the new modernist aesthetics and ideas.

William and Marguerite Zorach served as the poster children for modernism in the Provincetown of 1915. Unconventional in their lifestyle and dress as well as their ideas about art, they were recognizable characters in a town full of unconventional types. Reviewing a Provincetown Art Association show in August of 1915, a critic for the Boston *Globe* confessed, "The pictures by Mr. and Mrs. Zorach are way beyond me. I don't get 'em."[175] Marilyn Hoffman has pointed out that "in 1916, Georgia O'Keeffe, who was exactly Marguerite's age, was completely unknown, and Marguerite Zorach was the best known woman artist of her generation in America."[176] After growing up in California, she had gone with her aunt to Paris to study, eventually coming, like her future husband, to La Palette, the Fauvist art school run by the Scots artist John Duncan Ferguson. She began to paint in a Fauvist style in 1908 and, according to Hoffman, "her paintings of 1909 through 1913 are primarily derived from Paul Gauguin, Vincent Van Gogh, the Fauve landscapists and the German Expressionists. More the intellectual, and already a writer, Marguerite proselytized to William about the new art."[177] William has written that after he came to Paris in 1909, he became "fascinated by the bold and brilliant use of color by Van Gogh and Gaugin and the new conception of form through Cézanne. After all they were the true innovators."[178] Coming to La Palette, and encountering Marguerite's original use of color, William "became more intrigued by the bold surfaces patterned with black lines as well as with brilliant color. I, too, began to leave Impressionism as such behind and to paint in this freer manner."[179] Zorach's description of the simultaneous impact of Japanese, Post-Impressionist and Cubist artists on him in Paris gives a good sense of the eclectic aesthetics that fed American modernist painting during the early teens:

> In Paris I had realized the design quality of Japanese prints. It was a new point of view. Gauguin fascinated me, not only with his color but by his painting of a picture that had its own life. He saw with an inner vision of reality and not with an optic vision or a camera eye. Van Gogh and Cézanne I felt were basically realists – more like scientists exploring the development of new aspects of their surroundings. Gauguin took me into a mysterious inner world of the spirit. Picasso did, too, in his blue period and later on when he moved into Cubism. Braque had, for me, the same kind of expressiveness in his development of Cubism. I was stirred by Matisse's command of color but felt that he never quite rose above the ground when form was involved.[180]

Back in New York in 1913, Zorach was fascinated by "the sculpture of the Aztecs and the Mayans and the carving of the Eskimos in the Museum of Natural History" as well as the exhibition of African sculpture mounted by Marius de Zayas at 291: "It had an extraordinary magic and spiritual quality that is unequaled; it showed the spirit of man in all his terror and awe of the forces of the universe; it transcended the flesh; and it had almost unbelievable power, versatility, and imagination."[181] All of these elements went into the complex aesthetic the Zorachs called Post-Impressionism. Hoffman has commented that "it is unusual for two such talented artists to have shared the same training and influences and to have had such a parallel development for eight years, from 1911 through 1918. Although each diverged stylistically after 1918, during the years in question, the Zorachs' works are sometimes indistinguishable and their stylistic growth synchronous."[182] She has noted that the Post-Impressionism of the period, the term the Zorachs used for their own art, meant "not only the French painters we refer to today by that name, but also the Fauves, Cubists, Futurists, Synchromists and Expressionists." It was "the mainstream style of the avant-garde in the early teens." There were variations of style among the artists – Marguerite's was "flatter and more patterned than William's, which was more textured" – but all these artists were producing work "that could be termed provincial Fauvism."[183]

During the time they spent at Provincetown, the Zorachs were both experimenting with Cubism, a style neither of them embraced fully. For William, "pure Cubism was too coldly intellectual. Although William produced some fine Cubist works, he displayed a more impressionist, spiritual and humanistic side. Marguerite, who was inclined to flat decorative patterns and vivid colors, found pure French Cubism too architectonic."[184] According to Hoffman, "both Zorachs created remarkably original work at this time, combining Fauve color, expressionism and Cubist structures in a new way, and treating original subjects in a Cubist style." In Provincetown, they painted "boats in the harbor and seascapes that are unlike any French Cubist works. They fit comfortably, however, with what was then called 'Post-Impressionist' art by their colleagues in New York. This style encompassed all the artists of the Stieglitz group, such as Dove, Marin, O'Keeffe, and especially Hartley, who was painting similar subjects in Provincetown that summer."[185]

A sense of the aesthetic thinking behind the Zorachs' art during this period can be gotten from the essay William Zorach wrote for the catalogue of the Forum Exhibition in March, 1916, in which both artists were represented, although, interestingly, Marguerite, the only woman in the show, was also the only artist not to be represented with an essay. Hoffman suggests that "practically every artist's essay could readily describe the Zorachs' art, so similar are their tenets":

> Most of the artists stressed the importance of formal compositional devices: organization, pattern, and the rhythmical composition of forms.

Several discussed the quest for emotive power and the liberation of feelings. The breaking of laws, rules, and formulas was paramount, so that instinct, or the subjective, could result in an entirely personal and original creative expression. Freedom was the watch word – the artist was freed from the representation of the actual in order to invest the underlying life of the subject with vitality, invention and spiritual meaning.[186]

William Zorach's essay confirms that for him, it was the subjective element of his art, what he termed the spiritual and the emotional, that mattered most. His description of his artistic aims sets him clearly off from both the goal of "objective" representation in realism and the formalism that is often associated with high modernism: "It is the inner spirit of things that I seek to express, the essential relation of forms and colors to universal things. Each form and color has a spiritual significance to me, and I try to combine those forms and colors within my space to express that inner feeling which something in nature or life has given me."[187] The most familiar element in Zorach's aesthetics to readers acquainted with literary modernism is the conception of art as a creation of order within the chaos of experience, a concept that links Zorach's ideas with those of William James: "The moment I place one line or color upon my canvas, that moment I feel the need of other lines and colors to express the inner rhythm. I am organizing a new world in which each form and color exists and lives only in so far as it has meaning in relation to every other form and color in that space."[188]

The Zorachs were very close to the group of poets around the *Others* magazine edited by Alfred Kreymborg at this time, and both published some poetry in it. In gatherings at the Zorachs' apartment in New York, William reported, "we would all read poems and discuss them; Alfred Kreymborg, whose plays we produced, William Carlos Williams, Marianne Moore, Maxwell Bodenheim, Lola Ridge, Wallace Stevens, and Orrick Johns." The poets, he said, "liked the naiveté, the simplicity, and the direct expression of a mood"[189] in his poems. For him they were an analogue to the paintings he was doing in the medium of words. Kreymborg, Bodenheim, and Stevens would have plays produced by the Provincetown Players, through the influence of the Zorachs and John Reed, and Williams and Mina Loy would act in one of them. When the Zorachs first turned their attention to the theatre in the summer of 1916, however, it was because they were intrigued by the idea of being able to develop their Post-Impressionist art in three dimensions. "It was their first experience with the theatre and ours too," wrote William, "but we had no hesitation. We were full of ideas and eager to use them."[190]

The only one of the founding Provincetown Players with real experience in theatrical design was Brör Nordfeldt. In 1912, he had designed Euripides's *The Trojan Women* for the Chicago Little Theatre, a production that drew a great deal of praise and helped to establish the Little Theatre as a viable entity. Along with Cook and John Reed, Nordfeldt was among the hardest-working and most enthusiastic of the founding Players. He put a good deal of energy into making both the fish house on the wharf and the first theatre on Macdougal Street into theatrical spaces. Like the Zorachs, Nordfeldt was identified in the early teens as part of the insurgent Post-Impressionist group in Provincetown. Born in Sweden in 1878, Nordfeldt had come to the US in 1891 and grown up in Chicago. He studied at the Chicago Art Institute, but his most significant experience came when he was sent to Paris to oversee the installation of a mural he had worked on for the McCormick Harvester Company at the Paris Exposition. He taught and exhibited in both Paris and London, where he studied wood-block cutting and printing, a medium in which he became one of the most distinguished of American artists. During the first decade of the twentieth century, he traveled a good deal in Europe, including one trip to Italy, when he accompanied Mary Heaton Vorse, illustrating her series of travel articles for *Harper's* and *The Outlook* magazines. He became interested in the Little Theatre when he returned to Chicago in 1911, but soon left for more travel in the American West and in Europe, coming to New York from Paris only when World War I broke out in 1914. Between 1914 and 1918, he lived in Greenwich Village and spent summers in Provincetown. It was quite natural that he would become involved with the Provincetown Players.

Summing up his evolution as an artist in the years before he arrived in Provincetown, Nordfeldt's biographer Van Deren Coke wrote:

> Nordfeldt had moved from late nineteenth-century academic painting through a period of indebtedness to Whistler and Impressionism to a heightened awareness of post-impressionistic and Fauve-like bright colors. During his second visit to France in 1914 he had reinforced his interest in Cézanne's firmly and fully stated pictorial vocabulary. His paintings from 1912 to the end of World War I were usually characterized by brilliant color notations and loosely handled but affirmative drawing. In the best work of these years are found direct, bold application of paint – sometimes with shapes very heavily outlined – and freely applied strokes of high-key color. Through abrupt dashes of pigment

applied with a bristle brush in a loose and flowing fashion he gave a sense of mass to the forms in his pictures.[191]

In 1916, Nordfeldt's aesthetic ideas were quite similar to those of the Zorachs, and, like William Zorach in particular, he brought an element of emotional subjectivity to his painting. As Coke put it, "his intention was always to regenerate in pictorial terms his special emotional response to the raw material he took as his subjects."[192] Nordfeldt's strong personality, which was to come into conflict with the equally strong personality of George Cram Cook, is evident from Coke's description of his fiercely independent approach to his art: "He continually drew strength as an artist from his belief in himself, which sometimes took the form of sheer doggedness, and an inherent talent for handling paint and evolving strikingly simplified compositions." Coke characterizes the prevailing feeling of his work as "asperity and directness."[193]

The Post-Impressionism shared by the Zorachs and Nordfeldt had several anti-realistic elements. First of all, it eschewed any claim to objective representation. When William Zorach first noticed Marguerite Thompson at La Palette, she was painting a pink and yellow nude with a bold blue outline. Ascertaining that she knew just what she was doing and why she was doing it, Zorach knew "that was the beginning."[194] Second, it was frankly emotional and subjective. It attempted to convey an emotional reaction to what Zorach called "raw material" – whether the subject was a landscape, a person, or an object. Third, it followed a line of development from Matisse through Cézanne and the Fauvists in emphasizing form and color. And finally it was influenced by the Japanese print in its sense of composition and its lack of interest in academic perspective. All of these elements would be called into play when these artists set about designing in three dimensions for the theatre, and they were to have implications for acting and playwriting as well as the plastic elements of the theatrical production.

Charles Demuth, who was staying with John Reed and Louise Bryant in Provincetown during the summer of 1916, had many of the same ideas about art that the Zorachs and Nordfeldt had. Like them he had gone to Paris after early training in the US, in his case at the Pennsylvania Academy of the Fine Arts in Philadelphia. Demuth too was in Paris during the Fauvist period, studied at the Académie Moderne and Académie Julien, and he was a habitué of Gertrude Stein's salon on the rue de Fleurus. Critic Andrew Ritchie notes that Demuth's work from his first visit to Paris in 1907 reflects "direct contact with the *fauve* revolution which was then at its height in Paris, under Matisse's leadership."[195] Between 1907 and 1912, his work developed under the influence of John Marin, Matisse, and Cézanne, and he found much of his subject matter in café scenes and theatrical performance, particularly vaudeville turns and acrobats. Summing it up, Ritchie says that the years between 1907 and 1915 were spent "assimilating much that was to be learned from the *avant garde* in Paris, both as to expressionist freedom of color and cubist analysis of form," and after 1915, Demuth began to produce "a steady stream of increasingly brilliant work. The next five years, until 1920 when he was discovered to be suffering from diabetes, he was at the height of his powers."[196] Like Nordfeldt, Demuth was greatly interested in the Japanese prints he saw in Paris, and when he returned to the US in 1914, he and Helene Iungerich organized a show of "Living Japanese Prints" in Provincetown, an avant-garde series of tableaux vivants, one of which consisted of "Helene's foot sticking out at one side of the flies."[197] He was also influenced by Cubism, and was a close friend and champion of Marcel Duchamp, whose "Nude Descending a Staircase" was the most controversial piece in the Armory Show, and really defined Cubism for most Americans. Demuth's Post-Impressionist use of form and color in landscapes during the Provincetown period is similar to that of the Zorachs. Lawrence Langner describes watching him paint "a yellow sand dune at Provincetown by industriously painting what appeared to be large pink and blue worms on his white canvas."[198]

Although his techniques were avant garde, Demuth's sensibility was from a slightly older generation than that of the Zorachs, who epitomized the positive pole of the modernist spirit in their devotion to iconoclasm, change, and regeneration. Demuth, born in 1883, was really of the *fin de siècle* generation. He was, in a word, an aesthete, very much in the art for art's sake camp of the 1890s. As fellow art student and later Provincetown playwright Rita Wellman wrote of their group, "when we were very young, we were very old. We were all bored with life: knew everything there was to know; and only condescended to give our time and talents to painting because it seemed to our jaded spirits the one respectable calling left."[199] Demuth's sensibility is evident in his choice of texts to illustrate, a series of paintings he did for their own sake, without a commission. These included Walter Pater's *A Prince of Court Painters*, Henry James's *The Turn of the Screw* and *The Beast in the Jungle*, Zola's *Nana*, and Poe's "The Masque of the Red Death." The only modernist texts he chose to illustrate, Frank Wedekind's expressionist plays *Erdgeist* and *Pandora's Box*, reflect the darkest side of modernism, with its disillusionment and cynicism developing into a hysterical expressionist despair. Personally, Demuth was known as a good companion, quiet and agreeable, but remote and ultimately opaque. The subtitle of Emily Farnham's biography, *Behind a Laughing Mask*, expresses the general consensus of his friends. No doubt Demuth's wariness stemmed partly from the fact that he was living a closeted gay life, although he felt freer to express himself in Provincetown than in most places. Like Robert Edmond Jones, who often wore fanciful clothing in Provincetown, Demuth stood out from the crowd in the seaside vacation town wearing such costumes as a black shirt, white slacks, a plum-colored scarf tied around his waist, and highly polished black-laced shoes.

Demuth was generally silent in a large gathering, but he built up several intense individual relationships among the Provincetown group. It is probably not surprising that, of all the Provincetown Players, he became closest to O'Neill. According to Robin Frank, friends recalled Demuth rooming with O'Neill in the Francis Flats one summer, and later "always going over the dunes to see Agnes and Eugene O'Neill" after they had bought the Coast Guard station that had been renovated by Mabel Dodge.[200] He carried on an intimate correspondence with the O'Neills, particularly Agnes, through 1926, and, most significantly, depicted Eugene in two of the "Poster Portaits" that have become his best-known works. The two men went through a horrific experience together in 1918, when their friend Louis Holladay died from an overdose of heroin as they sat in a restaurant together. Accounts of the incident differ, but it is fairly clear that Demuth, who may have taken some of the heroin himself, stayed with Holladay, while O'Neill left, possibly right after Holladay took the drug and before it was clear that he was having a bad reaction. Whatever the details, the effects on both men were devastating. Hutchins Hapgood reported that he saw Demuth the next morning at the Hotel Brevoort, "looking like a crazy man. He literally seemed a being in hell. I never saw such a look of complete horror on any human being's face. He walked right by me without noticing my existence, or anything but the terrible image in his mind."[201] The effect on the sensitive O'Neill, with his family's history of drug addiction, can be imagined. After trying to drink himself into insensibility for a few days, O'Neill left for Provincetown with Agnes.[202] Demuth's friendship with O'Neill fell off during the late twenties after he left Agnes for Carlotta Monterey, who was rather determined to divide Eugene from his old friends from Provincetown and Greenwich Village.

Demuth did not design productions for the Players, as the Zorachs and Nordfeldt did, but he was a founding member, and actively participated in the renovation of both the Wharf Theatre in June and the new Provincetown Playhouse at 139 Macdougal Street in the fall of 1916. In the summer of 1916, he played Marmaduke, Jr., the young Post-Impressionist painter in George Cram Cook's *Change Your Style*, while Nordfeldt played Bordfelt. Along with O'Neill, Demuth was one of the few founding members who had published a play. His one-act comedy about Greenwich Village, *The Azure Adder*, was published in *The Glebe* in 1913. This little magazine was edited by Man Ray and Alfred Kreymborg, who was to join the Players in the fall of 1916, bringing several members of the New Jersey group of poets known by the title of their new magazine *Others*, including William Carlos Williams and Mina Loy. This group, to which the Zorachs and the young poet and actor Edna St. Vincent Millay were also drawn, was to introduce the most avant-garde aesthetics to the theatre created by the Players in 1916. An important point of connection among the artists, the poets, and the writers, the quiet Demuth was an integral part of the personal and aesthetic mix as the Provincetown Players was formed during the summer and fall of 1916.

2

The first plays

PERHAPS THE BEST SOURCE OF KNOWLEDGE ABOUT THE aesthetics of the founding Players is the group of plays they put on in the two summer seasons at Provincetown before they officially formed the Provincetown Players in September, 1916. These thirteen plays provide an excellent index to the eclectic mix of aesthetics and ideas that informed the group from its inception.[1] They are *Constancy* and *Winter's Night* by Neith Boyce and *Enemies*, a collaborative effort of Boyce and Hutchins Hapgood; *Suppressed Desires* by Susan Glaspell and George Cram Cook, *Change your Style* by Cook, and *Trifles* by Glaspell; *Contemporaries* and *"Not Smart"* by Wilbur Daniel Steele; *Freedom* and *The Eternal Quadrangle* by John Reed; *Bound East for Cardiff* and *Thirst* by Eugene O'Neill; and *The Game* by Louise Bryant. With the exception of *The Game*, all of these plays are within the realm of realism, although *Freedom* and *Thirst* push the boundaries of this aesthetic. Overall, the realistic plays try to produce a believable illusion that what is taking place on the stage is an objective representation of the audience's shared reality. They call for sets that will be accepted by the audience as a representation of some real contemporary place; they use dialogue that is within the realm of everyday speech; they have characters that an audience can accept as psychologically true-to-life human beings; they have plots that are within the possibility of contemporary human experience; they refer to the common ideas, concerns, and experiences that are shared by their largely middle-class, but progressive-minded playwrights and their self-selected audiences.

As was noted earlier, there is a wide spectrum of variety beyond this basic shared realism that reveals some meaningful differences among the playwrights. It is probably not surprising that a number of the plays in the first two summer seasons were essentially self-referential, depicting the same Greenwich Village artists and intellectuals who wrote, acted in, and watched the plays. The function of the realism in these plays was to provide as recognizable a semblance of the group as possible, in order to expose their peculiarities and failings to each other, the result being a ritual process of self-recognition, purgative laughter, and, presumably, change. It is important to remember, however, as J. Ellen Gainor has noted, that the dynamics of community theatre inflects the aesthetics of realism in important and fundamental ways. "In a community where the identities of the actors are known to the audience, where their status as members of the community doubles with their artistic identities of performers," she writes, "it is impossible for the audience to 'identify' with the characters, or for the production to convey an unfiltered mimesis, precisely because the audience will not suspend their knowledge of that duality – in fact, it is integral to their enjoyment of the art."[2] In other words, the fact that the actors and the playwright are known to the audience in real life makes it impossible for them to perceive the action on stage as an objective representation of reality, no matter how hard they try to suspend their disbelief. Major changes in the audience base altered the situation once the Greenwich Village Provincetown Playhouse was opened, in November of 1916, but for the first two summers, the Provincetown Players were just this kind of community theatre. As will be seen, many of the playwrights showed a sophisticated sense of the audience dynamics involved, and were adept at manipulating the audience's response to the actors' identities, which made for an additional interpretive layer in the audience's reaction to the performance.

Probably the most conservative playwright of the group, both aesthetically and ideologically, was Wilbur Daniel Steele. The son of a minister with a long and distinguished New England pedigree, Steele grew up in Colorado, and led a very conventional life until he met Mary Heaton Vorse, Brör Nordfeldt, and Nordfeldt's future wife Margaret Doolittle, while traveling in Europe with his mother and sister. Steele, who was then studying art, left the family group to travel with Nordfeldt and Vorse and study linoleum-block printing with Nordfeldt. His contact with the Greenwich Village–Provincetown group was a life-changing experience for Steele. With Vorse's encouragement, he began to write short stories, and finally gave up painting to pursue what he felt was his true vocation of writing fiction. By the time the Provincetown Players was formed, he had become a successful short story writer, publishing in *The Atlantic*, *Harper's*, and *Scribners*, the nation's premiere middle-brow magazines, as well as such disparate organs as *Success* and *The Masses*. His biographer

Martin Bucco contends that, "in the tradition of O. Henry, Steele wrote the best 'popular' stories of his day," serving as a "curious transitional figure" between "'old-fashioned' writers like Edgar Allan Poe, Nathaniel Hawthorne, Henry James, Jack London, and O. Henry and the 'modern' writers like Sherwood Anderson, Ernest Hemingway, Ring Lardner, F. Scott Fitzgerald, and William Faulkner." Bucco contends that Steele's "idiosyncratic Romantic Realism . . . bridges the 'old' and the 'new.'"[3]

Steele's brief contact with leftist circles came about largely through Vorse, with whom he had a love affair in 1912, after the death of her first husband, Albert Vorse. The couple lived together in her house in Provincetown, but unlike Mabel Dodge and John Reed, they maintained a conventional social front, using the cover story that Steele was a distant cousin visiting for the summer.[4] In 1913, Steele roomed with Sinclair Lewis in Provincetown before he married his first wife Margaret Thurston, the painter who was to be evicted from the wharf building so that the Provincetown Players could have a theatre in 1916. For the next few years, the Steeles had a cottage at the other end of the town from the more bohemian Greenwich Village group, and, according to Provincetown historian Leona Egan, they were driven out of Provincetown in 1923 by their distaste for the illegal activities during Prohibition, "to them a time of unlicensed behavior and 'Flaming Youth.'"[5] The increasing conservatism of Steele is evident in his novel *Meat* (1928), in which he spelled out his Nietzschean view of the relationship between the intellectual elite and the rest of society. Bucco describes *Meat* as a "bold (but perhaps ultimately vicious and self-defeating) indictment of the pernicious doctrine that the world should be made safe for the weak at the expense of the strong. Like Nietzsche, Steele shows how both the individual and the race – presumably the human race – stand to suffer from 'ethical' protective restrictions."[6]

As is evidenced by the Christian ideals in *Contemporaries*, in 1915 and 1916, Steele was much more in sympathy with those who were on the losing end of the existing societal structure, but his fundamental conservatism was also evident. *"Not Smart": A Farce in One Act* conveys Steele's skeptical view of Greenwich Village bohemianism, and irreverently exposes the hypocrisy that he saw operating in many Villagers' lives, as they espoused the "modern" ideas of a classless society, free love, feminism, and primitivism. *"Not Smart"* is a farce in the mold of the Howells magazine farces of the 1890s. A form of coterie drama, it functions as a comedy of manners in exposing the collective pretensions and bad faith within a self-defined social group and reveals the values that really motivate the characters' actions. In this case, the group is Greenwich Village artists and intellectuals, the very people who were both putting on the play and watching it. It is the cultural markers of modernity that are exposed as mere pretense in the play, and the middle-class Victorian values, which the characters claim to have left behind in their quest for modernity, that are revealed to really hold sway over their lives.

The characters in the play are a modern couple, Milo and Fannie, who are vacationing in a seaside cottage, and Mrs. Painter, the more conservative wife of one of their friends. Steele establishes the couple as intensely modern and opposed to "fog-bound superstitions of the mid-Victorian home"[7] in the opening scene, as Milo complains that the hero in a magazine story he is reading resists the temptation to follow an "ankle" he glimpses in the street and returns dutifully home. Milo insists that could never happen to him. Milo reminds Fannie that she should "always feel quite free, too" and "never let the silly little inhibitions" get the best of her (244). This concept of marriage as a union based on love rather than societal constrictions, in which the partners stay together by choice and are free to experiment sexually, was endorsed enthusiastically by people like Hutchins Hapgood and Floyd Dell in 1916, and less enthusiastically by people like Neith Boyce. While Boyce's plays reflect the struggle that couples such as she and Hapgood had in earnestly trying to live up to their principles of modernity, Steele is interested in suggesting they are unnatural and that it is silly to go against human nature by trying to live them out. Both Milo and Fannie instantly become jealous when there is any suggestion that the other may be sexually attracted to someone else. Steele takes a similar approach to other markers of freedom and emancipation. Fannie smokes cigarettes to show that she is an emancipated woman, but when the more conservative Mrs. Painter comes to the door, she rushes to hide her cigarette until Milo objects, and then "*shamed by his superior sense of honor, puts the cigarette between her lips and puffs conscientiously*" (251).

The two come into conflict over Fannie's assertion of class when she insists that their cook Mattie call her "ma'am." Milo objects, and Fannie in turn complains about his theories, to which he responds:

> My theories, Frances, are *identical* with yours; the only point of variance being that *I* am willing to practice them *at home*. (*Rising, he transfixes his wife with a didactic forefinger*) We all talk so largely of the Brotherhood of Man. And yet here is a young girl, a really splendid sort of creature in a

way, living close to the throbbing heart of Mother Earth . . . feeling the life-pulse of the Cosmos – well – damn it all – she's precisely the kind of thing we write about and talk about and make gestures about, the lot of us – *you* know. Only she *is* it. She *lives* it. She's got something we've lost.
(247–248)

In Milo, who is strikingly reminiscent of Steele's friend Hutchins Hapgood, Steele ridicules the patronizing attitude of one of the newest modern enthusiasms, that of "primitivism." In Greenwich Village, the "primitivist" conception of art derived from painters like Gauguin and Rousseau was well established, but a new primitivism associated with Cubism, and particularly Picasso's work, was first strikingly enunciated by Marius de Zayas, who brought a collection of African sculptures from Paris to New York and mounted an exhibition of them at Stieglitz's 291 in November of 1914. In the catalogue, he wrote:

> Modern art is not based on direct plastic phenomena, but on epiphenomena, on transpositions and on existing evolutions. In its plastic researches modern art discovered Negro Art. Picasso was the discover [sic]. He introduced into European art, through his own work, the plastic principles of Negro art – the point of departure for our abstract representation.
> Negro art has had thus a direct influence on our comprehension of form, teaching us to see and feel its purely expressive side and opening our eyes to a new world of plastic sensations. Negro art has re-awakened in us a sensibility obliterated by an education, which makes us always connect what we see with what we know – our visualization with our knowledge, and makes us, in regard to form, use our intellect more than our senses.[8]

Despite his respect and enthusiasm for African art, de Zayas's conception of it was a racist one, based on an assumption that the intellectual capacity and development of Africans was inferior to that of Europeans and Americans.

This mythologizing of the primitive was extremely attractive to thinkers like Hapgood and Dell, who eschewed the outworn culture of the nineteenth century and wanted to establish a new and original relation to the universe, and artists like the Zorachs, who were inspired by an art that they felt was closer to the natural sources of life. What Steele exposes, however, is a patronizing attitude that proceeds from a fundamental conviction of superiority which is not necessarily racist, but results from elitist views of class and education. Thus Milo speaks of Mattie as an Earth

Mother, "feeling the life-pulse of the cosmos" and claims to feel "a strange spiritual bond with that creature – something drawing me – irresistibly – like the pull of green things and the damp earth – weird – almost – ah – *Pliocene*" (248). He apostrophizes Mattie, asking if she knows how wonderful she is: "In a world staggering under a Freud, a Trotsky, a Marconi, the Republic of China, and the Imagist Poets – you've managed somehow to slip back to the great, all-brooding fundamentals – Food – Shelter – Procreation" (249). When Fannie expresses skepticism about applying these terms to their young servant, Milo retorts, "see here, Frances, you know what I mean as well as I do. For heaven's sake, after two years of our talks – our trying to find the – the – in our little group, you know – Look here, Fannie, you've talked as primitive as anyone" (250). The difference between Steele and the people he is making fun of is that he has no problem expressing his belief that Mattie is inferior. To him, she is a creature with a "*numb and docile brain*" (248) who simply doesn't know what these summer folks are talking about.

The major unmasking of Milo and Fannie's pretenses to modernity comes when Mattie says she is "not smart," a local euphemism for pregnancy. Milo has previously chided Mrs. Painter for sending her servant away to have her baby because she suspected her husband of being the father: "It seems to me you are missing the fundamental significance of life; that you are deliberately shutting the door on life; that you are throwing away an – experience! You three! Think of it! How wonderful a thing! Passing together, hand in hand, through the unfolding hours of a miracle! You three!" (253). When their turn comes, however, Milo and Fannie immediately revert to Victorian stereotypes. Fannie and Mrs. Painter stare accusingly at Milo, and then Fannie "*Sinks on her knees beside the desk, and hiding her face in her hands, shakes with the tumult of her woe*" (258). Milo accuses his wife of having a "*low – suspicious – mind*" and says "of course, the girl must be gotten away from here immediately" (258), while he keeps saying that he is not responsible for the pregnancy. Fannie recovers herself, and begins to have some fun with Milo, insisting that Mattie should stay with them, saying "We – you and I – are not going to miss the fundamental significance of life, are we?" (261), and reminding him of his desire that "theories are to be put in practice at home." Milo responds, "Theories! My God! Theories! Ideals! Dreams! Ah, if one could but afford to dream! (*With a heavy wistfulness*) But that is for the angels, and the young. Happy youth, unencumbered, foot-free" (261). Milo evokes such middle-class Victorian concerns as his career, their families, and "your good – name" (262) as considerations against carrying out his theory for experiencing life with Mattie, and when Mrs. Painter returns, she adds fear of violence to them, reminding him that the fishermen in the town may be "ignorant and uncouth," but they are avid about defending the honor of any of their womenfolks, especially from an outsider. Mrs. Painter apologizes for being "hopelessly middle-class" (265), but Milo now can't get Mattie out of the house fast enough. It is only when her husband comes to tell them that she isn't going to work now that she is pregnant that they realize they don't know the first thing about Mattie, and never thought to ask if she were married. Steele's exposure of the pretense of modernity is effective, and it is in keeping with the soul-searching accounts of trying to deal with these issues in such books as Boyce's *Autobiography* and Hapgood's *Story of a Lover*. His little farce reminded the group what most of them were, as Hapgood, who entitled his autobiography *A Victorian in the Modern World*, clearly understood. They were fascinated with modernity and with modern ideas, but it was difficult to escape being born and brought up as Victorians.

The least serious of the early plays is certainly Reed's *The Eternal Quadrangle*. Its subtitle identifies it as "*A Farce Adapted from the Wiener-Schnitzler*," which, as Barbara Ozieblo notes, is an "impish reference" to Arthur Schnitzler,[9] but the play is also modeled on Oscar Wilde's "trivial comedy for serious people." Like Wilde, Reed opens unexamined assumptions and social values up to scrutiny by upending convention and reversing the audiences's expectations. It has been suggested that Reed wrote the play as a response to the gossip about the affair between Eugene O'Neill and Louise Bryant that was going on while Reed was in the hospital having a kidney operation. Bryant had told O'Neill that Reed was unable to have sex with her, and so condoned her relationship with O'Neill. This seems to have been widely reported in the Village. The play, however, is much more reflective of Reed's relationship with Mabel Dodge before he met Bryant. Mabel Dodge was a well-known figure in the Village because of her salon and her patronage of such high-profile events as the Armory Show and the Paterson Pageant. She was a wealthy woman with intense passions and enthusiasms, which she would abruptly drop after a time to move on to other things. In 1913 and 1914, while she was married to the wealthy architect Edwin Dodge, she had a wildly romantic relationship with Reed, and lived openly with him in her villa in Florence, in Greenwich Village, and in Provincetown, apparently without objection by her husband.

After an opening vignette in which the butler, played by Reed, executes some fancy roller-skating tricks in the library, *The Eternal Quadrangle* opens with what appears at first to be a stock scene from the typical triangle farce. The wealthy businessman Robert Fortescue confronts his wife's lover, Freddie Temple, with the words, "Look here, Temple. My wife has been your mistress for the past six weeks!" (107). Instead of challenging him to a duel or exacting revenge, however, Fortescue complains that Temple seems to have broken off the affair, saying, "I've a notion to wring your neck, you little cad. How dare you throw my wife over?" (108). This reversal of expectations sets the tone for Reed's farce, in which the conventional triangle paradigm is exploded, and Reed substitutes the quadrangle instead.

In Reed's play, Fortescue is a man who is completely absorbed with business, and does not want to be bothered with the romantic demands of marriage. After his wife's affair ends, he complains to her, "I've got you on my hands again. How the devil do you think I can do any work with you concentrating your affections on me?" (109). His wife Margot, like Mabel Dodge, is a very romantic woman, who is entirely devoted to fads. She has broken with Temple because she "loved him for his dancing. He knew all the latest steps (*Wistfully*.) But now dancing is going out and skating is coming in ... and Eddie can't skate" (109). The intensity of her romantic demands is evident from Temple's description of the affair:

> I never heard of such a silly business. Secret letters! Clandestine meetings! Making me stand out in the snow at night and then climb up the side of the house on a grape-vine, when any policeman might have shot me, and anyway, you knew how susceptible I am to colds! And your husband knew all the time. (109)

This is very much like Reed's affair with Dodge, whose romantic arrangements included an elaborate "Arabian" tent set up on the dunes of Provincetown, and a rope ladder from which Reed was expected to descend each night from his bedroom in the Villa Curonia in Florence into hers.

Like Edwin Dodge, Fortescue is quite willing to have Margot engage in these practices, as long as it isn't with him: "I haven't time to waste on these continuous eruptions. The emotional basis of my life must be settled, or I'm good for nothing. I can't have you focusing your scattered personality on me" (111). His solution is quite practical, given the fact that Margot and he, being who they are, want to stay married: "You've got to get a job, my dear; and the only job you're trained for is love. So for heaven's sake find a man – but pick a stayer. I can't stand a bust-up every six months" (111). His proposal is that Margot have an affair with Archibald the butler. Archie is the perfect comic eiron character, appearing to be less than he is, for, as Fortescue notes, "he wears a mask as a well-trained servant should – and yet what must there be behind it! What a stranger, what an unguessed personality! I'll bet Archibald is no more what he seems than any servant" (111). Archibald agrees, "treat me as a servant, sir, and I know my place. Treat me as a human being, and believe me, I'm a bear." (112). Fortescue persuades Margot by reminding her of "the novelty of having an affair with your husband's valet under his very roof" (112). But Archibald is no stock comic "scheming valet." It is Temple who unmasks him as "Vladimir, the Fancy Ice-skating Champion of the World," who is working as a butler to get away from the public while he works on his new show. This, of course, makes him the perfect match for Margot, whose newest enthusiasm is skating, but a complication emerges in the fact that Archibald is married to Estelle the maid. Estelle, who has "read [her] Bernard Shaw" and knows that "servants always have the wildest times," is quite happy for Archibald to have an affair, saying "Archibald really ought to be psychoanalysed, but I think this will do just as well, and it won't cost so much" (114).

Reed upsets the audience's expectations a second time by not completing the quadrangle with an affair between Estelle and Fortescue. Estelle, who has taken Shaw to heart, believes that it is "for us Superwomen to make men what they will be" (115). Fortescue recognizes this as "real danger" from which "masculine dominance totters on its throne" (115). He is glad to be protected from the likes of Estelle, but it turns out that Margot's former lover Temple has been longing to be dominated: "I wish someone would love me to improve me. It's my only chance of being anything" (115). Estelle decides he is perfect material: "Youth, health, strength, and inexperience. And he's economically independent" (115). With the quadrangle complete, Fortescue is free to pursue business, the love of his life, and he leaves for a meeting as the two couples fall into each other's arms in an ending that echoes *The Importance of Being Earnest*.

The play succeeds at being an entertaining farce at the same time that it brings into the audience's consciousness some unorthodox ideas about marriage and the relations between the sexes. In a marriage like the Fortescues', why shouldn't the romantic Margot seek her fulfillment in an affair while her husband pursues his real passion, which is making money, in peace? Why shouldn't Archibald get a break from Estelle's "improvement" in a light-hearted affair with Margot while Temple gets the benefit of it? Deeper than this lie the kinds of social and cultural attitudes that are always at work in farce. In the need of Archibald and Fortescue to get away from their marriages, and from dominating women who either want to consume them with romantic demands or improve them so that "inside of a week ... you won't know yourself" (115) is the suggestion of a resistance to the commitment of marriage and fear of the kind of strong, feminist women that abounded in the Village and the Provincetown Players. *The Eternal Quadrangle* is a boyish play that celebrates freedom and autonomy and conveys a wariness in response to both women and social ties and constraints. It is an eloquent expression of John Reed's bohemian values.

Neith Boyce's play *Constancy*, the first to be produced in Provincetown, is also ostensibly based on the relationship between Reed and Dodge. It contains some telltale references that were well known in the Village, including one to the famous rope ladder, and the plot alludes to recent events, when Reed had returned to the US in January, 1915 after covering World War I in Europe for the *Metropolitan* magazine. Dodge had become increasingly unhappy with the peripheral place she occupied in Reed's life while the two were together in Paris in 1914, and had returned to the US, where she bought a house in Croton on Hudson and set about recouping emotionally away from New York. After a series of letters and cables, Dodge cabled Reed a final message in October that signaled the end of their romance. Reed quickly became involved with Freddie Lee, the wife of sculptor Arthur Lee, in a fast-moving romance that had them planning marriage within a few months. Both Reed and Freddie Lee wrote to Dodge, informing her of their love for each other, and she responded with understanding letters. This relationship soon broke up, however, and when Reed returned to New York, he bought two gold rings, planning to ask Mabel Dodge to marry him. Boyce's play dramatizes the scene when Reed came to Dodge's house in Croton and attempted to win her back. Dodge wrote in her memoir *Movers and Shakers* that she was flattered by his renewed ardor, but, having learned to resist her desire for him, she feigned indifference and refused every attempt to restore their old intimacy. When he produced the rings, she insisted that "it's all finished for us," and he kept demanding, "But *why*? What's *happened*? What has come between us?"[10]

Neith Boyce was one of Dodge's closest friends at this time. She had spent the summer of 1914 with her at her villa in Florence, returning to the US when the war broke out with Dodge's young son and Carl Van

Vechten, while Dodge went to Paris to meet Reed. Boyce was no doubt well acquainted with the story from Dodge's point of view when she wrote the play in the spring of 1915. But, as Ellen Trimberger has pointed out, the Dodge–Reed story is partly a cover for Boyce's working out of her own attitudes toward her husband's myriad infidelities during these years.[11]

Constancy is not so much a play as a dialogue focusing on the issue of infidelity.[12] The situation is that Rex has come back from "a long journey" and wants to renew his love relationship with Moira, despite the fact that he has fallen in love with someone named Ellen, and sent her a telegram saying "Let us part friends,"[13] while he was away. Rex insists that her having behaved so "well" (55) on receiving the telegram indicated that Moira too must have loved someone else. Moira tells him that this is not true, that she had forgiven him for the infidelity, but she "had ceased to feel about [him] as a lover" (60). Rex cannot understand this, insisting that if she no longer felt love for him she must never have loved him in the first place. He quotes Shakespeare to her – "love is not love that alters when it alteration finds" – and insists that "love never ends – real love" (61). Moira responds that she was faithful to him while their love relationship lasted: "I lived only for you for a year ... I was constant to you every moment, while I loved you" (61). To her way of thinking, it is of course Rex who has been unfaithful, since he has told her of his love for another woman and broken off their relationship, but he insists that, although he had loved Ellen "in a way," Moira ought to know that his love for her was constant: "that I have loved you ever since we met: that I never ceased loving you: that I could never love anyone else as I love you" (58). He insists that his desire to return to her is proof of his constancy: "I was always faithful to you, really. I always shall be. I would always come back" (59).

This is the crux of their fundamental disagreement. Rex's idea of constancy, as Moira puts it, "is to love a hundred other women and at intervals to come back – to me" (61). Moira's is to be faithful to her lover while she loves him. Rex insists that he is the constant one because his love for Moira endures throughout his romantic relationships with other women, and that she is inconstant, because she is changeable. In the end, Moira says, there is nothing more to say: "we have annihilated one another" (62). Rex leaves as they restate their positions, having found no resolution to the conflict.

Boyce implies that there is no resolution to what she sees as a fundamental conflict between essentialized male and female feelings about love, sex, and romantic relationships. *Constancy* is set up as a comedy, with Rex and Moira as humorously exaggerated versions of the male and female principles in the modern "war between the sexes," exchanging quick, ironic repartee that highlighted the absurdity of some of the ideas of the Provincetown group itself. But its lack of resolution is telling. This small society of male and female feminists and advocates of free sexual unions and equal marriages had not found a way to resolve their uneasiness around these issues. Boyce herself struggled throughout her marriage with her own response to her husband's double standard for sexual infidelity, leaving him for long periods, but never divorcing him. It is clear from the play that her concept of "constancy" differed from his, but she considered forbidding him to experiment sexually both futile and hopelessly Victorian. She did not condemn his behavior morally, but she felt that it was hurtful to her, and she could not understand why this was so. Her play universalizes their conflict into an inevitability, and it suggests that no end is in sight.

In *Enemies*, these issues are examined in a somewhat darker mood. Hapgood says in his autobiography that he and Boyce collaborated equally on *Enemies*, he writing the man's part and she writing the woman's, and that they "acted it together in the fish-house theatre."[14] The play has been compared to Strindberg's *The Stronger*, and there is something Strindbergian in its gender warfare despite its structurally comic resolution. This play, which Hapgood referred to as "a dialogue," does not pretend to be anything else. As it opens, a character called simply "She" lies on a chaise longue reading a book and smoking a cigarette – a marker of liberation and advanced views. Her husband "He" sits at a table trying to write an article of some kind. He keeps disturbing her reading with various complaints and accusations until she finally lays down her book and says, "I see you want to quarrel – so what shall we quarrel about?"[15] This apparently is their major mode of communication, and both are ready with well-rehearsed accusations. He complains that she has insufficient interest in housekeeping and in bringing up the children, as well as, most importantly, not enough interest in him: "All you want to do is to lie in bed for breakfast, smoke cigarettes, write your high literary stuff, make love to other men, talk cleverly when you go out to dinner and never say a word to me at home!" (120). He accuses her of being a "cold-blooded person," silent and uncommunicative, "unless we are quarreling" (123). "You have enslaved me," he says, "and your method is cool aloofness" (129). Although their tastes and their vices are "remarkably congenial," he contends, their "souls do not touch" (124). He accuses her of what he calls "spiritual infidelities" with other men, currently a man called Hank with whom she enjoys long afternoons of peace and quiet. The wife complains of her husband's sexual infidelities, most recently with a widow with whom he spent hours every day, his jealousy, and, more importantly, his attempts to dominate her: "what you want is to censor and control me, while you feel perfectly free to amuse yourself in every possible way" (128). His notion of loving her, she complains, is to "have tyrannized over me, bothered me, badgered me, nagged me, for fifteen years" (129). Because of his taking up her time and sapping her strength, she charges, he has prevented her from "accomplishing great works for the good of humanity" (129). Finally, she explodes: "You have crushed my soul, which longs for serenity and peace, with your perpetual complaining!" to which he responds, "Too bad" (129).

The fundamental difference between the two is in their world views. She is a pragmatist and a pessimist. He is an idealist and an optimist. She sees their perpetual quarrel as the inevitable result of their essential being. When her husband says that he is so rarely quiet with her because "you rarely express anything to me. I would be more quiet if you were less so – less expressive if you were more so," She responds that it is "the same old quarrel. Just the same for fifteen years! And all because you are you and I am I! And I suppose it will go on forever" (123–124). And She universalizes this condition to that of permanent and inevitable gender war:

> Men and women are natural enemies, like cat and dog – only more so. They are forced to live together for a time, or this wonderful race couldn't go on. In addition, in order to have the best children, men and women of totally opposed temperaments must live together. The shock and flame of two hostile temperaments meeting is what produces fine children. Well, we have fulfilled our fate and produced our children, and they are good ones. But really – to expect also to live in peace together – we as different as fire and water, or sea and land – that's too much! (130)

In their personal relations, She feels that a great distance has grown between them during their marriage, the inevitable result of their two identities. Her husband, She feels, is an idealist "longing for perfection in your soul" (134). She thinks He has treated their relationship and her as clay, modeling it "into the form you saw in your imagination." She insists, "You have been a passionate artist. But life is not a plastic material. *It* models us" (135). He agrees about the longing, but insists that it is "not for perfection, but for union ... No work of art is right, no matter how wonderful the material and the parts, if the whole, the unity, is not there" (134). She resists this desire, quoting his "favorite philosopher" against him, an inside joke because it is an allusion to Hapgood's favorite quotation from William James: "I cannot comprehend this wild swooning desire to wallow in unbridled unity" (131). In the end, however, these two self-confessed enemies do wallow in unbridled unity, as they come together in an "armed truce" and an embrace after She admits that she has always "adored the poet and mystic" in him and He admits that he has always "adored the woman" in her, "the mysterious, the beckoning and flying, that I cannot possess" (136).

In terms of the comic structure, this is a forced closure, a resolution in which nothing is really resolved. The same pattern of quarrel and truce will presumably go on the next day, and every day these two remain together. In comic terms, this suggests that the flawed order of things that exists at the beginning of the play, contemporary marriage, is irreparable, the gulf between men and women unbridgeable except in brief sexual interludes. In the context of the new view of marriage as a free union of

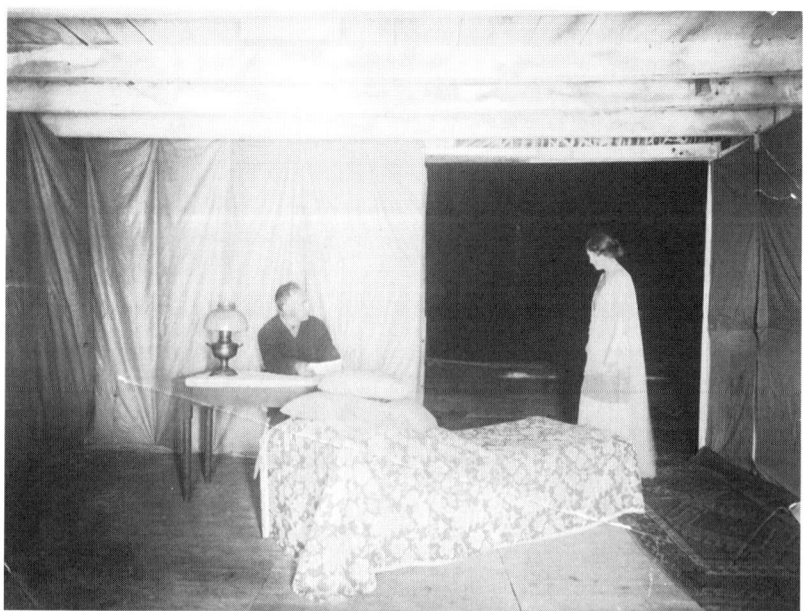

Figure 1. Hutchins Hapgood and Neith Boyce in *Enemies.*

equals that should be intellectual and emotional as well as sexual and economic, Hapgood and Boyce were sounding a distinctly pessimistic and conservative note here, despite the play's humor and its ostensibly comic form. Hapgood said that in writing the play, they were responding to "the latent feminism urging men to give up the ascendancy which women thought they had, and women to demand from men that which they didn't really want, namely so-called freedom from the ideal of monogamy." He thought the play "had a significance leading into the lives of many of my acquaintances and still further into a general situation between men and women," the total result of which was "a working-out of the situation into a more conscious companionship, greater self-knowledge, and a broader understanding of the relations between the sexes."[16] But it is clear that in 1916, this process had a long way to go.

The most conservative of the plays from the first two summers are the two comedies of manners with a satirical edge, *Suppressed Desires* and *Change Your Style*. The first takes on the fad of psychoanalysis that was rampant among Greenwich Villagers in 1915, and the second exposes some interesting cultural currents in the battle between the Academic and Post-Impressionist artists that was going on in Provincetown itself, and in fact included both audience members and actors among the principals. Susan Glaspell's explanation of the cultural phenomenon behind *Suppressed Desires* in *The Road to the Temple* is well known: "Those were the early years of psycho-analysis in the Village. You could not go out to buy a bun without hearing of someone's complex. We thought it would be amusing in a play, so we had a good time writing 'Suppressed Desires.'"[17] In the most informed and sophisticated analysis of the play to date, J. Ellen Gainor has noted that it "directly echoes" the ideas and concepts in popular articles on psychoanalysis by Floyd Dell and Max Eastman.[18] Appearing in December of 1915, Dell's article "Speaking of Psycho-analysis" is not a direct source for the play, but Max Eastman's "Exploring the Soul and Healing the Body," which appeared in the June issue of *Everybody's Magazine* could very well be.[19] Eastman's article is revealing in the context of the play's comedy, for it establishes directly several of the things that the play sets up for ridicule.

Most important in the context of *Suppressed Desires* is Eastman's extended discussion of Freud's case study of Elizabeth R–, who was relieved of her physical symptoms when she became conscious of a repressed desire for her brother-in-law, and his use of A. A. Brill's case study of a young woman who "dreamed that she was in a street with a large flock of chickens, who chased her, and the biggest one caught up with her and said something like 'Come with me into the dark.'"[20] The dream was interpreted to be an imaginary fulfillment of an unacknowledged wish to marry a rejected suitor. Eastman wrote that "all dreams can be proved to be such symbols, if the dreamer and the interpreter are willing to spend enough time unraveling the memories with which the objects in the dream are associated."[21] Glaspell and Cook's play opens with an argument between Stephen and his wife Henrietta over the validity of psychoanalysis, about which Henrietta has become very enthusiastic and is currently writing a paper to deliver to the Liberal Club. Stephen brings up "Art Holden's private secretary, Mary Snow, who has just been informed of her suppressed desire for her employer"[22] and Helen Dwight, who was "living, apparently, in peace and happiness with good old Joe" until she "went to this psychoanalyzer – and she was 'psyched,' and biff! – bang! – home she comes with an unsuppressed desire to leave her husband" (38).

In the course of the play, Henrietta decides that her sister Mabel is unhappy with her husband, and should get a divorce so she can be with a young man named Lyman Eggleston. Mabel has a dream: "I was pushing along through a crowd as fast as I could, but being a hen I couldn't walk very fast – it was like having a tight skirt, you know; and there was some sort of creature in a blue cap – you know how mixed up dreams are – and it kept shouting after me, 'Step hen! Step, hen!' until I got all excited and just couldn't move at all" (36). The comedy turns on several interpretations of the dream. Henrietta decides that dreaming she is a chicken means Mabel is harboring a "suppressed desire" for *Egg*leston. When Mabel mistakenly calls Mary Snow by her own name, Henrietta decides that she is suffering from the same kind of repressed desire that "was on the point of landing Mary Snow in the insane asylum" (39) and insists that she go to the psychiatrist A. E. Russell. To Henrietta's dismay, he tells her that Mabel has a suppressed desire for her brother-in-law Stephen (Step-hen) Brewster (Be-Rooster). The play implies that the most sensible interpretations of the dream are Mabel's naive associations, that she dreamed she was a hen because her sister had said she was "as mad as a wet hen" and she had dreamt about being told to "step hen" by someone in a blue cap because, as she says, "when I am getting on a street car it always irritates me to have them call 'Step lively'" (41–42).

Meanwhile, Stephen, an architect, has dreamt that the walls of his room have melted away and he is alone in a forest. This dream is interpreted by Russell as a suppressed desire to be freed from marriage, to which Henrietta has responded by saying that Stephen should leave her. When Mabel reveals the results of her psychoanalysis, however, Henrietta turns against psychoanalysis, saying the dream interpretation is based on "ridiculous coincidence" and a "trivial, meaningless play on syllables" (48). She says she is going to "stop talking psychoanalysis" because she has "seen what it does to people," and when Mabel asks what she is supposed to do with her suppressed desire, Steve gives her a "brotherly hug" and says, "Mabel, you just keep right on suppressing it!" (51).

Both Gainor and Fred Matthews have resisted viewing the play as a direct attack on Freudian psychology. Matthews suggests that "Cook and Glaspell were not ridiculing the New Psychology as such, but rather the pseudo-liberation of talk therapy and the dangers of liberation carried into narcissism."[23] Gainor also counters Arnold Goldman's earlier suggestion that the play is an attack on feminism, instead regarding Henrietta's quality as "the first in a series of Glaspell's female characters who embody extremes" as the focal point of criticism.[24] Gainor does somewhat reluctantly admit that the play's conclusion "could be viewed as 'conservative,'" however, noting that it is dramaturgically fitting, as "the classical comedy renews the heterosexual union, often through marriage."[25] I would suggest that, as a comedy of manners, the play's structure in fact pits psychoanalysis directly against the institution of marriage, suggesting that the new psychology is a direct threat to this institution, and, by extension, to social stability. In the play Henrietta is, as Gainor notes, the most unreliable of the characters, and her unbridled enthusiasm for the new psychology makes her dangerous to her family, in the persons of Mabel and Steve. While Mabel is a naive and passive victim of Henrietta's instability, Steve is a rational and controlled presence throughout. He begins by pointing out the errors and dangers of psychoanalysis, responds to Russell's suggestion and Henrietta's concurrence that he should leave by calmly planning a fishing trip, and ends in complete control by banishing psychoanalysis from the house and telling his sister-in-law to go back to the Victorian practice of suppressing her desires. It is the irrational, extremist Henrietta who speaks for psychoanalysis in the play, and the rational, controlled Steve who represents the opposition to it.

In the opening scene of the play, Henrietta complains that Steve has become "disagreeable. You certainly have got some sort of complex. You're all inhibited. You're no longer open to new ideas. You won't listen to a word about psychoanalysis" (35). Steve insists that he has listened to "volumes," and that he is only suffering "from a suppressed desire for a little peace" (35). When Mabel asks if psychoanalysis is the name of a new explosive, Steve responds, that "it *is*" (37) and calls it "the latest scientific method of separating families" (38), thus signifying both the danger of the new practice and the object of it. All of the examples of psychoanalysis in the play involve the potential breaking up of families: Mary Snow's desire for her boss, who has a wife and four children; Helen Dwight's divorce; Henrietta's insistence that Mabel must divorce her husband Bob if she harbors a suppressed desire for Lyman Eggleston; Russell's suggestion that Steve should seek his freedom from Henrietta; and Russell's suggestion that Mabel should leave her husband for Steve. The cavalier attitude that Henrietta expresses toward marriage and the family at first indicates the extent of the threat to the Victorian patriarchal structure: "Old institutions will have to be reshaped so that something can be done in such cases" (39). It is no accident that Cook and Glaspell have Steve, the architect, dreaming of the walls of his house melting away and putting the roof of the house he is designing in the cellar. The whole social structure based on the Victorian family is threatened by such thinking.

The answer they give is based on conservative, Victorian values. At the beginning of the play, Henrietta responds to Mabel's dismay that Helen Dwight has left her "good, kind husband" because of her psychoanalysis: "Oh, Mabel! 'Left her good, kind husband'? How naive – forgive me, dear – but how bourgeoise you are! She came to know herself. And she had the courage!" (39). At the end of the play, facing the threat that psychoanalysis poses to her own marriage, Henrietta says, "Mabel, have you thought of Bob – dear old Bob – your good, kind husband?" (49). It is Steve who takes control of the house, reestablishing the power hierarchy that had been undermined by Henrietta's intrusion of psychoanalysis into their relations. After exacting promises that she will "stop *talking* psychoanalysis," stop waking him in the night to find out what he is dreaming, and not only clear the psychology journal off Steve's work table, but burn it, Steve says, "My dear Henrietta, if you're going to separate from psychoanalysis, there's no reason why I should separate from *you*" (51) and they embrace, ardently. The play ends with Steve's telling Mabel to just "keep right on suppressing" her desires (51). In terms of comic structure, the social order has been restored with the reaffirmation of the heterosexual union, as Gainor has noted, but it is only through the purging of the new ideas about psychoanalysis, the institution of marriage, and the family from the household, and the reestablishment of the patriarchal power structure within the family, that this is made possible.

George Cram Cook's other comedy, *Change Your Style*, takes on the other pillar of modernity in 1915, Post-Impressionist art. As has been noted, Provincetown in 1915 was a well-established art colony and the site of fabled battles between the academicists allied with Charles Hawthorne and young insurgents such as Nordfeldt, the Zorachs, and Charles Demuth. In writing his one-act comedy about the artists, Cook chose to focus on the issue of economics that was central to many of their battles. In the play, the conflict between commercial and creative values in the production of art is neatly laid out by making Kenyon Crabtree, the Charles Hawthorne figure, an artist whose motives are completely commercial and Bordfelt, the figure that not only was based on Bröor Nordfeldt but was played by him in the production, an artist who is completely and inflexibly devoted to art as self-expression. Vacillating between them is young Marmaduke Marvin, Jr., who was played by Charles Demuth in the production. The play opens with a conversation between Marmaduke Junior and Bordfelt, in which Marmaduke Junior explains that he is about to lose his paternal subsidy because his father has given him three months to change his style from Post-Impressionism to something salable by studying under Crabtree, who produces the "deadest salon stuff."[26] Marmaduke Junior says that his father is reconciled to "the high-brow idea of having one painter in a banker's family – but a good, respectable, high-priced painter – like Crabtree. Not a painter like you, Bordfelt" (293). Bordfelt agrees with his disparaging view of the "old mummy" Crabtree, who runs a "Presbyterian art-school," but isn't quite sure that Marmaduke Junior is a painter like him, and Marmaduke Junior agrees: "No, I'm a free spirit, and you – you're an academician turned inside out " (293).

The conflict comes to life when two outsiders enter the scene, Myrtle Dart, a wealthy enthusiast of Eastern mysticism who is a send-up of Mabel Dodge, and Marmaduke Senior. Myrtle insists on buying a picture of Marmaduke Junior's because she believes it is "the spiritual form of the navel" (294). When Marmaduke Senior appears, he is angered to find that his son is still painting in the same style and looks around the studio muttering "Fifty dollars a month for this!" (295). He has a conversation with Crabtree in which the artist explains the economics of the art world to the banker, complaining that he has not sold a picture in a whole year because "this hectic stuff is all that gets talked about": "Not that people *like* this crazy stuff – it shocks them. But unfortunately – after the shock – they seem to lose all interest in sane art" (296). The banker's interest is piqued when he hears this, and he asks whether people buy the new paintings, to which Crabtree replies, "no, they are ruining us without in the least benefitting themselves. Nobody *buys* their stuff" (297). To this Bordfelt remarks, "I'm sorry, Mr. Crabtree, that we artists are hurting the picture business" (297). When Crabtree retorts that "failure to sell your pictures, Mr. Bordfelt, is not infallible proof that you are a true artist," Bordfelt responds, "to be more interested in selling one's pictures than in painting them is infallible proof that one is no artist at all" (297). At this point, Marmaduke Senior interjects an undeniable fact into the conversation, pointing out that "there's something wrong in the head of anyone whose income depends on the sale of pictures and is not interested in their sale" (297). This is the very trait that he has been worried about in his son.

When Marmaduke Junior reveals that he has actually sold a picture, and to Myrtle Dart, the terms of the conflict seem to shift, as suddenly it is he and not Crabtree who is the commercially viable artist. Marmaduke Senior expresses joy that his son's work has "begun to catch on" and tells him there is no need to change his style now. Crabtree decides it is time to "adapt ourselves to a changing world" and asks Nordfeldt to give him a few private lessons in Post-Impressionism, to which Bordfelt, inflexible, replies that "the new movement in art does not desire converts who join it for mercenary motives" (298). And Marmaduke Junior feels himself corrupted by the commodification of his art:

> I've had nothing but mercenary emotions since I sold that picture. It's transforming. It's like a cat's first taste of blood. I have a carnivorous desire to sell. I don't want to be carnivorous. I don't want to be caught by the horrible American moneylust. I don't feel like an artist any more. I'm commercialized. I might as well paint like Crabtree! (298)

Myrtle changes the matrix once again when she insists on giving back the painting, and demands that Marmaduke Junior, who has spent most of the money she gave him on his rent, pay her back the money. Marmaduke Junior is delighted that he is no longer a "commercialized" painter and need not paint like Crabtree. Crabtree decides that the economics of Post-Impressionism are a little too precarious for him. Marmaduke Senior the banker is astounded that his son would take back the picture. "Why didn't you tell her a sale's a sale? You! It wouldn't do you any good to change your style. You couldn't take care of yourself anyhow!" (299). He decides that "the revelation [his son] has made of his business capacity forces me to the conclusion that I owe it to society to support him – as a defective!" After Marmaduke Senior and Crabtree leave, Marmaduke Junior and Bordfelt end up drinking to "defective artists" (299).

In this little comedy, Cook reveals why the art world is a separate case that cannot be run on the principles of American business. In the Myrtle Dart exchange he shows the fickleness of the public and the tenuous relationship between the qualities of the art work and the reasons for its being sold. In Crabtree, he shows the emptiness of the so-called artist who works completely in response to an audience, only to produce a salable commodity, and in Bordfelt and Marmaduke Junior, the slightly deranged quality of the artist who works only to express himself, regardless of whether he has an audience or not. This dilemma had great implications for the participants in this production and for most of the audience that viewed it in 1915. It was a central issue for the artists of the Little Renaissance and it was to be a central conflict in the evolution of the Provincetown Players up until Cook left the company in 1922. In 1915, Cook's solution for the dilemma was to provide the *deus ex machina* of a patron who would free the artist to devote himself to expressing his own vision and yet still enable him to live a comfortable, middle-class life, something most of the artists in the group were reluctant to give up. Most of them, like Cook and Glaspell, and even Nordfeldt, were forced to devote a great deal of creative effort to writing and illustrating for magazines and newspapers that paid well in order to get a little time to do the work they wanted to do. There is a good deal of wish fulfillment in *Change Your Style*, but it is also a revealing look at some basic conflicts and values that prevailed in the group and its audience.

Wilbur Steele's *Contemporaries* was the first of the Provincetown plays to address a public issue beyond the special concerns of the self-defined group of Greenwich Village vacationers, and the only serious play produced during the Provincetown's first summer. It was based on a 1914 incident that was notorious in left-wing circles, and had been given considerable attention in *The Masses*. As a protest against the lack of attention being paid to the plight of the unemployed that winter, a young anarchist activist, Frank Tannenbaum, led a group of hungry and cold unemployed workers to seek shelter in St. Alphonsus church. Rather than helping the men, the Catholic priests called the police and had Tannenbaum arrested. He was convicted of disturbing the peace and sentenced to a year in prison. *The Masses* published two articles on the incident, including "The Tannenbaum Crime" by Max Eastman, and featured two drawings linking the teachings of Jesus with anarchist principles. Art Young's Christmas cover featured Jesus as a Nazareth carpenter sympathetic to the working man and John Sloan's *Calling the Christian Bluff* referred directly to the Tannenbaum case.[27] Drawing on his own religious background as the son of a minister, Wilbur Steele's play uses the incident to point out how far the institutional Church had strayed from the teachings of Jesus, especially when faced with concrete situations that called on it to practice them.

In its thematic strategy, *Contemporaries* is very much like a story by Steele or O. Henry. It uses sentiment to attach the audience's sympathy to some characters and alienate it from others, and then makes use of an ironic twist to convey its didactic message. In this case, however, the twist is not in the plot, but in the visual text on the stage, an indication that Steele's background and training in art had given him a much better sense of how the visual elements of the theatre might be used in drama than most of the Provincetown's playwrights had at the beginning. The play depends for its effect on being played in semi-darkness until the end. It is set in "*a congested quarter of the city; a single small room on the ground floor*"[28] of what appears to be an urban tenement. The curtain rises on a stage that is dark, "*save for a feeble jet of flame high on the back wall, right. A piece of board propped in front of this screens it from the eyes of the sleepers and further reduces its influence upon the gloom*" (64). The only light other than this comes from the single window in the back wall when "*an occasional pencil of brilliance*" (64) pierces the gloom as a light passes by in the street. Such a gleam of light allows the audience to see a tired and worn middle-aged woman move anxiously from window to door as she waits for her son to return. The other occupants of the room are her husband and a lodger who constantly complains about the bed bugs. In the course of the scene, the audience sees Sam, a boy, and Old John steal into the room in the dark. Sam is discovered by his parents, but John is unseen by the others.

Under questioning, Sam admits that he had been listening to an activist who has been organizing the working people: "I ain't ever heard a fellow talk like that one does. Comes right straight out about the churches and the priests and all, and they's scared to touch him on account of the mob, and the mob's with 'im" (67). The Lodger jokingly calls him "a regular anarchist" (67) and Sam's father, who works for the Church, is enraged that his son would put the family in jeopardy by attending such a rally. His fears are justified when a priest comes to the house in the company of policemen looking for a young man they accuse of inciting violence, as well as Old John. It turns out that Sam is not the boy they are looking for, but the priest takes the opportunity to make sure the boy will be beaten for going to the rally, and delivers a long speech linking obedience to the Church and obedience to the State. Sam is completely cowed by the priest, and agrees to serve as a spy for him, reporting any "wild, violent or sacrilegious talk" (73) he might hear in the street.

After the priest leaves, Old John is discovered trying to sneak out of the room, and when confronted, he defends the activist against the priest's accusations. In this speech, Steele manages to conflate contemporary anarchist rhetoric with the traditional teachings of Christianity and prepare the way for his "trick" ending. As the father kicks Old John out of the house, saying "we're going to clean out this town, and give decent men a chance to breathe," the dawn is breaking, and the room slowly brightening. The window begins to glow with red light. The father reveals to the audience its mistaken assumption about the time and place when he says, "I hear the camels gruntin' up out of the Vale of Kedron, an' the watchman cryin' already from the wall beyond Damascus Gate" (76). The mother lights an oil lamp and sits on the floor, beating grain with a pestle. The father opens the door, admitting "*the dull flush of dawn*" (76), which reveals his biblical clothing and beard as well as the ancient room behind him, and comments on the outside agitators who are invading the peace of the working man in Jerusalem. Finding out that the activist speech-maker is a carpenter from Nazareth, he says, "now why can't he stay up there, instead of botherin' us – stay up there and do his honest work in the world and have children and leave something behind him when he goes – something besides curses, and, maybe, a cross? I can't see . . . I can't understand" (77).

The ironic twist in the story is not only reflected in the stage lighting, it is brought about by it, for the truth presumably dawns on the audience as the light dawns on the stage. The play is heavily didactic. Its implied parallel between the teachings of Jesus and the teachings of anarchism is not to be missed, nor is its exposure of the unchristian attitudes and actions of the contemporary Church. For the early Provincetown Players, *Contemporaries* is an unusual play for several reasons. It is the first of the plays to use the theatre to make a serious statement about important events in contemporary society. Second, while it stays within the representational aesthetic of realism, it plays with the concept of representation, pushing the boundaries of the audience's shared perception and experience. With its didacticism, it confronts the audience directly, moving it out of the passive objectivity of simply observing and forcing it to respond to the implied challenge to its view of itself in Steele's analogy. Contemporary New York is like ancient Jerusalem, it says, and Frank Tannenbaum is like Jesus, and the contemporary priests who sent him to jail are like the priests and Pharisees who turned Jesus over to the Romans. It is up to the audience members to accept the analogy or reject it, and if they accept it, to respond to it in some way. Finally, Steele makes the theatrical elements of lighting, movement, costuming, and set design essential to conveying the play's meaning, and not just dialogue.

The three best plays of the summer theatre, and three of the best one-act plays American playwrights have produced, epitomize the maturing of realist aesthetics in the American theatre during the teens. O'Neill's *Bound East for Cardiff*, Boyce's *Winter's Night*, and Glaspell's *Trifles* may be seen as something of a culmination of the trend toward greater dramatic realism that grew out of American exposure to the turn-of-the-century American productions of Ibsen, Shaw, Hauptmann, Sudermann, and Strindberg, the tours of the Irish Players and the Moscow Art Theatre, and the enthusiastic praise by critics such as William Dean Howells and Brander Matthews for the realistic elements in the work of American playwrights like James A. Herne, Edward Sheldon, and Rachel Crothers. The American literary realists had called for a major shift in drama away from an aesthetics in which character, dialogue, and all the other elements were subservient to the pre-formed cookie-cutter plots of the well-made play. Howells called for an emphasis on character, and plots that were derived from life rather than imposed upon it. His concept of the ideal play was a completely believable representation of psychologically true-to-life characters in a recognizable contemporary situation through which significant psychological insights or sociological observations were revealed in the course of the action. By ignoring conventional dramatic plot paradigms and focusing on the interaction of their characters within a situation that has inherent importance, this is exactly what O'Neill, Boyce, and Glaspell accomplished in their plays. But more modern influences are evident in their aesthetics as well. Each of these playwrights made use of their characters and sets to suggest a realm of meaning beyond the accurate representation of aspects of contemporary society. It is in keeping with their realistic aesthetic that their mode of signification for this further meaning was metonymic – using synecdoche or metonymy – rather than symbolic. Using elements of the *mise en scène* in a figurative as well as representational way, they were pushing the boundaries of realism toward the symbolic, non-representational theatre of a Yeats or a Maeterlinck, the theatre that is usually characterized as modernist, but they did not go so far as to create a symbolist aesthetic. Their plays did not reference a disembodied conceptual world as symbolism does. The figurative language these playwrights produced, whether linguistic or visual, remained within the ontological world of the play through their skillful and sophisticated use of metonymic aesthetics.

O'Neill's *Bound East* has assumed the status of legend in the history of the Provincetown Players, largely because of Susan Glaspell's account of it in her memoir *The Road to the Temple*. Glaspell writes that she ran into O'Neill's friend Terry Carlin on Commercial Street early in the summer of 1916 and asked him whether he had any plays for the new theatre. Carlin suggested that his young roommate O'Neill had a "trunk full," and O'Neill was invited to read a play to the group. O'Neill being too shy, it was actor Fred Burt who read *Bound East*, and at the conclusion, in Glaspell's memorable phrase, "we knew what we were for."[29] Glaspell's version is the most arresting, and generous, for she characteristically places her own play *Trifles*, just as significant in putting the Provincetown Players on the map, in the background, placing all the focus on the dark young genius, O'Neill. It should be noted that there are other versions, however. The poet Harry Kemp, who played Davis in *Bound East*, has said that it was *The Movie Man*, his satirical play about the Mexican Revolution, that O'Neill first brought to the group, that it was rejected summarily by Jack Reed, and that *Bound East* was his second submission.[30] Hutchins Hapgood wrote that O'Neill first came to one of the group's meetings and "sat on the floor, perfectly silent, listening intently – a striking figure, his young face gaunt and taut-mouthed, his eyes burning." According to Hapgood, it was only after that meeting that he gave the manuscript for *Bound East*, interestingly, not to Glaspell but to Neith Boyce, to read: "Neith took it to Jig and said, 'We have got to do this play.' Jig read it and agreed, but said, 'I don't see how we can build that forecastle set in the fish-house.' But Jig loved problems; and he set to on this one and, within a day or so, he was building the set himself."[31] In themselves, the circumstances are not particularly important, but the various versions show how important the addition of O'Neill to the group was in its early myth-making.

As Louis Sheaffer has noted, *Bound East*, originally entitled *The Children of the Sea*, was an extraordinary accomplishment for the young O'Neill: "It is so markedly superior to *Abortion* and *The Movie Man* that it is difficult to believe that all three were written around the same time,"[32] in the spring of 1914. When examined in the context of the other plays put on by the Provincetown group that summer, *Bound East* is no less striking. Its detailed stage directions are as considered and as visually aware as those in O'Neill's mature full-length plays, which have become legendary for their detail and comprehensiveness. The set, though an ambitious undertaking for the amateur group, was elegantly simple, a representation of the milieu that it was possible to realize even on the crude stage of the Wharf Theatre. The play's action is at once the simplest and the most meaningful one can imagine. A man dies in the midst of the milieu in which he has lived a life that was the opposite of the one he had dreamed of. The action consists of his talking about it to his best friend. The characters are for the most part one-dimensional, but O'Neill develops the two main ones, the dying Yank and his friend Driscoll, with psychological and emotional complexity through dialogue that is completely natural within the situation. It is the play nineteenth-century American realists dreamed of.

The set for *Bound East* is a starkly realistic representation of the "*seamen's forecastle of the British tramp steamer* Glencairn"[33] at the same time that it is an eloquent visual synecdoche for the extremely confined and narrow milieu

Figure 2. A scene from *Bound East for Cardiff*.

that is the world of the lifetime sailor. The set consists of "*an irregular shaped compartment, the sides of which almost meet at the far end to form a triangle. Sleeping bunks about six feet long, ranged three deep, with a space of three feet separating the upper from the lower, are built against the sides*" (187). The space includes three or four portholes, a few wooden benches, a lamp, a water pail with a tin dipper, and the men's gear, such as oilskins, sea-chests, suitcases, and sea-boots, jammed in under the bunks. The far side of the forecastle "*is so narrow that it contains only one series of bunks*," and it is on the lower one of these that Yank lies dying from an internal injury sustained when he missed his footing on a ladder and fell into the ship's hold.

In this cramped space, five men sit talking and smoking pipes that fill the air with heavy tobacco smoke. The only alternative to this world for the men is going on watch up above, where there is "dirty weather." Every minute or so the steamer's whistle sounds. Before a word is said, the hellish confinement of life at sea is made clear to the audience. The play opens with the English Cocky, a "*weazened runt*," telling stories of adventures with exotic women in New Guinea, stories that none of the other sailors believe. It soon becomes apparent from their talk that this is a multiethnic group, including the Irish Driscoll and the dying Yank, an Englishman, a Scot, a Swede, a Norwegian, and a Russian. The play's irony turns on the fact that although these seamen have traveled the world and spend their days with men of many nations, they have the most limited of life experience. The men complain of the constant work, bad food, and incompetent officers they suffer as the inevitable state of things. When Yank and Driscoll reminisce, they talk of prostitutes and sailors' boarding houses that have swindled them, of fights they've been in, of getting drunk and sleeping on park benches and beaches. This and life at sea is the sum total of their world.

The play's realism functions partly to puncture any romantic dreams about life on the sea that the audience might have, but O'Neill also introduces irony and pathos into Yank's situation with the romantic dream that this hard-nosed sailor has built about the land. On his deathbed, he reveals his dream to Driscoll: "to stay on dry land all your life and have a farm with a house of your own with cows and pigs and chickens, 'way in the middle of the land where yuh'd never smell the sea or see a ship" (195). He dreamed of saving money and of going with Driscoll to "Canada or Argentine or some place and git a farm, just a small one, just enough to live on" (196). When Driscoll encourages him to think "it's a grand idea, and we'll be doin' ut sure if you'll stop your crazy notions – about – about bein' so sick" (196), Yank makes it clear that he knows it's too late. His only regret is that he will be buried at sea, on a "rotten night like this, with that damned whistle blowin' and people snorin' all around" (197), when he always wanted to be buried on dry land. Because of the weather, he can't even lie out on the deck and look at the stars, but must remain within the confinement of the forecastle, the visual synecdoche for his existential condition. When Cocky intrudes just as Yank has expired, calling Driscoll to "leave Yank for arf a mo and give me a 'and" (198), a moment of pathos and dignity is deflated by a reminder of the mundane and Yank's final inability to escape from the confines of his narrow world is brought home. But O'Neill also makes it clear that this life is not without significance. Both men stand in awe of the fact of death as a reminder of the supernatural. Driscoll makes a crude attempt to pray and Cocky ends the play saying in a hushed whisper, "Gawd blimey" (199). Yank's life may have been led within extremely constricted circumstances, and his dreams pathetic, but his passing is significant.

While O'Neill concentrates on the male homosocial society at sea, Boyce and Glaspell focus on the quintessential domestic setting, the kitchen, to establish a visual metonymy for the lives of their female characters. *Winter's Night* opens with Rachel Wescott's return to her home after a long, cold, winter ride. Her first line is, "Better blanket the team, Jacob. It'll be down to zero before morning."[34] At its opening, the play would seem to be a rather cozy, local-color domestic drama in the tradition of James A. Herne's *Shore Acres*. Rachel and Jacob seem to be a content and considerate domestic pair, as Rachel reminds Jacob about the horse and Jacob expresses concern about the long drive in the cold, and makes Rachel a cup of tea. Boyce describes her domestic setting in detail, indicating several elements that will have important thematic significance. The windows at the back show a dark landscape covered with snow, but within the kitchen, a fire glows in the stove, with "*a teakettle singing on top*" (41). The room contains a sewing machine and a basket "*piled with stuff*" as well as a shotgun. These last two items will become the poles of the conflict between the characters. When Rachel enters the room, Boyce notes that she is a middle-aged woman dressed in widow's black. The opening minutes could indeed be those of a Herne play, for they use his signature device of "quiet realism" as Rachel sits silently in her rocking chair and "*looks absently about the room.*" This action is a cue from Boyce to the audience to take notice of the surroundings that Rachel has created for herself and her family: "*In the light it is very attractive – the woodwork painted white, the curtains, couch cover and table cover of scarlet, several red and blue rugs on the floor, gay china showing in the cupboards, and some flowering plants on the windowsills*" (41). In contrast to the frozen landscape outside, Rachel has made a home that is vibrant and, with its potted flowers, literally full of life. Jacob, who, it soon becomes clear, is her brother-in-law, says that "liking colors the way you do, and fixing things up to look pretty" has "made a wonderful difference in this old house ... before you come into it, it was all gray and dull. You made it seem like a different place, all bright and cheerful, with flowers, too, even in winter" (43).

The death of Rachel's husband, a long-term invalid, has temporarily stilled Rachel's vibrant creative impulse, as she submits to the Victorian code of mourning. Surprised that Jacob removes his black coat immediately, saying "it's too tight for me," Rachel insists firmly: "I shall wear my crape a year for him, though heaven knows I've always hated black. But I always did my duty by my husband, and I shall now" (42). Boyce opposes the Victorian force of duty to Rachel's drive toward creativity and freedom metonymically through the objects on stage and their colors. Jacob knocks over a flower pot and breaks it, and he takes the red bow from her apron, foreshadowing the sexual threat that he will pose to her. He takes down the shotgun, saying that he is going to get the fox that has been after the "white pullets" (43), keeping it on his knee despite Rachel's protests. The actions and objects combine metonymic suggestions of sexuality in the red flower and bow and violence in the shotgun with the proverbial implication that Jacob is now the fox in the hencoop. The tensions come to a head when Rachel reveals her hopes for the future, now that she has done her duty by her husband. She tells of her plans to go to a city and start a dressmaking business. She says that, being childless, and having Jacob to take "all the care of the farm off me," she had taken up dressmaking, not because she needed the money, but "I like the work." Saying "I'm free now," she tries to explain to Jacob the drive for creativity that she wants to fulfill at last:

> I can have what I've always wanted – more life, something going on, and a business of my own – and, Jacob, you don't know how, all my life, I've loved colors and stuffs! ... Just to handle the velvets and silks and the rich colors would make me happy! I can't say why it is – it seems foolish – but a color I like – some of these deep reds or purples, why, it'll almost bring tears to my eyes, looking at it, I enjoy it so! (44)

Rachel's love of color, particularly vibrant reds and purples, and the joy of working with the medium itself echo the central aesthetic ideas of

Post-Impressionist art, particularly as expressed by the Zorachs. Boyce makes it clear that Rachel has the sensibility of an artist, and a modern one. Her dream is to devote her life to expressing it. But Jacob throws up an obstacle to Rachel by trying to get her to stay with him. He reveals that he has always loved her, despite the fact that she was married to his brother. He asks her to marry him, to which Rachel responds, "You're stark crazy!" (45). He insists that she will drive him over the brink of madness if she leaves him, and she tries to explain that, although she was fond of him "as a brother," she could never stay on the farm now that he has revealed his sexual feelings for her. When Jacob objects to her "meaning to go," she responds, "Why of course I mean to go! I'm in prison here, I have been for years!" (45). When she also refuses his pleas to take him with her, laughing a little, "*hysterically*," as she says, "two old people like us, we can't be thinking of such things," Jacob snaps, grabbing her. She breaks free of him and he sinks into a chair saying "Rachel – I wouldn't hurt you – don't be frightened – my dear, my dear – I'd never hurt you – I'll never say any more" (46).

Rachel's friend Sarah, who is to spend the night with her, finally arrives at this point, and Jacob takes the gun and goes outside. Sarah holds forth in a stream of conventional talk, which is meant to comfort Rachel, but only underlines ironically the emotional conflict between freedom and creative self-expression, and duty and imprisonment, that Jacob has imposed on her. At the end of this stream of talk comes the expected gun shot, much like that at the end of Ibsen's *Hedda Gabler*. Sarah asks what Jacob was shooting at, and Rachel replies, "It must be the fox – he was talking to-night about getting the fox" (46). When Sarah notices how shaken Rachel is by the shot, she goes out to investigate, and an offstage scream that became famous in the performance by Mary Heaton Vorse was heard before she came in and shrieked, "Down by the barn his head all blown to pieces – Rachel! Rachel!" (46). The debt to *Hedda Gabler* is obvious here, and the plot gestures toward melodrama as Ibsen's play does. But Boyce keeps her realistic aesthetic intact in this carefully motivated act and the response to it. While providing closure for the plot, she also completes the play's thematic statement at the figurative level with this act. In killing himself, Jacob has eliminated the threats of male sexuality and violence, figured in the fox and the shotgun, that are blocking Rachel's creative freedom. She is now free to leave. But he has also added a Victorian burden of guilt to her burden of duty.

Susan Glaspell's far better-known play *Trifles* has been analyzed from many perspectives, but, as Judith Barlow has suggested, viewing it in the context of *Winter's Night* is revealing.[35] *Trifles* was clearly written after Glaspell had seen *Winter's Night*, and with Boyce's play very much in mind. *Winter's Night* was produced as part of the first bill in the newly refurbished Wharf Theatre, on July 13, 1916, along with John Reed's *Freedom* and *Suppressed Desires*. The second bill, which Sarlós dates at sometime between July 24 and July 28, included *Bound East for Cardiff*, *"Not Smart"*, and Louise Bryant's *The Game*. In *The Road to the Temple* Glaspell is vague about chronology, but she is clear about the fact that she wrote *Trifles* after the production of *Bound East* in response to her husband's declaration that he had announced a play by her "for the next bill."[36] This would presumably have been in late July. When she protested that she had no play and didn't know how to write one, he responded that she would have to sit down the next day and begin one. She says that she wrote the play in ten days and that it was put into rehearsal while she was still finishing it.[37] *Trifles* was part of the third summer bill, opening August 8, along with *The Eternal Quadrangle* and a revival of *Constancy*.

Linda Ben-Zvi has analyzed Glaspell's use of her reportage on an Iowa murder case as a basis for *Trifles* and the later short story, "A Jury of Her Peers," and several critics have written about Glaspell's innovative use of the conventions of detective fiction in the play.[38] It is also profitably analyzed as a complement to, perhaps the obverse of, *Winter's Night*. Boyce's play is about a woman who is essentially freed by her husband's death from the "prison" of marriage and Victorian duty to express a creative gift that has found only partial outlets within her restricted life as a farm wife. Inspired by her vivid memory of a 1900 court case she had covered as a reporter in Iowa, in which Mrs. Hossack, a physically abused Iowa farm wife, was convicted of killing her husband with an ax, Glaspell takes the situation a step further in her play. Suppose Rachel had not had a comfortable home with an invalid husband and a devoted brother-in-law who delighted in the vibrant creativity she brought to her housekeeping and took the drudgery of the farmwork off her shoulders. Suppose she had been married to a mean-spirited, stingy, abusive patriarchal husband who stifled every impulse she had toward beauty and creativity. How could she have escaped from her prison then?

Glaspell's set, like Boyce's, is an example of the eloquent uses to which realism can be put. While Rachel's kitchen expresses her creativity and love of vibrant colors, however, Minnie Wright's is "*a gloomy kitchen, and left without having been put in order – unwashed pans under the sink, a loaf of bread outside the bread-box, a dish-towel on the table – other signs of uncompleted work.*"[39] Besides her domestic work having descended to chaos, Minnie's preserves have exploded as a result of the cold, leaving only one jar of cherries intact.[40] The play takes the form of a detective story, although, as J. Ellen Gainor has noted, it manipulates the conventions of detection in order to convey Glaspell's feminist point of view, implying that both male and female viewers must "learn to see as the women do, to become feminist spectators, and realize that this kind of seeing is different from, and in this case superior to, the men's way."[41] In the play, the Wrights' neighbors, Mr. and Mrs. Hale, have come with Henderson, the County Attorney, Sheriff Peters, and his wife so that the men can investigate the scene of the crime of John Wright's murder and the women can collect some clothes for Minnie Wright, who has been arrested for the crime. John Wright has been strangled with a rope placed around his neck in his sleep and the men do not believe Minnie's story that she knows nothing about it, having slept through it in the bed next to him. Henderson has said that "what was needed for the case was a motive; something to show anger, or – sudden feeling" (40). The men immediately leave the kitchen for the scene of the crime, commenting that "there was nothing important here – nothing that would point to any motive . . . nothing here but kitchen things" (38).

In the course of the action, the women find what they believe is the motive precisely by concerning themselves with the "trifles" of housekeeping in the kitchen. They note the dreariness of the kitchen, and comment on John Wright's harshness and stinginess. Mrs. Hale comments that "he was a hard man . . . just to pass the time of day with him – (*shivers*) Like a raw wind that gets to the bone" (42). The women find the "*bright pieces*" of a quilt Minnie was making, noting "it's a log cabin pattern. Pretty isn't it," and begin to exchange looks of understanding when they find that her even stitching had gone awry in the most recent work: "it looks as if she didn't know what she was about!" (41). Finding an empty birdcage with the door torn off the hinges, Mrs. Hale says she might have bought a canary from a peddler, "she used to sing real pretty herself" (42). Looking for Minnie's sewing things, they find the dead canary, its neck wrung, in a decorative box wrapped in silk, and "*their eyes meet. A look of growing comprehension, of horror*" (43).

Glaspell uses the bright quilt pieces and the bird metonymically, as Boyce uses the brilliantly colored material, the flowers, and the shotgun.

Minnie's artistic potential and her love of beauty, finally expressed only in these diminished ways, were ultimately destroyed by Wright. Mrs. Hale says, "No, Wright wouldn't like the bird – a thing that sang. She used to sing. He killed that, too" (44). With the implicit knowledge of who killed John Wright and why, the women feel a complicit understanding of Minnie Wright. Mrs. Hale berates herself for not coming to visit Minnie in a house she stayed away from "because it weren't cheerful – and that's why I ought to have come" (42). She decides "that was a crime ... I might have known she needed help" and she enunciates one of Glaspell's perennial monist themes: "we live close together and we live far apart. We all go through the same things – it's all just a different kind of the same thing" (44). The women cooperate in erasing the "trifles" that the men might possibly come to see as evidence, ripping out the awkward stitches and putting the canary in Mrs. Hale's pocket, although Mrs. Peters remarks, "wouldn't they just laugh! Getting all stirred up over a little thing like a – dead canary" (44). Glaspell underlines the irony of the men's ineffective investigation with the attorney's remarks as they are getting ready to leave: "It's all perfectly clear except a reason for doing it. But you know juries when it comes to women. If there was some definite thing. Something to show – something to make a story about – a thing that would connect up with this strange way of doing it" (44). In order to solve the mystery of Minnie Wright's action, the men would have to learn to see the world as she did, an impossible thing while they considered her world beneath their notice. As Gainor points out, Glaspell's subject is as much the way of knowing as the object of knowledge.

In the context of *Winter's Night*, Glaspell's play presents the situation of the creative woman in a much darker light than Boyce's does. Boyce presents the domestic demands of marriage and the restrictions on women's freedom by outmoded Victorian values as obstacles that can be overcome, although the act of overcoming may be fraught with guilt. Glaspell suggests that if the potential for creativity and the appreciation of beauty is chilled and stifled enough, the force that seeks life may turn to rage, and women will revolt against their obstacle, killing off their immediate oppressors, the patriarchal authority-figures in their lives. Boyce's is essentially an upper-middle-class reading of women's lives. Although putatively a farm wife, Rachel is free from the normal economic necessities and domestic demands that normally go with that job. She has a great deal of freedom to create even within the domestic sphere, the equivalent of "a room of one's own," and an economic base from which to stage her revolt when she decides to give up domesticity and go to the city where she can devote all her time to her creative activity. For Boyce, who grew up in comparative wealth, and whose experience with farm life was primarily as a carefree child on her father's ranch in California, the most imaginable domestic "prison" was an emotional and moral one.

Glaspell's Minnie is closer to the economic reality of the farm wife during the teens. The most immovable limitations on her freedom are economic. Her marriage to Wright sentences her to a life of hard work on the farm. It doesn't help that she has no money for decent clothes because he is so stingy, and so stays away even from church and the regular social gatherings of the community. Both physically and emotionally, she has far less freedom to move than Rachel. While Boyce's play is a hopeful message of liberation for the female artist, Glaspell's is darker, a call for understanding of female rage and of female solidarity in support of the women who find themselves in life situations like Minnie Wright's. And it does not suggest that there is any way of escaping them short of violence. To worry about Minnie Wright's wasted artistic potential would be a luxury, Glaspell suggests, while her sanity and her survival are at risk.

These three plays suggest the possibilities of a realistic theatre that makes full use of a metonymic aesthetic. Without sacrificing any of the audience's recognition of its representational fidelity to contemporary life, this drama suggests that there are many dimensions of meaning in the material facts of human existence. The first two summers of the Provincetown group also produced several plays that pushed the boundaries of realism further toward a non-representational theatre, essentially leaving the claim to representation of a shared experience behind. John Reed's *Freedom: A Prison Play* and Eugene O'Neill's *Thirst*, while tenuously within the realistic mode, both make a major move into abstraction, with metaphorical situations and characters that are unabashedly abstract types. Historically, readers of *Freedom* have come to it with the misconception that it was a radical left-wing play. This was produced first by Hutchins Hapgood's account that Reed

> wrote one or two short plays, which, according to our custom, he cast, produced, and also acted in. These plays were not successful and probably have not survived anywhere. Jack was keen about 'ideas'; not interested in any play, or probably in any other literary form, that did not carry a sociological thesis. He attempted to put over some of these ideas and in the attempt lost his quality as a writer, his feeling as a poet.[42]

This notion carried into the description of *Freedom* in Deutsch and Hanau's history as a "stirring, bitter prison play" and Gerhard Bach's statement that it "exemplifies this tendency toward kitchen-sink realism intermingled with traditional idealism."[43] It was not until Robert Sarlós summarized it in his 1982 history that *Freedom* came to be seen as "a hilarious farce."[44] It is something more than this, as well, for it is essentially the dramatization of a metaphor, and it unabashedly makes use of type characters that are identified by their names – "The Poet," "The Romancer" – in order to dramatize abstract cultural forces. *Freedom* was one of the plays rejected by the Washington Square Players before it was produced in Provincetown. It is based on Reed's experience when he was sentenced to twenty days in jail during the Paterson strike in 1913, an experience which, according to his biographer, had a profound effect on him. He had come to Paterson as a young reporter seeking the adventure of covering the strike. Jailed on what was as much a matter of pride as of principle, because he refused to move from the shelter of a porch roof when told to by a policeman, Reed found himself facing the realities of jail: confinement, dirt, vermin, inedible food, and boredom. As an editor of *The Masses*, he was a privileged character among the strikers in prison, and found himself vacillating between relishing his special status and being ashamed of it. He wrote to his friend Eddy Hunt: "My infernal sense of Romance and Humor makes me rather enjoy" the experience of jail.[45]

Rather than a realistic representation of Reed's experience in prison, *Freedom* is a dramatization of the conflicting responses that he felt toward it, responses that are abstracted into cultural phenomena so as to make a statement about the restrictions on freedom within the culture itself. As a number of observers have noted, John Reed was a complex and contradictory mix of many American attitudes and values. Daniel Aaron described him as "poet, adventurer, romanticist, collegian."[46] In *Freedom*, Reed wrote an early form of monodrama in which the conflicting attitudes and desires within his own personality are anthropomorphized and given full rein to interact as characters within the paradigm of a farcical comedy.

The main characters in *Freedom* are three prisoners, the Poet, the Romancer, and Smith, who are trying to make a jail break. They tunnel into the cell of the Trusty, an elderly prisoner who has earned a number of privileges by his good behavior, and has come to believe, as he tells a guard, that he is in prison because the Lord has taken vengeance on him, and the Law is "a revelation from on high."[47] In the course of the play, both the Poet and the Romancer display their weaknesses, as Smith, a self-described "low-brow that just wants to get out" (85), keeps complaining that they are holding up the jail break. The Romancer is a Tom Sawyer character who has gotten all his ideas about prison, and his lingo, from adventure books, and says things like, "Don't move. One step, damn you, and I'll blow you so full of holes you can't hold water!" (79). Like Tom Sawyer, he has paid a lot of attention to creating oaths which have to be signed in blood, having rope ladders smuggled into him in pies, and making a file out of a table knife by grinding it with his teeth. He insists, "we want to do it *right*, or not at all! If we can't do the thing properly, we won't do it. We're going to escape from here like gentlemen, or else we're not going to escape!" (85). The Poet is equally caught up in language, which he employs extravagantly: "Bright with the loathsome phosphorescence of putrescence! Adroit as the slimy members of a specimen of saurian reptilia!" (84). He has created an identity for himself while in prison, that of Jenkins, the Prison Poet, whose verses have appeared in "all the magazines." He says proudly that "it has been said that not since Oscar Wilde has anyone written so touchingly of Freedom. That's my line, you know – Freedom, Liberty, the Man in the Cage, the Iron Entering Into the Soul" (84). For Reed, who got himself arrested on principle for adventure and headed the letters he wrote from jail "Reading Gaol," there is a good deal of self-recognition and self-mockery in these portraits.

While the Poet and the Romancer hold things up quite a bit, Smith, the man of action, manages to keep the jail break going according to plan until they run into the Trusty and are ultimately unable to convince him to join them. He decides that he does not want to give up the position he has earned in prison, "a trusty, a man of responsibility in this community," a status he has "worked up to" from "the bottom ... with the help of the Lord God and His excellent Book" (89). He refuses to go with them because he is "well enough off here ... I'm a man of position in this jail, and if I go out into the world, I'll be nothing but a bum again" (89). Stirred by the Trusty's speech, the Poet decides that he would be making a "dreadful mistake" in leaving the prison: "I have told you my line was Liberty. For God's sake how can I write about Freedom when I'm free?" (90). Finally, the Romancer, finding that there is no resistance to their breaking out of jail, "no wall, no guard to shoot ... not even a little iron bar to file" (90), decides that he can't go through with the escape: "What's the use of escaping from a prison you can just walk out of? No man of honor would take advantage of such weakness" (91). Deserted by the others, Smith decides to take action on his own:

> Well the difference between you sapheads and me is that *I want to get out* and you just think you do. You're playing a little game where the rules are more important than who wins. I'm willing to grant you that you have it on me as far as honor, and patriotism, and reputation go, but all I want is Freedom. So, if you don't mind, gentlemen, I'll just be on my way.
> (91)

As Smith begins to climb through the window, the others decide that he has betrayed them and the code of the gentleman by taking action on his own, and they pull him back into the cell, calling him a coward and a traitor, and preparing to shoot him as a deserter. Smith responds, "You hypocrites! Just because you aren't as free as I am, you're jealous" (91). The others turn him in to the guard, who asks him what he has to say for himself, and Smith replies, "there's not a word of truth in it. I was trying to break into a padded cell so I could be free!" (92).

The implications of the play for American culture reflect its meaning for Reed personally. It was his experience in jail that made him decide to become a man of action in radical politics rather than a poet and an intellectual observing the action from the sidelines. The play is in one sense a metaphor for his breaking out of the prison of the conflicting identities among which he had vacillated since his graduation from Harvard. If he was to be judged as crazy for giving up his bourgeois lifestyle and respectable position as an editor of the *American* magazine, he was ready to embrace that identity in order to be free. In terms of its cultural implications, Reed was also sending a message to his fellow bohemians in Greenwich Village and Provincetown. Unless they were willing to live their radical politics, however mad that might make them appear to others, they would remain the prisoners of what he considered an outworn nineteenth-century culture. Viewed in this way, the little farce of *Freedom* rises to the status of a significant cultural metaphor for modernity. For John Reed, all the art and all the talk of Greenwich Village meant nothing without the will to take action that would change society.

In one of the early critical books on Eugene O'Neill, Olivia Coolidge remarked that his play *Thirst* "is not truly realistic, and yet not symbolic either."[48] This play, written during O'Neill's "apprentice year" of 1913–1914, when he wrote eight one-act and two full-length plays at breakneck speed, shows the influence of his reading of contemporary European playwrights, notably Strindberg and Maeterlinck, who wrote realistic plays with expressionist and symbolic elements. O'Neill's play is about three passengers from a sunken luxury liner who are adrift in a life raft, an unusual situation, but certainly not one beyond the bounds of contemporary experience, particularly with the recent sinking of the *Titanic*. As Reed does in *Freedom*, O'Neill uses his three characters, A Gentleman, A Dancer, and A West Indian Mulatto Sailor, in an abstract metaphorical way, while the action of the play maintains a tenuous hold on realism. The action takes place after the characters have been at sea for several days, surrounded by sharks, and, having run out of food and water, are going mad from the effects of thirst and the sun. In the course of the play, the Dancer and the Gentleman develop the delusion that the Sailor has stolen the last of the water and is holding out on them, and they try to get it from him. The Dancer, a beautiful young woman who has made her way by getting "gifts" from elderly gentlemen in exchange for her favors, first suggests that they steal the water, and then that they kill the Sailor to get it. The Gentleman agrees that he "deserves to be killed,"[49] but decides that they are too weak to do the job. The Dancer tries to get the Sailor to give her water, first by trading it for a diamond necklace that is the last of her possessions, and then by offering him her body. Although stirred briefly from his torpor by her second offer, he just keeps repeating his refrain, "I have no water." Finally driven mad, the Dancer tries to strangle the Sailor, and thrown to the deck, finally goes over the edge into madness, believing she is performing under hot footlights and dancing *"like some ghastly marionette jerked by invisible wires"* (50) until she finally falls back and dies. When the Sailor indicates cannibalistic intent, brandishing his knife and saying, "We shall eat. We shall drink" (51), the Gentleman is overcome with revulsion and pushes the Dancer's body overboard to the sharks. The enraged Sailor stabs the Gentleman, who falls into the water, and, with a last desperate effort, pulls the Sailor in with him. The sharks close in, and a *"black stain on the water widens. The fins circle no longer. The raft floats in the midst of a vast silence. The sun glares down like a great angry eye of God. The eerie heat waves float upward in the still air like the souls of the drowned. On the raft a diamond necklace lies glittering in the blazing sunshine"* (51).

In the broadest sense, the play is O'Neill's metaphor for the human condition. The characters play out a miserable existence with a certain end. As the Gentleman says, "what does it matter? – sharks or no sharks – the end is the same" (40). The sense of irony O'Neill creates is similar to that of Stephen Crane in writing about similar situations.[50] The Dancer wails, "God! Oh God! Must this be the end of all? I was coming home, home after years of struggling, home to success and fame and money. And I must die out here on a raft like a mad dog" (41). The Gentleman, too, notes the irony that this should happen as he was returning from his first vacation after a life of devotion to business: "Is this the meaning of all my years of labor? Is this the end, oh God?" (42). The answer is of course the eye of God looking down at the black stain on the water as the play ends. O'Neill's thematic statement echoes Crane's proto-existentialism in its implication that God is indifferent to the plight of individual human beings – a contradiction of the traditional Christian notions of Divine Providence and of the possibility for a personal relationship with God.

More specifically, O'Neill emphasizes the futility of the three approaches to life embodied in the three characters. The Gentleman expresses many of the traditional Victorian values of his class. With a sense of *noblesse oblige*, he expresses pity for the Sailor, who seems unable to speak clearly. He expresses moral judgments of the ship's Captain for having killed himself as the ship sank and justifies his willingness to kill the Sailor for his water with the moral judgment that he deserves it for having stolen the water from the group. He follows the code of the Gentleman in trying to protect the Dancer, shielding her from reality by lying to her that sharks never attack human beings, and finally dying for his values when he refuses to let the Sailor live by cannibalizing the Dancer's body. In the end, O'Neill suggests, it's all the same, the sharks get them all, so what is the difference if one lives by a code of values? By contrast, the other two characters seem to have no moral or social code inhibiting their self-interest. The Dancer, who has lived an essentially parasitical existence, prostituting her talent, is quite ready to steal, kill, or barter anything she has to survive. The Sailor, who seems to have no other thought than self-preservation, has no compunction at all about taking the most taboo of human actions to survive. Their existence suggests a deeper irony than the Gentleman's, since, after all, they do not survive. They represent human life spent entirely in the inherently futile pursuit of preserving itself. What's the point? O'Neill's ideas in the play may be seen as a fairly adolescent rebellion against unexamined values and received truisms. Like Stephen Crane, he expresses the anger of the young man who has been raised with the conviction of religious faith and finds that the facts of life don't seem to support it. Life should make sense, he suggests, it should be fair and moral, but it isn't. This play represents the beginning of a long journey of spiritual questioning by its author.

Besides his "modern" rejection of Victorian values and certainties, O'Neill's play also suggests an embracing of avant-garde dramaturgy. The move toward abstract types in the characters is a move toward the anti-representational techniques associated with symbolism. The stage directions are the play's most modern element, however. It is not only the ending that evokes a metaphorical visual image. O'Neill makes it quite clear from the beginning that his stage is an image of the universe of a pitiless God: *"The sky above is pitilessly clear, of a steel blue color merging into black shadow on the horizon's rim. The sun glares down from straight overhead like a great angry eye of God. The heat is terrific. Writhing, fantastic heat-waves rise from the white deck of the raft. Here and there on the still surface of the sea the fins of sharks may be seen slowly cutting the surface of the water in lazy circles"* (31). The stage directions gesture toward expressionism in conveying the subjective perception of the characters at the same time that they suggest a scenic image that conveys the play's central metaphor that life is hell, and the only escape is death.

Helen Deutsch and Stella Hanau suggest in their history that William Zorach recognized the nascent Post-Impressionist visual elements in *Thirst*, but was not allowed to develop them in a stage design: "Zorach was beginning to have ideas on what stage designs should be like – 'something related to art' – and he tried to follow up his success with 'The Game' by painting a backdrop of formalized waves. But Cook and Reed, who had given him *carte blanche* with 'The Game,' insisted that O'Neill was a realistic playwright. Crumpled canvas water was substituted and a realistic playwright Eugene O'Neill remained, until years later."[51] This rings true, since Zorach was impatient with O'Neill's adherence to realism when it came to staging. He told Arthur and Barbara Gelb that "the setting included a sea cloth with someone wriggling around underneath it to represent the ocean," something O'Neill "insisted on."[52] An avant-garde staging by the Zorachs might have done something for *Thirst*, by all accounts a failure when it was produced late in the summer of 1916, but it was never revived. Its clumsy aesthetic mix demands something other than the straight realistic production it apparently received. In the first critical book on O'Neill, Barrett Clark, who interviewed many of the participants about the early productions of the Provincetown Players, compared it to Jack London's *The Call of the Wild*, saying "the best that can be said of *Thirst* is that it is a forthright and daring melodramatic scene."⁵³

Louise Bryant's existential allegory, *The Game*, was one of the group's slighter efforts at playwriting during the first two summers, but because of her collaboration with William and Marguerite Zorach, it became their most important dramatic experiment. The play was barely accepted for production, partly because of the group's low estimate of Bryant as a writer. Cheryl Black has noted that Bryant was not much liked by the other members of the group, aside from Reed, with whom she was living, and O'Neill, with whom she had an affair in the fall, while Reed was in the hospital. Men in the group "characterized her as a 'bitch,' a 'nymphomaniac,' and a 'whore.'"⁵⁴ Women refused to take her seriously. Mary Heaton Vorse once remarked that Bryant "thinks the revolution is so everyone can have a fur coat" and Stella Ballantine expressed resentment over her favored status because of her attachment to Reed with her much quoted sentiment that "Bryant was not really a playwright, she only slept with one."⁵⁵

Few of the Provincetown writers saw anything of interest in the play, which even Bryant's biographer calls "a rather stilted attempt at parable."⁵⁶ From the perspective of the Zorachs, however, the script was a highly suggestive occasion for approaching theatre as a modernist work of art, an integrated symbolic structure, organic in form. William Zorach wrote about their discovery of the play in his autobiography:

> Louise Bryant had written a little English morality play called *The Game*. It was not much in itself, but she wanted to produce it and thought an exciting stage set might put it over. I must confess that we were as determined to do things our way as the playwrights were to do them theirs. Louise said we could do whatever we wished with her play and even asked me to act in it. We were delighted with the opportunity to put on a play and ruthlessly turned an English morality play into a sort of Egyptian pantomime.⁵⁷

The program for *The Game* contained a note that clarified the intention of the Zorachs, who both designed and directed the play. It said that the production was "an attempt to synthesize decoration, costume, speech and action into one mood," and made it clear that the production's aesthetic was a deliberate and complete break from representational realism: "Starting from the idea that the play is symbolic of rather than representative of life, the Zorachs have designed the decorations to suggest rather than to portray; the speech and action of the players being used as the plastic element in the whole unified convention."[58] This concise statement is a good description of the modernist aesthetic the Zorachs were trying to develop in the theatre. They were to meet discouragement with O'Neill, who apparently was not yet ready to break with representational theatre completely, but they would pursue their experiments with like-minded modernists like Alfred Kreymborg, William Carlos Williams, Mina Loy, and eventually Edna St. Vincent Millay, during the next few years.

The Game is a simple allegory in which two characters, a male Death and a female Life, are engaged in a game of dice, which must be played every day because "it's the law" (29). Each day they play for the lives of some human beings, and on this day, it is "The Girl," a dancer, and "Youth," a poet, whom Death describes as "a couple of suicides" and Life describes as "geniuses." In the course of the play, it comes out that the young man is suicidal; his lover has left him because "an ugly beast came and offered her gold" (33). Although Life explains to him that it was not love he felt, but only desire, he doesn't believe her until The Girl comes on the scene, and he discovers true love. She is smarter and more experienced than Youth, since she realizes that what the men who besieged her at the stage door every evening, sent her flowers, and jewels, and even killed themselves for was only desire, and "they wanted to buy me in order to destroy me" (36). Realizing this, she has rejected them all, but she is ready to kill herself because she thinks she will never find love. When she finds out who Youth is, she dances two of his poems for him, and he realizes that, unlike all the other women, she understands him. The Girl and Youth now hesitate in their intention to kill themselves. The Girl has found Youth, and Youth has found "Love – real Love at last" (38). Youth is determined that The Girl will not die because "Love is stronger than Death!" (38).

What follows is a debate about the value and meaning of Life. Death tries to convince The Girl that Youth doesn't love her, but only her art in service to his: "It is not you he loves, but your dancing of his songs. He is a Poet – therefore he loves only himself . . . you will one day be forgotten" (38). Life replies, "I can only give happiness for a moment – but it is real happiness – Love, Creation, Unity with the tremendous rhythm of the universe . . . What if it is himself he loves in you? That, too, is Love" (38). The Girl becomes a convert to this monist version of *carpe diem*: "To be supremely happy for a moment – an hour – that is worth living for!" (38). Offering a final peace, Death reminds The Girl of the torment of Life:

"she pours out the sunshine before you to make you glad; she sends the winter to chill your heart. She gives you Love and Desire – and takes them away. She brings you warm quietness – and kills it with hunger and anxiety" (38). The Girl disdains the idea of peace, but hesitates, acknowledging "Life is so cruel!" (39). But Death reminds Life that the game is incomplete. She has won the toss of the dice to save Youth, but they have not yet played for The Girl. They play, and Life wins, but Death reminds her, "some day we'll play for those two again – and then it will be *my* turn" (40). Youth replies, "Yes. But we will have *lived*. Until then, Death, you are Powerless. I fear you not, and I will guard her from you" (40).

Although the play remains in the realm of allegory, it does make a veiled allusion to the most obvious contemporary killer of youth that was staring its audience in the face, World War I. At the beginning of the play, Life offers Death "Kaiser Wilhelm, The Czar of Russia, George of England and old Francis Joseph" in exchange for the two young people, but Death refuses, saying "you're always trying to unload a lot of monarchs on me when you know I don't want them" (30). When she offers to trade them for a whole regiment of soldiers, Death responds scornfully: "Soldiers! What do you care about soldiers? ... You've been losing millions of soldiers in Europe for the past two years – and you're much more excited about these two rattle-pated young idiots" (31). At the end of the play, after Life has won the game for the two young people, Death asks her why she makes "such a fuss over dreamers" and cares so little for soldiers. She replies that "soldiers don't matter one way or the other to me; but some day the dreamers will chain you to the earth, and I will have the game all my way" (41). After Death has gone, however, she begins to count her losses, and the play ends with her line, "I must never let him know how much I mind losing soldiers. They are the flower of youth – there are dreamers among them" (42).

As noted above, the Zorachs' concept for the play was an Egyptian pantomime, which owed a good deal to the design that Léon Bakst had done for Diaghilev's ballet *L'après-midi d'un faune*. The ballet had caused quite a stir when it was produced in New York in January of 1916, and the final scene was altered because it was considered too suggestive by police censors.[59] Although the figures in the ballet are meant to be Greek, Bakst's design and costumes showed a marked Egyptian influence. Marguerite Zorach designed the backdrop for *The Game*, a stylized Egyptian-influenced scene which William described as "a decorative and abstract pattern of the sea, trees, the moon, and the moon path in the water."⁶⁰ The design for this backdrop, which, as William proudly noted, was used by the Provincetown Players as a decoration in front of the theatre in New York for years, was also executed as a linoleum block print by Marguerite for the program and was used as logo for the Players on brochures and announcements, a visual assertion of their claim to be a modern, experimental theatre. Robert Sarlós offers a good interpretation of the abstract backdrop, which was used in two Provincetown productions in July and September and in the New York production in November:

> Top center, the setting sun is framed in a diamond and surrounded by triangular hills. The sun's reflection lies heavily across the sinuous lines of waves from horizon to the bottom of the drop. Ten trees, symmetrically arranged on either side of the sun, resemble ancient columns, their foliage like so many fans. Dunes and stones in the foreground are painted with childlike simplicity of line and perspective.⁶¹

Zorach noted that "the costumes were slight and abstract and the movements were worked out in a flat plane in pantomime"⁶² like the figures in an Egyptian wall-painting. In Provincetown, the costumes were extremely simple. All the actors were barefoot. Zorach as Youth was stripped to the waist, wearing only a wrap tied around his waist with a sash. The

Figure 3. Marguerite Zorach's linoleum block rendering of *The Game.*

others wore simple tunics, with the Girl's belted at the waist and Life adding a sheer drapery over hers. As Death, Jack Reed wore the same costume in Provincetown and New York, the long tunic with a wide sash at the waist printed with a geometric design, and an executioner's mask. The costumes for the other actors in New York were a little more colorful and elaborate than in Provincetown, designed with a stronger suggestion of the Egyptian. Zorach's wrap had multicolored horizontal stripes and his sash was tied like those on Egyptian figures from the thirteenth century BC. Martha Ryther-Fuller, who played the Girl, had a two-piece costume with an abstract design at the hemline of both the over-blouse and the skirt. Black notes that Kathleen Cannell, "Who later became a fashion editor for the *New Yorker* in Paris, recalled constructing hers: 'I had an Egyptian costume and a marvelous wig of black knotted fringe which I made myself.'"[63]

Based on their Egyptian concept, the Zorachs developed a stiff, non-representational, abstract acting style for the play, which integrated well with Bryant's allegorical characters and pseudo-archaic dialogue. They directed the movement as a series of gestures based on poses from Egyptian friezes. In both the summer and fall productions, Jack Reed played Death and William Zorach played Youth. In the summer, the women's parts were played by two Provincetown women, Helene Freeman and Judith Lewis, who, as an artist's model, had a better sense of movement and the body than most of the amateurs. In New York, the Provincetown Players' system of having everyone involved in the production, and all the members of the Players, if they so desired, offer notes and suggestions on the productions during rehearsals, came into play. Kathleen Cannell, who was to have a career as a dancer under the stage name "Rihani," was a great resource for the Zorachs on the matter of movement. As Mary Pyne, soon to become one of the Players' best actresses, reported to Mary Heaton Vorse in September, "*The Game* has many more gestures in it, and two nice girls – Jack Reed rehearses his gestures between courses at meals."[64] Although not a particularly profound play, *The Game* succeeded as an arresting piece of theatre. In conceiving of the dialogue, the actors, the set and the costumes as elements of an integrated, non-representational work of art, Bryant and the Zorachs produced an example of the kind of "total theatre" that was being described by Max Reinhardt, Edward Gordon Craig, and the other practitioners of the "New Stagecraft," as well as a well-integrated synthesis of many elements of the newly emerging American modernism. Its combination of world-weary disillusionment and romantic idealism is a good example of the Zeitgeist of the Little Renaissance. Its recuperation and manipulation of medieval allegory and of early Egyptian art in order to construct a mythology for the modern age foreshadows a central aesthetic strategy of high modernism. The fact that the Players put it on their first bill in New York, along with *Bound East for Cardiff* and a new play by Floyd Dell, *King Arthur's Socks*, shows that they knew they had something unique in *The Game*, and something that would appeal to Greenwich Village.

3

Others *and the Other Players*

UNLIKE MOST OF THE PROVINCETOWN PLAYERS, ALFRED Kreymborg was a native New Yorker, born in 1883, the son of German immigrants. He grew up in his parents' tobacco shop at 1667 Third Avenue, living in the back and earning a reputation as a chess prodigy among the customers in the front. Kreymborg was hopeless at the business career his family wanted for him, dropping out of the commercial course in high school at the age of fifteen and failing at a series of entry-level jobs. A self-taught musician, Kreymborg found his niche in a store where he demonstrated and sold pianola rolls and taught himself the history of music. In his early twenties, he became interested in literature and followed a similar pattern, reading widely in a variety of national literatures from the classics to his contemporaries while he supported himself by playing chess and working as a secretary for a Wall Street power broker. Among his literary influences, he recognized Chekhov, Aristophanes, Verlaine, Cervantes, Goethe, Ibsen, Nietzsche, Hardy, Dostoevsky, Turgenev, Browning, Synge, Sterne, Fielding, Balzac, Flaubert, and Anatole France as well as Poe, Hawthorne, Emerson, and Thoreau, but he wrote that "these affections faded when Walt Whitman came."[1] Whitman remained a major inspiration throughout Kreymborg's life, but the primal effect that Whitman had on his sense of literature was matched by his discovery of modernism, when, in 1913, at the age of thirty, he finally stumbled upon the bohemian culture of Greenwich Village. He met the Boni brothers at the Washington Square Book Shop, and they introduced him to the Liberal Club, where he quickly became a member. He was at the founding meeting of the Washington Square Players, although he did not take an active part in this organization because he wasn't yet ready for the theatre. His closest ties in 1913 and 1914 were with the artists, particularly Marsden Hartley and the

Stieglitz group around 291, including Max Weber, John Marin, Arthur Dove, Marius de Zayas, Man Ray, and most importantly for this study, Charles Demuth and Marguerite and William Zorach.

Kreymborg became intrigued by the Post-Impressionist movement, and talked with the artists about his ideas for synthesizing poetry and music. Learning from Hutchins Hapgood about the prose poem, he thought:

> If he could get these things to move, this was the direction for him henceforth. Perhaps, if he began to divide the lines, in accordance with the cadences of speech, songs would evolve. He might employ a technical notation somewhat related to the mathematical system of a musical score: so many notes or syllables in the first measure or line, and similar divisions down the column. There would be whole tones, halves, quarters, eighths, rests and so on; and *tempi* in accordance with the movement of the mood, *tempi rubati*. He must be careful to resist a slavish imitation of music; and not fall between the stools of music and literature. The expression of a mood must be as natural as breathing; a matter of homogeneous speech throughout; a form *per se*, devoid of theories and other explanatory excrescences.[2]

With Man Ray, Kreymborg started a literary magazine called *The Glebe*, which featured Charles Demuth's play, *The Azure Adder*, in the third issue, and made its name with a complete issue that was sent from Paris by Ezra Pound, called *Des Imagistes, An Anthology*. It contained the work of Pound, H. D., Amy Lowell, Ford Madox Hueffer, James Joyce, William Carlos Williams and others, including Skipwith Cannell, the husband of Kathleen ("Kitty") Cannell (aka Rihani). Writing of *The Glebe*, the historians of the little magazine in America suggest that, "among the men active in literary protest, a few may be called the patron saints of the modern little magazine movement ... of them, Alfred Kreymborg was the first to enter a little magazine in the battle for a new literature."[3] *The Glebe* ended after a year in a disagreement between Kreymborg and the Boni brothers, who published it, but Kreymborg was soon to find a group of poets who were sympathetic to his experiments in the Walter Arensburg circle, a coterie that included Wallace Stevens, Mina Loy, Carl Van Vechten, Donald Evans, and Louise and Allen Norton. Van Vechten called the group "a 'post-decadent' circle," while Kreymborg referred to them as a "light band of esthetes, satirists, dandies, poets, dilettanti."[4] They and their short-lived poetry journal, *Rogue*, were more attuned to the *fin de siècle* than the new modernism, but they were interested in the French Symbolists and in Gertrude Stein.

Striking up a friendship with the wealthy Arensburg over chess, Kreymborg soon had him underwriting a new little magazine to be called *Others: A Magazine of the New Verse*. The only manifesto for *Others*, which began its life in July, 1915, was its motto, "The old expressions are with us always, and there are always others." Perhaps the best description of its editor's intent appears in a note published in the December, 1918 issue:

> It has been said in many places that the contributors to Others (magazine or anthologies) are members of a group, a school. This is not true. Collectively or separately, they eschew everything which approximates ismism. Any one is free to come in or stay out of the magazine, subject of course to the none-too-infallible judgment of the editors. The curriculum is taboo; the only question asked is: "Does a man express himself, and if so, how well?" If the editors escape seeing or hearing some worthy, set it down to temporary incapacity on their part, and pray for their early recovery. They do not sit on judicial or pedantic pedestals; primarily, they ask that they be permitted to evolve their own individualism, if they possess any, and to permit other folk to evolve theirs. They are editors in name only.[5]

Like *The Masses*, the Washington Square Players, and the soon to be constituted Provincetown Players, *Others* worked on the principle of cooperative, egalitarian editorship, and was more successful at it than most of these organizations. In the summer of 1915, Kreymborg was living in a loose sort of artists' colony in the woods of the New Jersey Palisades with Orrick Johns, Man Ray, and others in the modernist group. William Carlos Williams, who was to become a close friend and the chief editor of several issues, lived five miles away in Rutherford. During the summer, these people gathered at Kreymborg's cottage, and were joined by Marianne Moore and Mary Carolyn Davies, who came over from Chatham, NJ, and a number of people from the city, including Walter Arensburg, Marcel Duchamp, and Skipwith and Kathleen (Kitty) Cannell. They brought their submissions and listened while Kreymborg read them and others he had received from writers like Wallace Stevens and Maxwell Bodenheim. For Kreymborg, there was excitement in discovering and bringing together a group of people who were dedicated to what they called "the new verse," the modern and the spirit of experiment. He wrote that "each person present asked for every possible contact with other poets. The printed page was not enough; one wanted to greet the other fellow, and failing such a meeting, wished to hear about him, read about him, talk about him."[6] They read and commented on each other's poetry, and worked in various ways at getting the magazine out. Kreymborg has written that "among the first contributors to *Others*, no person gave as much of himself as Bill Williams."[7] Williams wrote in his autobiography that he was "hugely excited by what was taking place there ... on every possible occasion, I went madly in my flivver to help with the magazine which had saved my life as a writer. Twenty-five dollars a month kept it going, and the scripts began to come in. Kreymborg got the money somehow."[8]

Although it existed for only four years, *Others* published some of the most important work by many of the most significant American poets who are associated with modernism, including most of the early work of Williams, Mina Loy's "Love Songs," Wallace Stevens's "Peter Quince at the Clavier," "Domination of Black," and "Thirteen Ways of Looking at a Blackbird," T. S. Eliot's "Portrait of a Lady," and Marianne Moore's "Poetry" and "Critics and Connoisseurs." Beyond them, the list of contributors includes some of the most important early twentieth-century American poets: Ezra Pound, Amy Lowell, Carl Sandburg, Edgar Lee Masters, Conrad Aiken, H. D., Mary Aldis, Lola Ridge, Evelyn Scott, Vachel Lindsay. Kreymborg also published special issues devoted to Latin American and women poets.[9] More important in the context of this study is the substantial representation of poets who were or would be participants in the Provincetown Players: Kreymborg himself, Williams, Stevens, Loy, Maxwell Bodenheim, William Saphier, Mary Carolyn Davies, Djuna Barnes, William Zorach, Marguerite Zorach, Kathleen Cannell, Florence Kiper Frank, and Evelyn Scott. Kreymborg's interest in the theatre is reflected in the publication of plays by Williams, Barnes, Orrick Johns, and Bodenehim and Saphier. The theatrical spirit of the group is evident in Kreymborg's description of Kitty Cannell's interpretive dance contributions to the meetings: "among her impromptu performances, nothing gave greater pleasure than her exquisite mimicry of Ezra Pound. Skip and Kitty had just returned from London and Paris, where they had been in touch with the latest art movements, including the birth of Imagism, and the stay-at-homes revelled in their stories and pantomime and plied them for more."[10]

Others figured greatly in the conception of a new non-representational verse drama that was developing among the modernist poets, as well as Kreymborg's own development as a poet and playwright. An important influence was the October, 1915, issue, one of those wholesale contributions by Pound, who wrote a foreword to the collection of poems by the

"Choric School," consisting of three young poets, Hester Sainsbury, Kathleen Dillon, and John Rodker. Pound explained that he had seen Rodker's poetry before, but "could not make much of his cadence" until one evening when he saw "Miss Sainsbury and her company, including Miss Dillon," who "came in at the end of the hall and danced out their poems." It was only then that he understood "the curious breaks and pauses, the elaborate system of dots and dashes with which this new group is wont to adorn its verses." Noting the exploding popularity of modern dance, Pound explained that "their dancing is touched perhaps with the ubiquitous influence of Pavlowa and 'the Russians,'" but the "dance poems" were original: "it seemed certain that they had come on their form in no spirit of research, but simply because they wanted to dance and had no orchestra."[11]

In relation to Kreymborg's conception of theatre, John Rodker's composition, "Dutch Dolls," a Harlequinade whose characters are dolls with rhythmic, stylized movements, is particularly important. Kreymborg's theatrical imagination had begun its development through the puppet theatre he had played with as a child, a theatrical form that had a lasting impact on him. The new "Choric School" suggested a way in which Kreymborg's chosen media of music and poetry could be wedded to puppetry to create theatre. He said that when he wrote his first play, *Lima Beans*, in 1916, it was really a musical composition with puppets that was in his imagination, "a free verse experiment in which he treated the three characters of the plot as he might have handled a trio of instruments in a sonata movement, had music been his medium ... a light-hearted scherzo" in which he had "puppets partly in mind – dancing in accordance with the rhythm of the dialogue – he could have performed it with wooden beings." Writing with hindsight in 1925, Kreymborg explained his puppet aesthetic with lucidity:

> He had an affectionate recollection of his own paper outfit in childhood, but realized the present step was not a return to those days, but a recognition of certain symbols that lie between puppetry and mankind. He felt that, in those moments of detachment coming to people who reflect on their actions, one sees oneself as an infinitesimal individual in an environment of time and space in which the proportionate part one plays is so insignificant as to appear grotesquely tragi-comic. Starting with such an admission, one was assuredly an appropriate instrument for puppets to serve with fidelity. They are given a share in artificial time and space embryonic of the life allotted to people by the familiar fate

directing the strings that keep them in motion. People see and guess a great deal more than puppets are able to; otherwise, they are equally helpless, and out of this mutual helplessness comes that curious bond that lifts a man into an actor or a doll into an animated reproduction.[12]

Kreymborg was introduced to the Provincetown Players through William Zorach, who had both poetry and art work published in *Others*, as did his wife Marguerite. In New York, the Zorachs had a large group of friends that included painters from the Stieglitz 291 circle, poets from the *Others* group, and of course the Provincetown Players. The various groups often overlapped in their apartment, which was a social gathering place as well as a studio where they mounted shows of their work. After the great success of their Léon Bakst-inspired "Egyptian" design for *The Game*, which became the logo for the Players in the fall of 1916, the Zorachs were eager to do more experimental work with theatrical design, but were feeling frustrated by the bias toward realism that seemed to be emerging in the Players and the dearth of good experimental scripts to produce. When he learned about Kreymborg's *Lima Beans*, Zorach immediately suggested that he submit it to the Players. As both of them had feared, the play was rejected by the play-reading committee, but a champion arose in the person of Jack Reed, who threatened to resign if the play was not accepted. According to Kreymborg, "a compromise was reached ... if he would undertake producing the play himself, with some actors outside the personnel, no one of whom believed he could impersonate the lines, *Lima Beans* would have a place on the third bill of the season."[13] Elation at the thought that his play was to be produced was immediately followed by trepidation: "Where was he to find the actors, and, having enlisted them, how was he to direct them? ... As he had written the present scherzo with puppets partly in mind – dancing in accordance with the rhythm of the dialogue – he could have performed it with wooden beings. But where were the humans who would lower themselves to the level of puppetry and maintain a relationship to each other so harmonious as to admit no personal whim into the performance?"[14]

Enlisting Zorach to play the minor role of the vegetable Huckster as well as design the show, Kreymborg was to find his main actors among the *Others* poets, in Mina Loy and William Carlos Williams, both of whom had had some experience in amateur theatricals. As Kreymborg had unorthodox ideas about the acting style he wanted, their lack of theatrical training was as much of a bonus as their understanding of the free-verse line and how to read it. Williams, a physician with a practice in New Jersey, wrote that "it was tough, but I somehow got in to rehearsals from Rutherford three nights a week after office hours. It fascinated me ... who could tell? Here, perhaps, lay the future."[15] The historians of the Provincetown Players have focused on Kreymborg's remark that he began rehearsals "by taking out a pencil and beating time while Mina and Bill read their lines."[16] This made sense in terms of Kreymborg's conception of the drama as a "scherzo" for puppets, in which the rhythm and sound of the lines was an important element of the sense. Even his fellow poets took a little time to absorb the concept, however. Kreymborg wrote that "Bill resented the baton, charged Krimmie [Kreymborg] with the affectation of such a notion, but slowly and conscientiously fell in with the author's scheme. The part of the wife – much too light for a person of Mina's worldly experience – nevertheless appealed to her sense of comedy and she grew closer to the character with each rehearsal. As the huckster, Zorach sang with zest and vehemence."[17]

According to Kreymborg, the minimal set and props, designed and executed by the Zorachs, cost two dollars and a half.[18] In his autobiography, Zorach remembered the set with pleasure: "it was a lively production using colors in planes and angles with patterns of remarkable vegetables."[19] The curtain, with a big cornucopia bursting with vegetables painted on it, was listed on the program as a character in the play, and, under the inspired manipulation of Louis Ell, it served as a kind of punctuation to the free verse of the lines. The actors supplied their own costumes. Williams came up with "a weird concoction he had designed and executed himself." Mina Loy wore a green taffeta gown, gold slippers, and pieces from her jewelry collection, including a mosaic brooch, dangling gold earrings, and ornate English rings.[20] Kreymborg thought that, although the fashionable *décolleté* gown was not "in keeping with Mrs. Lima," on the beautiful Mina Loy it "served to fascinate the beholders."[21] Both Kreymborg and Williams have described the skeptical bemusement with which *Lima Beans* was received by the Provincetown Players in rehearsal. Williams spoke of the five performances at the beginning of December as "a qualified success,"[22] but Kreymborg recalled the opening night of December 1, 1916, in detail as a triumph over the skeptics:

> When the curtains parted, and Mina held back her first line to give the set time to take effect, Krimmie was delighted to hear it greeted with applause. Then the play began. People started to giggle. This wasn't so

bad. Then they were silent. This wasn't so bad either. Then came Zorach's booming sing-song about the vegetables. Bill Williams entered, stumbling a bit – an excellent effect – and the colloquy with Mina followed rhythmically and naturally. So far so good. Then followed the row over the bowl of string-beans, the husband's malediction, his irate exit, the collapse of the wife, and then the rondo – Mina alone, Zorach and the second duet, with its forgiveness and reunion. The actors were doing beautifully, and not a sound came out of the auditorium. Was the audience enthralled or bored? The final scene interrupted Krimmie's question. Taken at a breathless *tempo*, the lines scudded by, only to be interrupted by the curtains capering together. Even the stage-hand had played his part to the limit of accuracy.[23]

Kreymborg remembered wild applause and sixteen curtain calls on the opening night, and Zorach, who insisted that the author take a curtain call, sent up a huge basket of vegetables in place of flowers. Certainly for Kreymborg and for the Zorachs, a point had been made. The "associate members" that made up the New York audience for the Provincetown Players welcomed non-representational theatre that was truly experimental. Even Edna Kenton wrote that, for *Lima Beans*, "the Zorachs gave us one of the most effective sets we ever used, 'The Curtain' itself featured in the cast of players. Before it two poets and a poet–painter moved and spoke in a series of rhythms so carefully worked out between them, the Curtain and the author, that it seemed spontaneous play. Here was a clear case of what fine synthesis an experimental stage could give when a poet wrote, when poets spoke and when a poet–painter painted."[24]

The experimental nature of Kreymborg's artistic synthesis in *Lima Beans*, subtitled *A Conventional Scherzo*, is evident in his opening stage directions, where he says it can be defined as a "*pantomime dance of automatons to an accompaniment of rhythmic words, in place of music.*"[25] Beside Kreymborg's own musical background, the influence of the "choric school" poets, and of Kathleen Cannell's interpretive dance poetry, is evident in its composition. Drawing on the modernist influence of the harlequinade masque that was to have a significant presence in the Provincetown Players in the next few years, he suggests that the Husband and Wife might be Pierrot and Columbine, "*or preferably, two marionettes.*" For movement, he suggests a "*pantomime in the form of a semi-dance of gesture, in accordance with the sense more than the rhythm of the lines ... suggesting an inoffensive parody, unless the author errs, of the contours of certain ancient Burmese dances.*" The source for this is undoubtedly Kathleen Cannell's "static dances." To create a rhythm that was theatre rather than just music or just poetry, Kreymborg explained that "*the reading tempo varies, slow to fast, fast to slow, in accordance with the sense more than the rhythm; the gradations might be prompted by an invisible maitre-d'orchestre. Words, silences, pantomime – all should be presented inside a homogeneous rhythmic pattern*" (131). Rhymes within the lines, he notes, are incidental. In structural terms, the piece consists of a short monologue or aria by the Wife, a brief duet by the Wife and the Huckster, the major duet by the Wife and the Husband, a reprise of the duet by the Wife and the Huckster, followed by a monologue by the Wife, and the final duet by the Wife and the Husband.

In literary terms, *Lima Beans* is an epithalamium, or bridal song, about a young couple who are just two weeks married.[26] At the literal level, the plot is the light-hearted nonsense that is suggested by Kreymborg's calling it a "rondo." The Wife is seen setting the table and wondering what to give her husband for dinner: "roses for hearts, ah, / but food for the appetite! / Mammals are happiest after dark!" (132). She worries that they have had lima beans every night since their wedding and that "one more lima would shatter his love!" (132). After hearing the Huckster's litany of his wares, she chooses string beans, and sits down to string them, relapsing into "*a gentle rocking as she strings the beans to this invocation*":

> String the crooked ones,
> string the straight –
> love needs a change every meal.
> To-morrow, come kidney beans,
> Wednesday, come white or black –
> limas, return not too soon!
> The string bean rules in the
> vegetable kingdom (133)

When her husband returns, tired from work, they twice engage in a ritual of kissing delicately six times, followed by dialogue about the meaning of kisses and of love. Then the Husband announces that he is now hungry, and is incensed to find that his wife is offering him, not lima, but string beans. The Wife explains that they have had lima beans every night since their marriage, and "I thought you'd have to have a change" (136). The Husband throws the bowl of beans out the window after banishing string beans "from this domicile, / dedicated, / consecrated, / immortalized / in the name of Hymen!" (138), and storms out, calling his wife a traitress. After the Wife collapses in woe, the Huckster appears again, offering her his litany of fruits and vegetables. This time she insists on lima beans. She sits down and begins splitting the beans, intoning a monologue to the effect that all beans are alike to her, but she will be glad to serve her husband limas if that's what he wants. The man returns in a contrite mood and approaches, calling her "Beloved, / dear, dearest wife!" and saying that if she will forgive him, he will "eat all the beans in the world" (140). When the Wife shows him that she has made lima beans for him, he becomes "rapturous," and they intone a bantering love duet, shell the beans together, and then go through their kissing ritual again. The curtain quivers, and then closes on their talk of kisses and love.

At the literal level, the play is a little parable about marital forbearance. In giving up their individual desires, Husband and Wife find a greater bliss in their union. Kreymborg's text also figures more mischievously at the metaphoric level. The vegetative profusion obviously suggests the procreative character of the marriage, and Kreymborg uses the lima bean and the string bean as metaphors for female and male sexuality. The husband calls the lima "the godliest of vegetables":

> that soft, soothing,
> succulent, caressing,
> creamy, persuasively serene,
> my buttery entity (136)

On the other hand, he describes the string beans as "elongated, cadaverous ... Worms, / snakes, / reptiles, caterpillars" (137). In offering the string beans in place of his beloved limas, the suggestion is that the Wife is offering him some variety in their love-making that does not include intercourse. As she says, "love needs a change every meal" (133). Banishing the string beans from the house in the name of Hymen suggests that the Husband wants no part of sexual variety in his marriage. Indeed, it is clearly the wife who is more sexually experienced, as she sings:

> Lima beans, string beans,
> kidney beans, white or black –
> you're all alike –
> though not alike to him.
> ...
> Heighho, it's all one to me,
> so he loves what I do,

> I'll do what he loves,
> Angry boy? No, a man
> quite young in the practise
> of wedlock – and love! (139)

Though he finally expresses his willingness to "eat all the beans in the world" (140), if that's what she wants him to do, it is clear from his rapture that it is limas he wants, and she makes it clear that she is delighted to indulge him once she knows that he does not crave variety. With its implication of fertility, the playful vegetable metaphor is entirely appropriate for the epithalamium, a song in honor of the god Hymen in celebration of marriage. There is also the sense, however, that the Wife is more wise in the ways of the world than her ardent husband, and that the attractive list of fruits and vegetables that is intoned by the Huckster will be sampled eventually in all its variety, regardless of his love of lima beans.

With the success of *Lima Beans*, Kreymborg was made a full member of the Provincetown Players and appointed to the play-reading committee. He and the Zorachs had hopes of influencing the group to become more "daring and elastic" in their selection of plays. Kreymborg later wrote a little bitterly that he "had no objection to the fairly constant production of plays by the regulars" or the "arbitrary selection" of plays "by the two or three most powerful members," but "he was given the impression his notions were 'rather queer,' and his own love of experiment, seeking more room for poetry in the theatre, was not seriously encouraged."[27] Actually Kreymborg was successful in persuading the Players to accept a few scripts by the *Others* poets which were poetic experiments in non-representational theatre. *Knotholes* by Maxwell Bodenheim and William Saphier and Bodenheim's *The Gentle Furniture-Shop* were produced along with O'Neill's *Ile* beginning on November 30, 1917. Kenton maintained that "the Bodenheim fantasies missed the mark, if any, at which the author aimed in writing them and at which we aimed in producing them," admitting that "they were the stepchildren of this bill, were hustled off into corners and let shift for themselves." Although she acknowledged that *Ile* was "a typical O'Neill melodrama," she credited it alone with "swelling the subscription audiences to such an extent that for the rest of the season we played seven nights regularly."[28] In January of 1918, the Players included Mary Carolyn Davies's poetic allegory,

The Slave with Two Faces, with music written and played by Kreymborg, on a bill with two light comedies, Grace Potter's *"About Six"* and Floyd Dell's *Sweet and Twenty*, which proved successful. This time the success was attributed to Edna Millay's acting in Dell's play.

The next play that Kreymborg himself submitted, *Manikin and Minikin*, was rejected by the Players "because of the rigid static demands made upon the actors, 'a stillness,' he was advised, 'no New York audience would sit though.'"[29] Frustrated by the attitude of the Players, Kreymborg and the Zorachs decided to try an experimental bill on their own, as the Other Players. After several discussions with Cook, they convinced the Players to rent them the Provincetown Playhouse for a nominal sum between the production of Cook's *Athenian Women* that ended on March 7 and the bill of one-act plays that began March 29. This gave a very short time to secure scripts and get the theatre up and running. The Zorachs offered their services for the design and execution of the sets and costumes. Kathleen Cannell offered to contribute original dances and choreograph the movement for Kreymborg's "pantomimes." A young composer, Julian Freedman, set to work turning Kreymborg's *Jack's House: A Cubic Play*, "a tragi-comedy in the language of a primer concerning a 'one-room-home,'" into a "melodrama."

Looking for actors among the Players, Kreymborg approached Edna Millay, who had just made a great hit in two Floyd Dell plays. Kreymborg wrote that,

> while on the reading committee of the Provincetown Players, [he] had enjoyed a morality comedy of hers, *Two Slatterns and a King*, that would complete the Other bill with an appropriate lightness. It was fortunate that Edna, like the Other Players, was anxious to experiment with poetry in the theatre. The chance to put on her play under her own direction and take part in it with her sister appealed to her.[30]

Zorach remembered the selection of Millay's play, written while she was a student at Vassar, in a less positive light. In his words: "We put on a school-girlish play by Edna St. Vincent Millay, *Two Slatterns and a King*. We had to do this in order to get Edna to act in *Jack's House*. It wasn't much of a play but it was fun."[31] The selection of the Millay play may also have meant the loss of a play by William Carlos Williams, who wrote that, after the experience with *Lima Beans*, "I too wanted to have play on that stage."[32] Although Kreymborg does not seem to have been aware of it, in Williams's eyes, the choice of the Millay play did irreparable damage to the relationship between the two poets, and probably was involved in Williams's eventually washing his hands of *Others* magazine in July, 1919. In his autobiography, he wrote that Kreymborg lost one script that he had given him to submit to the Provincetown Players, and Williams was "sick over it." The two poets then had planned to do a bill together, presumably the Others bill. Williams thought it "a wonderful chance. But nothing happened." When Kreymborg finally told him he was instead "putting on a bill with Edna St. Vincent Millay, a play called *Da Capo* and did I mind? . . . it knocked me cold. I saw the bill and really enjoyed it, but from that time on Kreymborg and I didn't get on so well."[33] From the vantage point of 1951, Williams may have been confused about the name of the play (*Aria da Capo* was not produced until 1919), but the effect was still there. The play Kreymborg passed up was probably *The Comic Life of Elia Brobitza*, which was published in *Others* magazine in 1919. Williams later published *Many Loves*, a volume of his plays, but none of them were to be produced by the Provincetown Players.

The casting of the three plays came from an overlapping Others and Provincetown Players group. Kathleen Cannell played Jack in *Jack's House*, "a speaking part affording her opportunities for pantomime," and Edna Millay played Jack's wife with what Kreymborg considered a complete understanding of the pantomimic demands of the part. With Cannell's choreography, he was pleased to see that she and Millay "looked and acted like puppets, the illusion being heightened by the picturesque circumstance that the former, with her stature of an overgrown boy, was two or three heads taller than the latter, who reduced Jack's large, dreamy gestures to a minimum – the broad legato broken up into its component staccato bits."[34] Manikin was played by Marjory Lacey-Baker, a newcomer to the Players, who came from Boston and had the flawless diction Kreymborg desired for the play. Minikin was played by Louie Earl, a young English woman who reminded Kreymborg of a Chelsea figurine and whose accent blended well with Laccy-Baker's. In *Two Slatterns and a King*, the Millay sisters played the two girls, Tidy and Slut, Marjorie Lacey-Baker played Chance, and Zorach enjoyed himself hugely as the King. He wrote later that he "wore a robe of purple and ermine made by Marguerite. Instead of a modest crown, I made one twenty inches high and a magnificent scepter from a bed post covered with tinsel and designed with colored papers. The Cubist painter Gleizes was visiting here and was so fascinated with my scepter that he took it back to Paris with him."[35] Kreymborg said that Zorach was "absurdly droll with his exaggerated stolidity and the measured solemnity of his quatrains."[36] To complete the program, Kathleen Cannell, under her stage name Rihani, performed some of her "static dances" to the music of Grieg and Cui. In a letter to Robert Sarlós she explained why the dances were called "Static":

> I never moved from one spot, all the movement was for the head, torso, arms and hands, as in certain Persian dances. In one dance, the Sphynx, I started standing and finished on the floor in the attitude of the title. At other times I began on the floor and rose to my knees or to my feet. This was before Modern Dancers came along using the floor as an intrinsic element of the dance, so caused quite a lot of comment.[37]

Kreymborg has described the opening night of the program to a standing-room-only audience: "*Manikin and Minkin*, Rihani's beautiful static dances, Edna's rollicking morality play, *Jack's House*, with Julian playing the music on a piano behind the Zorach set – passed on their way to the final curtain and left an infectious path behind them." To the group's delight, "the evening was an intoxicating success," as were the other three performances.[38] They announced a second program for the second week of April, and immediately thought about ways of extending the run of their successful bill. According to Kreymborg, "the leaders of the older group turned a deaf ear to any rental of the theatre in the near future,"[39] so they invested the profits of their first four performances in renting the Bramhall Playhouse on East 28th Street. Unfortunately, this was a huge miscalculation. There was a small, self-defined audience that came to Macdougal Street to see experimental theatre. The part of the Broadway audience that was interested in the theatrical experiments had already subscribed through the New York Stage Society, which had been persuaded by Jack Reed to buy 400 associate memberships when the Provincetown Players moved to Macdougal Street. A friendly notice by Heyward Broun in the New York *Tribune* may have unwittingly contributed to their failure by scaring off the uptown theatre audience, for it described the group as "the latest and most ultra-modern of the little theatres, with free verse dramatists, Futurist scenic artists and Cubist dancers. Its programme is a combination of plays, poems, music and dances, and it aims at the synthesis of the arts."[40] William Zorach, who later considered *Jack's House* "one of the most interesting things Marguerite and I did ... the first Cubist play ever produced in New York," put the case plainly: "the critics were excited over *Jack's House*. There was much publicity and the scenes and sets were reproduced in color in the Sunday supplements. But the public was indifferent. They found it confusing and it meant nothing to them."[41] This was the kind of thing arty New Yorkers might go to Greenwich Village for, but very few people came to 28th Street to see the Other Players, who lost all of their investment on the one-week run. It was to be their first and last producing venture.

Despite the sad financial story, the Other Players were an important artistic force. The group served as a focal point for other artists who were interested in creating experimental theatre, both inside and outside the Provincetown Players, and the innovative techniques in the plays, which did, as Broun said, aim at a synthesis of the arts in production, are worth noting. Edna Millay's allegorical fairy tale and the five plays by the poets of the *Others* group show the wide range of modernist experimentation that was being applied to the theatre in the Provincetown Playhouse during the 1917–1918 season. Kreymborg's *Manikin and Minikin: A Bisque Play in One Act* is a combination love duet and philosophical dialogue that takes on some of the issues that Pirandello was to examine in *Six Characters in Search of an Author* several years later. Kreymborg gave a description of the literal situation of the play in his autobiography:

> Two inanimate porcelain figures, a boy and a girl he called Manikin and Minikin, were sitting on an old mantelpiece and talking back and forth to the metronomic accompaniment of the clock standing between them. They had been sitting up there for over a hundred years, with their backs to each other or facing each other – in accordance with the whim of the servant who took them down and dusted them off each morning. On this particular morning, in replacing them, she had carelessly turned them apart, and there they sat trying to touch each other through talking. The more they talked the more it became apparent that, though they had each other up there even when they couldn't see each other, they went right on longing for closer embraces. Loneliness of one sort or another held them apart though they loved nothing but each other and had nought but the maid to disturb them.[42]

In production, with a set designed and executed by the Zorachs, the play raised immediate issues of perception and subjectivity. The set consisted of one of the walls of a parlor, seen through an oval frame, which included only the shelf of a mantelpiece within the frame. The framing of the image, so important to the Zorach's Post-Impressionist aesthetic, brought the fact of the artists' and the spectators' subjective perception immediately to mind. The oval picture frame also served as a reminder that the proceedings on stage were art, not life, an overt statement of the piece's non-representational aesthetic. The two actors, both women, were seated on pedestals at the ends of the "mantelpiece," two static figures turned away from one another. They were made up and costumed as "*two aristocratic bisque figures, a boy in delicate cerise and a girl in cornflower blue.*" Casting an ominous mood over the piece, "*their shadows join in a grotesque silhouette*" and inserting a jarring mechanical presence, "*in the center, an ancient clock whose tick acts as the metronome for the sound of their high voices.*"[43]

The spectators are brought into further play with subjectivity as the play opens, when they are invited to see the "yankee salon" where the bisque figurines have ended up after 170 years of existence from the figurines' point of view:

> Oh, these Yankees! – and I see
> the everlasting rattan rocker,
> the everlasting samovar,
> the everlasting noisy piano,
> the everlasting portrait of milady –
> (2)

Thus the tables are turned, and these inanimate objects have the power of perspective and judgment that the spectators had thought unique to their own privileged point of view as subjects, rather than objects, animate rather than inanimate beings. This becomes the central point of opposition in the play, couched in the context of the love duet between Manikin and Minikin. The inanimate figurines are at the mercy of chance, in the person of the maid, who has turned them away from each other, and the lovers are suffering an agony of separation. What's more, Minikin claims to be tortured by doubt of Manikin's love, and jealousy, thinking that the "human creature" surely loves him and that he might return her love. She feels that she is at a disadvantage in the competition, with "poor dead me in her live power!" and tells Manikin, "If you could see me / the way you see her, / you'd still love me" (7). Manikin retorts that "I see you – / see you always – / see only you!" (7), thus establishing the conflict between physical sight, which is fleeting and changeable, and subjective vision, which is eternal and immutable. Minikin, rather like Mrs. Lima, believes that "It's a change, it's a change, / you men ask of women!" (9), fearing that "You're eye-sick, heart-sick / of seeing the same foolish porcelain thing, / a hundred years old" (10). Manikin responds that he doesn't and can't love the maid because,

> To begin with –
> I dislike, suspect, deplore –
> I had best say, feel compassion
> for what is called, humanity –
> or the animate, as opposed to the inanimate –
> (11)

He gives several reasons for the inferiority of the animate. First, mutability is a negative thing to him, for "that which is able to move / can never be steadfast" (11). Second, there is the matter of movement, which means that one's perspective on, and therefore vision of the animate object is constantly changing. "I can only see part of her at once. / She moves into my vision; / she moves out of my vision; / she is doomed to be wayward" (12). Third, there is physical change, for "humans change with each going moment." Just as he sees "that creature" only "when she touches my vision," so he could "only see her once, were she beautiful – / at best, twice or thrice." By contrast, Minikin, the immutable art work, is "more precious than when [she] came" (13). Finally, and most importantly, there is the changeable "inner life" of human beings, which "changes far more desperately" (14) than the outer. Human beings are subject to moods, and although they may be telling the truth "passionately, tenaciously, tragically," when they say, "I love you," they can only say it "so long as the mood breathes." When "the mood languishes," Manikin says, they have to say "I do not love you" if they are honest, or they have to say "I love you" to someone else (14). Manikin and Minikin, on the other hand, have said "I love you" to each other constantly for 170 years, for as unchangeable works of art that figure lovers, "we've had to say it . . . and we'll have to say it always" (15). Manikin sums up the fundamental contrast between animate and inanimate, mutable and immutable, human being and work of art, as decidedly in favor of art:

> The life of an animate
> is a procession of deaths
> with but a secret sorrowing candle,
> guttering lower and lower,
> on the path to the grave –
> the life of an inanimate
> is as serenely enduring –
> as all still things are. (15)

Finally, Manikin avers the superiority of the inner subjective vision over the physical. When Minikin asks whether, even though he hasn't seen her with his "dear blue eyes" for "hours, days, weeks," he can still see her with his "hidden ones," he replies that he can, and no matter which way his inanimate figure is turned, "I look at you. / I see you" (17). The philosophical discussion having put to rest Minikin's doubts and jealousy, the play ends with her confession that she was never really jealous of the maid, but just wanted to hear Manikin talk, because he talks so wonderfully. In this little play, which Kreymborg and his wife Dorothy later put on many times with puppets, he manages to combine an experimental approach to theatre in "static drama" with dialogue that raises several aesthetic and philosophical issues that were vital to the new ways of thinking about art and life. A contemporary critic summed up the uniqueness of Kreymborg's art as a synthesis of techniques that served his vision of the "miniature universal experience":

> Music and language, fancies and metaphors are homogeneous in his expressions and true to his experience. No note is forced. The music remains discreet, light, low, free of over-emphasis, almost conversational in its reticence. Its very key symbolizes matters small in scale and not eternally serious; and balances exquisitely between pathos and humor, satire and pity. The irreconcilable contradictions of life are in it as neat little counterbobs and balancement; the eternal dialogue of tiny head and heart, of porcelain him and her ... Satire tweaks a string or two in a corner of the brain, then pauses innocently and mischievously. The very words, polysyllabic though many of them are, achieve an entirely laconic and monosyllabic effect, stand separate and clipped as nouns in a child's talk. It is a very large child which speaks.[44]

Jack's House: A Cubic Play is reminiscent of *Lima Beans* in its domestic focus, but while the earlier play is a development of the vegetative metaphor, *Jack's House* combines elements of early theatrical expressionism with Cubist dialogic experiments reminiscent of Gertrude Stein's contemporaneous work, which was well known to the Others group. The Zorachs entered enthusiastically into Kreymborg's expressionist vision of the set. On the curtain was a design of various shapes – squares, triangles, rhomboids, etc., which foreshadowed the geometrical patterns of movement and the gestures of the actors, choreographed by Kathleen Cannell, and executed brilliantly, in Kreymborg's estimation, by Cannell as Jack and Edna Millay as Jack's Wife. The Zorachs created an expressionist set for the "one-room home" that is both the locale of the play and its subject. The room, with its one window in the rear, contained one table, one chair, one couch, a stove on which one kettle was boiling, all of them undersized, except the chair, in which both Jack and Jack's Wife sit at one point. In contrast to the diminutive size of most of the room's appointments are two unnaturally large objects that dominate the opening stage image, a broom and the "*ponderous volume*" labeled "HOUSEHOLD ACCOUNTS"[45] that Jack is studying. These two objects figure expressionistically the preoccupation that is weighing on Jack's mind, his and his new wife's failure as yet to create a home in the room where they live. Further stressing the subjectivity of the expressionist aesthetic, Jack's Wife does not speak, but expresses herself only through pantomime, in which she increasingly imitates Jack as the play progresses. Jack's dialogue is addressed directly to the audience. Thus the staging implies that the action is by no means meant to suggest "real life," but rather a daydream of Jack's in which he comes up with a possible solution to his problem and allays his anxiety.

Jack's opening monologue, as he studies his accounts, suggests his preoccupation with his anxiety about his marriage. Among the figures, "two and two are four, / four and six are ten," several lines are inserted: "Wife is only twenty ... I hope she'll do the housework soon ... house without housework is no house at all" (62). When his "adorable" wife arrives, Jack greets her ardently and daintily, and then leads her to two unfinished cushions on the couch, which he hopes she will begin to work on. When she stubbornly shakes her head, he indicates some curtains that need to be sewn, but she is even more stubborn. Then "*he indicates the wooden spoon, and stirs the contents of the kettle with truly magic persuasiveness. She turns her back on him*" (63). She responds similarly to his pantomime of setting the table. He falls into despair, but "*a sign of extraordinary good cheer not unmixed with whimsic shrewdness, breaks his mood*," and he begins to sing her a love song as the two take each other's hands and dance in geometrical figures around the room, finishing with the thought that "Love, liebe, amore, amour / is a dear little word / for to hold a lady" (64) and also to hold a lord.

Before the dance is over, Jack's Wife has become more responsive to his suggestions, and when he leads her to the table, she participates in the pantomime of setting the table this time, although reluctantly. After a cubist verse that plays variations on the statement that "we have no dishes to eat our meals from because we have no dishes to eat our meals from," Jack places the chair for his wife and serves the meal, which they eat sitting companionably together on the chair. This is followed by another cubist verse on the theme of the "one-room home," in which Jack insists that they have a one-room home because that is what they want, and if they had more, they would need more. Jack then tries to interest his wife in washing the dishes with him, but she will have none of it, and wanders away, tracing shapes on the window with her finger. Singing a nonsense verse about his love for her, he continues on with the dishes. As his wife moves to the couch and tentatively fingers one of the cushions, Jack addresses his song to her:

> And-she-sol-la-ci-do-ci-la?
> *[They exchange sidelong glances. Jack smiles; so does His Wife. He quickens the tempo of his tune and goes to the drawer*:
> loves-ci-do-ci-la-sol-fa-mi?
> *[He sends her a glance. She nods and he pulls open the drawer and gets her work basket* (66)

Won over to the idea of making a home by the dance and the love song, Jack's Wife takes her sewing basket from him and begins to work on the cushions as he sweeps the floor and intones a verse to the audience about the two green pillows on their black couch that contrast with the "cerulean bolsters / on your lemon silk divan" (67). Kreymborg is again announcing his values to the presumably middle-class audience. The preferred bohemian scheme of decoration – black with splashes of bright colors in simple materials – contrasts with the conspicuous consumption they renounce. Jack does not oppose their bourgeois values, he just doesn't want them imposed on him:

> Have cerulean bolsters
> on your lemon silk divan
> and let us have
> two green pillows
> on our black couch (68)

Having finished the pillows, Jack's Wife begins sewing the curtains, while he looks around for other housekeeping chores. It is here that she becomes an active partner in the one-room home, for she motions to him that he could wash the window and "*Jack is so surprised she has to repeat her pointing several times*" (68). Delighted, he goes to wash the window, but draws back and explains to the audience that he can't wipe away the "figures she has blown on it / with her breath / on which a spirit has blown – / a spirit? a saint? a sprite?" (69). Now Jack's Wife insists on hanging the curtains herself, while Jack delivers another cubist verse to the audience on his delight that "she *likes* to make shades, / yellow shades for the window" (70). Happily exhausted from their efforts at making a home for each other, they end the play snuggling on the couch as Jack says,

> this room
> is our cradle.
> It will rock
> in our memory
> no matter what
> we grow to. (70–71)

While the play is a celebration of domesticity, it is also mildly subversive in its insistence on the bohemian values of simplicity and resistance to conspicuous consumption as opposed to what the play assumes to be a middle-class disapproval of their flouting of conventions in choosing to live in a one-room apartment with only the bare necessities. In 1918, the suggestion that husband and wife are equal partners in making the home, especially with Kreymborg's suggestion that the husband might cook the meals and serve them to the wife, was fairly shocking, although perhaps less so in Greenwich Village than elsewhere. More fundamental is the subversion of the conception of marriage as an institution that exists for the creation of children. The play depicts a bohemian couple of equals, both of whom are presumably artists. Jack confronts the audience about the issue of children:

> We have many, many children
> I would sing you of,
> but you would not call
> them any, any children.
> And what is it to you how
> many, many children we have
> (68)

This was a statement that directly confronted basic middle-class values and resisted them. These two artists create, but their "children" are presumably the products of their art. Jack asserts their right to choose this form of creation in place of the traditional one. Thus Kreymborg's conception of the "one-room home" is more than a hymn to love and home. It is a statement of bohemian values in opposition to those of the middle class, and an assertion that bohemia's lifestyle can produce just as much of a home as the conventional middle-class domesticity that most of the residents of Greenwich Village had fled in choosing to live as free-spirited artists.

In her allegorical fairy tale *Two Slatterns and a King*, Edna Millay composed another light-hearted assault on middle-class values. Here she presents the traditional good girl and bad girl of the fairly tale, but rather than traditional morality, she uses housekeeping skills as a scale of value. The two girls, played by Norma and Edna Millay, are called Slut and Tidy. As might be guessed, Tidy exhibits the middle-class virtues of cleanliness, orderliness, and hard work: "From my outside to my in / Clean am I unto my skin."[46] She gets up before dawn every day and washes before she tends to her housekeeping in her spotless and orderly kitchen, which she calls the pride of her life. Slut, on the other hand, confesses herself a slattern:

> I spend my days in slovenly ease;
> I sleep when I like and I wake when I please.
> My manners, they are indolent;
> In clutter and filth I am quite content. (6)

Slut's disorderly kitchen is filled with stale food, dirty dishes, and broken crockery. Chance, played by Marjory Lacey-Baker in the production, enters into their lives in the person of a puckish figure who is seen by the audience but not by the characters. As the play begins, the King, played by William Zorach in the production, enters declaring his sovereignty:

> I am the King of all this land:
> I hold a scepter in my hand;
> Upon my head I wear a crown;
> Everybody stands when I sit down.
> (3)

But the King is not happy, and Chance plants the idea that it is because he doesn't have a wife. He decides that, in order to ensure that he will not choose a slattern for a spouse, he will go from house to house appearing unannounced so "that maid whose kitchen's neatest / Will I have to be my sweetest" (7). Chance intervenes mischievously to make Tidy and Slut appear the opposite of what their true natures are. Tidy enters in great disorder, explaining to the audience that she has had a terrible day. Her milk has spoiled in the sun, and she has become all dirty and bedraggled chasing the neighbor's dog, which had run away with the duck she had broiled for dinner. Her clean laundry has fallen in the mud, her baking has burned, her jelly has boiled over, and, while trying to clean it up, she has slipped and turned the table over with everything on it. At this point, of course, the King enters and chides her on her poor housekeeping: "Untidy Spill-time, it is easy to see / That my fair bride you never will be" (9). Tidy pleads that it is by unlucky chance that he has seen her in this unlikely state, but it is too late. He tells her, "Vain, wench, your lies and your pretense! / I see what I see and I hie me hence!" (10).

Slut, on the other hand, he finds in an unusual state of cleanliness because she had gotten so bored that she decided to clean up just for the novelty of the experience. She assures the audience that "in a room as clean as this / My bones ache and I find no bliss" (11), so it will soon appear "much less orderly and drear" (11). When the King sees her clean kitchen, he decides that Slut must be his bride, and he marries her. He realizes his mistake the next day when he sees Tidy back in her accustomed state, "the tidiest lady in the land" (12), and wishes he could marry her, but it is too late. Slut reappears in her original slovenly state and drags him off as he whines, "Oh, woe is me, what a life will be mine!" while Tidy concludes the play, "A slattern is a fearful sight, – ah, me! / What pleasure it gives so tidy to be!" (13).

Millay's prologue for the little play, which is spoken by Chance, suggests that chance is the subject of the play. She reminds the audience that "It is through me you met your wives" and "one and all, through me, to-day, / Hither you came to see the play" (3). According to Chance, the moral of the play is clear:

> You shall be taught what way a King
> Though a sublime and awful thing
> And even wise, may come to be
> A laughing-stock, – and all through me!
>   (3)

The play certainly illustrates the powerful and potentially devastating effect of Chance on human life. It also shows the futility of trying to control or order one's environment, as Tidy does. For all her effort and anxiety, her rather arrogant claim to have ordered her particular chunk of the universe proves hollow, and this through a few chance occurrences on a single morning. On the other hand, Slut, who takes things as they come and never lifts a finger to alter them, has ended up with the prize, which Tidy surely "deserved" and would have won in a just and orderly universe. Given the power of Chance, however, Millay implies the futility of all the striving for control and order that underlies conventional middle-class virtues, most of which seem to be aimed at producing a neat and tidy order, whether it be in one's soul or in one's little corner of real estate. What does it matter that cleanliness is next to godliness if Chance rules? Thus Millay pokes fun at the overhang of Victorian domestic virtues in a society that claims to have left its underlying religious value structure behind. Like *Jack's House*, *Two Slatterns and a King* sets the freedom of bohemia against the domestic conventions of the middle class directly for its audience and presents it with a light-hearted challenge to examine its fundamental values. A secondary theme is the perennial modernist concern with issues of perception, appearance, and reality. The King is following the direct, empirical evidence of his eyes, which tell him that Tidy's protests are "lies and pretense," when in fact her story is the truth, and the appearance of Slut is the "lie." By stressing the fact that we cannot trust the evidence of our senses in making judgments, Millay undercuts further the arrogant and foolish position of those who would demand order in a universe that is ultimately governed by chance.

Besides the single bill of the Other Players, at Kreymborg's urging, the Provincetown Players also produced plays by several *Others* poets during the regular season. These included Mary Carolyn Davies's *The Slave with Two Faces: An Allegory* (January, 1918), Maxwell Bodenheim's *Knotholes* (November, 1917), and *The Gentle Furniture-Shop* (November, 1917), by Bodenheim and William Saphier. Davies had the distinction of the lead poems in the first volume of *Others* in 1915, a group of lyrics called "Songs of a Girl." Having been a student at the University of California, she had come to Greenwich Village seeking the bohemian artist's life. Kreymborg remembered her as the "lanky Oregonian" who sometimes accompanied Marianne Moore to editorial meetings. She was eventually to edit her own poetry magazine, *Quill*, and to publish six volumes of poetry. She never married. Her early poems express what Cheryl Black refers to as "girl consciousness."[47] The lyrics in *Others*, written from the point of view of a girl or woman, express a *carpe diem* view of life. It is not surprising that her play should focus, not on the relationship between a young woman and a man, but on the relationship of two young women, one of whom serves as mentor to the other. The meaning of the play is figured in their simple costumes: "*The girls wear that useful sort of gown which, with the addition of a crown, makes a queen – without, makes a peasant.*"[48] The First Girl wears a crown, while the Second Girl carries hers. The lessons that the First Girl imparts all serve to teach the Second Girl how to deal with life. The first is that she must wear her crown always: "That is all of wisdom – the wearing of crowns before the eyes of Life" (184). Although we all long for Life, she tells her, "when he comes, he hurts us, he tortures us. He kills us, unless we know the secret" (184), which is that he is a slave, and that he is afraid only of those who know his secret. On the other hand, to those who are afraid of him he is a tyrant. He only obeys "Kings and Queens," which is why the Second Girl must never let him see her without her crown.

When Life appears, the spectators are allowed to see his two faces. At first, he saunters along the path, walking "*like a conqueror. But there is something ugly in his appearance.*" When he sees the girls, "*just as a sudden sun-ray catches the jewels of their crowns,*" he "*cringes and walks like a hunchback slave. He is beautiful now*" (185). The reversal of expectations in the response to the figure of Life is emphasized by the First Girl as she reminds her student, "Remember! You are only safe – as long as you remain his master. Never forget that he is a slave and that you are a queen" (185). She says that Life is very beautiful as long as he remains a slave, and stages a demonstration for the Second Girl, demanding that Life bring her opals and pearls, and a strawberry tart, and "a fair prince to think tinkling words about me" (186). As Life assents, the Second Girl begins to get the idea, and demands a gown of gold, a little garden, a gray steed, and a little page with two dimples. As Life turns to go in order to fulfill their demands, the girls keep calling him back and demanding more, and each time he bows and turns to obey. Finally, the girls, "*convulsed with mirth at the adventure and its success,*" let him go, after the First Girl has snatched a gold chain from his neck and a bracelet from his wrist. She tells the Second Girl, "What you see you must take," because Life, being a slave himself, does not like beggars (186–187). She tells her that Life is the only person to whom one should be rude, and that she must be on guard because he is always watching for the first sign of fear, which is a thought. While thoughts are dangerous, words are even more so, for "if we say we are afraid we will be more afraid, because whatever we make into words makes itself into our bodies" (187).

Having received her instructions about how to master Life, the Second Girl is shown a demonstration of what happens when one fails to do so. Life crosses the stage like the devil in a medieval mystery play, "*with a whip of many thongs driving a huddled throng of half crouching men and women. They kneel and kiss his robe … He is hideous*" (188). Life demands that a young man hand over his ideals. To an old woman, he says, "for twelve hours you shall toil at what you hate. For an hour you shall work at what you love, to keep the wound fresh, to make the torture keener" (188). When the people beg for a dream, for love, for a little rest, he only lashes them with the whip and dances a mocking dance, which works him into a greater fury until, "*laughing terribly*," he lashes out at them and kills several, finally driving the living off the stage, dragging the bodies along with them. This horrific spectacle has its effect on the Second Girl. She takes to heart the assurance of the First Girl that she will never see this hideous face of Life, "unless you kneel – never kneel, little queen" (189).

With the departure of the First Girl, the Second Girl's trial by temptation comes. When she hears Life's voice offstage, she cowers at first, but recovers in time to demand a necklace from him and to snatch a ring from his finger. The beginning of her downfall comes when she looks toward the place where the bodies were and involuntarily shivers with horror. Life raises his head in time "*to see the look of horror. From this moment his aspect gradually changes until from the slave he becomes a tyrant*" (189). Life launches his attack on the girl first by flattering her and telling her how beautiful she is. Taken off guard, the girl responds by trying to please him with a conventional feminine confession of weakness: "I think he wants me to be afraid, so I will say it. I have heard that men are like that. I am not afraid, but I will say it to please him." When she tells him she is afraid, he responds, "that pleases me." The girl is delighted that she is able to please him, and she expresses doubt about the First Girl's warning that "whatever I make into words makes itself into my body." She says, "it is so pleasant to please him – And so easy! I am not afraid of him. I have only *said* that I am afraid" (190). Life then flatters the girl into taking her crown from her head so that he can look at her beautiful hair. He insists that she dance for him in order to get it back, and then throws it away. He promises to be kind if she will call him master, which she does. Assuming more power over her, he threatens her with his whip until she kneels to him. When she starts to beg for pity, he beats her, and finally chokes her to death, and leaves "*laughing horribly*" (193).

When the First Girl returns, singing a merry song about the lovely April day, she sees the body and kneels beside it, saying, "She was young [...] he was cruel ... Life has broken her [...] Life has broken them all [...] some day [...] I am afraid" (194). While she cowers over the body, Life enters, but, seeing him a second before he sees her, she recovers "*just in time to be her scornful self before his eyes light upon her. As she speaks Life becomes a slave again*" (194), and she demands that he bring her a fresh rose. With Life played with relish by Ida Rauh, Davies's feminist allegory had the raw theatrical power of the kind of medieval morality play it was meant to resemble. Like an Everyman figure, the Everywoman figure of the Second Girl goes through the various stages of temptation that test her faith in a wisdom that will save her from being destroyed by the villain Life, but, there being no divine grace to save her from her own weakness, she fails in the end. The message to the audience is that it had better follow the example of the First Girl, no matter how demoralizing Life is, and refuse to acknowledge fear of Life; "take what you see" and never beg for it; beware of flattery; never play at weakness; and be very careful of the words you use. Davies's "gospel" is a message of strength, assertiveness, and self-reliance for women in opposition to the traditional Victorian values of deference to men, self-effacement, and placing themselves in a position of bad faith by using "feminine wiles" to get what they want while they are denying what they really think and feel. In the world Davies creates in this play, men are decidedly secondary. It is women who confront Life as a sisterhood.

Maxwell Bodenheim was a more fanciful poet than Davies, and his two brief poetic allegories, as Kreymborg wrote, "mystified the subscribers

Figure 4. A scene from *The Slave with Two Faces.*

and scared off the group from a repetition of such an adventure."[49] Bodenheim's plays must have seemed strange to the 1917 audiences, particularly in juxtaposition with the rest of the bill, O'Neill's psycho-melodrama *Ile* and a naturalistic study of the deleterious effects of bohemian life on family values, Rita Wellman's *Funiculi-Funicula*. Like Robert Frost's 1916 poem *Mending Wall* and Edna St. Vincent Millay's 1919 play *Aria da Capo*, Bodenheim's collaboration with William Saphier, *Knotholes*, plays on the common World War I figuration of the wall to indicate the obstacles that modern social and political structures present to human communication and understanding. In *Knotholes*, a Jaunty Bricklayer tries to persuade a Sleepy Mayor to replace the old wooden fence, full of knotholes, that stands behind the village cemetery, with a modern brick wall. The Mayor hesitates because he sees the wooden fence as a living thing, covered with an endless whisper, while the wall is silent. The Bricklayer accuses him of being sleepily sentimental, and insists that he has come to wake him up, but their argument is interrupted by the appearance of two ghosts who look like some romantic figures out of *The Three Musketeers*, dressed in black capes, gray tights, and wide, black-plumed hats. They tell the Mayor that he must keep the fence, with its knotholes, for it is through these tiny windows that they live a second life, watching mothers with their children, young men and women in love, and even men like the Bricklayer, who they say are walking coffins carrying dead children around with them.[50] Telling the Bricklayer that there is a dead child within him that needs to be awakened, the ghosts take hold of him and make him dance with them. Afterwards, he feels light and free, and the Mayor tells him his "child" is awake. The Bricklayer decides that he likes the fence, and, looking up, says that he sees the moon for the first time. The play ends with the Mayor and the Bricklayer looking up at the moon with their arms over each other's shoulders. Thus the romance of the past, figured by the ghosts, awakens the imagination of the Bricklayer, who is able to appreciate that it is not the walls dividing people that are important to civilization, but the "knotholes" that allow people to perceive each other, and to enter imaginatively into each other's lives. Bodenheim and Saphier were writing long before the concept of the "inner child" became a cultural cliché, but they were looking to convey something similar. It is only through the reawakening of a childlike openness to the imagination, they suggest, that this civilization can once again embrace the romance of the past and become open to both human communication and wonder at the beauty of the world.

The Gentle Furniture-Shop offers a retail metaphor for the stages of life. Three shops are juxtaposed on one street: the Dancing Robe shop for young women, the Fortune-Telling Booth for middle-aged people, and the Gentle Furniture-Shop for old people. The action takes place in the furniture shop, the inventory of which is an abundance of chairs "*of every shape and color.*"[51] Two furniture salesmen begin the day with a conversation about the moon they have eaten for breakfast, and one remarks that the old people who come to the shop "can never buy what they want; they must take the chairs we give, or leave empty handed" (180). It becomes evident that the chairs represent the given circumstances of one's existential condition, for as the salesman tells a customer, "Life rules this shop and we must obey him" (181). Thus an old man who wants a chair that is stiff-backed, because he dreams best when he is slightly uncomfortable, and green, because he wants to be reminded of "the green grass where I once sat and told Death what a fool he was" (180), is given a high-backed, low-seated, deep crimson chair. The salesman tells him that, because his life has always been "stern and clear," he needs "the touch of beginning laughter" that he will get each time he sits down in the chair.

The old woman with him wants a little chair, round because "my heart once swelled round with surprise when some one told me he loved me," and with green and purple upholstery because "they are both colors of blossomed regret" (180). She is given the stiff-backed chair the man had wanted instead because her life has been "too often rounded and unmoving" and she needs the "restless awakening" the chair will bring. As they are resigning themselves to the choices the salesmen have made for them, a Young Girl dances in, and is told that she is in the wrong shop, but she dashes in and picks out a slender black chair, skipping out past the "amazed merchants" without paying. After a short silence, the old man is emboldened to object to the crimson chair he is being forced to take, and the proprietor (Life) responds: "Take what you like, old man. This Gentle Furniture-Shop is a fraud [...] Shops of all kinds exist, I suppose, to unknowingly deceive their customers" (182). Although the form of his play is quite different, the import of its metaphor is similar to that of Davies's play. One has to seize control of life in order to be happy, and those who passively sink into whatever circumstances they are given are bound to be dissatisfied. The old man's gesture toward self-assertion and free will at the end suggests that there is hope for self-determination at any stage of life.

Edna Kenton's remarks on Bodenheim's plays in various places demonstrate why they were treated as "the stepchildren" of the bill and "hustled off into corners and let shift for themselves."[52] In her article about the Provincetown Players published in the Boston *Transcript* in April, 1918, she said of *Knotholes* and *The Gentle Furniture-Shop*, "the less said the kinder," opining that "because poetic and fantasy plays require above all things deft though not necessarily involved stage mechanics to produce in unillusioned minds the effect of illusion, their failures with this sort of play have been marked and almost invariable," a rather odd statement for an article that was meant to bring positive attention to the Players. Further indicating the lack of interest in their modernist efforts among the group, Alfred Kreymborg and Marguerite and William Zorach were demoted, along with Charles Demuth, Harry Kemp, and Mary Heaton Vorse O'Brien, from "Active" to "Club" Members of the Provincetown Players in March of 1918, signifying that they no longer had any official influence on its activities.[53] In the following season, there seems to have been a concerted effort on the part of the play-selectors to move away from non-representational dramaturgy. With the exception of O'Neill's *Where the Cross Is Made*, the influence of modernism is absent from the plays of that season, among which ethnic realism is the dominant new note. There are plays centered on Irish Americans (Alice Rostetter's *The Widow's Veil* and Mary Barber's *The Squealer*), on Jewish Americans (Florence Kiper Frank's *Gee-Rusalem* and Bosworth Crocker's *The Baby Carriage*), and on the Japanese (Rita Wellman's *The String of the Samisen*). Besides O'Neill's play, Edna Millay's fairy-tale fantasy, *The Princess Marries the Page*, and Robert Parker's futuristic satire *50–50* were the only plays that diverged from representational realism.

In 1919, however, the Provincetown took a renewed interest in modernist aesthetics when Cook, at Glaspell's urging, took a "sabbatical" from the group. Growing impatience with the haphazard management and "paternalism" of Cook among the younger members of the group had produced dissension which, by its third New York season, could no longer be ignored.[54] Cook was also feeling depressed and frustrated that his concentrated work on the productions had kept him from completing his full-length play, *The Spring*. So Cook and Glaspell went to Provincetown to write, while the Provincetown Players was placed under the joint directorship of James Light and Ida Rauh, in an experiment that was dubbed "The Season of Youth," something of a misnomer, since Rauh, only four years younger than Cook, was definitely part of the old guard. The dual directorship was probably meant to assure Cook of some control over Light, who, although he was a favorite of O'Neill's, did not get along with Cook and Glaspell and their friends Kenton and Rauh. Sarlós notes that, although he was recognized as "talented, well educated, and dedicated to the acquisition and application of craftsmanship in the creative process" and "became one of two outstanding directors to rise from the ranks of the amateur group," the older members accused Light of bringing "a sneering, wisecracking atmosphere into the younger part of the group," which undermined Cook.[55] The sharing of power, probably doomed from the outset, ended with Rauh's abrupt departure after the second bill in December, 1919, although she remained nominally a member of the group's executive committee.

Rauh's departure gave Light free rein, and he encouraged the *Others* group to return to the theatre, with immediately positive results. The set design for Winthrop Parkhurst's *Getting Unmarried*, a rather old-fashioned play that Alexander Woollcott called "a bit of 1896 insurgency,"[56] was designed by Marguerite Zorach and executed by William Zorach, producing a set that Kenneth Macgowan called "so striking that it ought to ruin its play by drawing all the attention from the actors," but instead "the eternal vitality of a human being on a lighted platform dominates ... honor to the Zorachs for reasserting it."[57] During this season, Light gave equal space to realist and modernist plays. From the Others group, he produced three plays by Djuna Barnes, *Three from the Earth*, *An Irish Triangle*, and *Kurzy of the Sea*; Wallace Stevens's *Three Travelers Watch a Sunrise*; and Alfred Kreymborg's *Vote the New Moon*. He also produced Edna St. Vincent Millay's best play, *Aria da Capo*. All of them brought elements of modernist experimentation to the stage of the Provincetown.

Wallace Stevens, the most significant *Others* poet to have a play produced by the Provincetown Players, had met Alfred Kreymborg and William Carlos Williams through Walter Arensburg, whom he had known during his undergraduate days at Harvard. Born in 1879, he was older than most of the poets, and as a corporation lawyer who was working his way up to a vice presidency at the Hartford, one of the most venerable companies in the "Insurance City," he lived even more of a double life than William Carlos Williams, the general practitioner from New Jersey. After his 1916 move to Hartford, Stevens came to New York regularly on business, where he would spend time in the Arensburg salon and look up Kreymborg to get the latest gossip from the literary world while leaving his staid, upper-middle-class life back in Connecticut. Unlike Arensburg, he never went to New Jersey to attend the open editorial meetings of *Others*, but he published some of his most important poems in the magazine between 1915 and 1919. Significantly for Stevens, however, his first play, *Three Travelers Watch a Sunrise*, was published not in *Others*, but in the more mainline and more prestigious *Poetry*, edited by Harriet

Monroe in Chicago. In fact, the play had won the first professional prize of Stevens's career when it was selected from among eighty one-act plays submitted in a contest sponsored by the Players' Producing Company of Chicago. Stevens was very happy about the $100 validation of his work, and agreed to make some revisions in the play before it was published in the journal. Stevens wrote to Harriet Monroe that he was willing to revise it because he wanted "to have the play a play and not merely a poem."[58]

In the early teens, Stevens, like Kreymborg and Williams, was very enthusiastic about the literary possibilities in the new art theatres, and thought his own future might lie there. His enthusiasm for taking part in theatrical productions was erased by his first direct experience, when he participated in the Neighborhood Playhouse's production of his second play, *Carlos Among the Candles*, in 1917. Stevens had worked hard to get the right staging for his play, negotiating with the painter Bancel LaFarge to do a set of sketches for the backdrops, which were "extremely delicate and extremely suggestive." When the designs were executed, by a "school boy," he recalled eighteen years later, the result was just the opposite. He also remembered that the actor playing the main character forgot three of the twelve pages of dialogue during the first and only performance and "the whole thing became ridiculous."[59] This experience, which gave the sensitive Stevens "the horrors" in 1917, was probably what kept him from going to see the Provincetown Players' production of *Three Travelers*, undoubtedly arranged by Kreymborg, whose *Vote the New Moon* appeared on the same bill, which opened on February 13, 1920, and ran for two weeks. He wrote to Monroe, "I was in New-York while they were doing the play but did not have an opportunity to see it or even to see anyone to make inquiries. So much water has gone under the bridges since the thing was written that I have not the curiosity even to read it to see how it looks at this late day." He insisted that his indifference was "truth, not pose,"[60] but it probably stemmed from his "horror" at the earlier production.

As Robley Evans has pointed out, Stevens's conception of drama and theatre in *Three Travelers* owes a good deal to Maeterlinck's symbolist plays, especially the self-enclosed, lost or wandering groups of characters in *The Blind* and *The Intruder*.[61] Ruth M. Harrison has shown in detail the influence of the Japanese Noh theatre, "by way of Ezra Pound's translations of and writings about the Noh that appeared in *Poetry* magazine in 1914 and 1915."[62] And, as Maureen Kravec has noted, the play evinces "the early modernist fascination with chinoiserie."[63] The aesthetic ideas that the play theatricalizes and develops, however, are quintessential Stevens, and in this sense the play is a very effective original use of the techniques of non-representational theatre, newly discovered on his part. Glen MacLeod has shown that Stevens was preoccupied with several interrelated aesthetic and philosophical questions at this time: "To what degree do external things exist separate from our perceptions of them? To what degree do our perceptions alter the things perceived, and vice versa? Stevens posed these epistemological questions in a variety of ways during the 1910s."[64]

In *Three Travelers*, Stevens combines favorite symbols, the candle and the jar, with a shocking but familiar contemporary image, that of a body hanging in a tree, which the audience could hardly avoid connecting with the plague of lynchings by the Ku Klux Klan during the first two decades of the century. Stevens, who was from Reading, Pennsylvania, must have been aware of the infamous lynching in nearby Coatesville in 1911, which was the occasion of John Jay Chapman's famous 1912 speech, published in *Harper's Weekly*, a classic civil rights document.[65] In the play, the jar, a red porcelain water bottle, becomes a contemporary instance of Keats's Grecian urn, with the important difference that there are no figures painted on the jar. The candle becomes associated with the sun as a figuration of light and revelation. The hanging body signifies the "invasion of humanity" into the realm of pure beauty.[66]

The plot of the play is simple, and the action nearly static. The characters consist of First and Second Negro, First, Second, and Third Chinese, and Anna, a young girl. The scene, significantly, is a hilltop in eastern Pennsylvania at four a.m. The stage is dark when the curtain rises, and the creaking of a tree limb is heard, a sound that will be repeated at strategic times throughout the play. First Negro hears the sound, crosses over to the trees and raises his lantern: "*Discerning a dark object among the branches, he shrinks back, crosses stage, and goes out through the woods to the left*" (127). The association of the locality and the object in the tree, horrific to the Black character, with lynching would have been natural to an audience in 1916, when the play was written, and even in 1920, when the Provincetown production opened. Second Negro enters with two baskets, followed by the three Chinese characters, one of whom carries a lantern. Second Chinese, "*of middle height, thin and turning gray; a man of sense and sympathy*," is the first to speak: "All you need, / To find poetry, / Is to look for it with a lantern" (127). Thus, Stevens's Diogenes figure is in search, not of an honest man, but of poetry, which he expects to find by bringing a light into the dark world. Third Chinese, on the other hand, is a poet not unlike Stevens, "*a young man, intent, detached*." He says that he could find poetry on an August night without a lantern "If I saw no more / Than the dew on the barns" (128). First Chinese, "*short, fat, quizzical, and of middle age*" (128), is the hedonist of the group, which has come to the hilltop to watch the beauty of the sunrise. He is the only one of them who has never seen it. Third Chinese sets his red porcelain water bottle on the ground with the statement: "This fetches its own water" (129). He tells his companions:

> I drink from it, dry as it is,
> As you from maxims *(to Second Chinese)*
> Or you from melons. *(to First Chinese)*
> (129)

Second Chinese reads from his book the sentence that defines the central issue about art in the book: "The court had known poverty and wretchedness; humanity had invaded its seclusion, with its suffering and its pity" (129). First Chinese, however, is skeptical. Practically, he gives the Second Negro a jug and sends him off to find water. Then, lighting a candle, he sets it on the ground next to the porcelain water bottle.

The proximity of the candle and the water bottle provides the visual image for one of Stevens's major statements about art and reality, one that foreshadows Kreymborg's treatment of it in *Manikin and Minikin* and Pirandello's in *Six Characters in Search of an Author*. Third Chinese remarks that "There is a seclusion of porcelain / That humanity never invades," which is like "the seclusion of sunrise, / Before it shines on any house" (130). While First Chinese scoffs at this statement, Second Chinese explicates it:

> This candle is the sun;
> This bottle is the earth:
> It is an illustration
> Used by generations of hermits.
> The point of difference from reality
> Is this:
> That, in this illustration,
> The earth remains of one color –
> It remains red,
> It remains what it is.
> But when the sun shines on the earth,
> In reality
> It does not shine on a thing that remains
> What it was yesterday. (130)

While the work of art, the bottle, remains fixed, reality is flux. Thus there are "indeterminate moments" before sunrise, before one can tell "What the bottle is going to be – / Porcelain, Venetian glass, / Egyptian" (131). These are the moments when the sunrise "finds itself in seclusion," and "Shines, perhaps, for the beauty of shining." That, he says, "is the seclusion of sunrise / Before it shines on any house" (131). This seclusion of sunrise, existing only for beauty, or art for art's sake, is inferior for Second Chinese because it lacks the element of the human. It is like the experience of the court in its "windless pavilions," where it saw only "chosen porcelain" on "chosen mornings," always "of the same color, / And well shaped, / And seen in a clear light" (131). Because the court knew only beauty, there was much that it never saw in the flawed jars, the weak colors, the "contorted glass," the poor light that are part of ordinary human experience. Second Chinese's position might be seen as the antithesis of the formalism that is often associated with modernism. He believes that the meaning of art comes through its expression of human experience:

> When the court knew beauty only,
> And in seclusion,
> It had neither love nor wisdom.
> These came through poverty
> And wretchedness,
> Through suffering and pity.
> *(He pauses.)*
> It is the invasion of humanity
> That counts. (132)

Applying his criterion to the art object at hand, Second Chinese suggests that the invasion of humanity, in the form of figures painted on the porcelain, would give the porcelain jar meaning for a spectator, in the form of an emotional response to the image. The spectator would "wonder" if the three of them were painted as they were, or would "tremble" if they were painted as warriors, or would "sorrow" if they were painted as three dead men. The emperor himself "would forget the porcelain / For the figures painted on it" if it were he who held the candle that illuminated it (133). Thus the most effective art is not created for the beauty of form alone, but compounded of form, imagination, and human feeling.

Third Chinese's response to this point of view is skeptical, but not hostile. He is not convinced that art cannot exist for beauty alone:

> Let the candle shine for the beauty of shining.
> I dislike the invasion
> And long for the windless pavilions.
> And yet it may be true
> That nothing is beautiful
> Except with reference to ourselves (133)

A second major aesthetic issue arises with the revelation of a third group of characters. Second Negro returns from the woods "*somewhat agitated*," with the jug of water but without his lantern, which he has left behind. A reminder of the subjectivity of the artist, the lantern becomes to Third Chinese "like evening Venus in a cloud-top" and to First Chinese "like a ripe strawberry / Among its leaves" (135). With First Chinese's ballad about an "Italian" who disappeared with his neighbor's daughter comes the invasion of humanity. The young man has been seen to climb the hill "in the manner of a tragedian / Who sweats" and "*Un miserable*" (136). As for the young girl, "There are as many points of view / From which to regard her / As there are sides to a round bottle" (136). First Chinese says that she has been "represented" to him as beautiful, beautiful as a porcelain water bottle, and young. At this point the creaking tree limb insinuates itself into the audience's consciousness. All three of the Chinese characters, seated on the ground, make note of it, and the audience's attention is drawn to "*a dark object, hanging to the limb of the tree*" (137), as the morning sky grows constantly brighter. The characters, who can't see the tree, dismiss the sound as they continue to speculate about the girl and the "sweaty tragedian," whether it was an elopement or something else. Third Chinese, who reminds the others that they have come "for isolation, / To rest in sunrise," wants to forget about the ballad, but Second Chinese insists on bringing the human element into their aesthetic experience: "this will be a part of sunrise, / And can you tell me how it will end?" (138). He reminds Third Chinese that in the meantime he has his experience of beauty; the candle shines for the beauty of shining.

The invasion of humanity comes in the person of First Negro, carrying two lanterns, presumably his own and the one Second Negro has left in the woods. As Second Negro jumps up and moves away from the Chinese characters to join First Negro, they all look up, and in the morning light "*see the body of a man hanging to the limb of the tree.*" First Chinese, "*moved*," recognizes "the young gentleman of the ballad" (139) and Third Chinese realizes that this is the ending to the story of the Italian and Anna. As the candle and the lanterns are being put out, they discover

Anna, sitting under the tree where the body hangs. She tells them her version of the ballad, which is both simpler and more baffling than the elopement described in the conventional ballad sung by First Chinese:

> He asked me to walk with him
> To the top of the hill.
> I felt the evil,
> But he wanted nothing.
> He hanged himself in front of me.
>   (141)

Third Chinese recognizes that the invasion of humanity against the "seclusion of porcelain[. . .] / Seclusion of sunrise" (142) has created something new. The sun will shine soon

> And find a new thing
> *(indicating the body)*
> Painted on this porcelain,
> *(indicating the trees)*
> But not on this,
> *(indicating the bottle)*
>   (142)

The bottle, the work of art, remains as it was, beautiful in form, but untouched by the human emotion which makes for such complexity of experience. Accepting the implications of this, he places the bottle on the ground again as the morning sky reddens. Stevens ends the dialogue by bringing rhetorical closure to the second aesthetic issue the play raises, that of perception. Picking up the book of maxims, Third Chinese reads that red is not only the color of blood, or of a man's or girl's eyes, but

> as the red of the sun
> Is one thing to me
> And one thing to another,
> So it is the green of one tree
> *(indicating)*
> And the green of another,
> Without which all would be black.
> Sunrise is multiplied,
> Like the earth on which it shines,
> By all the eyes that open on it,

> Even dead eyes,
> As red is multiplied by the leaves of trees.
> (143)

Although this statement of the multiplicity of perception, and therefore interpretation, ends the dialogue, it does not end the play. It is not Third Chinese, but Second Negro who is the final character on the stage. He picks up the musical instrument on which First Chinese has been playing his ballad and strikes it a few times. Then he hears the crack of a whip, at which he stands up, and walks to the side of the road, where he remains as the curtain falls. The ending, reminiscent of the ending of *The Cherry Orchard*, underlines another subtext, or in the terms of the play, another point of view from which to regard the bottle.

While the words of the play have been centered on the Chinese characters, the Black characters have been the subject of its most compelling visual text, and an "invasion of humanity" at least as unsettling as that of the Italian and Anna. At the opening of the play, First Negro sees the "*dark object among the branches*" (127) of the tree that to him, a Black man, immediately signifies a lynching. It is no surprise that he disappears into the woods. Likewise, Second Negro, having gone into the woods with his lantern, has probably also seen the body, which explains his agitated state and his leaving the lantern behind when he comes back with the water. When First Negro comes out of the woods with both of their lanterns, he sheds light on the scene for both groups of characters. Second Negro immediately leaves the Chinese characters and comes to the side of the other Black man, who stands looking at the group and then at the body. As they find Anna, and she explains that the hanging was a suicide, the two Black men revert to their roles as servants, but with a level of wariness to which the spectator has been made sensitive, although the Chinese characters are oblivious to it.

When Second Negro hears the crack of the whip at the end of the play, the audience cannot help but understand that he is thinking of lynching, and the image of the dead body, the visual invasion of humanity in the scene, represents the social horror of lynching as well as the private horror of the suicide in the story of the lovers. Thus Stevens has used the resources of the theatre to make the piece into a self-reflexive performance of its major aesthetic statement. The two sets of characters are like two different sets of figures painted on a porcelain jar, evoking two different emotional responses from the audience. An overt demonstration of the aesthetic principle Stevens explains in the dialogue, the object in the tree is invested with multiple meanings, depending on the subjective perception of the characters, and the spectators, who observe it, and these subjective perceptions depend in turn on the "invasion of humanity," the life experience they bring to it.

To be effective, a production of *Three Travelers* requires an understanding of the issues Stevens was dealing with in the play, an appropriate approach to non-representational acting, and an expert technical execution of his staging requirements. A total theatre synthesis, including effective presentation of the creaking tree limb, the gradually lightening sky, and the all-important objects, such as the body in the tree and the porcelain water bottle, is necessary for the play to have its full meaning for an audience. With no help from Stevens in explaining his ideas of theatre to them, the Provincetown Players' production fell short of this. Designed and directed by Charles Ellis, the production was amateurish. *Poetry* editor Harriet Monroe approved of the "not too elaborate setting" as appropriate, but complained that "the sunrise, instead of approaching slowly, with gradual revelation of the dead figure among the branches, appeared with the sudden flare of an electric light."[67] No doubt the production would have been more effective if Ellis had had at his disposal the lighting effects of the famous plaster dome that was installed in the Provincetown Playhouse the next year for *The Emperor Jones*. According to Monroe, the acting was strong, with the exception of Kathleen Millay, who played Anna. Although the three travelers, played by Remo Bufano, William Dunbar, and Harry Winston, "uttering their beautiful lines, had woven a spell which no later inadequacy could destroy," Millay "seemed merely a high-school amateur."[68] The Black characters were played by Ellis and James Butler.

The other plays on the bill with *Three Travelers*, Lawrence Langner's *Pie* and Alfred Kreymborg's *Vote the New Moon*, were far less demanding stuff than Stevens's play. *Pie* is a straightforward realistic comedy of manners with a conservative perspective, which mocks Greenwich Village feminism. Clifford Quilter leaves his home, which his wife Diantha, an editor of *House Beautiful*, has decorated impeccably but is almost never in. He leaves her to live in a little apartment with Annie Mulligan, their former cook, lured by her true homemaking skills, represented by her apple pie, while Diantha is happy with an affair that does not include any domestic responsibilities.[69]

Kreymborg's play makes use of the new non-representational theatrical aesthetics that he was developing in a cause that was uncharacteristic for him, political satire. An important context for *Vote the New Moon* is an anecdote that Kreymborg tells in his autobiography, *Troubadour*. In 1916, he was serving as personal secretary to a Wall Street power broker with ties to the Democratic Party. When his employer, a Hungarian whose English was broken, was asked to submit a speech in competition for the keynote that was eventually delivered by former New York governor Martin H. Glynn, at the national convention in St. Louis, he gave the task to Kreymborg. The most apolitical of poets, Kreymborg reports that he had no idea how to write such a speech, for "he could detect no fundamental differences in the respective party ideals. The more he read the more he felt the two were identical."[70] He was taken by his employer to Chicago to see the Republican convention in order to get an idea of the competition's rhetoric, a trip which gave him the opportunity to spend most of his time with the group of poets associated with *Poetry* magazine. He claimed that he could only attempt the kind of political rhetoric he heard "through the most carefully veiled satire" and "it was in this mood he wrote what Mr. Krauss had asked him for." He presented the speech to his employer "praying that the old man would not detect the parody between the lines."[71] The parody was not detected, and, to his surprise, the speech was accepted as the keynote.

What Kreymborg does not say is that the speech caused a sensation at the convention, "one of the most dramatic scenes in the history of national conventions," in the opinion of the *New York Times* reporter.[72] The official keynote of the convention had been designated as "Americanism" in order to counter the Republican charges that Woodrow Wilson was not enough of a patriot. This note had been sounded to less-than-enthusiastic response by the speakers leading up to Glynn's keynote speech. What took the Party leaders by surprise was the "spontaneous and electrifying enthusiasm" of the crowd when Glynn spoke of peace. The crowd broke into wild applause at the statement that it was "an American policy not to fight unnecessarily" and the "presentation of precedents to prove that whenever possible it was an immemorial American position to stay out of war even under provocation." The defense of peace was completely unexpected by the leadership, which passed notes to Glynn telling him to get back onto the theme of Americanism. But Glynn, who, according to reports, "had intended to omit large parts of this section of his speech, thinking it would be uninteresting to hear," instead responded enthusiastically to the crowd's demands that he repeat sentences and even paragraphs that supported the case for peace.[73] The result was a shift of the campaign's emphasis that is epitomized in Wilson's re-election slogan, "He kept us out of war."

It might be assumed that, when he saw the immediate effect of his political speech-writing, Kreymborg was impressed by the power that one man could have in the democratic process, but his skepticism about politics was confirmed when Wilson, elected on the slogan of peace, almost immediately plunged the country into World War I. *Vote the New Moon: A Toy Play* reflects both frames of mind. Like his earlier plays, it is a form of theatre that could easily be played with puppets, and its style is that of a children's story. The set is bare, except for a set of children's building blocks, out of which the five houses of a town are constructed. The characters pop out of their houses like Jacks-in-the-box. The play opens with the Town Crier announcing that it has been dark a long time, "since the old moon fell" and was flung into the river and gobbled up by "the Fish." Since a moon "helped us ever to see in the dark," it is time for the citizens of the town to vote a new moon.[74] The Town Crier wakes two citizens, Burgher, who lives in a blue house, and Burgess, who lives in a red one. He chastises them for being so lackadaisical about voting on election day, and they somewhat reluctantly begin the election process by hoisting red and blue pennants from their respective houses, and hitting each other over the head with their "party hammers," as they repeat over and over, "one for the red – " and "one for the blue – " (12). They continue this activity with waning enthusiasm while the Town Crier explains to the audience the advantages of their democratic system for electing the candidates, who will in turn choose the new Burgomaster to run the town: "the simplest, the most naive process in history – / of – one for the blue – one for the red – / of citizen smiting citizen on the head – / until one or the other falls insensible" (13). The Candidate who wins will be able to vote for the new Burgomaster, while the one who loses will be thrown into the river to be gobbled up by a monstrous Catfish, along with the old moon and the old Burgomaster.

The Crier becomes agitated when the citizens, who have absent-mindedly transposed their red and blue votes, become lively and "impudent." The Crier wants to know "what treachery is this? . . . what regicide is this?" (14). The citizens tell him that they're tired of the old moons, and they want a new one that is neither red nor blue. They are "tired of the old ways . . . laws, customs, routine" (16). They want a change. The Crier awakens the

Red and Blue Candidates, who immediately want to know which of them has won and which of them will die. The Crier tells them that the election has been interrupted and they have been betrayed by their red and blue constituencies. They want to go back to bed, but he reminds them: "Dark is dark without a moon ... A burg is blind sans burgomaster" (18). He tells them that their haranguing of the voters has been "non-sufficient – non-alluring – " (21), not enough to sway the hearts of two dolts, and they will have to harangue all over again. Wearily, the Candidates begin their harangues:

> BLUE: I come to you to-day –
> RED: I come to you this day –
> BLUE: With a profound appeal to your discrimination –
> RED: With the lofty purpose of lifting your thoughts on high –
> BLUE: With the special intention of nobly catechising you –
> RED: Towards the duties and pleasures of the honored –
> BLUE: In the duties and joys of those conferring honor – (22–23)

After they listen for a while, it dawns on the citizens that the Candidates are "in league" and conspire, because "each speaks like t'other ... Each mouths like t'other" (23). They accuse them of being "fraudulent ... frauds" (24), and they revolt against the system, damning them both to the river and the Catfish. The Crier cries "mutiny – insurrection – revolution – homicide – fratricide – patricide!" and calls on the "sacred purple Cat – sacred purple Fish" (25) for pardon and mercy. He cries "Sacrilege!!" when the Candidates and the citizens call together "Damn the Catfish!!" (25).

At this point, the Catfish makes itself known, as a crescendo of sounds comes from the river along with a weird violet light. While the Crier begs them to "vote – harangue – harangue – vote" in order to escape the death and perdition that comes from the Catfish, the citizens start casting their votes for the purple, and the Candidates start telling them to "vote for the Fish" rather than the red or blue. The citizens first turn on the Candidates, killing them with their hammers, and gobbling them up, and then eat each other, crying "Crunch for the purple" (27). When the Crier asks which of them swallowed which, the Catfish is heard saying "I swallowed them all!!!" (27), and makes his appearance, a huge, misshapen purple figure four times the size of the citizens and Candidates, with whiskers, fins, and a tail. The Crier recognizes him as his "Master – King" and, as the Catfish enters the Burgomaster's house from which he will rule the town, a purple moon appears, which the Burgomaster calls "The new M-moon! / Purple! / Color of kingship! / Woe!!" (28).

The general political import of this rather lurid fairy tale is that the political process of democracy is rife with corruption, its institutions so outmoded and its politicians so mendacious that it seems pointless for the average citizen to participate. This situation is dangerous, for if they are disillusioned enough, the citizens may become so bored with business as usual that they demand a radical change, and throw out democracy altogether. This is the frame of mind that leads to revolution, or, as the rise of the Catfish suggests, some form of demagoguery or fascism. As long as the people believe they are voting for nothing more significant than red or blue, while the candidates and the parties remain essentially the same, this danger will persist. Kreymborg had experienced this disillusionment personally when the peace platform he elucidated in Glynn's speech was endorsed spontaneously and enthusiastically by the people, and then promptly discarded after it had been used cynically by the party leaders to get their candidate elected. Prone to political apathy himself, Kreymborg was well aware of its danger in a democracy, but he located the responsibility for it more in the parties than in the average citizen: "Dolts can't move dolts!" (21).

The best piece of non-representational theatre the Provincetown Players produced was also a political satire, but it was a great deal more. While her two earlier plays were youthful efforts, written while she was at Vassar, and earlier, Edna Millay's *Aria da Capo* was a product of the early Greenwich Village period when she was at the height of her creative powers. Having written it in the winter of 1919, she immediately recognized that it was "a peach – one of the best things I've ever done."[75] The most literarily sophisticated of the Provincetown plays, *Aria da Capo* is, as its name suggests, a three-part lyric, with the musical form A–B–A. It consists of a duet between Pierrot and Columbine, interrupted by a duet between Corydon and Thyrsis, and ending with a reprise of the opening motif between Pierrot and Columbine. In literary terms, it draws on two well-established traditions, the harlequinade, which has its origins in the *commedia dell'arte*, and the pastoral dialogue, stemming from Virgil's Eclogues. Its satirical targets are multiple, including most importantly war, and the conception of nationalism that leads to it; the Zeitgeist of modernity, particularly within the contemporary theatre; and most directly, the Provincetown Players themselves. Its form is a modernist bricolage, a juxtaposition of fragments from two venerable literary traditions which organically expresses one of the piece's major themes. As the tragedy intrudes on the harlequinade, the awareness of the dark side of the human spirit expressed in war inevitably intrudes itself upon the light-hearted and self-centered bohemian lifestyle of Greenwich Village.

Aria da Capo begins in the spirit of light self-mockery that was familiar and comfortable territory to the Provincetown audience. Millay shapes Pierrot and Columbine, traditional lovers from the harlequinade, into representatives of the modern version of *carpe diem* that characterized the typical Greenwich Village bohemian. Mary J. McKee has described the traditional Pierrot and Columbine, valet and serving maid from the *commedia*, as "prototypes of all men and women cut off from the joy and sorrow of their fellowmen and from inquiry into the metaphysical sense of life ... they lack good will, warmth, love of fellowman, and easy emotional flow; instead, they have a certain kind of charming and disarming Charlie Chaplin helplessness."[76] In his historical study of Pierrot, Robert F. Storey has traced the evolution of the character from the *commedia* to its modern manifestations in the work of T. S. Eliot and Wallace Stevens. In the mid-nineteenth-century Pierrot, he notes the traces of the morality-play vice. This Pierrot is "ingenuous like a child, cowardly, crafty, lazy, mischievous by instinct, obliging, jeering, gluttonous, thieving, blustering, greedy, clumsy, ingenious in the arts that tend to the satisfaction of his tastes: he is a naïve and clownish Satan."[77] In the hands of Verlaine at the end of the century, he has been somewhat domesticated, but exudes a spirit of amoral self-indulgence: "happy, without envy, eating everything, drinking everything, cowardly but prudent, libidinous but outwardly continent ... he has not a care ... no remorse, no regret for anything."[78]

Millay was quite familiar with the tradition of Pierrot and Harlequin and their rivalry for the favors of the coquettish Columbine. In her notes for the published edition of *Aria da Capo*, she describes Columbine as "pretty and charming, but stupid; she never knows what Pierrot is talking about, and is so accustomed to him that she no longer pretends to understand him; but she is very proud of him, and when he speaks she listens with trustful admiration." Not unlike Millay herself, Columbine "believes men prefer women to be useless and extravagant; if left to herself she would be a domestic and capable person."[79] Her Pierrot epitomizes the modern spirit of self-centeredness through the traditional amoral indulgence of the character: "Pierrot sees clearly into existing evils and is rendered gaily cynical by them; he is both too indolent and too indifferent to do anything about it," although he does occasionally express "his conviction that all beauty and romance are fled from the world." And the traces of the medieval vice are with him as well: "although he speaks very gaily his malice must be apparent almost even to [Columbine]. Columbine bores him to death."[80]

As the play opens, Pierrot and Columbine are sitting at a table that is spread with a banquet of persimmons, pomegranates, grapes and other exotic fruits. The characters are dressed in their traditional costumes, Pierrot in a smock with wide trousers and a ruff and Columbine in a tight bodice and tarlatan skirts over ruffled bloomers, but the colors are modern, Pierrot in lavender and Columbine in pink and cerise. The opening dialogue suggests that the audience is about to be entertained with a witty modern version of the traditional harlequinade which trains a knowing eye on the fads and affectations of Greenwich Village. Columbine speaks of macaroons and artichokes that she can't live without and Pierrot says that he will kiss her if it's Tuesday. A more serious note creeps into their dialogue with Pierrot's complaint, "I am always wanting / A little more than what I have – or else / A little less. There's something wrong."[81] Millay exploits traditional characteristics of Pierrot, his pedantry and changeableness, to mock the most recognizable touchstones of avant-garde modern culture in 1919. Pierrot says he has become a painter who plans a painting of "six orange bull's-eyes, four green pinwheels, / And one magenta jelly-roll – the title / As follows: *Woman Taking In Cheese From Fire-Escape*" (220) – an obvious shot at Cubism. In quick succession, he decides that he has become a pianist who composes "on a new scale [...] without tonality" (220); a socialist who loves Humanity but hates people; a philanthropist "because I feel so restless" (221); and the manager of Columbine, who he thinks will make a wonderful actress because she's blonde and has no education. Then he decides he will be a critic because "there is nothing I can enjoy" (222). Alluding to the tradition of Pierrot as a moonstruck lover, Millay has him eschewing even the romance of love, telling Columbine that he will not swear his love to her by the "black moon," because "I always lied about the moon and you. / Food is my only lust" (222).

Having established the context of modernity, Millay puts an end to the light-hearted harlequinade by reminding the audience that it is in the theatre. Pierrot and Columbine are interrupted by Cothurnus, the spirit of tragedy, in a dull purple toga and buskins, who walks onto the stage in the middle of the scene. Pierrot breaks character, saying, "what's this, for

God's sake? – / What's the matter? / Say, whadda you mean? – Get off the stage, my friend" (223). Cothurnus says that he is tired of waiting to do his scene, and that Pierrot will have to do his later, and then calls Thyrsis and Corydon from their dressing room, where they had been quietly resting. When they tell him that their scene is set down for later, he replies, "that is true; / But we will play it now. I am the scene" (223). Millay plays the audience on multiple levels here. With the disruption of the harlequinade comes a disruption of generic expectations. The conventions of the theatre piece are no longer clear, and the audience's confidence in its knowledge of the aesthetic context and its implications is shaken. What's more, for the insider audience at the Provincetown Playhouse, the situation has an immediate reference to the Players themselves. Because of the limited rehearsal space and the bills consisting of two or three one-act plays, the actors often found themselves in close and incongruous juxtaposition. Several Players have commented on the jarring effects of this, as, for example, when the *Lima Beans* cast tried to rehearse their rhythmic modernist lines in the hall while Eugene O'Neill's father James, the great melodramatic actor of *Monte Cristo* fame, was giving rather unwelcome pointers to the actors in his son's Strindbergian monologue *Before Breakfast*.[82] Millay, who had acted in six plays at the Playhouse and directed one, was well aware of the strange juxtapositions that occurred, and used it to great theatrical and thematic effect in this scene. For it is tragedy that intrudes itself upon the carefree, self-involved bohemians before its stated time and insists on playing its scene, even against the protests of its own actors, Thyrsis and Corydon. Corydon complains that "this is the setting for a farce. / Our scene requires a wall; we cannot build / A wall of tissue-paper" and Thyrsis says that "we cannot act / A tragedy with comic properties" (224), but the director Cothurnus tells them to "try it and see. I think you'll find you can. / One wall is like another" (224). The tragic mood intrudes itself into the Zeitgeist of the Players and Greenwich Village as the tragic play intrudes upon the harlequinade that it displaces on the stage.

The Thyrsis and Corydon section of the play is a parable about war, or more specifically, the darker human traits that produce it. Cothurnus, whom Millay places on a raised dais at center stage, presides over the proceedings and several times prompts the actors when they are about to diverge from the tragic plan. Thyrsis and Corydon are drawn from the pastoral tradition, specifically, from Virgil's seventh Eclogue, in which they engage in a singing competition while they watch their flocks. Millay draws on the pastoral tradition, with perhaps an allusion to Kreymborg's *Vote the New Moon*, in her costumes for them, which "in striking contrast to the elegance of those of Pierrot and Columbine, should be very simple, and very roughly made," short rough tunics and sandals, with the only color being Thyrsis's cloak of "raw bright red" and Corydon's of "brilliant blue." Millay made a point that "there must be no red or blue used anywhere in the entire play excepting in the blue and red of these two cloaks."[83] As in *Vote the New Moon*, the red and blue come to stand for the two sides of a meaningless battle in the play, a competition for its own sake.

Like the harlequinade, the pastoral begins within the confines of a familiar convention. The two shepherds move the table and chairs from the earlier scene out of the way and seat themselves on the floor, propped up by pillows that are meant to represent rocks. They begin a pastoral dialogue about the landscape and Corydon suggests that they make a song about a lamb that thought himself a shepherd. Thyrsis at first agrees, but prompted by Cothurnus, instead proposes a game: "Let's gather rocks, and build a wall between us; / And say that over there belongs to me, / And over here to you!" (225). It is likely that the audience would have recognized an allusion to Robert Frost's "Mending Wall," published in *North of Boston* three years before the play was produced. Both the poem and the play take the simple premise of the building of a wall between neighbors as a metaphor for human interaction. Within the context of World War I, Millay implies the basic impulses behind nationalism in the building of the wall.

Once they have built their wall from crepe paper, Thyrsis and Corydon separate to "sit alone / A little while, and lay a plot whereby / We may outdo each other" (225). Thyrsis immediately thinks better of having proposed this game, saying "what is the sense of saying / I do not want you on my side the wall? / It is a silly game" (225). He proposes that they give it up and instead make up the song about the lamb. Significantly, Corydon forgets his line until, prompted by Cothurnus, he says, "How do I know this isn't a trick / To get upon my land?" (226), introducing the poison of suspicion into the heretofore loving relationship of the two friends as well as the concept of ownership in relation to the land. From this beginning, a number of ugly feelings grow up between the friends as a result of their having built the wall. The water is all on Thyrsis's side, and Thyrsis is willing to let the sheep on the other side go thirsty because "they're not my sheep" (226). He threatens violence if Corydon tries to lead his part of the flock over the wall. Corydon thinks that the game is getting too serious, and proposes dropping it, but as they reach over the wall to take each other's hands, Cothurnus prompts Thyrsis to ask suspiciously "how do I know this isn't a trick / To water your sheep, and get the laugh on me?" (227). Corydon replies that his suspicion has to be conquered by trust:

> You can't know; that's the difficult thing about it.
> Of course, – you can't be sure; you have to take
> My word for it. And I know just how you feel.
> But one of us has to take a risk, or else,
> Why, don't you see? – the game goes on forever –
> (227)

Thyrsis recognizes that it is an ugly game, and offers to end it and allow Corydon to come over and water his sheep, but Corydon realizes that the wall has changed them. He no longer trusts Thyrsis: "I think / I am afraid of you! – You are a stranger!" (228). He refuses to bring the sheep over because he is afraid that Thyrsis will mix them up with his and try to keep them.

Distrust and fear harden into hatred when Corydon discovers jewels on his side of the wall and is glad the wall was up before he found them so he doesn't have to share them. Thyrsis offers him water for the jewels, but Corydon doesn't care about the sheep now because he has become a merchant and is deciding how to spend his money. While Corydon naps, Thyrsis looks for jewels on his side of the wall, and, unable to find them, digs a poisonous black weed instead, thinking it would be "a speedy remedy" for "a festered pride and a feverish ambition" (230). Corydon, awakening, now finds that he himself is thirsty, and offers Thyrsis a bowl of jewels in exchange for some water. Thyrsis gives him water infused with the poisonous root and Corydon strangles Thyrsis with the necklace of jewels he gives him in payment. In the spirit of tragedy, Corydon recognizes too late that his love for his friend is stronger than the game and breaks through the wall, where he falls on Thyrsis's body and dies, whereupon Cothurnus closes his promptbook with a bang and matter-of-factly places the table from the harlequinade over the two bodies. Millay comments that "these two characters are young, very simple, and childlike; they are acted upon by the force [Cothurnus] that sits on the back of the stage behind them. More and more as their quarrel advances they begin to see that something is wrong, but they have no idea what to do about it, and they scarcely realize what is happening, the quarrel grows so from little things into big things."[84] Thus from the building of the wall and the consequent establishment of the concepts of "mine" and "yours" come suspicion, selfishness, alienation, fear, greed, pride, ambition, and murder, with the result that the human race destroys itself.

The third part of the play returns to the mood of the first, but the bodies of the two shepherds serve as a reminder of the human tragedy. Pierrot tells Cothurnus he will drag the bodies away because the audience wouldn't stand for their sitting down to eat with two dead bodies lying under the table. But Cothurnus assures them that if they pull the tablecloth down and "hide them from the house, / And play the farce. The audience will forget" (234). Pierrot agrees, and after arranging the table, the actors reprise their opening lines from the harlequinade:

> COLUMBINE: Pierrot, a macaroon! I cannot *live*
> Without a macaroon!
> PIERROT: My only love,
> You are *so* intense [. . .] Is it Tuesday, Columbine?
> I'll kiss you if it's Tuesday. (234)

As Nancy Milford has remarked, *Aria da Capo* is "a deadly little play."[85] After the Thyrsis and Corydon section, the effect on the audience of returning to the mood of the beginning is devastating. It is an exposure not only of the theatre, and perhaps specifically the Provincetown Players, which continues its self-involved, lighted-hearted aesthetic play in the midst of a world that has been devastated by world war and the utter disillusionment it has occasioned, but also of the pre-war Zeitgeist of Greenwich Village bohemia, which appears escapist and frivolous rather than daring and unconventional in this context. Something new is needed, Millay suggests, something more serious than simple rebellion against the traditions and values of the past. Like T. S. Eliot in *The Waste Land*, Millay juxtaposes fragments of the old traditions to shore against the ruin of Western civilization. It is hardly a statement of values, but it is a suggestion that humankind needs to have them.

The staging, designed and executed by Charles Ellis, contributed to the impression of the play's arresting modernity. As Millay prescribed, it was "a merry black and white interior" (219). Rather than a backdrop and wings on the tiny stage, Ellis used black screens of various sizes on which he painted a design in white. In her staging notes, Millay specified a black table with a table cloth covered with black and white spots and striped

Figure 5. Norma Millay and Harrison Dowd in a rehearsal for *Aria da Capo*.

ends. Cothurnus's chair was set on a platform draped with a black cloth. The color was supplied by the costumes – lavender and pink for Pierrot and Columbine, and red, blue, and purple for Thyrsis, Corydon, and Cothurnus – as well as the bowls of fruit and the confetti representing the jewels. According to Norma Millay, who played Columbine, Ellis painted a proscenium border of colored fruits and flowers, "cut as though they were hanging down."[86] *Aria da Capo* was recognized immediately as one of the most original of the Provincetown plays. Alexander Woollcott wrote in the *New York Times* that it was "the most beautiful and most interesting play in the English language now to be seen in New York," suggesting that "it would pass over the heads of the average unthinking audience, but surely no mother from a gold-starred home, who saw the war come and go like a grotesque comet and who now hears the rattle-pated merriment of her neighbors all the more distinctly because of the blank silence in her own impoverished home – surely no such mother will quite miss the point of 'Aria da Capo.'"[87]

Although Woollcott considered Millay the better playwright, he was equally enthusiastic about her chief rival among the Players, Djuna Barnes. In April of 1920, Woollcott wrote that one of the chief attractions of the Provincetown was "the refreshing sight of Miss Djuna Barnes, bounding up and down the centre aisle like an artless antelope – a compensating privilege accorded to the Provincetown Playwrights on first nights, presumably in lieu of royalties."[88] To those most familiar with the brittle, acerbic, sophisticated and alcoholic Barnes of the thirties, the Barnes who wrote the classic modernist novel *Nightwood*, the image that she had in Greenwich Village in the early teens may come as a surprise. In Guido Bruno's words, she comes off as the epitome of the female "merry Villager":

> Red cheeks. Auburn hair. Gray eyes, ever sparkling with delight and mischief. Fantastic earrings in her ears, picturesquely dressed, ever ready to live and to be merry: that's the real Djuna as she walks down Fifth Avenue, or sips black coffee, a cigarette in hand, in the Café Lafayette.[89]

Barnes, who had moved to Greenwich Village from her mother's apartment in the Bronx in 1915, was building a successful career as a journalist in the early teens, probably the most successful of the women among the group. As a young reporter, she made a name for herself with her interviews with famous people, particularly artists, theatre people, and writers, and the kind of stunt journalism made popular by Nelly Bly, including going into a cage with a baby gorilla and being force-fed like the hunger-striking suffragettes in order to report on the experience. As she grew older, Barnes became something of a celebrity journalist, commanding as much as $1,000 for an article in *McCall's* in 1920. Her easy access to the newspapers also gave her the opportunity to practice the creative writing that she saw as her true vocation. Many of her early short stories appeared in newspapers, as did several short plays, beginning in 1916. It is significant for an ambitious free-lance writer like Barnes that her first play with aspirations to literary merit, *A Passion Play*, was published by Kreymborg in the February, 1918, issue of *Others*, which of course did not pay its contributors. Barnes had three plays produced by the Provincetown Players, all in the 1919–1920 season. They were *Three from the Earth*, *Kurzy of the Sea*, and *An Irish Triangle*.

Like all of Barnes's serious work, her plays are imaginative expressions of a deeply troubling personal history that obsessed her as an artist. At this point in her life, the sunny mask of the Village bohemian hid a recent familial past to which Barnes was just beginning to find access through art. She had grown up in a household headed by her grandmother and her bigamous father, who had two sets of children, the "legitimate" offspring of Djuna's mother to whom he was married, and the children of another woman whom he had moved into the household when Djuna was five years old. He continued to have children by both women, who at one point, when Djuna was ten, gave birth within twelve days of each other, events at which Djuna was required to assist. The family was kept isolated in rural households in Cornwall-on-Hudson and on a farm on Long Island, and the children were for the most part kept out of school to avoid contact with the neighbors. Within this setting, Djuna was sexually abused by her grandmother, a writer and spiritualist, over a long period of time and by her father at least once.[90] Djuna, who detested her father but felt that she had a special bond with her grandmother, felt utterly betrayed when the two decided that Djuna's mother and her four children would leave the farm that Djuna's mother's money had paid for and go to live in New York, on the charity of relatives and what Djuna, aged twenty, could earn, while her father would divorce her and legally marry his bigamous "second wife," Fanny.

It is this familial history that lies below the surface of *Three from the Earth*, the first play that Barnes had produced by the Players, in October, 1919. This play consists of a dialogue between Kate Morley, a beautiful, seductive woman of forty, and the three Carson brothers, James, Henry, and John, tall, rather heavy young men ranging in age from nineteen to twenty-five, who "*look like peasants of the most obvious type.*"[91] While this play remains within the boundaries of representational realism, it pushes those boundaries toward the grotesque and the symbolic. The three young men, precursors of the brothers in O'Neill's *Desire Under the Elms*, suggest farm animals. They have a look of "*formidable grossness and stupidity*," and are stoop-shouldered, with "*excessively ugly*" hands. They have sandy, sun-bleached hair that sticks straight up, oily, sweaty skin, large hanging lips and small eyes with whitish eyelashes. The are "*clumsy and ill-clothed*," despite their grotesque efforts to appear "*well-dressed*" – each wears a purple aster and has on a tie "*of the super-stunning variety*" (69). The youngest, John, says that their work as farmers is to "go down on the earth and find things, tear them up, shaking the dirt off" (73). Barnes suggests in the stage directions that the animal element so evident in the three is at war with something else: "*their eyes are intelligent, their smiles gentle, melancholy, compassionate*" (69). Although they have been doing farm work for their father, who lies in bed all day, they are familiar with literary figures like Anatole France and Rémy de Gourmont.

The parallel between these figures and Barnes's half-brothers, who had remained on the Long Island farm with her father and tried to make a business of growing vegetables while she and her siblings went to the city, is suggestive, as is the description of their father, a grotesque representation of Barnes's father Wald, who had with his mother Zadel frequented the decadent *fin de siècle* salons of London before establishing his "bohemian" rural households in New York. Kate describes the brothers' father as wearing a green cloth suit and carrying white rats on his shoulders. In a foreshadowing of the representation of her father in the novel *Ryder* and the play *The Antiphon*, Barnes gives her a diatribe against the "mighty righteous and original father" who is responsible for the young men being "ugly and clumsy and uncouth. You grunt and roar, you wear abominable clothes – and you have no manners":

> He called himself "The little Father," as one might say, "The great Emperor." Well, to have a father to whom you can go and say, "All is not as it should be" – that would have been everything. But what could you say to him, and what had he to say to you? . . . Then he becomes the gentleman farmer because he discovers he cannot be the Beloved Fool. Suddenly he is the father of three creatures for all the world like Russian peasants – without an idea, a subtlety – it's wicked, that's all, wicked.
> (75–76)

Kate suggests that each of the three men may have had a different mother, and "I might be the mother of one of you", to which John, the youngest replies "[*significantly*] So I believe, madame" (76). In a slam at her stepmother, Barnes has Kate identify the men's mother as a part-time prostitute and "dancing girl without a clean word in her vocabulary, or a whole shirt to her name" (71) who has, like the obese Fanny Barnes, a "gross stomach" (78). In the course of the play, the young men reveal that they have come on their bicycles to see Kate in order to retrieve their father's letters to her. Kate, who is about to be married to a Supreme Court justice, decides to trust them, and gives them the letters, as one would "give the oxen the rope, [so] they won't run away" (74).

As the foreshadowing has indicated, one more piece of business remains between them, and John abruptly rises to transact it. Picking up a photograph of Kate with a baby, he says "You have posed for the madonna?" (77). Kate replies that every woman has, and that she posed for the picture while she was playing in an amateur theatrical, "Crown of Thorns" (77). John reveals that their father has died, cutting his throat with a knife, freeing the men from the farm. Responding to Kate's desire to "clean house" before she marries, John says that "it won't be quite cleared out until [the photograph] goes" (79). Taking it out of the frame, he finds the inscription, "Little John, God bless him" (79). He takes the photograph, and the men get up to leave against Kate's protest, "gentlemen, gentlemen, not this way" (80). Saying "Well?" John takes Kate in his arms, raises her face, and kisses her on the mouth. When Kate cries out, "Not that way! Not that way!" James ends the play with "That's the way you bore him!" (80).

Reviewers of the play confessed that they did not understand its meaning, although they found it a compelling piece of drama. Given its references to Barnes's private experience, this is not surprising. While it has a hidden frame of reference in a perhaps imagined meeting between Barnes and her half-brothers, the play suggests the universal implications of myth through its carefully crafted simplicity. The natural, which is also the primitive, wars with the civilized within the spirits of the brothers. Now that they have been freed from their ogre father, they are going abroad to "listen," to absorb the culture of Anatole France and Rémy De Gourmont, but they are still the farm animals their father raised them to be. The result is a typically Barnesian grotesque image of humanity, in which the animal element is given equal acknowledgment with the intellect and the imagination. The father–daughter incest that was Barnes's "crown of thorns" comes full-circle in *Three from the Earth*, with the suggestion of mother–son incest initiated by John. The suggestion that the sins of the fathers will not only be visited upon the children, but will be repeated by them, is not only ancient wisdom, but the modern wisdom of social scientists who have studied the data related to incest. While audiences did not necessarily decode the surface meaning of the play, it is clear that they responded to it at the more visceral level where myth reaches us. As Robert Sarlós has said, the play "confounded yet delighted audiences and critics alike."[92] Woollcott took the production as proof of "how absorbing and essentially dramatic a play can be without the audience ever knowing what, if anything, the author is driving at."[93]

Of all the Players, Barnes was the most influenced by the art of the Abbey Players, and most specifically, the work of their most important playwright, John Millington Synge. In 1917, Barnes wrote an admiring article about Synge for which she prepared with uncharacteristic thoroughness, reading critical and biographical studies as well as Synge's work, which she clearly knew well. What had first captured her interest was Synge's dialogue. She wrote that there was "nothing in the English language that sets my whole heart to singing as his lines." But a deeper affinity emerged in what she saw as his vision of life: "He realized that grim brutality and frankness and love are one, the upper lip is romance, but the under is irony, and he knew 'There is no timber that has not strong roots among the clay and worms.'"[94] In the next two Barnes plays produced by the Players, the influence of Synge is unmistakable, although the elements that Barnes appropriates from his aesthetic, a rather awkward imitation of his poetic "Irish" dialogue and plots that draw on a putative folk tradition, are put to service in a uniquely Barnesian way.

Like *Three from the Earth*, the pseudo-Irish *Kurzy of the Sea* is based on a disturbing chapter of Barnes's personal history. At the age of seventeen, while the two branches of the family were still living under one roof in Long Island, she was induced, chiefly by her grandmother, to enter into a common-law marriage with Percy Faulkner, the 52-year-old brother of Fanny. As Barnes recalled the incident later in life, she believed that her father had more or less sold her to Faulkner, as he had tried to do with a neighbor, also three times her age, when she was sixteen. As was typical, she tended to downplay the role her grandmother had played in the transaction, blaming chiefly her father and her mother, who let it happen despite her objections. According to Barnes's biographer, both father and grandmother were eager to get Djuna out of the house, if just to have one less mouth to feed.[95] After living with Faulkner in a transients' hotel in Bridgeport, Connecticut for about two months, Barnes returned home to the farm on Long Island, where she remained until the eviction of her mother two years later.

Kurzy of the Sea is set in a poor Irish household that includes a married couple, Molly and Pat McRace, who are eager to get their son Rory married off, and an old woman named Betsy Keep, who is reminiscent of Barnes's grandmother Zadel, "*keen of tongue and quick of mind. She is always 'coming over' for the good of the 'world.'*"[96] It is Molly who is most eager to be rid of Rory, for "it's not the rest of his life I can be cooking for him and his father feeding him, great stupid that he is" (84). If he is not married by sundown the next day, the realist Molly threatens to kick Rory out of the house. She complains that "it's fairy tales has got him by the ear" (84), and that he has been so bewitched by the tales of the local story-teller that he will not marry unless "we give him a Queen or a Saint or a Venus, or whatever it is comes in with the tide" (85). Right on cue, Pat appears with Kurzy, who he says is a mermaid that was caught in his fishing net. Kurzy tells Rory that she came to shore because she had been watching the family and "got tired of seeing your mother, and her all dressed up, standing on the hill top, making incantations and signs, and you, going down into the bogs, with your fists clenched" (90). When Rory suggests that it was spite that brought her to the surface, she answers, "it's spite that does be bringing a woman up through thirty fathoms of water, but it's love I'm thinking, does be driving her to shore" (90).

When Rory carries Kurzy off for a ride on the gray mare his parents have promised them for a wedding present, Molly expresses relief that he will be out of the house and making his own living, but also regrets that "it's a hard word here, and a hard word there I've been putting past our Rory's ear, that he'll have difficulty forgetting perhaps" (92). Pat is glad that marriage will put an end to Rory's "dreaming and nonsense," and that he will have to turn a deaf ear to the story-teller "when he does be coming singing down out of the hills with the foolish eyes of him all lit up from below and shining, and words coming out of him with a great rattle and a hurry and a sorrow surely" (93). With that Rory returns alone, explaining that he threw Kurzy back into the sea to test her, for if she was "a saint," she would swim, and if not, she would drown. With pride he recounts Kurzy's reply, that he was a dreamer or a fool, but in either case, he could keep her petticoat. Without her long petticoat, Kurzy was revealed to be "in a neat little bathing suit like they keep at Shannon's" (93) as she swam away. She told Rory she was a barmaid at the local pub, and challenged him: "'It's long distance swimming you'll be learning this summer, but it will do you little good,' she says. 'For by the time you can hold your own, I shall be halfway to Cork with a lover on my arm'" (94). Having told the tale, Rory heads for the door and says, "You can keep your horse, mother, for it's a boat I shall be needing" (94).

In this imaginative revisiting of her own experience, Barnes suggests that Rory has been the victim not only of his parents' determination to be rid of him, but of the fantastic romantic stories that suggested to him he might have "a Queen or a Saint or a Venus" for his mate, and so set him up to be satisfied with nothing less. His parents are duped by Kurzy's scheme out of self-interest – they want her to be what she says she is so they can be rid of Rory. Betsy and Molly both see that Kurzy has "a bit too human look," but Molly suggests to Pat that "perhaps it'll wear off" (92). Although they are skeptical, they are quite ready to exploit Rory's romantic dreams. Rory first declares that he won't believe the story because Kurzy "isn't real" (88). Vulnerable to the art of story-telling, however, he is convinced by his father's narrative of catching Kurzy in his nets, saying, "Ah, saints save us, it's a real spirit she is, and I'm lost" (89). Trembling at the thought that Kurzy is indeed a supernatural being, Rory is empowered by his discovery of her humanity. This can occur only after Kurzy declares her love for him, revealing that she has human feelings, and therefore, vulnerability. Rory's test for whether she is a "saint" results in a symbolic simultaneous revelation of her humanity and her sexuality when she voluntarily removes her petticoat. This action and her challenge to him frees Rory from his seeming enchantment by the romantic stories as well as his dependence on his family, and he is determined to follow and win her himself.

For Barnes, the play acts as a symbolic embracing of the natural and the human in opposition to her family's claims to "specialness," whether in her grandmother's spiritualism or her father's unsupported claim to artistic genius. These romantic fantasies are exposed as a lie, paralyzing and regressive to the person who invests in them. Having been led into the situation through false promises of Percy Faulkner's romantic love for her and his desire to give her the chance to develop her artistic gifts, Djuna Barnes had fled back to her family circle to escape the rather dreary reality of her life in a seedy hotel with a soap salesman, who was three times her age and not really very interested in her soul. The play exposes the danger of the romantic lies on which the family circle was based. It is only by recognizing one's common humanity, suggested here by the healthy sexuality of a local barmaid, that one can be freed from the kind of spiritual paralysis that grips Rory at the beginning of the play. Not surprisingly, Rory's transformation from trembling son to ardent lover is similar to that of Synge's Playboy. It is the joyful expression of his own desire that empowers him in the end to go out and seek his lover, and to reject the parental deception that had kept him fearful and obedient. Rory's pursuit of Kurzy on his own terms represents his coming of age and his rejection of his self-interested, deceitful parents.

A third play produced by the Provincetown in the 1919–1920 season, *An Irish Triangle*, has a much different tone from the *unheimlich* suggestion of the murky depths of the human psyche that lurks in the plays based on Barnes's family experience. In this lighthearted treatment of an unorthodox marriage, guaranteed to *épater le bourgeois*, Barnes makes little use of Synge, except for her rather inaccurate version of his Irish dialogue. *An Irish Triangle* is a brief dialogue between Kathleen O'Rune, an Irish peasant, and her friend Shiela, over tea. In the course of the conversation, it becomes evident that Kathleen has been discovering the finer things in life, such as the joys of reading great literature, of wearing stylish clothes, and of behaving with middle-class manners, as a result of her husband John's dalliance with the lady of the manor house. Kathleen insists that she does not regret the fact that John has "gone up on the hill and found her ladyship beautiful,"[97] because he has reported to her everything he has learned about the lady of the manor and her way of life. Because there is no better, "more remembering, more observing" man than John, Kathleen says, "if there's anything her ladyship knows above me now, it's John has no words for the repeating" (240).

A sort of chorus figure representing the village consciousness, Shiela is shocked and mystified by Kathleen's tolerance of the affair, insisting that she should consider the "honor" of the other women in the village if not her own: "Where would the likes of the glory of Ireland and its women be if they were all as strange as yourself" (241). Kathleen refuses to be bound by these outmoded ideas, and insists that the women of Ireland would be better off if they embraced her attitude: "you'd be smiling with the straight smile that knows no sorrow, and the glint in your two eyes, and you would by lying down in the dark and rising up in the dawn with a sense in you that you had not stopped the great progress of the world by turning on your lean sides, dropping down tears, and lamenting out of your shallowness and your astounding ignorance" (241). Ireland, she says, is "in need of education . . . and the refinement that comes down out of the hills, from behind grand doors" (241). Shiela recognizes Kathleen's happiness: "the sorrow has gone out of your eyes, and your smile that used to be crooked with sadness, is glad and straight and does by [sic] 'sassing' the sun" (238). But she remains mystified by her attitude toward her husband's infidelity, unable to break out of her conventional view of marriage and sexuality. The play ends with Kathleen's suggestion that she is preparing to flaunt convention more actively, for she has bought some new underclothes, and "it's a grand night coming on, and it's the moon and I will be climbing the hill, for I've nothing more to learn, but John is rare ignorant" (242). The implication is that Kathleen is now going to perform the same service that John has done for her, for "it's the master of the Manor himself who is soft of tongue and charming, and John says there's a way he's dying to know, the master has of wrapping his puttees, that can be learned by close contact only" (241).

As in *Kurzy of the Sea*, Barnes's implication here is that the power of sexuality should be a liberating force, not one that condemns a woman to humiliation and sorrow. By embracing it, and by unlinking it from the conventional expectations of marriage, she suggests, it can be put to good use. The idea of marriage described here in the simple terms of the folk tale is quite close to that promoted by Hutchins Hapgood and other Greenwich Village proponents of open marriage and "free love." In their view, the bond of marriage should be separated from sexuality, which might have many outlets that would serve to enrich the experience of each partner and thus make the marital relationship more varied and interesting. Similarly, while Kathleen can say that "it's John I'm better pleased with than any man in the country, for he's a good husband and a generous" (239), she does not see why that should require sexual exclusivity from either of them. They use sex as Hapgood suggested it should be used, to broaden one's experience, although he had in mind more an emotional experiential realm and Barnes suggests a much more practical one. Barnes was the only woman among the players to write so openly in favor of free love. Most, like Hapgood's wife Neith Boyce, were extremely ambivalent about sexual exclusivity in marriage. But for Barnes, whose sex life was anything but conventional, restricting sex to one partner was an outmoded and rather quaint notion.

Although the level of achievement by the Provincetown was characteristically inconsistent in the 1919–1920 season, as Robert Sarlós has noted, under James Light's leadership, "the Young Turks … carried the season to conclusion barely scathed and had both artistic and fiscal laurels to show for their trouble."[98] The treasury had a favorable balance after receipts of more than $14,000, more than double the income from the previous season. Nonetheless, Kenton and the rest of the Cook faction were incensed that Light had diverged from the group's principles by producing a foreign play, Arthur Schnitzler's *Last Masks*, and that Light had, in their view, frittered away money that might have gone to the building fund by paying the actors small salaries. In her words, "Jig and Susan came down from Provincetown towards the end of the season – definitely and desperately sent for"[99] – one can imagine by whom. For the next season, Cook and Light were made co-directors. The executive committee was expanded to seven, with James Light and Charles Ellis being added to the previous committee of Cook, Kenton, Rauh, Millay, and the new Secretary–Treasurer, Eleanor Fitzgerald. As events would prove, however, this combination of the old and the new would prove unstable. With O'Neill's tacit assent, the Cook faction tried increasingly to diminish Light's power and influence, and finally oust him from the group, during the following two seasons, as they had the Nordfeldts in 1917, while Light, allied with Fitzgerald, Charles Ellis, Norma Millay, and costume designer Blanche Hays, stubbornly refused to go.[100] It was under these conditions that the Provincetown Players did their most significant work.

4

Glaspell and O'Neill

One-act plays

In 1916, with Glaspell's *Trifles* and O'Neill's *The Moon of the Caribees*, the last of the plays set on the SS *Glencairn* to be written, the Provincetown's two major playwrights had produced plays that brought the techniques of dramatic realism to full realization on the stage. O'Neill believed that, in contrast with *In the Zone*, which he thought "a conventional construction of the theater as it is," *The Moon of the Caribees* "works with truth ... the impelling, inscrutable forces behind life which it is my ambition to at least faintly shadow at their work in my plays."[1] Reflecting their knowledge of the modernist theatre of Kreymborg and the rest of the *Others* group, the work that both playwrights did after 1916 shows an increasing awareness of the possibilities of extending their dramatic aesthetics beyond the strictly representational. The development of Glaspell and O'Neill as playwrights during the five years between 1916 and 1921 was nothing short of extraordinary, and both of them show the unmistakable influence of the modernist writers with whom they were now associating at the Provincetown.

The first two plays that Glaspell wrote after *Trifles*, *The People* (March, 1917) and *Close the Book* (November, 1917), are well-crafted one-acts that succeeded well at the Provincetown, but artistically are something of a reversion to the spirit of *Suppressed Desires*. *The People*, a satirical treatment of the *Masses* group, exhibits the in-group mentality of coterie drama, but shows elements of Glaspell's later method in that it moves from a satiric mockery of the flaws in the group to an earnest and mystical suggestion of how they can be ameliorated. The play begins with comedy of manners among recognizable characters based on Max Eastman (played by Cook), Floyd Dell, John Sloan, Hyppolyte Havel, Mary Heaton Vorse, and John Reed, and becomes more serious as Glaspell introduces characters who emblematize elements of the magazine's readership, a Woman from Idaho (played by Glaspell), a Man from the Cape, and a Boy from Georgia. The slight plot is that Ed, the editor has returned from an unsuccessful fund-raising trip feeling jaded and disillusioned with the magazine's stated purpose: "The more I looked the more ridiculous it seemed to me that we should be giving our lives to … The People – A Journal of the Social Revolution." One by one, however, the readers arrive at the office, offering to volunteer their efforts to the great cause that Ed has described in an editorial, which reads much more like Cook and Glaspell's Nietzschean–monist gospel of mystical unity through nature than like Eastman's philosophical socialism:

> We are living now. We shall not be living long. No one can tell us we shall live again. This is our little while. This is our chance. And we take it like a child who comes from a dark room to which he must return – comes for one sunny afternoon to a lovely hillside, and finding a hole, crawls in there till after the sun is set. I want that child to know the sun is shining upon flowers in the grass. I want him to know it before he has to go back to the room that is dark. I wish I had pipes to call him to the hilltop of beautiful distances. I myself could see farther if he were seeing at all. Perhaps I can tell you: you who have dreamed and dreaming know, and knowing care. Move! Move from the things that hold you. If you move, others will move. Come! Now. Before the sun goes down.[2]

The Woman from Idaho, whose chief aim in life had been to leave enough money behind her for an impressive tombstone, says that the words have inspired her to throw over her old life: "they're like a spring – if you've lived in a dry country, you'll know what I mean. And they made me know that my tombstone was as dead as … a tombstone" (54), so she has come East in search of a better purpose for her life. On the journey, looking at the same people that Ed had looked at with jaded eyes, the Woman has become inspired by "the truth – the truth – the truth that opens from our lives as water opens from the rocks." She urges the editors to continue their mission to "let life become what it may become! – so beautiful that everything that is back of us is worth everything it cost" (58). Reinspired by the faith of their readers, the editors decide to continue on with the magazine. More deftly developed, this trajectory from representational realism to abstract mysticism was to inform several of Glaspell's most significant plays, particularly *The Outside* and *The Verge*. In using abstract, emblematic characters, she had taken an element of the non-representational drama of Maeterlinck, witnessed at Provincetown in the work of Louise Bryant, Mary Carolyn Davies, and Alfred Kreymborg, and put it to effective use within the representational framework. She also suggested a way in which the representational might be fused with the non-representational to create the new dramatic idiom that she was to make her own.

Close the Book is a less imaginative effort dramaturgically, but the idea behind it was to be developed into the full-length *Inheritors*. Glaspell wrote it during a trip back to Iowa when she was induced by Cook's mother to make the rounds with her in Davenport society, an obvious attempt to establish Glaspell's social position as her son's wife, and to recuperate Cook's social position, which had suffered after he had divorced his first wife in order to marry Glaspell. Barbara Ozieblo has noted the irony of Glaspell's position as she returned to a town where, as a marginal farmer's daughter, she had yearned to be part of the social circle to which the Cooks belonged.[3] Now a successful author, she was welcomed by all the women's clubs from which she had been excluded, but now wanted no part of them because she thought them narrow, provincial, and silly. *Close the Book* exposes the triviality of small-town social pretensions at the same time that it pokes fun at what might have been Glaspell's own position, that of the "radical" who wants to divorce herself from her past and her roots, but finds it impossible. In the play, a radical young student, Jhansi, an orphan who believes she is descended from Gypsies and thus naturally a free spirit, is taken to meet the family of her new fiancé John, a professor at the local university, who comes from one of the state's most powerful families. Anxious to establish her social respectability, John's relatives reveal that she is actually part of a respected family in the state, and even produce some long-lost relatives to prove it. Reluctant to join a social establishment she loathes, Jhansi does not believe them until they back up their story with a volume called *Iowa Descendants of New England Families*. They try to win her over with stories of war heroes and Christian missionaries, but Jhansi only embraces her ancestors when she finds that her grandfather had burned down his neighbor's house because he had chased his pigs and that John's ancestors included a grave robber and someone who had built the family fortune on selling whiskey and firearms to the local Indians. Their relatives insist that it is time to "close the book" on this unwanted knowledge, but Jhansi says, "whenever we feel a bit stifled we can always find air through our family trees."[4]

Both of these well-crafted plays were popular at the Provincetown, and they contributed to Glaspell's growing reputation as a playwright. It was *The Outside*, however, produced in December of 1917, that was to be Glaspell's breakthrough play, the one in which she established her own original theatrical idiom, successful in modernist terms at making the drama into an organic form, a natural expression of the play's thematic import. The situation in *The Outside* was suggested by a real occurrence in Provincetown, when Mabel Dodge had renovated the abandoned life-saving station that stood alone and isolated at the furthest reach on the "outside" of the Provincetown peninsula. After spending the summer of 1914 with Jack Reed in a rented cottage, Dodge had decided to go in for something more grand the next summer. She talked Sam Lewisohn, a millionaire friend, into buying the life-saving station that was being abandoned by the Coast Guard so that she could renovate it as a vacation home that both of them could use. With the long-suffering John Francis as agent and contractor, Dodge had the station renovated to her specifications over the winter, all of the building supplies and furniture being dragged over the two miles of sand dunes between the town and the Point by horses. The result was the beautifully appointed, modern cottage Peaked Hill Bars, which James O'Neill bought for Eugene and Agnes as a wedding gift in 1919. In the summer of 1915, however, Dodge, still depressed over the end of her relationship with John Reed, stayed in the cottage with her new lover, the painter Maurice Sterne, who would become her second husband. Reed was living in the village with Louise Bryant. Dodge, however, was still hoping to reconcile with him somehow. At one point, when they met on the street, she alluded to the open secret of Bryant's affair with O'Neill, and told him that she was waiting in the wings to console him if he broke with Bryant.

Dodge's frame of mind that summer was not good. She quarrelled with her only real friends in Provincetown, Hutchins Hapgood and Neith Boyce, soon after she arrived in her chauffeur-driven Pierce Arrow. Dodge distanced herself from the rest of the Provincetown summer people, partly because of her possessiveness of Sterne, and probably also because of the unflattering portrait of her in Boyce's *Constancy*, which she couldn't fail to know about. In her memoir, *Movers and Shakers*, she says she stayed on her veranda overlooking the sea and read to Maurice from the *Upanishads*. One horrific moment occurred when Sterne, Mabel's son, and Robert Edmond Jones, who was staying with them, nearly drowned in the surf near the cottage. The Provincetown *Advocate* reported that the Coast Guard worked on Sterne for twenty minutes before he was revived. Mabel had witnessed the scene from a distance, as she struggled over the sand dunes in a white lace dress and French heels. Her description of her reaction to the scene betrays a peculiar frame of mind:

> The body of Maurice, as it lay swollen and shapeless over a barrel with its discolored face and swinging arms, had lost its charm . . . Feeling, then,

coldly embarrassed and detached from that scene of resuscitation I turned and walked away home.[5]

She had been furious with the three of them, and Jones, who often told the story, reported that she had shown them "the most horrible face I ever saw in my life."[6] As Leona Rust Egan has suggested, renovating the station had been "a challenge for Mabel, a way to fight her depression." But, "what should have been a triumphant summer" for her "ended in a fiasco."[7] Still, it is hard to comprehend her reaction to the near-drowning of a loved one.

It is perhaps here that Glaspell began with her play *The Outside*. The set for the play is "*a room in a house which was once a life-saving station*."[8] Unlike Peaked Hill Bars, however, "*since ceasing to be that it has taken on no other character, except that of a place which no one cares either to preserve or change*" and is still painted "*life-saving grey*" (48). Of great thematic importance in the play is the view seen through the big sliding door in the back wall of the room – the dunes, and beyond them the woods: "*At one point the line where woods and dunes meet stands out clearly and there are indicated the rude things, vines, bushes, which form the outer uneven rim of the woods – the only things that grow in the sand. At another point a sand-hill is menacing the woods*" (48). Because the life-saving station is located "*on the outside shore of Cape Cod, at the point, near the tip of the Cape, where it makes that final curve which forms the Provincetown Harbor*" (48), the sea is also seen through the open door. Glaspell is specific in describing the beach grass that grows in the dunes: "*struggle; dogged growing against odds*." The play begins with the futile attempt by male life-savers to resuscitate a man who has drowned in front of the house, "not forty feet out" in the surf (48). They have brought the drowned man to the former station out of habit, and, kicking in the door, have laid him just inside the house in order to revive him. As the men work, they comment on the forbidding atmosphere the place has acquired since it has been taken over by Mrs. Patrick, a city woman who seems pathologically withdrawn from human society. As one of the men says, "in my opinion the woman's crazy – sittin' over there on the sand – (*a gesture towards the dunes*) what's she *lookin'* at? There ain't nothin' to *see*" (49). They also think that Allie Mayo, the local woman she hired to work for her because Alice never spoke an unnecessary word, is crazy.

Mrs. Patrick appears, and demands in an increasingly "*wild way* ... I must have my house to myself!" (50). After she leaves, one of the men explains that she used to be "all right." She and her husband were summer people who had bought the house as a cottage, but that she had shown up in November and insisted on moving in alone, getting the local grocer,

Bill Joseph, to haul the things that she needs across the sand for her. Tony, a local Portuguese sailor, sets up the dissonance of male and female space in the play when he says, "this not like a place where a woman live. On the floor there is nothing – on the wall there is nothing. Things ... do not hang on other things" (49). Mrs. Patrick has invaded the male space of the life-saving station, but has refused to transform it into something recognizably female. In turn, the men have invaded her house as if it were still theirs, a violation that she protests in vain. The play's natural imagery conveys a similar sense of invasion and violation between the forces of life and death: "What's the matter with the woman? Does she want folks to die? Appears to break her all up to see somebody trying to save a life ... I've seen her – day after day – settin' over there where the dunes meet the woods; just sittin' there, lookin' ... I believe she *likes* to see the sand slippin' down on the woods. Pleases her to see somethin' gettin' buried" (50). J. Ellen Gainor has noted that the controlling metaphor in the play is that of liminality. In the set, she contends, Glaspell's

> focus on the threshold of the room, the large sliding door in the rear wall, serves to highlight its literal and figurative status as a point of transition: from the man-made to the natural world, from salvation to danger, from male to female, from "inside" to "outside." The liminality of this point carries over to the environment beyond, however, with its concentration on the line separating dunes from woods, a point of continual struggle that takes on even greater connotative, symbolic value in the drama.[9]

As the play moves forward, the men go back to town for transportation, leaving the dead body behind in the house. With their departure comes a marked change in the dialogue, beginning with Allie Mayo's first "unnecessary word," "Wait" (51), spoken to keep Mrs. Patrick from going back to the dunes for her customary solitary contemplation of the battle between the dunes and the woods.

Allie confides to her that "for twenty years, I did what you are doing," after she had lost her young husband at sea: "The ice that caught Jim – caught me" (52). She tries to shake up Mrs. Patrick with the reminder, "you're not the only woman in the world whose husband is dead!" but she responds "(*with a cry of the hurt*) Dead? My husband's not *dead*" (52). This leads to a moment of silent understanding between the women, perhaps an imaginative expression of the understanding that Glaspell now had for Mabel Dodge's ordeal, the subject of jokes and laughter in 1915. By 1917, Glaspell's relationship with Cook had changed markedly from what it was in 1915 because she had lived through a year of his infidelities, particularly his affair with Ida Rauh. As Barbara Ozieblo notes, "the humiliation of the deserted wife haunted Glaspell. She herself had taken Cook from another woman, and ... the fear that history would repeat itself would never leave her. Jig constantly gave her cause for concern."[10] In the play, the two women share an understanding that is expressed through images rather than through the logocentric language the men use. Allie tells Mrs. Patrick that, after keeping still for twenty years, she knows things she didn't know she knew: "I know why you're doing that" (52). She tells her, "Don't bury the only thing that will grow. Let it grow" (52). She knows what Mrs. Patrick is trying to do when she watches the sand dunes slowly engulf the trees and swallow up the woods: "Bury it. The life in you. Bury it – watching the sand bury the woods. But I'll tell you something! *They* fight too. The woods! They fight for life the way that Captain fought for life in there!" (53).

The rest of the scene is an extraordinary modernist text, a dialogue that is carried out completely within William Carlos Williams's dictum, "No ideas but in things." Through imagery alone, the two women carry on a debate over the efficacy of the force of life in opposition to the force of death. When Mrs. Patrick insists that the sand will win because she has "walked on the tops of buried trees," Allie says "that vines will grow over the sand that covers the trees, and hold it. And other trees will grow over the buried trees" (53). Foreshadowing Glaspell's later development of the theme in *The Verge*, Allie speaks of the vines, "strange little things that reach out farthest ... and hold the sand for things behind them. They save a wood that guards a town" (53). Mrs. Patrick insists that she is at the "outer shore where men can't live. The Outside" (53), but Allie insists that the Outside is "but an arm that bends to make a harbor – where men are safe" (53). The argument eventually comes down to two conflicting images:

> MRS. PATRICK: This is the Outside. Sand ... Sand that *covers* – hills of sand that move and cover.
> ALLIE MAYO: Woods. Woods to hold the moving hills from Provincetown" (53)

Allie sends Mrs. Patrick back to "your edge of the woods that's *the edge of the dunes*," and the women meet in a moment of understanding, as Mrs. Patrick recognizes that the line is "the edge of life," and Allie, "*big with the sense of the wonder of life*," recognizes that it is "not worth a name. And – meeting the Outside" (53).

Insisting on the power of life to resist death, Allie tells Mrs. Patrick that she will not find peace among the dunes again, but should go back and "watch them *fight*" (54). Mrs. Patrick at first resists the knowledge of life, saying, "I didn't *go* to the Outside. I was left there ... Everything that can hurt me I want buried" (54). She had felt spring coming that morning "coming through the storm – to take me – take me to hurt me. That's why I couldn't bear ... things that made me know I feel" (54). She says that Allie is cruel to face the things that had been safely buried, saying "What did you ever find after you lost the thing you wanted?" and Allie responds, "I found – what I find now I know. The edge of life – to hold life behind me" (54). When Mrs. Patrick says she is "like this Cape. A line of land way out to sea – land not life," Allie responds with a series of images in which Glaspell has invested the whole import of the play: "Outside sea – outer shore, dark with the wood that once was ships – dunes, strange land not life – woods, town and harbor. The line! Stunted straggly line that meets the Outside face to face – and fights for what itself can never be. Lonely line. Brave growing" (54). Allie insists that "life grows over buried life" and that "Springs will come when you will want to know that it is Spring" (54). Through this series of natural images, and without the rational argument associated with male discourse, Allie succeeds in conveying to Mrs. Patrick the same faith in the force of life to overcome death that she has attained. When the men return with their stretcher to retrieve the body, she at first mocks them as "savers of life! 'Meeting the Outside'" but then "*she cannot say it mockingly again; in saying it, something of what it means has broken through, rises. Herself lost, feeling her way into the wonder of life*) Meeting the Outside! (*It grows in her as CURTAIN lowers slowly*") (55).

In her analysis, which focuses on the disjunction between the male and female realms in the play, both spatially and linguistically, Gainor has noted that the language in *The Outside* is marked by gender: "The male characters, intentionally, are not part of the symbolic linguistic realm of the play. They neither speak in poetic images nor envision their world through symbolism."[11] She stresses the "symbolic resurrection" in the ending: "Mrs. Patrick and Allie Mayo, both of whom have given up on life, each help to 'save' the other, much like Mrs. Hale and Mrs. Peters discover a bond through their examination of 'trifles.'"[12] This contrasts with the men, who are unable to save the drowned man. Veronica Makowsky, who calls the characters "two aspiring, but temporarily stymied, female modernist artists-in-life," maintains that "Glaspell ... suggests that the woman artist should neither be isolated from other human beings nor disconnected from the past, though this alienation may be a necessary stage of recovery on the way to the future."[13] Female bonding is at the heart of this play, in which Allie Mayo acts as an experienced guide and mentor to Mrs. Patrick in the life-changing process of meeting "the Outside."

This was in line with the feminist thought of Glaspell's friends at Heterodoxy, and also personally significant for her at a time when she and her close friend Neith Boyce were going through similar experiences of alienation from philandering husbands, who did not live up to their high ideals for radically altering the relations between the sexes by eliminating the double sexual standard and building companionate marriages based on true intimacy and equal support for each other's work. As time went on, however, Glaspell's vision would become more radical than that of her feminist friends, who for the most part sought to remake the society in which they found themselves rather than to reinvision the terms of their being in the world. In her most ambitious, and perhaps most personal play, *The Verge* (1921), it is the Nietzschean Glaspell that we see, as she tests the idea of the female artist as *Übermensch*, the lone creator who ventures beyond the edge vines to make a form of life that is truly new.

Like *The Outside*, O'Neill's early forays into non-representational theatre in search of a greater truth than the illusion of objectivity could afford also focused mainly on the individual consciousness in distress. From *Ile* (1917), through *Where the Cross Is Made* (1918), to *The Emperor Jones* (1920), O'Neill can be seen experimenting with the possibilities of theatricalizing madness. *Ile* is essentially a melodrama, although it makes use of a detailed realism in setting and character. Although the play ends in an emotional climax complete with the wild organ-playing of Mrs. Keeney, the sea captain's wife who has gone mad while on a whaling voyage with her husband, O'Neill is interested in providing psychological explanations for the conditions of the characters, which have been recognized as early disguised portraits of his parents. Just as the young O'Neill believed that his father James was fixated on the money that his successful career in the theatre as a swashbuckling matinee idol brought in, Captain Keeney is fixated on bringing in a full cargo of whale oil, refusing to turn back after two years at sea and months of being caught in the ice, despite the threat of mutiny from the crew and his wife's increasingly fragile mental condition. Like Ahab fixed on Moby Dick, he "don't see nothin.' . . . He just walks up and down like he didn't notice nobody – and stares at the ice to the no'the'ard."[14] The sailors think the captain is unbalanced. As one of them says, "Did ye ever hear of a man who wasn't crazy do the things he does? . . . Who but a man that's mad would take his woman – and as sweet a woman as ever was – on a stinkin' whalin' ship to the Arctic seas to be locked in by the rotten ice for nigh on a year, and maybe lose her senses forever – for it's sure she'll never be the same again" (493). In terms of the family biography, well known from *Long Day's Journey Into Night*, O'Neill seems at this point in his life to be holding his father responsible for his mother's dissociation from reality. But the play does not completely objectify Captain Keeney. O'Neill allows him a moment of self-revelation in a speech to the first mate. "It ain't the damned money what's keepin' me up in the northern seas," he says, "but I can't go back to Homeport with a measly four hundred barrel of ile. I'd die fust. I ain't never come back home in all my days without a full ship" (497). It is his pride of profession that drives Keeney more than the money itself, and the determination not to hear the other captains "laughin' and sneerin'" (497) at him for coming back home a failure. "I got to git the ile! I got to git it in spite of all hell, and by God, I ain't agoin' home till I do git it!" (498). While Captain Keeney is presented as responsible for his wife's madness, his monomania is treated with a measure of sympathy and understanding.

Unlike Mary Tyrone, Mrs. Keeney is held entirely blameless for her condition, which is the result of her husband's refusal to take her home, where she longs to be, despite her telling him, "it's killing me, this life – the brutality and cold and horror of it. I'm going mad" (504). The play ends with heavy irony. Just as Captain Keeney is about to relent, the word comes that the ice is breaking up, and he is once again seized by his mania to get the oil as his wife *"passes her hand across her eyes – then commences to laugh hysterically and goes to the organ,"* where she starts to play an old hymn (505). When her husband comes back, she doesn't know him, and the play ends with her wild, discordant playing of the organ as her husband goes back on deck, determined to get the "ile."

Crude though it is, this play may be seen as O'Neill's earliest attempt to achieve an imaginative understanding of the great shadow that hung over his life and work, what he came to see as the familial tragedy that had befallen the O'Neills. In this play, both parents are victims of a psychosis over which they have no control, although the father is guilty of not saving the mother. In the years that followed, O'Neill was to view his father more sympathetically and his mother more judgmentally, achieving finally the "forgiveness" that pervades *Long Day's Journey Into Night*, but in 1917 this process had just begun. At this time, he had begun to draw closer to his father, and the two would continue to develop a companionable relationship that ended with James's death from cancer in 1920. James became increasingly proud of his son and generous to him and his new wife, Agnes Boulton, as is evidenced by his gift of Peaked Hill Bars. It is clear from his work in these years that O'Neill's newfound sympathy for his father was a motivating force for his attempts to penetrate the human psyche imaginatively in his plays and find a theatrical language through which to express this "truth" on the stage. In relation to his father, he was also trying to understand himself, for in these years, he found himself following in the paternal footsteps more than he had ever expected to, and he feared the outcome.

In February, 1917, James O'Neill had played his last Broadway role in *The Wanderer*, a biblical epic by Maurice Samuels that was based on the parable of the Prodigal Son. The elder O'Neill played the father who welcomes his wayward son back with lavish forgiveness, a part that O'Neill biographers have noted as particularly galling to his two sons, who thought of him as a tight-fisted miser, unwilling to share with his sons the fortune that he had earned in the theatre.[15] During the period between 1917 and 1920, O'Neill grew closer to his father, spending time with him at his suite in the Prince George Hotel when he was in New York, and gradually forming the understanding of his character that is evident in *Long Day's Journey Into Night*. In these years, Eugene O'Neill was also energetically pursuing a career in the Broadway theatre where his father had prospered materially, and becoming ever more distant from the Provincetown Players, even while he tried to keep up his ties with the group as an experimental theatre where he could try out his new ideas. In the years between 1918 and 1920, while he was growing closer to his father, most of O'Neill's energy went into trying to get professional productions, in what the Players referred to as the "commercial" or Broadway theatre, for his three full-length plays: *Beyond the Horizon*, which was written in 1918 and produced by John D. Williams to great critical acclaim in February, 1920, eventually winning the Pulitzer Prize; *Chris Christopherson*, which was written in 1919 and produced by James O'Neill's old friend George Tyler in 1920, but closed before it reached New York; and *The Straw*, which was written in 1918 and also produced by Tyler in 1921. At the same time that he actively pursued Broadway productions for his plays, and for those of other Provincetown playwrights, such as Glaspell,[16] he continued to write plays intended for the

Provincetown Players, including *The Dreamy Kid* and *Where the Cross Is Made* in 1918, *Exorcism* and *The Rope* in 1919, and *The Emperor Jones* and *Diff'rent* in 1920.

O'Neill expressed a deep sense of bifurcation in himself at this time, describing his divided self in terms of Dr. Jeckyll and Mr. Hyde:

> One part of me fiddles betimes while Rome burneth and while the other part perishes in the flames – a martyr giving birth to the soul of an idea. One part of me is the author of my life-play tearing his hair in a piteous grimace as he watches his "worser" half playing the lead and distorting the theme by many strange grimaces.[17]

While this sense of division will be recognized as a perennial basis for O'Neill's self-conception, informing later plays such as *The Great God Brown* and *Days Without End*, at this early stage in his playwriting career, it had a direct and practical application. Eugene O'Neill wanted above all to become a successful playwright, which meant moving into the "big time" of Broadway, with fully funded professional productions in large theatres. But he was also repelled by the mercenary values of this world that he associated with his father's having sold out a promising acting career to make a fortune playing the Count of Monte Cristo for thirty years. On the other hand, he had a great affinity with the Provincetown Players' ideas about the sacredness of art and the responsibility of the artist to put his gift for creation in its service, as well as a sense of indebtedness to the group, and particularly Cook and Glaspell, who had given him the first opportunity to see his plays fully realized on the stage. But he spoke of the production values of the amateur productions at the Provincetown Players with a dissatisfaction bordering on contempt. Although he didn't voice it directly to them, he had a clear sense that his plays deserved better.

During these years, O'Neill was truly divided as a playwright, pursuing two distinctly different lines of playwriting. One was focused on revising *Beyond the Horizon* and *Chris Christopherson* to get them into a form that would be acceptable to the Broadway producers, the more ambitious project in the sense that he was writing full-length plays for professional production, but, because of the perceived limitations of Broadway audiences, much less ambitious than he would like it to be aesthetically. The other line was that devoted to the art of the amateur, taking time to consult with Nina Moise on the production of *The Rope*, and to write one-act plays like *The Dreamy Kid* and *Where the Cross Is Made*, so that the Provincetown Players would have their "O'Neill play" to headline each season. This line allowed the artist much more latitude for experimentation, but was inevitably frustrating in execution, as the amateurs never lived up to O'Neill's vision for the productions. At this point in his career, O'Neill was unable to commit to defining himself in terms of either one of these versions of the theatre, and his work shows that he was tortured by his internal division.

O'Neill worked out this conflict imaginatively in the Provincetown plays he was writing during this period, particularly *The Rope* and *Where the Cross Is Made*, which dramatize a fear of the mercenary, of becoming obsessed with "gold," that is associated with a father figure. In both plays, the son is drawn to these values by the father, thereby placing himself in grave danger. In *The Rope*, produced in 1918, O'Neill combines two biblical stories about fathers and sons, the parable of the Prodigal Son (Luke 15, 11–32) and the story of Abraham and Isaac (Genesis 22, 1–19). It involves a miserly old farmer, Bentley, who has driven his son Luke away from home after he stole money from him. Bentley has hung a noose in the barn, by which he says he will hang Luke if he ever returns. When Luke does return, Bentley welcomes him by quoting from the story of the Prodigal Son about bringing out the fatted calf and celebrating his return. It seems a joyful reunion until Bentley gets Luke to put his head through the noose, and keeps insisting that he knock the chair he is standing on out from under him and literally hang himself. Luke naturally refuses, and joy at the reunion having turned to spite, plans with his brother-in-law to torture the old man until he tells them where he has hidden his money. O'Neill's parable ends with heavy irony as Luke's young niece, swinging on the noose, pulls down the bag of gold coins to which it is attached, and happily throws them, one by one, over a cliff into the ocean so she can watch them skim across the water.

O'Neill reverses the story of Abraham and Isaac so that it is the son who is tested rather than the father. Unwilling to die at his father's request, Luke fails to win the treasure that would have been his reward. And for making the request, Bentley is to suffer torture at his son's hands. In this strange little play, O'Neill expresses a perhaps unconscious fear of succumbing to his father's values. As his father urged him to leave the amateur art theatre behind and put his fate in the hands of producers like Williams and Tyler, O'Neill sensed that his artistic self was undergoing a kind of ritual death. He was willingly putting his head in the noose, and the promised reward was a bag of gold, the ultimate value of which he deeply questioned. In 1918, O'Neill was extremely anxious about making this choice. The "commercial" theatre could be a noose for an artist. It certainly had been for his father. But if he rejected it, as Luke does with a great show of bravado, he could be tossing the treasure away. In the play, there is a sense of release as little Mary claps and sings and throws the golden coins into the water. But Mary is a simple-minded child who doesn't know what she is doing. Meanwhile, father and son have been revealed as deeply perverted by the money. It is clear that O'Neill was not able to toss the money of Broadway over a cliff even if he felt that he was sticking his head in a noose to try to get it.

Where the Cross Is Made, O'Neill's first experiment in using the expressionistic techniques he was familiar with from Strindberg, dramatizes both the fear of madness that is evident in *Ile* and the fear of becoming obsessed with money that is expressed in *The Rope*. The play was written during the summer of 1918 in Provincetown, where O'Neill was staying with his new wife Agnes and, for a long period, his brother Jamie. The play was based, according to Agnes, on a short story she was writing, called "The Captain's Walk."[18] O'Neill told George Jean Nathan that he had always conceived of it as the last act of the full-length play that became *Gold* in 1920: "I merely took the last act situation and jammed it into the one-act form because I wanted to be represented on the Provincetown Players' opening bill."[19] The play is about an old sea captain, Isaiah Bartlett, who has been in a shipwreck seven years previous to the play's action, which only he and six sailors survived. After drifting at sea for days, "mad from thirst and starvation,"[20] they finally landed on a barren island, where three of the sailors died, possibly "killed and eaten" (699), as Bartlett's son Nat suggests. When he was picked up at last and brought home, Nat says, "we hardly recognized my father. He had been through hell and looked it. His hair was white ... And the others – they were all a bit queer, too – mad, if you will" (699).

After his return, Bartlett had told his son that he was to be "heir" to a secret, a treasure the crew had found on a shipwrecked Malay prau, and buried, complete with a map marked with a cross. Four years later, Captain Bartlett had mortgaged his house to send the other three on a voyage to look for the treasure on the schooner *Mary Allen*, which has since been lost. He has spent the last three years watching for the return of the *Mary Allen*, even though he knows the ship has been lost, "*knows* – but he won't *believe*. He can't – and keep living" (697). As the play opens, Nat is about to have his father committed to the local asylum. He tells the doctor the story, and reveals that he knows the treasure is worthless junk, having had a jeweler look at the bracelet that his father had given him in proof of the story.

In dialogue with his sister, significantly named Sue,[21] Nat reveals that he is literally selling his father out by having him committed, because the owner of the mortgage has offered him $2,000 above what is owed and will allow him to stay on in the house if he will get rid of his father, who is an embarrassment to the neighborhood. Staying in the house will allow Nat the chance to finish the book that is "three-fourths done – my book that will set me free!" for he believes that he couldn't finish it "outside of this house where it was born . . . so I will stay – in spite of hell!" (704). In terms that are reminiscent of Jamie's complaints against James Tyrone for forcing him on the stage in *Long Day's Journey*, Nat bursts out violently against the "damned sea he forced me on as a boy – the sea that robbed me of my arm and made me the broken thing I am! . . . He took me from school and forced me on his ship, didn't he? What would I have been now but an ignorant sailor like him if he had had his way?" (703). Both Jamie and Eugene O'Neill had been expelled from college by their own doing, but James O'Neill insisted at various times that both of them join his theatrical troupe on tour, and kept a close rein on Jamie's career as an actor, placing him in small parts when he couldn't be hired elsewhere.

The severed arm is obviously symbolic. Nat says that his father's forcing him on the sea has made him a "cripple" and a "wreck." It is only by writing his book that he can separate from his father and make himself whole. More significantly, Nat reveals to Sue that, although he knows his father is delusional and the treasure is worthless, he still carries the map with him:

> It stands between me and my book. It stood between me and life – driving me mad! *He* taught me to wait and hope with him – wait and hope – day after day. He made me doubt my brain and give the lie to my eyes – when hope was dead – when I knew it was all a dream – I couldn't kill it! *(his eyes starting from his head)* God forgive me, I still believe! And that's mad – (705)

It is his share in his father's madness, the everlasting hope of the big payoff, that keeps Nat from realizing his potential as an artist and finishing the book that will finally free him. He admits, "I do hate him! He's stolen my brain! I've got to free myself, can't you see, from him – and his madness" (705). To do so, he finally burns the map, saying, "see how I free myself and become sane . . . it must all be destroyed – this poisonous madness" (706). For O'Neill, this is perhaps an admission that, like his seventy-year-old father, he is desperately hoping for the big hit that will make his fortune in the theatre as James had in his youth with *Monte Cristo*. Constantly reminded by his friends at the Provincetown of the low artistic standards of the Broadway theatre and of their own devotion to art, he feels he is crippled as an artist by the drive for commercial success. He would like to turn his back on his father's obsession with money, for which he feels he is, as Captain Bartlett calls Nat, a "Judas" (707). The burning of the map is suggestive of the destruction of much of his early work, short plays for vaudeville, scenarios for motion pictures, and other things written solely to make money.

Sue is repelled by Nat's plan to get his father out of the way, but she is not tempted by the desire for gold as he is. In fact she represents a point of objectivity as the action goes forward, for Nat is drawn into his father's madness when he enters and announces that the *Mary Allen* is approaching. Nat sees the ship as well, but Sue does not. And O'Neill employs some expressionistic staging so that the audience is drawn into Nat's subjectivity. As the captain watches for the sailors to come up the path, Nat strains forward in his chair and "*the sound of the wind and sea suddenly ceases and there is a heavy silence. A dense green glow floods slowly in rhythmic waves like a liquid into the room – as of great depths of the sea faintly penetrated by light*" (709). Thus the audience shares Nat's view: "See how the light changes! Green and gold! ... Deep under the sea! I've been drowned for years! (*hysterically*) Save me! Save me!" (709). But Sue sees nothing, telling him it's "only the moonlight ... it hasn't changed."

The spectators witness the full delusion that Nat and Captain Bartlett share as the three sailors "*rise noiselessly into the room from the stairs*" (709), carrying two heavy chests.

> *Water drips from their soaked and rotten clothes. Their hair is matted, intertwined with slimy strands of seaweed. Their eyes, as they glide silently in to the room, stare frightfully wide at nothing. Their flesh in the green light has the suggestion of decomposition. Their bodies sway limply, nervelessly, rhythmically as if to the pulse of long swells of the deep sea.* (710)

Captain Bartlett, who has heard part of Nat's conversation with Sue and repudiated him with the name of Judas, goes up into his "captain's walk" lookout with the three sailors and the treasure, saying "he has no right, now. Come. The treasure is ours only" (710). In a frenzy, Nat calls after him, "Father!", but perceives that the trap door is shut against him. Although they have the testimony of Sue that all of this is delusional, the spectators have the evidence of their eyes that it has really happened to Nat. When the doctor arrives, however, he demonstrates that the trap door is open, and finds that Captain Bartlett has died of heart failure. Completely delusional, Nat pries the map out of his dead father's hand and insists that "it isn't lost for me after all! There's still a chance – *my chance!*" (711). The play ends with Nat vowing to go and find the treasure and Sue begging him to "come away" (712).

Even more than *The Rope*, *Where the Cross Is Made* conveys a deep sense of danger connected with the father's obsession with money and what seems the son's doomed efforts to resist it. Having recently sold *In the Zone*, which he considered the weakest of the SS *Glencairn* plays, "a conventional construction of the theatre as it is,"[22] to vaudeville for a profitable run, O'Neill was staring directly at the division between art and commercial success in the theatre that summer, and his enthusiastic pursuit of Broadway productions for the three long plays in the next two years shows that he was committed to success. But he also feared it, as he watched his father become increasingly regretful for having thrown over his promising career as a serious actor for success as a matinee idol. According to O'Neill, his father's last words to him were "Eugene – I'm going to a better sort of life. This sort of life – here – all froth – no good – rottenness!"[23] Responding to a note of condolence from Nina Moise, the Provincetown director he most respected, he wrote, "you'll be pleased to know that I'm not compromising, but 'hewing to the line,' and not trying to get too wealthy although, as you can imagine, the opportunities to sell myself have not been lacking of late."[24] Fortunately for O'Neill, this troubling division was to resolve itself as he became the first American playwright whose aesthetic experiments were enthusiastically welcomed by both admiring critics and the paying public, but this ideal outcome seemed impossibly out of reach in 1918.

What O'Neill got for *Where the Cross Is Made* was an amateur production by the Provincetown Players that was willing in spirit but impossibly weak in execution. According to Edna Kenton, most of the group thought the experiment in expressionist theatre unworkable in their technically crude theatre. O'Neill's hope was to draw the spectators into the illusion that they shared Nat's subjective reality through the staging. He told the doubters: "This play presumes that everybody is mad but the girl, that everybody sees the ghosts but the girl. Everybody but the girl means everybody in this house but the girl. I want to see whether it's possible to make an audience go mad too. Perhaps the first rows will snicker – perhaps they won't. We'll see."[25] Later, he told George Jean Nathan, "it was great fun to write, theatrically very thrilling, an amusing experiment in treating the audience as insane."[26] In practice, the experiment was not so much fun. Kenton described the rehearsals as "one prolonged argument" in which O'Neill invoked the provision in the Provincetown bylaws that "the author shall produce the play without hindrance, according to his own ideas."[27] The Players were unable to produce the subjective lighting effects that the stage directions describe, but the biggest sticking point was the ghosts, which are to "*rise noiselessly*" and "*glide silently*" into the room. The Players found this impossible to do on the creaky little stage in Macdougal Street, and many were afraid that the audience would laugh at the effect rather than be drawn into the characters' delusion, as O'Neill was hoping. According to Kenton, "the play would be wrecked by the noisy ghosts, the actors would be laughed at and our best friends would say, 'Whatever in the world made you think you could get away with that?'"[28] The result was not as bad as Kenton remembered it, and *Where the Cross Is Made* was successful enough to be revived by the Players in the spring of 1920 after its original production in November, 1918, but O'Neill's sense of the amateur art theatre as inadequate for the full realization of his dramatic experiments was once again confirmed. On the other hand, when the full-length play *Gold*, from which the one-act was taken, was given its full commercial production, minus the expressionist experiment with the ghosts, in June of 1921, it closed after only thirteen performances. In his experience with this play, O'Neill was looking at frustration on both sides of the balance scale between art and commerce.

The Emperor Jones

In 1920, two watershed events in O'Neill's career, and one in the Provincetown's, were to change the terms of O'Neill's relationship with the theatre irrevocably. One was the critical acclaim at the opening of *Beyond the Horizon* in February and the awarding of what O'Neill described as "the Pulitzer Prize of one thousand dollars for the best American play"[29] in June, combining critical validation with monetary reward for a work he had written for the "commercial" rather than the art theatre. O'Neill proudly reported that it was the greatest satisfaction his father knew that he "had made good in a way dear to his own heart . . . he was in a box at the opening matinee and wept his eyes out."[30] The near adulatory critical response to the play was the dream of every young playwright, greeting O'Neill as the long-hoped-for savior of the American stage, a truly world-class American playwright. Although it was not a big hit in a commercial sense, *Beyond the Horizon* had a respectable Broadway run of 111 performances and paved the way for Broadway productions of *The Straw* and *Gold*. Eugene O'Neill had become a Broadway playwright. The other major event of 1920 was the production of *The Emperor Jones* by the Provincetown Players in November, a breakthrough play for both the playwright and the theatre that resulted in extraordinary publicity and a move from Macdougal Street to Broadway for the production, where it ran for more than 200 performances. This event changed the character of the Provincetown Players, and some older members like Kenton considered that "the very success of *The Emperor Jones* was the last push downhill"[31] for the amateur art theatre.

After this, long plays with one-act curtain raisers became the rule at the Provincetown, in place of the bills of three or four one-acts that favored artistic experimentation. And the other playwrights were clearly aiming at the Broadway success that O'Neill had won. Following *The Emperor Jones* in the 1920–1921 season were five full-length plays: O'Neill's *Diff'rent*, which transferred to the Princess Theatre for a 100-performance run, George Cram Cook's *The Spring*, Evelyn Scott's *Love*, and Susan Glaspell's *Inheritors*. After failing to persuade the Players to transfer *The Spring* to Broadway, Cook financed and directed a production himself under the name of the Provincetown Players, a failure that closed after twenty-one performances.[32] In Kenton's opinion:

> Values had shifted overnight, astonishingly. To go uptown with our first success was higher honor than to stay down town with our experiments. It was human; it was natural; we had worked and waited a long time – was the work and the waiting again and all humanly for "success"? – we were a little drunk with the wine of applause and we lost our balance and fell. We had ceased to be one thing purely; we began just there to be divided in purpose, mixed in motive. We were still, oh, so insistently, "experimental"; but the chemicals we worked with, though labeled by old names, had somehow caught from the air of "expansion" a foreign ingredient that blurred results.[33]

In the following and final season of the Provincetown Players, four one-acts were given secondary status to the four full-length plays that were produced: Glaspell's *The Verge*, which Deutsch and Hanau report was announced for an uptown showing even before the first curtain, Theodore Dreiser's *The Hand of the Potter*, O'Neill's *The Hairy Ape*, and Glaspell's *Chains of Dew*. The group had come to be dominated by Cook, Glaspell, and O'Neill, three playwrights whose major drive was to write full-length plays and have them produced on Broadway.

In the summer of 1920, O'Neill, Cook, and Glaspell had been in Provincetown working on plays that were all, to a greater or lesser degree, indebted to Nietzsche. Cook's *The Spring* and Glaspell's *Inheritors* both work with the concept of eternal recurrence in the context of the history of the American Midwest. Although Cook brought paranormal psychic phenomena into the stage reality of *The Spring*, both it and *Inheritors* are within the realm of representational realism. With *The Emperor Jones*, however, O'Neill was working to fuse many of his intellectual and artistic influences into a form of theatre that was authentically his, and thus truly original. In this play, Brutus Jones, an African American former Pullman car porter, who landed on a Caribbean island "as yet not self-determined by White Marines"[34] after escaping from prison in the US, has joined with the white Englishman Smithers as traders to fleece the black local populace. Building on this success, Jones has made himself into the "Emperor" of the island, and has placed a fortune in an offshore bank account from his exorbitant taxation of the populace, bolstered by a self-created myth. When one of the local men had tried to shoot him early on, the gun had misfired and Jones had shot him instead. Jones told the people that he had survived because he had a charm that warded off death, and he could only be killed by a silver bullet. In the course of the play, Jones flees from the local insurgents who are preparing for attack with war rituals involving a steadily beating drum. Jones's well-planned escape is foiled, however, when he gets into the night forest, going around and around in a circle as he becomes increasingly exhausted, and begins to see hallucinations, which he calls "h'ants." In five scenes, O'Neill takes Brutus Jones from his present state of rising fear back through his own history and that of his African American ancestors. He hallucinates, seeing creatures identified as "little formless fears," and then a crap game where he revisits killing a man named Jeff, a prison scene where he revisits killing a guard, and then a slave auction and a scene from the middle passage, in which he is treated as a slave. In the midst of these hallucinations, he gradually fires each of

Figure 6. The middle-passage scene from *The Emperor Jones*.

the lead bullets from his gun, so that he is left only with the silver bullet with which he plans to shoot himself if worse comes to worst. This he shoots at a "crocodile god" to whom he is about to be sacrificed by an African "witch doctor." The play ends with a final scene in which the insurgent leader Lem shows Smithers that they have succeeded in killing Jones because they made silver bullets with which to shoot him.

A number of critics have explored the intellectual context of *The Emperor Jones*. Robert Sarlós has noted "O'Neill's vivid interest in primitive ritual [which] was accentuated by William Zorach, who shared with the playwright a fascination with cubist features in African masks."[35] More specifically, Travis Bogard wrote that O'Neill was influenced by a book of photographs of African sculpture by Charles Sheeler, suggesting that "the heart of darkness resides in these images."[36] The book to which Bogard refers is *African Negro Wood Sculpture*, which appeared early in 1918. A rare privately printed book, it includes twenty 8 by 10 inch photographs tipped into the volume.[37] The subjects are objects in Marius de Zayas's collection, most of which are sculptures from West and Central Africa. As noted in chapter 2, de Zayas had mounted the first important exhibit of African art in the US at Stieglitz's gallery 291 in 1914, and he had written his seminal article, "African Art: Its Influence on Modern Art," in 1916. Tracing the influence of African art through Matisse, Brancusi, and especially Picasso, he was a major force in introducing it to American artists like Zorach, whose sculpture was deeply indebted to African forms.

Unfortunately, de Zayas's attitude toward the art that he championed combined extraordinary racism with a passionate response to the beauty of the work, and his attitude toward its creators did much to establish the primitivism that is characteristic of American Modernism. In the context of *The Emperor Jones*, de Zayas's racist description in his introductory note for the catalogue of the 1914 exhibit is worth noting: "Negro art, product of the 'Land of Fright,' created by a mentality full of fear, and completely devoid of the faculties of observation and analysis, is the pure expression of the emotion of a savage race – victims of nature – who see the outer world only under its most intensely expressive aspect and not under its natural one."[38] It is likely that O'Neill, who lived in Greenwich Village in 1914, would have seen the exhibit. Having seen the rare Sheeler book with its introduction by de Zayas, probably through Zorach, O'Neill certainly was aware of de Zayas's ideas about the African "mentality." The play has been duly criticized for its reflection of these ideas. On the other hand, as J. Michael Dash has noted, "O'Neill's play is singular in its attempt to see a black protagonist not simply as a natural primitive but in terms of a larger human tragedy." Calling O'Neill's use of Haitian material for serious literary purposes "remarkable" for the time, he wrote: "This use of Haitian themes to depict a journey into the forest of the unconscious is a unique departure from the cult of the primitive that could only serve to justify the 'salutary lesson' that the Occupation [of Haiti by the US] was expected to administer to Haitians."[39] Far from representing Jones as a stereotypical stage Negro driven by a fear of ghosts, O'Neill was using the character to explore the nature of human fear.[40]

As Dash's comment suggests, the conception of Africa as the "Land of Fright" fed into another of O'Neill's interests at this time, Jungian psychology. Because of his deep interest in dramatizing the human psyche, O'Neill was constantly asked in interviews whether he was influenced by Freudian psychology. He always claimed to be "no deep student of psychoanalysis," as he told Barrett Clark: "As far as I can remember, of all the books written by Freud, Jung, etc., I have read only four, and Jung is the only one of the lot who interests me. Some of his suggestions I find extraordinarily illuminating in the light of my own experience with hidden motives."⁴¹ Doris Falk was the first critic to analyze the extent to which Jungian psychology informs *The Emperor Jones*, and particularly "Jung's fundamental premise – the existence and power of the collective unconscious." As translated into the theatrical idiom of O'Neill's play, the Jungian "suggestions" are quite straightforward. As Falk puts it:

> the mind of a given man contains ideas from the collective unconscious which come to him simply by virtue of his membership in the human race, as well as ideas inherited from his own specific race, tribe, and family. His mind contains, in addition, unconscious ideas and symbols arising from his unique personal situation to make up the structure of his personal unconscious. Finally, from this personal unconscious emerges his own consciousness, his ego.⁴²

Falk reads the experience of Jones as a "progress in self-understanding": "the stripping off of the masks of self, layer by layer, just as bit by bit his 'emperor's' uniform is ripped from his back, until at the end he must confront his destiny – himself – in nakedness."⁴³

The Jungian trajectory of Jones's progress from self-described Emperor to sacrificial victim is represented by the gradual casting off of the artificial accoutrements of the Emperor – western-style uniform, sword, boots, and spurs – to become the nearly naked "primitive man" who is sacrificed by the group to appease the gods for his betrayal. O'Neill begins in his throne room as Jones's black "subjects" are deserting him, leaving only the exploitative white colonial Smithers to prop up his ego and assure him that he still fears him as Emperor. At the threat of insurgency, Jones leaves the throne room, his imitation of the Western accoutrements that signify power, and goes into the dark forest, a powerful Jungian image of the unconscious. Here he progressively encounters his personal fear and guilt, in the little "formless fears" and the two homicides he has committed, and then participates in the iconic experiences in the collective history of his African American ancestors, being sold on the auction block and enduring the horrors of the middle passage. Finally, he is brought back to Africa, where the last trace of his Western identity, his Baptist Christianity, is pitted against the pantheistic religion that O'Neill imagines for his ancestors. Jones's fear, his essential driving trait, is closely associated with his sense of guilt, a guilt that O'Neill suggests is grounded in his fundamental betrayal of his own people, from the killing of Jeff to the subjugation of what he calls the "ign'rent bush niggers" (1040) on the island. As Jones calls on Jesus to save him, the witch doctor mimes the demands of the African religion:

> *There is a salvation. The forces of evil demand sacrifice. They must be appeased. The witch-doctor points with his wand to the sacred tree, to the river beyond, to the altar, and finally to Jones with a ferocious command. Jones seems to sense the meaning of this. It is he who must offer himself for sacrifice.*
> (1058)

In resisting this, and using his silver bullet on the crocodile rather than on himself, Jones enacts his last betrayal of his people, and the rejection of his authentic self. The irony is that it is this act that destroys him, for he now lies defenseless on the ground, having given away his position to the insurgents. Lem and his men have no trouble killing him with their silver bullets.

It is at this point that a third powerful influence on the play is most intensely present, that of Nietzsche's *The Birth of Tragedy*. Calling *The Emperor Jones* an attempt "to fuse a Nietzschean perspective with the myth of an American Eden," Michael Hinden has argued persuasively that the play should be "set in the context of [O'Neill's] sustaining effort of the twenties – an attempt to invent a mythic framework for American history incorporating Nietzsche's insights concerning Greek tragedy and culture." In Hinden's view, it is not "the collective unconscious of the American Negro," as many of the earlier critics of the play suggested, that Jones is exploring, so much as "the collective conscience of Americans," and our national original sin, slavery.[44] Hinden, and other critics, see Jones's journey in the forest as a progress from the false Apollonian mask of control that he assumes as Emperor, signified in the trappings of office that he gradually sheds during his night in the forest, toward the primal Dionysian ritual that should enable the discovery of his authentic identity. Hinden notes that "Jones *wastes* his silver bullet, the symbol of his myth-making ability, his creative imagination, by firing at the apparition of the crocodile – the final clue to his identity." The crocodile, he says "is the symbolic epiphany of the false god Mammon, upon whose altar Jones has sacrificed throughout his life," in the form of the "long green," as Jones often puts it.[45]

Jones's self-betrayal is the self-betrayal of the nation, as O'Neill saw it, a self-betrayal he summed up in quoting the biblical statement: "For what shall it profit a man if he shall gain the whole world and lose his own soul?" This, we have seen, was the fundamental lesson O'Neill derived from his father's life, and it was the central theme of his most ambitious work, the projected play cycle *A Tale of Possessors Self-Dispossessed*. As he told Hamilton Basso in 1948, he believed that some kind of retribution was coming for all Americans:

> This country is going to get it – really get it. We had everything to start with – everything – but there's bound to be a retribution. We've followed the same selfish, greedy path as every other country in the world. We talk about the American Dream, and want to tell the world about the American Dream, but what is that dream, in most cases, but the dream of material things? I sometimes think that the United States, for this reason, is the greatest failure the world has ever seen.[46]

Having risen from Pullman car porter to Emperor, Brutus Jones is the epitome of the materialistic American Dream that O'Neill describes, and he has learned its rules directly from the "white quality" on the Pullman cars. As he tells Smithers: "Dere's little stealin' like you does, and dere's big stealin' like I does. For de little stealin' dey gits you in jail soon or late. For de big stealin' dey makes you Emperor and puts you in de Hall of Fame when you croaks" (1035). In the course of the play, Jones is proven wrong, at least in the context of the Caribbean. Like the United States, which had recently begun its nineteen-year occupation of Haiti, Jones enters his Caribbean Island with contempt for its inhabitants and a plan to exploit them. In O'Neill's imaginative construction of history, retribution is swift.

The most immediately recognizable modernist element in *The Emperor Jones* is its expressionist staging. As Timo Tiusanen has pointed out, however, there is an important difference between O'Neill's expressionism and the more familiar German form: "Both O'Neill and the German expressionists rebelled against objective realism, which they felt to be a limitation on their freedom; and they rebelled under the flag of Nietzscheism. Yet under the influence of the recently initiated American realism, O'Neill was closer to Strindberg's 'psycho-expressionism' than to its German variant, to be called 'socio-expressionism.'"[47] As Tiusanen noted, the play has many of the elements commonly associated with expressionism: "Stream of consciousness is expressed in 'terms of stage symbols'; inner reality is suggested in dream-like fashion; the scenes are brief; they alternate between reality and fantasy; stage reality becomes subconsciousness; and sources of conduct are explored." But unlike his German counterpart, "the hero does not become a mere abstraction." This is because "*The Emperor Jones* belongs to that sect of expressionism, sometimes called 'monodrama,' where the distortion is motivated 'by a character's state of mind,' and where that character is still a human being."[48] The reason for this is not hard to determine. O'Neill made use of expressionist techniques in *The Emperor Jones* precisely because he was interested in the individual psyche, not in the social abstraction. He was looking for the links between individual fear and guilt and collective human experience, but always in terms of the individual. Expressionist techniques were useful to him because they allowed him literally to put the subjective events of a man's consciousness on the stage for the spectators to see, and in some sense, to experience. Much more effectively than in *Where the Cross Is Made*, O'Neill tried to make the audience go mad along with Jones by seeing what he saw and, in the case of the famous drum, hearing what he heard, thus making his subjective experience their own. This could best be done through expressionist techniques.

The most obvious expressionist element in the play is of course the drum, which "*starts at a rate exactly corresponding to normal pulse beat – 72 to the minute – and continues at a gradually accelerating rate from this point uninterruptedly to the very end of the play*" (1041). In 1922, Isaac Goldberg recognized that the drum was "part and parcel of the psychological action; at first it is the call to war; then it merges into the Emperor Jones's vision of the slaves rolling to its beat [on the slave ship]; finally it becomes his own throbbing, feverish temples, and all the while it is our heart beating more and more rapidly as we follow his fate."[49] A second element is the "little formless fears," the first hallucination that appears to Jones at the beginning of his night in the forest. These were probably derived from a hallucinatory dream in Frank Norris's *McTeague*.[50] In the play, O'Neill rather riskily presents them to the audience, with the aim of drawing them into Jones's subjectivity, much as he used the ghosts in *Where the Cross Is Made*: "*the litte Formless Fears creep out from the deeper blackness of the forest. They are black, shapeless, only their glittering little eyes can be seen. If they have any describable form at all it is that of a grubworm about the size of a creeping child. They move noiselessly, but with deliberate, painful effort, striving to raise themselves on end, failing and sinking prone again*" (1045–1046).

More conventional expressionist elements occur in the hallucinatory scenes, in which the characters often move in unison and with the "*regular, rigid, mechanical movements of an automaton*" (1047). Perhaps the most effective integration of these elements occurs in scene 6, aboard the

Figure 7. The auction scene from *The Emperor Jones*.

slave ship, when Jones is drawn into the group of slaves as they change from a collection of individuals in various despairing attitudes to a unified group through their swaying in unison to the roll of the ship and the rising of a rhythmic "*melancholy murmur*" that becomes a "*tremulous wail of despair*" in time with the drum, as it "*beats louder, quicker, with a more insistent, triumphant pulsation*" (1056). Each of these elements serves the overall purpose of forcing the audience to share the subjective experience that Jones is going through.

In the staging of the play, O'Neill for once received energetic and effective support from the Provincetown Players. Beginning with Edna Kenton's partisan pro-Cook account, the historians of the Players have treated the story of *The Emperor Jones* primarily as the story of the dome, a structure which George Cram Cook insisted on constructing for the play against the vote of the Executive Committee. It was modeled on the *Kuppelhorizont* that became common in German theatres after Max Reinhardt installed one in the Grosses Schauspielhaus in 1919, and that had been known in the US at least since the exhibit of New Stagecraft designs sponsored by the New York Stage Society in 1914, which featured the model of a plaster dome by designer Sam Hume. Ronald Wainscott has noted that "because its reflective properties were prodigious, it was greeted with considerable enthusiasm, but only the Neighborhood Playhouse tried it out, installing a partial dome in 1915."[51] The Provincetown Playhouse was the first in New York to install a full dome. Robert Sarlós describes it as "a segment of a true dome, made of plaster, the inside of which is used as a reflecting surface to represent the horizon. A combination of vertical and horizontal curvatures can achieve an illusion of greater depth than a cyclorama hung flat, even on a shallower stage" (126).

James Light, and probably Donald Corley, both of whom had studied architecture, were on hand to help with the technical aspects of building the dome, and it proved extremely effective in creating the illusion of limitless space on the tiny stage of the Provincetown Playhouse. According to Kenton, Cook directed the production, although there was no directing credit listed on the program. Amateurs always, the Players, including Cook, clearly had little idea what to do with their new toy once they had built it. As Kenton describes it, "we were all there, all over the place. The group spirit was rampant, and to play with the lights on the dome was the best game of all."[52] Five days before the production was to open, however, Cleon Throckmorton arrived from Washington, DC, to take charge of the sets and the lighting. According to Kenton, he tore apart the "childish" sets the group had constructed and redesigned and rebuilt them along much simpler lines in order to make better use of the dome and the lighting.[53] Kenton, viewing the construction of the dome as Cook's triumph, reported the opening of *The Emperor Jones* as the opening of the dome. After the applause for the play, she reported, the audience would not go home, so the stage was cleared of scenery and "the dome was put through a series of lighting effects so far as we knew them then – we never exhausted them."[54]

In general the critics concurred that the dome, the first in New York, had made for some extraordinary effects in the theatre. Heywood Broun wrote that, despite long waits between scenes that "prey upon the attention" of the audience, "the setting of the play on the little stage is fine and imaginative and the lighting effects ucommonly beautiful."[55] Kenneth Macgowan, an enthusiastic supporter of the "new theatre" who recognized the German model from which the dome was drawn, wrote that the Players were able "to accomplish two silhouette episodes of glorious beauty, while the lighting of the scene of the dream convicts makes another picture remain as long in the mind as any moment of 'The Jest' or 'Richard III.' "[56] But they and other critics all expressed a response to the production best articulated by Alexander Woollcott in his inimitable way in the *New York Times*:

> The Provincetown Players have squanderously invested in cushions for their celebrated seats and a concrete dome to catch and dissolve their lights, so that even on their little stage they can now get such illusions of distance and the wide outdoors as few of their uptown rivals can achieve. But of immeasurably greater importance in their present enterprise, they have acquired an actor, one who has it in him to invoke the pity and the terror and the indescribable foreboding which are part of the secret of 'The Emperor Jones.'[57]

Other critics joined unanimously in the praise for Charles Gilpin, a veteran actor whose art had never had the broad exposure it was to get from playing Brutus Jones.

The major praise was for O'Neill's play, however, which Broun described as "the most interesting play which has yet come from the most promising playwright in America,"[58] and Woollcott called "an extraordinarily striking and dramatic study of panic fear" which "reinforces the impression that for strength and originality [O'Neill] has no rival among the American writers for the stage."[59] Lest one get as carried away with the excitement over the dome as the Players were, it needs to be remembered that *The Emperor Jones* ran for six weeks at the Macdougal Street theatre and then was transferred uptown and ran for 204 performances, first at the Selwyn, and then at the Princess Theatre, where it generated even greater excitement and critical praise, without the dome.[60] Of course, it is to be expected that the Broadway production of an exciting new play by a newly emerged young playwright would draw more attention than the production in a little theatre in Greenwich Village, but it is important to note that *The Emperor Jones* did not need the dome to be recognized as exciting, innovative theatre. In terms of the realization of the play on the stage, Throckmorton's design and lighting were at least as important as the Provincetown's dome. And the response of the critics suggests that Charles Gilpin's performances as Jones was the most exciting element of the production for audiences. The Provincetown Players' Scrapbook, at the New York Public Library for the Performing Arts, bears witness that the attention he received in the press far outstripped even that given to O'Neill, let alone the scenic effects.

Bernice

Glaspell's most original play, *The Verge*, has a number of similarities to *The Emperor Jones*. Both create original ways of using the theatre to represent the consciousness of a protagonist at the far edge of sanity. Both embody a Nietzschean sense of Dionysian creative power. Both present Nietzschean protagonists who see themselves as beyond good and evil. And both plays are the result of long contemplation of, and experimentation with, techniques for dramatizing the unconscious on the stage. In this context, it is important to look at *The Verge* along with Glaspell's first full-length play, *Bernice*, produced by the Players in March of 1919, in the same season as *Where the Cross Is Made*. *Bernice* was written in the winter of 1918, the only one of Glaspell's plays to be written in New York rather than in Provincetown. It has long been noted that *Bernice* is a fuller realization of Glaspell's techniques for developing an absent character, techniques first seen in *Trifles*.[61] Both plays are written within the mode of representational realism, and both make use of a realistic scenic image in the setting to convey the subjectivity of the absent character. There is a great difference in the dramatic impetus of the two plays, however. The subjectivity of Minnie Wright is *acted upon* in *Trifles*, as the women unravel the clues she has left behind in her kitchen in order to solve the mystery of her motive for killing her husband. In *Bernice*, the absent character becomes the *moving force*, acting upon the other characters from beyond the grave. This play is also an imaginative theatricalization of Glaspell's own desire to affect those people closest to her, a kind of wish-fulfillment written at a time when she was unhappy with many of the aspects of her married life.

In the fall of 1918, Glaspell had stayed in Provincetown alone for months after Cook and most of their friends had moved to New York. Week after week dragged by as it became progressively more uncomfortable in the drafty cottage, and she received letters from Cook telling her not to come to the city yet, where he was ostensibly kept busy with the renovations of the new building the Provincetown Players were moving into at 133 Macdougal Street, but she knew he was caught up in his relationship with Ida Rauh. When Glaspell did come to New York in November, it was to co-direct the production of *Tickless Time*, a collaborative play by the two of them that had taken up much of her summer. They had begun the play as a kind of therapy when, as Barbara Ozieblo notes, Cook had "transferred his personal fear of aging into an obsession with the mechanics of timekeeping," and wanted to throw out all their clocks, keeping time by the cycles of nature represented by a sundial. Ozieblo suggests that, because "she knew better than to deny him the euphoria of sharing his conceits with her," Glaspell started working with him on the play as a way of "channeling his sophistry into more profitable paths," as she had with *Suppressed Desires*. After enjoying the game of coming up with humorous observations on time, nature, and eternity, however, Cook had "enjoined his wife to transcribe their exchanges and create the play he could only talk of." *Tickless Time* "was the play that sprang from Cook's obsession during the summer of 1918."[62] After her recent experimental work on *The Outside*, it can be imagined that Glaspell had little interest in returning to the spirit of *Suppressed Desires* with this little satire of "advanced ideas" or in playing second fiddle to her husband in the production process. What's more, *Tickless Time* could only be seen as a regression after what she considered Cook's real artistic achievement in *The Athenian Women*, a non-comic reworking of *Lysistrata* in which he insisted on casting Rauh in the female lead opposite himself as Pericles. *The Athenian Women* was the first full-length play to be produced by the Provincetown Players, and Cook and Glaspell considered it an artistic success even though Cook's own performance was weak. As the usually sympathetic Heywood Broun put it, Cook "was not able to make Pericles seem much more than a very recently commissioned second lieutenant in the reserve corps."[63] Ozielbo notes that Glaspell was "always jealous" when Cook rehearsed with Rauh.[64] In contrast to his collaboration on this work, which he considered his best, the work with his wife on *Tickless Time* was trivial for both of them, and moreover, it interrupted Glaspell's own work.

It was in this frame of mind that Glaspell wrote *Bernice* that winter. It was at one level a therapeutic exercise for her, as *Tickless Time* had been for her husband, but it evinced a much deeper and much darker self-analysis. At its most obvious, the play may be seen as wish-fulfillment for Glaspell, a Tom Sawyeresque imagining of one's own funeral, expressing the well-suppressed but understandably somewhat passive–aggressive feeling of a self-sacrificing woman, that if she deprives her loved ones of her presence, they might begin to appreciate her. *Bernice* takes place after the death of the titular character, as her father, her husband Craig, a writer, and her best friend Margaret, a social worker, gather for her funeral. The characters are easily recognizable as Glaspell, Cook (who imagined himself to be the American Edward Gordon Craig), Glaspell's mild and rather ineffectual father, and Lucy Huffaker, Glaspell's closest friend since they were in college together. Glaspell suggests through the staging that the characters are in Bernice's control even after death. The stage directions indicate that Bernice has so created the environment that she still lives there: "*You feel yourself in the house of a woman you would like to know, a woman of sure and beautiful instincts, who lives simply.*"[65] The characters feel themselves unable to escape the sense that "Bernice made this house ... Everything is Bernice" (160). Even when they rearrange the furniture, her father says, "you can't get Bernice out of this room."

The characterization of Craig is a devastating analysis of Cook at this point. Craig has missed Bernice's death because she told her father not to telegraph him. He explains, "she didn't want to hurry you away from New York ... I supposed you were doing something that she knew about and did not want to interrupt" (168). Later her friend Margaret says that "Craig stayed in New York with May Fredericks – and he doesn't pretend anything else. Stayed there with May Fredericks, continuing an affair that has been going on for the past year. And before it was May Fredericks it was this one and that one" (185). Glaspell provides an analysis of Craig's infidelities in his confession of an inadequacy with regard to Bernice. Bernice is too self-sufficient, "she never seemed to need me. I never felt she – couldn't get along without me" (170). He tells Margaret that he never "*had* Bernice" because something in her resisted his desire to "reshape" her (173–174). He tells Margaret that "there was something in her that had almost nothing to do with our love ... that isn't right, Margaret. You want to feel that you *have* the woman you love. Yes – completely. Yes, every bit of her!" (197). Margaret suggests a motive for his affairs: "So you turned to the women you could have ... you 'had' all of them simply because there was less to have. You want no baffling sense of something beyond you" (197).

Craig's other weakness is as an artist. Margaret says that Bernice would have been "a wonderful wife for a real writer" (188), but that she didn't value Craig's work because he had failed to meet the challenge of "strong free minds that might go – we know not where! Might go into places where the light of a mind has never been" (189), but had been satisfied to do what he could do easily. Margaret's critique of Craig, with its imagery of fog, already associated with O'Neill from *Thirst* and *Fog*, and light, associated with the detested Jimmy Light, might be Glaspell's indictment of the Provincetown Players as well:

> You write so well, Craig, but – what of it? What is it is the matter with you – with all you American writers – most all of you. A well-put-up light – but it doesn't penetrate anything. It never makes the fog part. Just

shows itself off – a well-put-up-light. [*Growing angry.*] It would be better if we didn't have you at all! Can you see that it would? Lights which – only light themselves keep us from having light – from knowing what the darkness is. [*After thinking.*] Craig, as you write these things are there never times when you sit there dumb and know that you are glib and empty? ... you do this just to cover the fact that you can't do anything? Your skill – a mask for your lack of power? (199)

This devastating statement implies a great deal about Glaspell's attitude toward Cook and toward the work of the Provincetown Players at this point: O'Neill unable as yet to get through the fog that clouded his vision, and Cook having been reduced to his primary function in the theatre, producing plays like *Tickless Time* that did not aim much beyond entertainment, a role that Glaspell associated with the new ambitious would-be professional element in the Provincetown Players. That she would associate Cook with the likes of Jimmy Light in her mind shows the extent of her disillusionment with Cook's much articulated lofty artistic ideals. In the most devastating bit of analysis in the play, Margaret goes on to suggest that Craig's love affairs are "like your false writing – to keep yourself from knowing you haven't power," judging his life one "long attempt to appear effective – to persuade yourself that you *are* something" (201). In contrast to Craig are the real writers, those who try to "get a little farther than others can get – get at least the edge of the shadow" (102).

In the play, Bernice takes a final action before her death that is meant to redeem Craig from his failure as an artist. She tells her servant Abbie to say that she had killed herself. As expected, Craig leaps to the conclusion that "Bernice *killed* herself because she loved me so!" (176). This is in effect Bernice's last act of self-sacrifice, the surrendering of the sense of self that had kept her from being completely dominated by Craig. Yet it is also an exercise of power. Now that Craig believes that Bernice reserved nothing from her love of him, he says, "it is a different world. Life will never be – that old thing again" (225). Now that he is confident of Bernice's love, he need never return to the old life of "pretending. Fumbling. Always trying to seem something – to feel myself something." He has no need to go back to "my make-believe, now that I've got *to* life" (226). He tells Margaret that it consoles him for the loss of Bernice that "this comes crashing through my make-believe – and Bernice's world gets to me" (227). By taking this action with her death, Bernice has wrought the transformation in Craig that she had longed for in life. What had been a wasted talent and a hurtful life now has the potential to be that true "light" that will penetrate to the edges of the fog, a life dedicated to art.

But the play has an ironic twist as well. Margaret, who knows and understands Bernice far better than Craig does, cannot believe that anyone who valued life as she did would kill herself: "It's inconceivable that she should – cut off her own life. In her lived all the life that was behind her. You felt that in her – so wonderfully" (183). Abbie finally discloses that she is right, that Bernice had not killed herself, but begs her not to tell Craig out of loyalty to Bernice. Thus Bernice exerts her power over Margaret as well. Margaret, who values truth, must collaborate in the lie that Bernice leaves about her life. As Craig says, "You say life broke through her – the whole of life. But Bernice didn't want – the whole of life. She wanted *me*" (203). Margaret says that Abbie is telling her that "Bernice's life was *hate*": "You are telling me she covered hate with – with the beauty that was like nothing else?" (206). But after seeing the change in Craig, she comes to understand that what she had done was not out of "hate," or destructiveness, but "a gift to the spirit. A gift sent back through the dark. Preposterous. Profound," musing "Power. Oh, how *strange*" (229). She ends the play with a paean to Bernice's "tenderness of insight" and courage, saying she held out her hands "with gifts she was not afraid to send back," and recognizing that "she loved you, Craig … and more than that. [*Her voice electric.*] Oh, in all the world – since first life moved – has there been any beauty like the beauty of perceiving love?" (230).

The Verge

Bernice is a kind of hybrid play that pushes at the edges of representational theatre through its experiment with characterization and realizes aspects of the very male Nietzschean concept of the will-to-power in the female character Bernice. The play finally remains within boundaries of dramatic convention, however, with its redemptive ending, conveying a nineteenth-century message of the value and efficacy of female self-sacrifice, a theme that had preoccupied Glaspell since her first novel *Constancy* (1909). With *The Verge*, produced by the Provincetown Players in November, 1921, Glaspell clearly broke through the boundaries of theatrical convention to the "outside," creating an original and uniquely personal form of theatre in which to express her vision of the female artist. *The Verge* is the most modernist play the Players produced, both as an example of non-representational total theatre and as a dramatic text that conveys and realizes some of the fundamental concepts in modernist thought. It is a startling example of what came to be known among modernists as organic form, for the play embodies in its own form Glaspell's Nietzschean theme of the need for the artist–creator to break though established patterns, whether traditional aesthetic forms or the boundaries of society, in order to exercise her will to create. As an artist in horticulture, Claire Archer "breaks things up" in order to create a new plant, the Breath of Life. Glaspell breaks through the traditional representational theatrical conventions with which the play begins, and moves progressively into the realm of the artist's subjectivity, ending with an original form of theatre. The final act of *The Verge* fuses expressionist staging techniques, experimental dialogue that includes free verse, and a structural closure that is neither tragic nor comic nor melodramatic, but expresses the madness or visionary ecstasy of the Nietzschean artist.

The Verge begins in Claire's greenhouse, which Glaspell makes clear is "*not a greenhouse where plants are being displayed, nor the usual workshop for the growing of them, but a place for experiment with plants, a laboratory.*"[66] The mood is that of light comedy, as it becomes apparent that her husband Harry is determined to invade the greenhouse along with their houseguests, Tom Edgeworthy and Dick Demming, to eat their breakfast, because Claire has diverted the house's heat to the plants on this snowy day, leaving the rest of the rooms too cold for comfort. There is a good deal of comic business involving the men's inability to communicate through the glass walls and the failure to get salt for their eggs. During the first act it emerges that Claire is completely involved in her experiments, particularly two plants, the Edge Vine, which was her last creation, and the Breath of Life, "*a plant like caught motion, and of a greater transparency than plants have had. Its leaves, like waves that curl, close around a heart that is not seen*" (62). The Breath of Life is expected to bloom the following day. Claire considers the Breath of Life her most important creation, for "if the heart has . . . held its own," it will be "alive in its otherness." The Edge Vine, however, has proven a disappointment, for it "is running back to what it broke out of" (62). In the course of the first act, it emerges that Claire has been having an affair with Dick, a modernist painter, and that Tom is an intimate friend who understands some of her vision as a creative artist. Her sister and her daughter also arrive, and it becomes clear that Claire has no interest in the seventeen-year-old who has been brought up in her sister's home, because she has become so conventional. Act 1 ends with Claire pulling up the Edge Vine, saying, "Why did I make you?

To get past you! ... Oh, I have loved you so! You took me where I hadn't been," and then nearly hitting her daughter with it for saying "it would be better not to go there" (78).

The expressionistic elements in the set for Act 2 begin to take the play out of the representational mode. On the afternoon of the following day, Claire is in "*a tower which is thought to be round but does not complete the circle. The back is curved, then jagged lines break from that, and the front is a queer bulging window – in a curve that leans. The whole structure is as if given a twist by some terrific force – like something wrong*" (78). As in *The Outside*, the dialogue becomes increasingly subjective as Claire becomes increasingly unnerved by her interactions with the other characters. First her sister Adelaide and her husband Harry take her to task for being "monstrous" (79) for wanting to cast off her child. Then, as she tries to draw Tom into a physical relationship that will match the intensity of their emotional intimacy, her dialogue drops the witty banter of society comedy and becomes increasingly poetic. Two speeches are in free verse. When Harry and Adelaide come in with Dr. Emmons, a "nerve specialist," Claire's dialogue becomes fragmented and disjointed, a series of images that have a meaning for her, but for none of the other characters. Accusing her sister of "smothering" things with "the word for it," for example, she says: "Yes, she can hurt it! Piling it up – always piling it up – between us and – What's there. Clogging the way – always (*to Emmons*) I want to cease to know! That's all I ask. Darken it. Darken it. If you came to help me, strike me blind!" (91). The act ends with Claire being placed in the hands of Dr. Emmons because, as Harry says, "You're sick, Claire. There's no denying it" (92).

In Act 2, which takes place in the greenhouse, the Breath of Life has bloomed, and Claire's creation is what she has hoped it would be, both "stronger" and "more fragile" than anything before it. She says to the plant, "You weren't. You are" (96). Even Harry and Dick see that she has created something entirely new. Harry says, "I never saw anything like that before! There seems to be something alive – inside this outer shell" and Dick, the painter, says "it's quite new in form. It – says something about form" (96). After they leave, Tom tells Claire that he wants their relationship to be physical after all, for "as you stood there, looking into the womb you breathed to life, you were beautiful to me beyond any other beauty. You were life and its reach and its anguish" (97). Claire, however, now feels trapped by Tom's love, which has become stereotypically male. He says: "I will threaten you. I'm here to hold you from where I know you cannot go. You're trying what we can't do ... I love you, and I will keep you – from fartherness – from harm. You are mine, and you will stay with me! . . . I will keep you – safe" (99). Claire is now repulsed by Tom, saying: "Now I know who you are. It is you puts out the breath of life. Image of beauty – *You fill the place – should be a gate*" (99). Driven to a "*last passion*," she chokes Tom to death, saying "Breath of Life – my gift – to you!" (99). When Harry comes and asks how he can save her now, she responds, "Saved – myself" (100). The play ends with her broken singing of "Nearer My God to Thee."

While it maintains a hold on the illusion of objective reality that is fundamental to realism, *The Verge* pushes through the conventional boundaries of this mode to encompass a highly subjective and abstract dramatic idiom as well. Tom, Dick, and Harry, for example, are individualized characters and also a generalized male principle that the female artist Claire is up against in the various manifestations of husband, lover, and confidante. The husband Harry, an aviator whom Claire married because she thought he would "smash something" (69), shows elements of Cook. Claire is as disappointed in Harry as Glaspell was in Cook's inability to realize his visionary statements about art and the theatre: "I thought flying would do something to a man. But it didn't take us out. We just took it in" (69). Tom Edgeworthy, who is "always going to the ends of the earth to – meditate about something" and who had the "best kind of family connections" in the "very good business his father left him" (66), suggests the young O'Neill, with whom Glaspell had had a particularly intimate friendship during the years just before she wrote the play. It was also under the influence of O'Neill's success on Broadway that she had written *Chains of Dew* the previous year, a comedy involving the birth-control movement with her old theme of the redemption of a male artist through female self-sacrifice, which was unabashedly aimed at the Broadway theatre. O'Neill had obligingly used his family connections to get a reading of play with two producers who had options on his own work, John D. Williams and George C. Tyler, as well as advising her to submit it to the Theatre Guild, but none of these producers were interested in the play.[67] Dick could have been based on a number of artists that Glaspell knew in Provincetown and Greenwich Village, their affair real or imagined. In the play, the men are fully individualized characters, but become symbolically charged as the action goes on, and each inhabits the role that Claire gives them in her subjective drama. Claire's sister Adelaide and her daughter Elizabeth also migrate from individualized characters to the reality they have in Claire's mind, the embodiment of conventional morality and social attitudes. Similarly, the plants are real

Figure 8. The expressionist set of *The Verge*.

and visually startling plants, but they also have an abstract meaning that is so overdetermined as to be beyond symbolism. They mean what Claire sees them to mean, the "edge" and the "breath of life."

In keeping with Glaspell's dramatic idiom, the staging also incorporates both objective and subjective reality, as the social action in Act 1 moves into the more subjective experience in Act 2, which has an expressionistic set. As Ronald Wainscott puts it:

> *The Verge* stands in part as an early American experiment in expressionistic technique, predating all American dramaturgical attempts (unless we label *The Emperor Jones* expressionistic) ... Strictly speaking, the play is not expressionistic in the way German plays of the style are, but the scenic needs, especially of the second act, and the protagonist's spiral into madness, which is complicated at times with her breaking into spontaneous lyrical verse, sets it apart from realistic presentations, including the productions of all Glaspell's other plays.[68]

In another powerful element of the play's organic form, Glaspell uses the setting to express what Margit Sichert has noted as her radical revision of

Nietzsche's philosophy. In opposition to Nietzsche's "low estimation of women," and his "particular aversion to those with artistic ambition," Glaspell establishes a woman "as the paragon of superhuman endeavour in a play she used as a laboratory for Nietzschean idea/l/s," thus going "far beyond Nietzsche's reversal of all values."[69] This step was a major one for Glaspell, freeing her from the stultifying devotion to female self-sacrifice that she had valorized in both *Bernice* and *Chains of Dew*. According to Nietzsche's *Zarathustra*, "The happiness of man is, 'I will.' The happiness of woman is, 'He will. Lo, now hath the world become perfect!' – thus thinketh every woman when she obeyeth with all her love."[70] Sichert notes that Glaspell overcomes his "narrow patriarchal view by presenting the opposite in Claire Archer: *she wills*." Thus Claire "goes the way of the creator." She "*wills* to give spiritual birth to the ideal of the overman – to a male idea, which according to Nietzsche is reserved only to men. Claire becomes the *actor of her own ideal*."[71] And of course, Glaspell the playwright wills too. Her writing of the play with the female creator as protagonist is her own acting of an ideal. It is a feminist appropriation of Nietzsche's philosophy, which is given elegant expression in the first act's scenic image. Here it is Claire who inhabits the traditionally male space of the laboratory where creation is going on. It is the men who perform the usually female function of domesticating the space, as they invade the greenhouse with their breakfast, endangering the plants with their heedless opening and closing of the doors to the outside. When he gets there, Harry makes demands on Claire that she place her domestic duties above her work, reminding her of her role as hostess and insisting, "I am not a flower – true, but I too need a little attention – and a little heat" (59). Sichert notes that a power struggle takes place within the greenhouse, where "different values confront each other: the greenhouse becomes the stage for a battle between opposite world views … this power game becomes more and more serious."[72]

Claire's desire to "break things up" establishes her as a Nietzschean lawbreaker, but in her case, what she wants to break up is an inherited patriarchal culture. When Harry calls her the "flower of New England," and "what came of the men who made the laws that made New England … the gentleman of culture who … moulded the American mind," Claire says that is exactly what she wants to get away from: "I want to break it up! If it were all in pieces, we'd be (*a little laugh*) shocked to aliveness" (64). She wants to break out of the "forms moulded for us. There is outness – and otherness" (64). In willing to break things up, she wants to break out of the mold that Nietzsche prescribes for women as well as the other outmoded cultural forms. Claire's rejection of the forms of the past leads her to the rejection of conventional morality expressed by Nietzsche, for "morality is a hindrance to the creation of new and better customs: it makes stupid."[73] But it takes her further than this, to the unexpected rejection of motherhood, which the audience, and many critics, join Harry in judging "monstrous," and, on the heels of the global catastrophe that was World War I, of embracing war, as a "stunning chance! Mankind massed to kill" (70). She sees it as the equivalent of the "big leap" that plants take when they "explode their species – because something in them knows they've gone as far as they can go ... so – go mad – that life may not be prisoned. Break themselves up into crazy things – into lesser things, and from the pieces – may come one sliver of life with vitality to find the future. How beautiful. How brave" (70). She believes that humankind missed its chance to explode the species and move on to something better because it exhausted all its energy in the killing and "didn't say – 'And then' – The spirit didn't take the tip" (70). In exploding two of the cherished sentimental beliefs about women – their innate nurturing instinct and their revulsion against violence – Glaspell was presenting a female protagonist who did break the mold of patriarchal expectations, thus breaking the mold herself.

The new forms that Claire creates, the two plants, signify the emergence of the female artist as Nietzschean creator, a form of divinity. Expressing the patriarchal attitude, Harry wants Claire to "make the flowers as good as possible of their kind. That's an awfully nice thing for a woman to do – raise flowers." He expresses an uneasiness with what Dick recognizes is "creating," the "changing things into other things – putting things together and making queer new things ... it's unsettling for a woman" (65). Claire, however, knows exactly what she is doing, in creating "otherness." Her creations, she says "have been shocked out of what they were – into something they were not; they've broken from the forms in which they found themselves. They are alien. Outside. That's it, outside" (76). Denying her daughter's suggestion that the object of the experiment was to "make them better plants," she responds with a speech that is reminiscent of *The Outside*:

> Out there ... lies all that's not been touched – lies life that waits. Back here – the old pattern, done again, again, and again. So long done it doesn't even know itself for a pattern – in immensity. But this – has invaded.

> Crept a little way into – what wasn't. Strange lines in life unused. And when you make a pattern new you know a pattern's made with life. And then you know that anything may be – if you only know how to reach it.
>
> (77)

She says that she has to destroy the Edge Vine because it "isn't – over the edge. It's running, back to – 'all the girls' " (77), her daughter's sources for all her tastes and opinions. It is when her daughter says that "this is *wrong*" (77) that Claire recognizes her "hymn-singing ancestors" in her, and finally drives her away by nearly hitting her with the Edge Vine she has pulled up. Sichert notes that she is obeying a law of Zarathustra when she destroys the Edge Vine, for "whoever must be a creator in good and evil, verily, he must first be annihilator and break values." In killing the Edge Vine, Sichert contends, "Claire plays God – not satisfied with her creation, she destroys it in order to live up to her ideal. She has succeeded in creating her own law: she feels good having done what is evil for the others. Now she feels in harmony with God, with her God, who for the others can only be the devil – or madness."[74] Thus, Claire has passed beyond good and evil into the realm of the creator.

The Breath of Life is a form that is "further out" than the Edge Vine. Claire describes the intent of her experimental form to Tom:

> It's a secret. A secret? – it's a trick. Distilled from the most fragile flowers there are. It's only air – pulsing – playing; except, far in, one stab of red, its quivering heart – that asks a question. But here's the trick – I bred the air – form to strength. The strength shut up behind us I've sent – far out ... And I have another gift for Breath of Life; some day – though days of work lie in between – some day I'll give it reminiscence. Fragrance that is – no one thing in here but – reminiscent ... We need the haunting beauty from the life we've left. I need that. (86)

With the Breath of Life, Claire attains her status as a true Nietzschean creator. Having broken up the dead forms of the past, she has literally created a new form of life. When the plant flowers, it is clear to Tom that Claire has embodied the "breath of the uncaptured" (96). She has broken through to something new. But the plant still lacks "reminiscence." Claire says that "What has gone out should bring fragrance from what it has left ... Breath of Life may be lonely out in what hasn't been" (63–64). Sichert has noted that, in suggesting this need for the new to contain a trace of the past, Glaspell is echoing Nietzsche, who held that genius must contain a reminiscence of "past cultures and their powers,"[75] that is to say, a sense of history carried forward into the future. Monomaniacally fixated as she is on the breaking up of the old forms and the creation of something new, Claire has been unable to bestow "reminiscence" on her new life form, as she is unable herself to find any grounding in the past for her creation, which is made of air, and thus utterly fragile.

Claire's experiment with the plant is reflected in Glaspell's experiment with her play, as she breaks up the familiar pattern the audience expects. Like the set, which morphs from realistic greenhouse to expressionistic tower, the play's action begins on the familiar ground of society comedy, and, with Claire's "monstrous" casting off of her daughter, becomes something else. When Elizabeth evokes conventional morality to express her doubts about Claire's experiment, suggesting that it would be "better not to go there," Claire, like King Lear, casts off her child with the venomous language, "To think that object ever moved my belly and sucked my breast!" (78). This places her beyond the pale as a heroine for society comedy. Her alienation from human society, and presumably the audience, increases in Act 2 as she rejects the claims of family, society, and conventional morality, finally declaring, "all I ask is to die in the gutter with everyone spitting on me" (92). Rather than providing closure through an established pattern of resolution in the plot, punishment of Claire or redemption through self-sacrifice, for example, Glaspell takes the play into unexplored territory by having her behave in a completely unexpected way. Rather than being brought to regret her transgressions and reconciled with society, Claire further transgresses by killing Tom in the last act, and ends in an ambivalent state that has been interpreted by audiences and critics as either a descent into madness or an ascent into Dionysian ecstasy. Thus Glaspell's play is ultimately a modernist tour de force, a work of art whose meaning is finally a matter of subjective perception on the part of the spectator.

From a Nietzschean perspective, the killing of Tom is the act that takes Claire the creator beyond good and evil. Tom now wants to enforce his will over Claire by keeping her "safe" from "fartherness," which is just where she, as an artist, needs to go. She sees that it is he who "puts out the breath of life" by filling "*the place – should be a gate*" toward "radiance lighting forms undreamed" (86). In order to fulfill her creative potential, or destiny, Claire has to destroy Tom Edgeworthy as she has destroyed the Edge Vine, and the act of destruction gives her the same kind of Dionysian ecstasy, as she gives her "gift" to the Breath of Life. Claire's final fragmented dialogue is the endpoint of Glaspell's organic form. She articulates three concepts that are the keys to her further creativity: "Saved – myself"; "Out"; and "Reminiscence" (100). Having passed beyond good and evil, she is clearly beyond the self-sacrifice of Glaspell's earlier female protagonists. The recognition that she is not the means toward a man's creativity but a creator in her own right makes saving herself more important than Tom's life. In killing him, she has passed to the "outside" at last, as has Glaspell, in leaving behind the outmoded notion of self-sacrifice and affirming self-interest as the obligation of the female artist as well as the male. Having passed to the outside, it seems, Claire is now able to provide "reminiscence" to her creation in a characteristically modernist way, by appropriating a cultural myth for her own purpose. Her singing of "Nearer My God to Thee" might be seen as ironic, since she has left the moral principles of her New England forebears far behind. But what Glaspell suggests is that Claire the creator is now nearer to divinity herself, having smashed through conventional morality and established her own morality as a Nietzschean *Übermensch*. In taking Claire beyond good and evil, Glaspell also takes the play beyond the boundaries of the commonly accepted social and moral structure upon which representational realism depends. Glaspell suggests that the only criterion for judging Claire is the originality of her art. By extension, the same could be said of Glaspell's play.

It is not surprising that there is a good deal of critical disagreement over the ending of the play. In Gainor's view, "Claire's final evocation of an emblem of the Protestant Church points toward the ultimate inescapability of patriarchy."[76] Thus Claire has not triumphed but been defeated, reduced to madness by an established patriarchal order she cannot overcome. In her Nietzschean analysis, Margit Sichert contends that in the end, "Claire becomes a vengeful god, full of madness and frenzy and saves herself. She saves her ideal, finds her own god within herself: the Dionysian God."[77] Most critical responses seem to be at one of these two poles.[78] The Provincetown's production evoked a similar range of responses, although most critics reported that audiences were delighted with the show. The degree of clarity the critics saw in the play depended in large part on the extent to which the critic shared Glaspell's Nietzschean perspective on Claire. One critic suggested that Glaspell's pathfinding in the "unexplored regions of mental experience must be exceedingly puzzling to the Broadwayite," although the piece was "befogging delighted audiences at the Provincetown Playhouse."[79] Kenneth Macgowan, who knew his Nietzsche, acknowledged that *The Verge* was "the most difficult play that any American, and perhaps any European has ever written," but urged audiences to stay with its "attempt to make the theatre say things about the quivering soul of life," suggesting that "it tries to say that if we destroy perhaps we shall achieve creation."[80] The most positive response to *The Verge*, however, may have been by Stephen Rathburn, who wrote that "the play is an extraordinary study of the superwoman. Its heroine strives for the absolute freedom of the individual; freedom from heredity and the vast heritage of the past, and freedom even from the present, from environment, from duties, conventions, family ties and all the other obligations of society." Acknowledging Claire's insanity, he wrote "Three cheers for Claire! If she is insane let us have more insanity! Freedom is the greatest of all words ... Claire made her own great charter, and we should all pray for strength to follow her example. If we could, there would follow a race of supermen that Nietzsche himself would have applauded."[81]

The Hairy Ape

Probably the best-known statement O'Neill made about expressionism was his response to Barrett Clark's question in 1929 whether "European Expressionism" had influenced his work on *The Emperor Jones* and *The Hairy Ape*:

> The first Expressionistic play that I ever saw ... was Kaiser's *From Morn to Midnight*, produced in New York in 1922, after I'd written both *The Emperor Jones* and *The Hairy Ape*. I had read *From Morn to Midnight* before *The Hairy Ape* was written, but not before the idea for it was planned. The point is that *The Hairy Ape* is a direct descendant of *Jones*, written long before I had ever heard of Expressionism, and its form needs no explanation but this. As a matter of fact, I did not think much of *Morn to Midnight*, and still don't. It is too easy. It would not have influenced me.[82]

O'Neill's denial of European influence on his expressionism tended to increase in vehemence the further he got from the experience of writing and producing *The Hairy Ape*. O'Neill had in fact had an eager interest in German expressionism in 1921 before he wrote the play. As early as July, he had asked Kenneth Macgowan to bring him some illustrated pamphlets on the German theatre.[83] When he wrote the play, in three weeks during December, 1921, he was fresh from encountering full-blown expressionism in a reading of *From Morn to Midnight* and the film *The Cabinet of Dr. Caligari*, first shown in New York in April, 1921, a film he admired very much. As Louis Sheaffer has pointed out, "the new O'Neill play ... resembles the Georg Kaiser work: in both the lowly protagonist is jolted out of his rut by encountering a 'Lady' and at last finds peace, after a series of bewildering experiences, in death."[84]

The Hairy Ape begins in the forecastle of a luxury ocean liner, where the stokers are preparing for their shift. As in his other maritime plays, O'Neill represents the group of sailors as a geographical and ethnic microcosm. Prominent in the scene are Paddy, a survivor from the old days of the sailing ships, and Yank, whose identity is completely tied up in being the most powerful of the stokers who provide the power for the ocean liner. Paddy sings sea chanties and gives a rhapsodic monologue about the old days of the "fine beautiful ships" and the "fine strong men in them – men that was sons of the sea as if 'twas the mother that bore them." In those days, he says, "you worked under the sky and 'twas work wid skill and daring to it ... 'Twas them days men belonged to ships, not now. 'Twas them days a ship was part of the sea, and a man was part of a ship, and the sea joined all together and made it one."[85] Yank dismisses Paddy contemptuously, insisting that his way of life "it's dead, get me? Yuh don't belong no more, see. Yuh don't get de stuff. Yuh're too old." Yank says he is the one who "belongs" now. "Sure I'm part of de engines! Why de hell not! Dey move, don't dey? Dey're speed, ain't dey? Dey smash trou, don't dey?" (129). In the modern industrial order, Yank insists, he is the most important element:

> Sure, on'y for me everyting stops. It all goes dead, get me? ... Everyting else dat makes the woild move, somep'n makes it move. It can't move witout somep'n else, see? Den yuh get down to me. I'm at the bottom, get me! Dere ain't nothin' foither. I'm de end! I'm de start! I start somep'n and de woild moves! It – dat's me! – de new dat's moiderin' de old!
>
> (128)

As the men shovel coal into the engines, Mildred Douglas, the spoiled daughter of a steel magnate, is escorted down into the stokehold to satisfy her curiosity, and confronted by Yank's appearance and his tirade of invective against the engineers who are driving the men too hard, cries out "Oh, the filthy beast!" and faints. In the next scene, back in the forecastle, Yank, sitting in the attitude of Rodin's "The Thinker," contemplates revenge on Mildred for making him feel like a "hairy ape" instead of a man: "Who give her de noive to look at me like dat? Dis ting's got my goat right. I don't get her. She's new to me" (142). The next scene has Yank on Fifth Avenue in New York, escorted by Long, the socialist among the sailors. Long wants to raise Yank's class consciousness so he can understand the oppression by people like Mildred of the working man in general. In the expressionist scene, the two men are completely ignored by the wealthy passers by, masked and all wearing evening wear in the Provincetown production, even when Yank deliberately bumps and punches them after they all get excited about a store window displaying monkey fur. It is only when he inadvertently causes one of them to miss his bus that the police are summoned and Yank is thrown in jail.

The jail scene, a "*a row of cells in the prison on Blackwells Island*," which "*do not stop, but disappear in the dark background as if they ran on, numberless, into infinity*" (149–150), mimics the forecastle scenes in which tiers of narrow, steel bunks create the effect of "*a cramped space in the bowels of a ship, imprisoned by white steel . . . the steel framework of a cage*" (121). Here Yank resumes his Thinker posture for a while, and then shakes the bars, saying, "Steel. Dis is de Zoo, huh?" (150). One of the inmates reads an attack on the IWW from a newspaper, which says that if the radicals get control of the government, they will reduce civilization to a shambles, "a desolation where man, God's masterpiece, would soon degenerate back to the ape!" (153). This gives Yank the idea to join the IWW, where he is welcomed at first. When he offers to blow up the headquarters of the Douglas steel company, however, the men decide he must be a government spy and throw him out. Yank decides that they are only interested in "tree square a day" and a "lousy vote," but that doesn't get at what is really bothering him: "I don't tick see? – I'm a busted Ingersoll, dat's what. Steel was me, and I owned de woild. Now I ain't steel, and de woild owns me" (159). In desperation, he goes to the zoo, where he hopes he can get some understanding from the gorillas: "And why wouldn't yuh get me? Ain't we both members of de same club – de Hairy Apes?" (161). Freeing the gorilla from his cage, he puts out his hand to him, but the ape grabs him and crushes him in a "*murderous hug*," throws him in the cage, and walks off as Yank dies proclaiming himself as the "one and original – Hairy Ape" (163).

In a 1922 interview, O'Neill complained that many spectators thought the forecastle scenes in the play were meant to represent "an exact picture of the reality. They don't understand that the whole play is expressionistic."

He went on to say that "Yank is really yourself, and myself. He is *every* human being ... His struggle to 'belong,' to find the thread that will make him a part of the fabric of Life – we are all struggling to do just that."[86] Pointing out typical examples of expressionist techniques, he complained that people thought it was "an actual custom aboard ship" for the stokers to "all stand up, come to attention, then go out in a lockstep file," missing the implication that it is "symbolic of the regimentation of men who are the slaves of machinery. In a larger sense, it applies to all of us, because we all are more or less the slaves of convention, or of discipline, or of a rigid formula of some sort." He also pointed out that stokers do not really shovel coal the way it is done in the play ("*They bend over, looking neither to right nor left, handling their shovels as if they were part of their bodies, with a strange, awkward, swinging rhythm ... the men shovel with a rhythmic motion, swinging as on a pivot from the coal which lies in heaps on the floor behind to hurl it into the flaming mouths before them*" [135]): "It is done in the play in order to contribute to the rhythm. For rhythm is a powerful factor in making anything expressive. People do not know how sensitive they are to rhythm. You can actually produce and control emotions by that means alone."[87]

Just two years after the play was produced, O'Neill was distancing himself from German expressionism, primarily because he thought that "expressionism denies the value of characterization." He countered that "I personally do not believe that an idea can be readily put over to an audience except through characters. When it sees 'A Man' and 'A Woman' – just abstractions, it loses the human contact by which it identifies itself with the protagonist of the play."[88] Of course O'Neill had experimented with this kind of abstraction in early plays such as *Thirst* and *Fog*, but his target here was *From Morn to Midnight*. He said that the "real contribution of the expressionist has been in the dynamic qualities of his plays. They express something in modern life better than did the old plays." Acknowledging that he had "something of this method in the Hairy Ape," he insisted on the difference that "the character Yank remains a man and every one recognizes him as such."[89] At the same time that he insisted on the individuation of Yank, O'Neill said that "*The Hairy Ape* was propaganda in the sense that it was a symbol of man, who has lost his old harmony with nature, the harmony which he used to have as an animal and has not yet acquired in a spiritual way. Thus, not being able to find it on earth, nor in heaven, he's in the middle, trying to make peace, taking the 'woist punches from bot' of 'em.'"

While he wanted the audience to perceive Yank as an individual, O'Neill was frustrated that "the public saw just the stoker, not the symbol, and the symbol makes the play either important or just another play." In O'Neill's view, the meaning of the play was universal despite the exceptionalism of his choice of protagonist:

> Yank can't go forward, and so he tries to go back. This is what his shaking hands with the gorilla meant. But he can't go back to "belonging" either. The gorilla kills him. The subject here is the same ancient one that always was and always will be the one subject for drama and that is man and his struggle with his own fate. The struggle used to be with the gods, but is now with himself, his own past, his attempt "to belong."[90]

What may seem a contradiction in the play's aesthetics is perhaps what makes for its strength as drama. O'Neill's use of expressionist techniques really is original because the play is not "all expressionist" as he said in 1922, nor is it a conventional progression from a representational frame story into the subjective reality of the protagonist, like *The Emperor Jones*, *From Morn to Midnight*, and the early expressionistic works by his admired Strindberg. *The Hairy Ape*'s aesthetics are a dialectic between realism and expressionism that emphasizes O'Neill's fundamental theme in the play, Yank's inability to "belong."

It is clear that O'Neill was aware of what he was doing from his communication with Macgowan, who was, by December of 1921, a trusted critic of his work and his most valued link to knowledge of the "new theatre." The day he finished the first draft of *The Hairy Ape*, he wrote Macgowan that the play was "at least astonishing, whether for good or evil," adding "I don't think the play as a whole can be fitted into any of the current 'isms.' It seems to run the whole gamut from extreme naturalism to extreme expressionism – with more of the latter than the former. I have tried to dig deep in it, to probe in the shadows of the soul of man bewildered by the disharmony of his primitive pride and individualism at war with the mechanistic development of society."[91] Timo Tiusanen has noted that there is "an incongruous element in each of the eight scenes: Paddy in the forecastle, Mildred both on the deck and in the stokehold, Yank wherever he turns, after the crushing moment in Scene iii [the confrontation with Mildred]. Contrasts between the images extend their influence over scene lines and help to form new images full of inner tensions."[92] Tiusanen sees the strongly discordant images as a weakness in the play, because they overpower Yank's monologue, but

I would argue that they are an important element in the play's fundamental aesthetics, a dynamic interaction between expressionism and realism, subjectivity and objectification. The play's dialectic aesthetics reflect the dynamic of Yank's interaction with the external world, which is symbolized in the two images he inhabits bodily on stage, the Thinker and the Ape. Is Yank a man, *homo sapiens*, or is he, as Mildred names him, and as the industrial society she represents has seemingly made him, a "filthy beast"? When his humanity is denied by the world with which he interacts, Yank sees the world in nightmarish terms. O'Neill forces the audience to share Yank's subjective vision through his use of expressionistic techniques. In the forecastle, the noise the men make is meant to rise to "*a confused, inchoate uproar swelling into a sort of unity, a meaning – the bewildered, furious, baffled defiance of a beast in a cage*" (121). Likewise, the steel framework of bunks is meant to resemble a cage, and "*the ceiling crushes down upon the men's heads. They cannot stand upright*" and "*the men themselves should resemble those pictures in which the appearance of Neanderthal Man is guessed at*" (121). This is a world in which Yank literally thinks of himself as "steel," a part of the engine. It is even more dramatic in the stokehold, where the men behave as automatons, feeding the insatiable engine in response to the insistent whistle from above. It is only after the confrontation with Mildred that Yank assumes the "Thinker" position and begins to express an alienation from his dehumanizing work on the ship.

In the rest of the play, Yank's quest to be a man, to find somewhere to "belong" in the world of human beings, is emphasized by the dialectic between the realistic and the expressionistic. Scene 5, the Fifth Avenue scene, begins with the realistic interaction between Long and Yank, as Long tries to get Yank to see the bigger picture of his humiliation by Mildred Douglas. Unlike the nightmarish sets on the ship, the Fifth Avenue set represents "*a general atmosphere of clean, well-tidied, wide street; a flood of mellow, tempered sunshine; gentle, genteel breezes*," although "*a background of magnificence [is] cheapened and made grotesque by commercialism, a background in tawdry disharmony with the clear light and sunshine on the street itself*" (144). When the people appear, and don't recognize that Yank and Long exist, the scene becomes increasingly expressionistic. When the crowd emerges from church, the people saunter "*slowly and affectedly, their heads held stiffly up, looking neither to right nor left, talking in toneless, simpering voices. The women are rouged, calcimined, dyed, overdressed to the nth degree. The men are in Prince Alberts, high hats, spats,*

Figure 9. The Fifth Avenue scene from *The Hairy Ape*.

canes, etc. *A procession of gaudy marionettes, yet with something of the relentless horror of Frankensteins in their detached, mechanical unawareness*" (147). Thus they appear in Yank's imagination, lashed to fury by their complete refusal to recognize his existence, even when he pushes and shoves them. It is only when one of them runs into him, and misses his bus, that he is noticed, and the nightmare closes in on Yank again as a "*platoon of policemen rush in on Yank from all sides. He tries to fight but is clubbed to the pavement and fallen upon.*" Meanwhile, the crowd "*have not moved or noticed this disturbance*" (149). The trope of the cage is repeated in the scene in the jail that follows, and once again the figure of Yank as the Thinker contrasts with the dehumanizing environment in which he has been placed. His conclusion is that he has been put in the zoo. In the Provincetown production, the expressionism in this scene was emphasized by the shadowy lighting, the distorted angles and dimensions of the set, and the perspective that suggested the row of cells went on into infinity.

The penultimate scene, in the IWW headquarters, is a return to the representational, as Yank interacts with the men on an equal basis.

The room, "*which is general assembly room, office, and reading room, resembles some dingy settlement boys' club.*" It is "*decidedly cheap, banal, commonplace and unmysterious as a room could well be*" (155). When he is called a "brainless ape" by the Secretary and thrown out for offering to blow up the steel headquarters, Yank once again assumes the Thinker attitude, trying to decide whether there is any place for him in the world at all. His answer comes from a policeman who tells him to "go to hell" (160). In the final scene, of course, the trope of the cage is brought into its full realization in the zoo. O'Neill indicates that only one cage should be visible, on which there is "*a sign from which the word 'gorilla' stands out.*" A "*spot of clear gray light falls on the front of one cage so that the interior can be seen*" (160). Emphasizing Yank's subjective identification with him, the gorilla "*is seen squatting on his haunches on a bench in much the same attitude as Rodin's 'Thinker'*" (160). The final scenic image is of the dying Yank, crushed by the gorilla, pulling himself up on the bars and saying "In de cage, huh?" then sliding to the floor as he proclaims himself the "one and original – Hairy Ape" (163). As, rather crudely, in *Where the Cross Is Made* and more effectively in *The Emperor Jones*, O'Neill's design is to force the spectators to share the protagonist's subjective perception of the external world, but here he plays it against continual reminders of "objective" reality. *The Hairy Ape* is not the representation of a dream or hallucination, but of the perception of the modern industrial world as seen from the bottom of the heap.

Although the production process of *The Hairy Ape* was rather chaotic, it was the beneficiary of some of the most imaginative collaboration the Provincetown Players enjoyed. O'Neill realized from the beginning both that mounting an effective production of *The Hairy Ape* was beyond the capabilities of the Provincetown Players and that the play could probably not be launched successfully on Broadway without first succeeding in the little experimental theatre in Greenwich Village. Since he had first had the idea for the play, O'Neill had been writing about it to Charles O'Brien Kennedy, an old friend of his father's who had directed his realistic psychological study of a sexually repressed woman, *Diff'rent*, for the Provincetown the previous season, as well as Dreiser's *The Hand of the Potter* and a revival of *The Moon of the Caribees*. Besides being involved with the Provincetown Players, Kennedy was also on the staff of Arthur Hopkins, the most distinguished producer of "literary" drama in New York at the time. O'Neill wanted Kennedy to direct the play, but, as Louis Sheaffer reports, "Jig Cook was so eager for the assignment that

O'Neill, against his better judgment, yielded."[93] Suffering from a bout of depression after the ignominious uptown failure of *The Spring*, Cook was also drinking heavily. He was hardly in shape to conceive or supervise the complex production of an experimental new work like *The Hairy Ape*.

When rehearsals began, O'Neill, who had been acting as producer, assumed greater and greater control over the direction of the play, leaving Cook feeling "diminished, slighted, relegated to a corner."[94] It was at this point that Cook decided to pull up stakes and go to Greece, taking Susan Glaspell with him, of course. Mostly in order to keep James Light, whom Cook, Glaspell, and Edna Kenton detested, from taking over the Players, on February 23rd, they engineered an incorporation of the Provincetown Players, with the intention of reserving the use of the name after the group had disbanded. They set sail on the SS *Themistocles* on March 1.[95] The direction of *The Hairy Ape*, which opened on March 9, was assumed by O'Neill, with the assistance of Light and Arthur Hopkins, who was partially funding the Provincetown production with an eye toward bringing it to Broadway. There was no directing credit listed on the program, and Light was listed as "Stage Manager." In an interview with Robert Sarlós, Light later said that he had taken over direction of the play from Cook, but that, under the circumstances, "collective credit seemed preferable to naming them both."[96] With Louis Wohlheim, a Hopkins actor, as Yank, the collaboration proved fruitful. The design was also the production of talented collaborators. Cleon Throckmorton, who had become the Provincetown's technical director after working his five-day wonder on *The Emperor Jones*, was joined by Robert Edmond Jones, now a successful Broadway designer, who had been lured back to the Provincetown group after seven years by the experimental possibilities of O'Neill's expressionistic script and the new dome. The result was a design that was even more effective than that of *Emperor Jones* had been. The characteristic minimalism of Jones worked extraordinarily well in the series of expressionistic images the two designers created and realized on the stage. As costume designer, the veteran Player Blanche Hays made her own contribution to expressionism, for it was she who came up with the idea of using masks for the procession of "gaudy marionettes" in the Fifth Avenue scene. "I suggested using masks, and Gene was delighted," she said.[97] This was the beginning of O'Neill's long fascination with masks and dual identities in his plays, and he wrote years later that, "in *The Hairy Ape* a much more extensive use of masks would be of the greatest value in emphasizing the theme of the play. From the opening of the fourth scene, where Yank begins to think, he enters into a masked world; even the familiar faces of his mates in the forecastle have become strange and alien. They should be masked, and the faces of everyone he encounters thereafter, including the symbolic gorilla's."[98]

Edna Kenton claimed that *The Hairy Ape* "wrecked us with its questions of directorship and problems of production."[99] Louis Sheaffer suggested that the Cooks departed so precipitously because "they did not want to be around to witness the acclaim they expected for *The Hairy Ape*."[100] These are perhaps two subjective perceptions of the same reality. The production of the play certainly was a difficult experience for the group, especially the Cook faction, but in many ways, its collaborative process, drawing on a wide range of available talent to create something new in the American theatre, was much truer to the group's original purpose as an experimental theatre serving the American playwright than most of the recent productions of the Players had been. And there is no doubt of its artistic success. Noting that O'Neill "dove deep into Bobby Jones's locker" for the scene design of the play, Alexander Woollcott, after seeing the production at the Provincetown Playhouse, praised the "new evidences of O'Neill writing not in isolation, as has been his wont, but on the very stage where his world was to be played. The new play suggests a greater familiarity with the theatre, as an instrument, and, as all plays should be, was evidently worked out in collaboration with the artists who would make it visible and the actors who would give it body."[101] Having seen *The Hairy Ape* after its move uptown to the Plymouth Theatre, Walter Prichard Eaton, who understood what O'Neill was after in his "expressionistic tragi-comedy of modern industrial unrest," wrote that "no such fusion of dialogue and scenery, of the intellectual, the emotional, the spiritual, and pictorial, into a single thing which is only to be described by the word *theatrical*, has ever before been accomplished by an American playwright." He continued with the confirmation that "in Eugene O'Neill the new art of the theatre in America has found the new playwright at last. To see 'The Hairy Ape' is to see the bright promise of what is to come, not the pale reflection of what has been."[102] The production had certainly realized the original aspirations of the Provincetown Players, if it had indeed wrecked the organization built up by George Cram Cook and his allies.

The departure of Cook and Glaspell and the end of the Provincetown Players was the culmination of their thwarted attempt to remove James Light, Cook's young rival for influence and control, from the Players as they had the Nordfeldts in 1917. In a meeting similar to the "massacre" of March, 1917, Cook, Glaspell, and Kenton had taken advantage of Light's absence when he remained for several months in Europe after the run of *The Emperor Jones*, to oust him from power. In the 1920–1921 season, Cook and Light were co-directors of the Provincetown Players. Light naturally assumed that this arrangement would continue when he returned from Europe in January. In September, 1921, however, a meeting of the Executive Committee, which by then had reached the unprecedented size of twelve members – Cook, Kenton, Rauh, Glaspell, O'Neill, Light, Eleanor Fitzgerald, Edna Millay, Charles Ellis, E. J. Ballantine, Jasper Deeter, and Cleon Throckmorton – was called. The meeting consisted of Cook, Kenton, and Fitzgerald, with proxies from O'Neill, Glaspell, and Rauh. At the meeting they voted that the double signatures of Fitzgerald and Cook were to be required on all checks disbursing funds; that the Executive Committee be reduced to five: Cook, O'Neill, Glaspell, Kenton, and Fitzgerald; that "there be one director of the Provincetown Players and that one to be George Cram Cook"; and that Kenton be given an official paid position with the Players as play reader. With this coup, the Cook faction had simply ousted Light and his allies from power and invested complete control in the people who profited the most from the organization, the two major playwrights and three paid officers.

In February, 1922, when O'Neill, who seemed to play all sides to his advantage, took the direction of *The Hairy Ape* out of the hands of Cook and gave it, at least partly, to Light, the Cook faction was not only demoralized, but more determined than ever to keep the Provincetown Players out of the hands of Jimmy Light. Before Cook and Glaspell left for Greece on March 1, a secret meeting of the Executive Committee was called, on February 13, at which it was voted to incorporate the Provincetown Players, thus reserving the name of the company for future use; to authorize Edna Kenton to sign checks in place of Cook; and to suspend operations of the theatre until the fall of 1923, subletting the building for the 1922–1923 season. On March 1, the Executive Committee approved the incorporation of the Provincetown Players as a membership corporation, with the members to be Cook, O'Neill, Glaspell, Fitzgerald, Kenton, Cleon Throckmorton, and attorney Harry Weinberger. In Kenton's view, the committee had "decided on the pilot for the rest of the disastrous voyage; I would take Jig's place and do what I could to hold the wheel more or less steady to the end."[103] This was a rather inflated view of her authority to sign checks in Cook's absence. To her credit, however, she tried conscientiously to act in the interest of Cook and Glaspell, which for her was acting in the interest of the Provincetown Players, preparing Susan Glaspell's *Chains of Dew*, the play that O'Neill had tried unsuccessfully to place with a Broadway manager in 1918, for the theatre's final production, and working hard to see that the theatre was rented, while keeping it out of the hands of Jimmy Light.[104]

Before he left for Greece, George Cram Cook had written a "valedictory" circular in which he said that the Provincetown Players would reopen in October, 1923, but this was not to be. Cook and Glaspell remained in Greece in 1923, and many of the other members had moved on by then. The one remaining founder, quietly and tenaciously working in the background to keep the experimental theatre going, was, perhaps surprisingly, Eugene O'Neill. Along with Robert Edmond Jones, who had become interested in the new scenic possibilities of the Provincetown Playhouse as well as O'Neill's turn toward the new expressionistic drama, O'Neill recruited Kenneth Macgowan, who had graduated from Harvard a year after Jones and John Reed. By 1922 a respected theatre critic and an editor of *Theatre Arts* magazine, Macgowan was quite familiar with the new developments in the theatre. Hiram Moderwell, who introduced the new European developments to Americans in 1914 with his *The Theatre of Today*, had been Macgowan's roommate at Harvard. Macgowan's 1921 *The Theatre of Tomorrow* was "frankly a sequel" to Moderwell's book.[105] In March of 1921, O'Neill had approached both Jones and Macgowan for help with the play that would become *The Fountain*. Asking Macgowan to suggest anything that "might be of help in the way of atmosphere, mood, method or myth," he noted that he had also asked Jones to suggest things and was hoping to "combine" with him in working "this thing out in harmony from our respective lines in the theatre."[106] He also asked Macgowan to visit him in Provincetown, which he did, sowing the seeds for theatrical collaboration and beginning a lifelong friendship between them. In January, O'Neill read Macgowan's book, writing "now that I have 'got' it as a whole for the first time," he had the feeling "of having seen a thing in its entire significance which before was scattered about and had meaning only in its episodes."[107] In the spring of 1922, Macgowan and Jones made a tour of European theatres together, which informed their collaborative work on the modernist developments in European theatre, *Continental Stagecraft* (1922).

By the spring of 1923, Macgowan had proposed a scheme for taking over the Provincetown Players, to which O'Neill had responded that

Macgowan could "rely on my being all for it and cooperating as actively as possible in every way. It seems to me the only way to save the P. P. theatre and stimulus."[108] The plans proceeded, with Macgowan to become the new director of the Provincetown, and O'Neill, Jones, and the designer Norman Bel Geddes associate directors. In September, the lawyer Harry Weinberger wrote to O'Neill, "as I see it, the Provincetown Players are going on. Mr. Macgowan is to have absolute power as a director just the same as if we had hired Mr. Stanislavsky or Mr. Reinhardt, to be assisted by all the great dramatists of the world including Eugene O'Neill."[109] Much more sensitive to the issues behind the name of the Provincetown Players, and disturbed by Macgowan's plan to issue a circular headed "Macgowan, Jones, and O'Neill Announce," O'Neill complained to Macgowan, "things are happening a bit as I had dreaded, and I already see a wild-eyed Jig Cook returning hot-foot from Greece to denounce the kidnapping of his child." He balked at any formulation "where any of the old bickering has a legal right to operate," and urged Macgowan to drop the name of the Provincetown Players.[110] He wrote Weinberger that, "having cabled Jig and being advised by him to let the theatre go … if we're going to turn the name – purely for its financial help – over to Macgowan let's turn it over with no strings of the old bickering democracy attached."[111]

On November 8, 1923, Robert Edmond Jones and Kenneth Macgowan were added to the member list of the Provincetown Players, Inc., and a statement signed by Kenton, Throckmorton, Weinberger, and Fitzgerald said "we agree that Kenneth Macgowan be appointed director of the production season 1923–1924, at the Provincetown Theatre, and that he be given full and final power both in production and business management."[112] As O'Neill had expected, much wrangling and confusion about the use of the name "Provincetown" followed over the next few years. Although the new group was officially named the Experimental Theatre, Inc., it freely used the name of the Provincetown Playhouse in its advertising. Glaspell and Kenton, in particular, resisted the new group's use of the Provincetown name after Cook's death in Greece in 1924. Macgowan, who confessed to being "irritated" at their refusal to let him use the name, took pleasure in "seeing the public ignore their wishes." But he also said that he came to understand only upon reading Deutsch and Hanau's history of the early years "the peculiar creative spirit of the Provincetown … It had done its work. We carried on to useful ends, but they were not the ends of Jig Cook and the Provincetown Players."[113]

O'Neill, however, had accomplished his goal. He retained his experimental stage in the new Experimental Theatre, Inc., and the new plays that were produced by this organization, *The Ancient Mariner*, *All God's Chillun Got Wings*, *The Fountain*, *Desire Under the Elms*, and *The Great God Brown*, were well served by the professional artistry of the productions. In perhaps a final blow to the old guard, Jimmy Light was made stage manager of the new group, and an Associate Director the following season. In 1926, O'Neill continued to consider him "'aces' compared to any [director] I know" and "fine for me to work with."[114] In 1925, Light and Eleanor Fitzgerald were put in charge of a more experimental season at the Provincetown Playhouse, while Macgowan, Jones, and O'Neill oversaw major productions at the Greenwich Village theatre.

5

The legacy

Macgowan, Jones, and O'Neill

With the building of the Experimental Theatre, Inc. (ETI) out of the ashes of the dead Provincetown Players, O'Neill had a stable producing organization where he could work with theatre artists he trusted and with whom he felt comfortable, theatre artists who thought of themselves frankly as responsible professionals rather than as inspired amateurs. With collaborators committed to modernist experiment, O'Neill produced new plays that were among the most experimental of his career. Robert Edmond Jones served this work literally to exhaustion. For O'Neill, he directed and designed *Desire Under the Elms* (November, 1924), *The Fountain* (December, 1925), and *The Great God Brown* (January, 1926) for the ETI, and designed *Welded* (March, 1924) independently. In addition, for the ETI he designed, alone or in collaboration, Strindberg's *Spook Sonata*, the very successful revival of Mowatt's *Fashion, or Life in New York*, Molière's *George Dandin*, translated by Stark Young, O'Neill's adaptation of Coleridge's *The Ancient Mariner*, Stark Young's *The Saint*, Hasenclever's *Beyond*, and Congreve's *Love for Love*, all while carrying on with his regular design work for the "commercial" Broadway theatre. In 1926, he finally broke under the stress, and went to Zurich, where he underwent psychoanalysis by Carl Gustav Jung. Jimmy Light co-directed *The Ancient Mariner* (April, 1924), for which he also designed and constructed masks, as well as *All God's Chillun Got Wings* (May, 1924), *S. S. Glencairn* (November, 1924), and a revival of *The Emperor Jones* (May, 1924) with Paul Robeson.

The theatrical innovations O'Neill imagined for these plays are a logical development of the experimentation he had begun with the Provincetown Players, and exhibit a modernist preoccupation with dramatizing the subconscious through expressionist staging, lighting, and the use of masks. In *Welded*, for example, O'Neill indicated an expressionist use of the newly developed follow spot on the two main characters, Eleanor and Michael Cape. When Michael enters, "*a circle of light appears with him, follows him into the room. These two circles of light, like auras of egoism, emphasize and intensify Eleanor and Michael throughout the play. There is no other lighting.*" The staging of a dual monologue in which the two characters speak their thoughts anticipates the more complicated technique O'Neill developed for *Strange Interlude* several years later. The two characters sit in chairs facing front, staring straight ahead and remaining motionless as "*they speak, ostensibly to the other, but showing by their tone it is a thinking aloud to oneself, and neither appears to hear what the other has said*" (243). Although O'Neill complained that they were never executed as he imagined them,[2] the famous elm trees of *Desire Under the Elms*, with the "sinister maternity in their aspect, a crushing, jealous absorption" and the "appalling humaneness" with which they "brood oppressively over the house ... like exhausted women resting their sagging breasts and hands and hair on its roof" are a scenic representation of the raw subjectivity that broods over the whole play, the spirit of Eben Cabot's dead "Maw."[3]

In *The Fountain*, which Macgowan called a dramatization of "one of the oldest of race-myths,"[4] an established device of expressionism, the hallucination, is invested with a subjective symbolism. Juan Ponce de Leon, devastated when he finds that a spring in the forest is not the fountain of youth, sees a series of apparitions. The figure of his beloved Beatriz is transformed into the spirit of the fountain. He sees a Chinese poet, a Moorish minstrel, a Native American whom he has tortured, and his Spanish friend Luis, who are transformed into a "Buddhist priest," a "priest of Islam," a "Medicine Man," and a "Dominican monk": "*Each one carries the symbol of his religion before him. They appear clearly for a moment, then fade from sight, seeming to dissolve in the fountain.*"[5] Juan perceives that, as they vanish, all religious faiths become "one and equal," and he perceives the fountain as the figure of divinity: "O God, fountain of Eternity, Thou art the All in One, the One in All – the Eternal Becoming which is Beauty!" (226). O'Neill had used expressionistic techniques to draw the audience into the protagonist's subjectivity in earlier plays – to try to make the audience "go mad" in *Where the Cross Is Made* and to participate in Brutus Jones's terror in *The Emperor Jones*. In *The Fountain* he used them to draw the audience into Juan's Nietzschean epiphany, his discovery of the inadequacy of organized religion and of the divinity of Eternal Becoming.

All God's Chillun Got Wings also used established expressionistic devices in some new ways. The juxtaposition of highly schematized black and white communities in the opening scene and the scene in which the black character Jim marries the white character Ella performs the simultaneous function of calling the audience's attention to the racism of the community and externalizing the racism that exists in the characters' minds, whether they are conscious of it or not. In the opening scene, four children, two black and two white, play together, seemingly innocent of the racism that pervades their environment: "*People pass, black and white, the Negroes frankly participants in the spirit of Spring, the whites laughing constrainedly, awkward in natural emotion. Their words are lost. One hears only their laughter. It expresses the difference in race.*"⁶ From one side of the street comes the sound of a high-pitched nasal tenor singing "Only a Bird in a Gilded Cage," and from the other comes a rendition of "I guess I'll Have to Telegraph My Baby," ending with the laughter, "*distinctive in quality*" (279), from both sides. Through these carefully selected, exaggerated details, O'Neill establishes an image of a racially segregated, but mutually tolerant, community.

In scene 4, as Jim and Ella are about to marry, the neutrality of this image has changed as it is invested with the subjectivity of the young interracial couple that is about to be ostracized: "*The buildings have a stern, forbidding look. All the shades on the windows are drawn down, giving an effect of staring, brutal eyes that pry callously at human beings without acknowledging them ... The district is unusually still, as if it were waiting, holding its breath*" (294–295). A blues song with the line "sometimes I wish that I'd never been born" is interrupted by "*one startling, metallic clang of the church-bell*," and, as if on a signal, people pour from the two tenements on the two sides of the church, blacks on one side, whites on the other. As "*they hurry to form into two racial lines on each side of the gate, rigid and unyielding, staring across at each other with bitter hostile eyes*," the doors swing open, emitting Jim and Ella, and "*the doors slam behind them like wooden lips of an idol that has spat them out.*" As the young couple stands "*in the sunlight, shrinking and confused,*" all the "*hostile eyes are now concentrated on them.*" Afraid to pass through the two lines of hostile eyes, "*they hesitate and tremble; then stand there staring back at the people as fixed and immovable as they are*" (295–296). An organ grinder plays "Old Black Joe," ending with the clang of the church bell. Scenically, O'Neill theatricalizes the trait of racism through the simple hostility of the two lines of people. He also invests the scene with the subjectivity of the young couple, who perceive the rejection of the community and of the church in the very buildings themselves. Similarly, O'Neill uses scenic distortion to represent the characters' state of mind in the course of their marriage. In scene 2, "*the walls of the room appear shrunken in, the ceiling lowered, so that the furniture, the portrait, the [Congo] mask look unnaturally large and domineering*" (305). In scene 3, six months later, "*the walls appear shrunken in still more, the ceiling now seems barely to clear the people's heads, the furniture and the characters appear enormously magnified*" (311). Both Jim and Ella feel trapped by the circumstances of the marriage, Jim by the burden of expectation that has been placed on him in this hostile world, and Ella by her inability to escape from the racism that taints her attitude toward Jim despite her love for him.

O'Neill makes use of a favorite image in the African mask onto which Ella projects her racist hatred. Continuing to believe that she loves Jim, and that Jim is "white," she addresses the mask: "What have you got against me? I married you, didn't I? Why don't you let Jim alone? . . . He's white, isn't he – the whitest man that ever lived," whereas she sees the mask as "Black! Black! Black as dirt! You've poisoned me! I can't wash myself clean! Oh, I hate you!" (312). In the climax of the play, she stabs the mask, telling Jim, "It's dead. The devil's dead." If Jim had passed his bar exam, she says, "it would have lived in you. Then I'd have had to kill you, Jim, don't you see! – or it would have killed me. But now I've killed it (*She pats his hand*.) So you needn't ever be afraid any more, Jim" (314). The stabbing of the mask is an externalization of Ella's pathology, which the play suggests is brought on by the racist community in which she is raised.

The use of the mask was a major feature of the ETI, one in which O'Neill, Macgowan, Jones, and Light were all keenly interested. In 1923, Macgowan had written his *Masks and Demons*, a heavily illustrated volume "intended to tell the man who looks at a mask drawn by Craig or a mask made by Dulac, Stern, or Benda various facts that he should know about their ancestors, the holy masks of simpler men."[7] The depth of O'Neill's interest may be measured by the three pieces on masks he wrote for the magazine *American Spectator* in 1932 and 1933, several years after he had finished his work with the ETI. He wrote that he considered the use of masks in *The Hairy Ape*, *The Ancient Mariner*, *All God's Chillun Got Wings*, *The Great God Brown*, and *Lazarus Laughed* "uniformly successful," and the only change he would make in the future would be "to call for more masks in some of these productions and to use them in other productions where they were not used before."[8] James Light echoed Macgowan's *Masks and Demons* and Nietzsche's *Birth of Tragedy* in a program note he wrote for *The Ancient Mariner*, writing that a mask is "the embodiment of a dramatic quality in a medium which has a spiritual texture. The mask is primarily the face of the god, the ritual reincarnation of Dionysus, the ceremonial appearance among men of the god himself ... the mask alone is constantly true, the sublimation of the attributes of the god in a face that human eyes can bear."[9]

O'Neill recognized two fundamental uses for masks in the modernist theatre, both of which are evident in his work with the ETI: "One's outer life passes in a solitude haunted by the masks of others; one's inner life passes in a solitude hounded by the masks of oneself."[10] The first is evident in the masked Fifth Avenue crowd of *The Hairy Ape*, and epitomized in *Lazarus Laughed*, which has the most elaborate system of masks in all of O'Neill's work. On the one hand, O'Neill sought to make the crowd in *Lazarus* an image of all humanity. His stage directions call for forty-nine different masks among the crowd in each scene, representing seven periods of life from boyhood or girlhood to old age, and, within each age group, seven different masks of "*general types of character*," including: "*the Simple, Ignorant; the Happy, Eager; the Self-Tortured, Introspective; the Proud, Self-Reliant; the Servile, Hypocritical; the Revengeful, Cruel; the Sorrowful, Resigned.*"[11] As the scene shifts from Bethany to Athens to Rome, new sets of masks are called for, exhibiting the ethnic characteristics of the place. In masking the crowds for this play, O'Neill was "visualizing an effect that, intensified by dramatic lighting, would give an audience visually the sense of the Crowd, not as a random collection of individuals, but as a collective whole, an entity." When the Crowd speaks, he "wanted an audience to hear the voice of Crowd mind, Crowd emotion, as one voice of a body composed of, but quite distinct from, its parts."[12]

On the other hand, O'Neill thought the whole "new psychological insight into human cause and effect but a study in masks, an exercise in unmasking," impressing "the idea of mask as a symbol of inner reality upon all intelligent people of today."[13] The fullest theatrical expression of this idea, of course, is *The Great God Brown*, which Macgowan claimed was the first "play of modern life to use masks at all to any extent" and the first play "in which masks have ever been used to dramatize changes and conflicts in character."[14] In *Brown*, the masks serve the function of psychological masking and unmasking that O'Neill alluded to. As Macgowan put it,

"O'Neill uses the naked face and the masked face to picture the conflict between inner character and the distortions which outer life thrusts upon it." Beyond this obvious use, however, the masks take on a power that is detailed in Macgowan's *Masks and Demons* and suggested in his program note for the play. O'Neill, he wrote, "goes on to use the mask as a means of dramatizing a transfer of personality from one man to another" when Bill Brown steals Dion Anthony's mask in order to inhabit his identity after he kills him. Macgowan hints at the spiritual depths of this use of the mask in his reference to the use of the mask by "primitive peoples" for demonic possession: "The skull or the mask of a dead man grips his soul, and whoever puts it on must be ready to have that soul enter into his body."[15] This happens to Bill Brown when he takes on Dion Anthony's mask.

In *The Great God Brown*, masks themselves also have an animating spirit apart from the character, so that the removal of the mask often suggests a literal splitting into two people that can be deeply disturbing to view in its physical manifestation on stage. In Act 2, scene 2, Dion reads aloud from the *Imitation of Christ* to his mask, which is lying on the table. In Act 3, scene 2, Brown lays his own mask, that of the self-assured, successful businessman, on the desk next to the cynical mask of Dion that he has stolen and addresses a long monologue to Dion's mask, at one point gesturing as if he were going to strangle the mask, and then reaching out "*for the mask of Dion like a dope fiend after a drug. As soon as he holds it, he seems to gain strength.*"[16] In Act 4, scene 1, Bill stands with one hand on each of the masks, hesitating between the two identities he wants to assume, while the spectators see that "*his real face is now sick, ghastly, tortured, hollow-cheeked and feverish-eyed*" (525), embodying the anguish of his spiritual struggle. It is hard to imagine going beyond the different scenic complexities of *Brown* and *Lazarus* in the use of physical masks, and so it is no surprise to find O'Neill thinking of *Strange Interlude* as "an attempt at the new masked psychological drama ... without masks"[17] and dropping his earlier idea to use physical masks in *Mourning Becomes Electra* in favor of the "mask-like" faces of the Mannons. He did say a few years after the first production that he would "like to see *Mourning Becomes Electra* done entirely with masks, now that I can view it solely as a psychological play, quite removed from the confusing preoccupations the Classical derivation of its plot once caused me."[18]

Another preoccupation of the ETI was its aim to produce its own version of the total theatre advocated by Edward Gordon Craig and Max Reinhardt, by whom Jones and Macgowan were deeply influenced.

Making a clear distinction between the Provincetown Players, also known as the Playwright's Theater, and the theatre under the management of the Triumvirate of Macgowan, Jones, and O'Neill, Macgowan wrote that the Provincetown Playhouse and the Greenwich Village Theater were "dedicated to the art of the whole theater and not to the art of the playwright alone."[19] Robert Edmond Jones wrote that, in contrast to the thinking of the previous generation, when plays "were conceived for the most part in terms of painting," the theatre artists of the current generation, under "the influence of the continent . . . have arrived at the 'plastic' theater. The director of today often thinks in terms of sculpture and arranges his actors in powerfully expressive groups as a sculptor might wish to arrange them. The playwright sees his characters in the round. The scene-designer models with light."[20]

Writing to Macgowan about the plans for a production of *Lazarus Laughed* that never materialized, O'Neill insisted that it "be made plain on the program – this is *important* to me! – that masks, chorus, etc. are all in my script, that they are in my design of this play for an imaginative theater. I want to be known as having done this, for better or worse, so there can be no mistake in people's minds as to the materials I work with."[21] This was followed by a reference to the "confusion" surrounding "Bobby's house" in the set for *Desire Under the Elms*, a reminder that the idea for the simultaneous staging in that play, the set for the house which enabled the shift from kitchen to bedroom to parlor to be made instantaneously, was O'Neill's and was indicated in his preliminary drawings for the play. Jones had developed the idea in his design and been credited with innovative staging that changed the nature of the play. O'Neill wanted it clear that the conception for a piece of total theatre could as naturally come from the playwright as from the theatre artists with whom he collaborated.

The Theatre Guild

The Washington Square Players (WSP), forerunner of the Provincetown Players, disbanded in 1918, to be reorganized after the war into the Theatre Guild, the most prolific producer of literary drama in the history of the United States, operating successfully from 1919 until 1950. Just as the WSP had served the founders of the Provincetown Players as a model, the Guild, established in 1919, served in some ways as a model for the ETI. Unlike the earlier organizations, it was not democratic, but was run from the top down by a board of directors, including playwright and lawyer Lawrence Langner, director Philip Moeller, play reader Theresa Helburn, designer Lee Simonson, actor Helen Westley, and banker Maurice Wertheim. The new organization signaled the Guild's determination to be a professional producing organization rather than an amateur art theatre, but one that produced the best modern plays with the highest artistic standards in production. They were happy to produce both European and American plays that met their standards, and to help promising American playwrights along, as when they opened their Garrick Theater to matinee performances of *The Verge* in 1921. During their first three seasons, the Guild produced literary but safe playwrights like Shaw, Strindberg, Tolstoy, Andreyev, St. John Ervine, David Pinski, A. A. Milne, Ferenc Molnar, and Arnold Bennett. The success of the Provincetown's experimental productions, particularly *The Emperor Jones* and *The Hairy Ape*, had a clear influence on the Guild. This can be seen most immediately in the one-act plays that Lawrence Langner himself had produced at the Provincetown. In 1919, he wrote *Pie*, a realistic play in which a bohemian writer is seduced into domesticity by the quality of his cook's pastry.[22] In November, 1920, his *Matinata* was produced as the curtain-raiser for *The Emperor Jones*. Like *Aria da Capo*, it is a modern harlequinade. In it Harlequin tries to lure Columbine away from her bohemian life with Pierrot, who is a writer, with promises of a prosperous and stable life, but fails.[23] It seems that Langner himself was being seduced by the modernist theatre.

After the success of *The Hairy Ape* in January, 1922, and the subsequent discussion of expressionism in the press and the middle-brow magazines, the Theatre Guild moved quickly to include the new drama in its repertoire. In May of 1922, the Theatre Guild produced Kaiser's *From Morn to Midnight*. In the following season, it introduced Karel Čapek's *R. U. R.* to the New York stage, and premiered Elmer Rice's *The Adding Machine*, the most "American" of the expressionist plays. These were followed in the next two seasons by Ernst Toller's *Man and the Masses* (April, 1924) and John Howard Lawson's *Processional* (January, 1925). Set among plays by Ibsen, Shaw, Galsworthy, Sidney Howard, and Rogers and Hart in the Guild's season, these plays now took on an air of middle-brow respectability, and expressionism became a technique of the mainstream theatre rather than an avant-garde shocker. It was used seriously and effectively by former Provincetowner Sophie Treadwell in *Machinal* (1928) and again by Elmer Rice in *The Subway* (1929). It also quickly became the target of parody in the hands of George S. Kaufman and Marc Connelly in *Beggar on Horseback* (1924), and from then on was freely used, often for humorous purposes, in theatre, film, and television.

After the Triumvirate broke down in 1926, Langner worked hard to bring O'Neill to the Theatre Guild, which he managed to do by agreeing to produce the expensive *Marco Millions* (January, 1928) as well as *Strange Interlude* (January, 1928), which he was very eager to get. *Marco*, like *Lazarus*, is a work conceived as total theatre, which requires a full integration of all of the elements of the theatre and a full collaboration among the artists to be successful. The Theatre Guild production, directed by Rouben Mamoulian and designed by Lee Simonson, with Alfred Lunt in the lead role, was a qualified success, both artistically and financially.[24] *Strange Interlude*, however, which Langner judged "one of the greatest plays of all time," repaid his confidence.[25] This play, in which O'Neill refined his conception of masks as a vehicle for the revelation of the character's "inner thoughts" into the stylized asides that he called the "*Interlude*" technique," is the most significant achievement of American modernist playwriting and the most original of O'Neill's modernist works. Interestingly, Macgowan had predicted O'Neill's dialogic innovation in *The Theatre of Tomorrow* (1921). Writing about the "form of the future" in the modern theatre, he predicted that

> the soliloquy will return again as a natural and proper revelation of the mind of a character. Even the aside may redevelop as a deliberate piece of theatricalism. It will not be the slovenly device of a playwright for telling us something that he is too lazy or inexpert to impart in any other way, but a frank and open intercourse between the actor and his audience, a reaffirmation that this is a play which is being acted, a remarkable game between these two.[26]

It was the mutual understanding of what the modern theatre was and what it was trying to do that was responsible for the startling agreement between critic and playwright here. In a sense, O'Neill's collaboration with Macgowan and Jones came to fruition in his work with the Theatre Guild and director Philip Moeller and designer Lee Simonson, as well as Jones. His productions with the Guild also included the expressionist *Dynamo* (1929) and *Mourning Becomes Electra* (1931).

Diaspora

The various lines of development modernism took in the theatre that felt the impact of O'Neill and the Provincetown can be seen in the work of three of the second-generation playwrights whose plays were produced at the Greenwich Village Theater and at the Provincetown Playhouse under the aegis of the ETI: Edmund Wilson's *The Crime in the Whistler Room* (Provincetown Playhouse, October, 1924), Stark Young's *The Saint* (Greenwich Village, October, 1924), and e. e. cummings's *Him* (Provincetown Playhouse, April, 1928). Edmund Wilson, a classmate and friend of F. Scott Fitzgerald's at Princeton, was already making his way as a critic when he began his association with the Provincetown through Edna Millay, with whom he was romantically involved in the early 1920s. His real ambition was to be a successful novelist and playwright, and *The Crime in the Whistler Room* was the first of his plays to be produced. Its technique is that of a straightforward expressionist dream play. Its opening scene suggests sociologically leaning realism. A young woman, Elizabeth ("Bill") McGee is being made the object of charitable attention by the "old-money" Streetfield family, who are having her stay with them while she learns the etiquette of American bourgeois living and is tutored for Vassar's entrance exam. The burning question of the Streetfields' lives is whether a gate-leg table should be left against the wall, where it balances a Whistler etching aesthetically, or moved to the center of the room, where it will be more useful. Bill has fallen in love and become pregnant by a rather wild and irresponsible young writer named Simon Delacy, who is modeled on Scott Fitzgerald.

After setting up the situation and establishing the characters realistically, Wilson has Bill fall asleep, and dream an expressionist dream, in which, a program note clarified, "the dramatist has tried to stick close to the [psychological] processes of the dream": "it is the business of the first scene to provide characters, ideas, even phrases, for the mind of the heroine to make over into sharp, contrasting images in her dream. The special problem of the playwright in working out this dream-technique has been to escape equally from the literal and the obscure, and to make his play live in a world of both allusion and illusion."[27] The scenes of the dream begin with a long, dark corridor, down which Bill, in a waitress's uniform, is trying to escape with a package in which a guard accuses her of carrying her baby. It shifts to the edge of a forest, where Bill sits in a waitress's uniform, watching people in evening dress party to "*the strains of The Sheik – thrilling, heady and somehow sinister*" (41). In the most famous scene of the play, the partiers leave, and a wolf's howling, associated with Bill's fears about Simon, is heard:

> *The tree-trunks seem to prolong themselves upward as if Bill were sinking into the earth. Then, against a background entirely black, appears on the right*

Figure 10. Cleon Throckmorton's drawing for *The Crime in the Whistler Room.*

a high narrow door opening out on a sky, white and sheer, which might be the infinitude of space, and framing the silhouette of a thin oldish man on a high stool behind a high desk. The desk stands between him and us and he is beating a Devil's Tattoo on it with his fingers, but he is gazing out through the door: his profile seems turned away. Bill stands working at an enormous blackboard covered with very large chalked figures: she is trying to balance an equation. The music is still heard playing quite loudly as at the end of the scene before.[28]

Bill is trying to make her side of the equation balance with that of a former boyfriend who loved her more than she did him. She frets that she can't make "Simon's side balance with my side! I can't find out the value of X... Won't you tell me the value of X that makes the equations come out all right?" (48). Unable to find it, she goes to the Streetfield living room, where the family is sneering at her fast-talking father's attempt to amuse them with a magic act. He is dragged away by policemen, and Bill is accused of killing Schuyler Streetfield, a character who is a parody of

Henry Adams. She says, "we killed him so that we could live" (64), and is accused by the family of being horrid and ill-bred, but the supposedly dead Schuyler goes on to give a long monologue about his place in history. Pressed by the Streetfields to study for college, she rebels, saying "I *won't* be a college girl! And I *won't* be a waitress" (68). The final scene of her dream is a tranquil room by the sea where she is living happily-ever-after with Simon and her child. At the end of the play, the scene returns to reality and the Streetfield living room. After trying unsuccessfully to get Bill to have an abortion, Simon becomes reconciled to the idea of marriage and a baby, saying "Farewell! house of starvation and decay! We leave you for a house of our own!" (83). The play ends with the Streetfields admiring their Whistler. Thus Wilson combines what is essentially a romantic drama with some social commentary and a dream sequence that depicts his vision of Bill's unconscious working out of her life questions.

In *The Saint*, Stark Young, a veteran theatre critic and former professor of literature who had directed O'Neill's *Welded* in March of 1924, made it clear that he aimed to create the kind of total theatre that the Triumvirate sought in its productions. In his Preface to the published play he wrote, "I have always tried to create into every part and element making up the play a statement of the essential idea in terms of that part."[29] The theme of the play as he stated it was "continuity, going on, the long line of the soul's days that makes life possible to bear" (9). It enacts the experience of Valdez, a young seminarian in the Southwestern town of Las Flores, who falls in love with Marietta, a member of a traveling show called Thompson's Variety. Torn between his devotion to the Virgin Mary and his passion for Marietta, Valdez leaves the seminary and joins the show, where he makes a great success with his Charlie Chaplin impersonation. Marietta, however, is disappointed in him as a lover, and eventually runs away with the resident knife-thrower, ending up in Las Flores. Valdez pursues them there with the idea of shooting Marietta, but decides it isn't worth it. Watching a religious procession pass by, he finds he no longer feels a devotion to the Blessed Virgin, but shifts instead to the statue of a bleeding Jesus: "*The tragic figure of the cruelty of life and death, the pain, the sense of time and the earth of the dream, the rapture, the silence and pause following the vision that has been seen*" (138). Finding in this image the courage to face life, Valdez decides not to go back to the seminary, but turns his face toward the world and more of human experience.

Young wrote that his intention was to carry "one man's life from one spot in its course to another, passionately and grotesquely filled with struggle, with the wings of his soul and the flight of his blood, the clutter and fire of the world around him, the old forces of life within him, from one spot in his course to another, never to an end but always going on" (9). The theme of continuity was to extend "into the motifs and appearances of the play. It is stated in the procession going past, with that figure of the eternal mother and the pale body of that dead young man, divine dreamer, images going on forever through time and the world" (9). It is also stated "in that stream of music through the streets; I want the whole play to move in music and in the rumor and memory of the earth" (9). Although the play is not expressionist, Young made it clear that "technically the intention in *The Saint* is never realistic. It never intends to reproduce the sheer surface of life but intends to find, in the region of the real, such words and acts as will express and embody in some concentrated and receivable form the life behind them" (11). He makes it clear that some of his characters are to be seen as "grotesques." American Pigeons, who has a pigeon act in the show, is "*a tragic grotesque, she is one of those machines [?] in whom life is consumed by that which it is nourished by . . . she appears as a distorted mask of her own intensity and rightness*" (10). The show's owner Tip Thomson is a big man with a ruddy face and a Texas drawl, but "*the streak of an artist in him breaks out in two spots: a huge ring with a Mexican opal and instead of a belt a striped cravat about his waist . . . essentially, however, Tip is a grotesque, as Pigeons is: he is a mask under which life moves, a rough cast above a tender, burly, vain creature within*" (52). In characters like these, precursors of the characters in the later plays of Tennessee Williams, for example, can be seen elements of the modernist theatre that would blossom after World War II, which is called absurdist and postmodern.

The most ambitiously modernist of all the plays of the ETI was the play that caused the last critical controversy at the Provincetown Playhouse, e. e. cummings's *Him*. Cummings's play is a piece of pure non-representational theatre in every element. His program note for the production included this "warning": "Him *isn't a comedy or a tragedy or a farce or a melodrama or a revue or an operetta or a moving picture or any other convenient excuse for 'going to the theatre' – in fact, it's a PLAY, so let it PLAY; and because you are here, let it PLAY with you . . . DON'T TRY TO UNDERSTAND IT, LET IT TRY TO UNDERSTAND YOU.*"[30] The play, in twenty-one scenes, touches realism and expressionism occasionally, but is not bound by the conventions of either one. It has a frame story, in which the young writer Him is trying to write a play, but is unable to do so, coming to understand that his inability to write is tied up with his inability to solve the complex problem of his love relationship with Me, a young woman who has another lover besides Him, and can't decide between them. The staging is never realistic. The play begins with a scene in which there is "*a flat surface upon which is painted a DOCTOR anaesthetizing a WOMAN. In this picture there are two holes corresponding to the heads of the physician and of the patient, and through these holes protrude the living heads of a man and of a woman. Facing this picture, with their backs to the audience, three withered female FIGURES are rocking in rocking chairs and knitting.*"[31]

The woman in the carnival picture is Me, which provides the suggestion that the play might be her hallucination under the anaesthesia. The doctor shows up in various other roles, including that of a patent medicine barker. The three female figures, images of the Fates who are at times called the Miss Weirds, appear at intervals throughout the play, often in their rocking chairs on a bare stage. Their dialogue is in a mode that would be called absurdist after 1950. For example:

> SECOND: I can sympathise with you, my dear. All my children were killed in the great war.
> FIRST: That's perfectly marvelous! How many did you have?
> SECOND: At one time I had over eighty boys.
> THIRD: Boys are the naughtiest little creatures – didn't you find them a bother?
> SECOND: Not a bit, I used to keep mine out on the fire-escape.
> FIRST: Male or female?
> SECOND: Female, so my husband says. (17–18)

The other major set is a room with three visible walls and an invisible wall facing the audience. This set appears four times, and each time, the room is revolved so that a different wall becomes the invisible one. This room is the site for the scenes in which Me and Him discuss their relationship and his inability to write his play. In scene 2, the first time this set appears, the wall with a mirror is the invisible wall, and Me spends a good deal of time looking out into the audience as if into the mirror. In a later scene Him says, "this play of mine is all about mirrors" and the hero is "the sort of a man – who is writing a play about a man who is writing a sort of a play . . . this hero is called 'Mr. O'Him, the Man in the Mirror'" (30). The heroine, he says, "lives over there – (*points to mirror*) . . . Me, the beautiful mistress of the extraordinary Mr. O'Him" (30).

In Act 2, the curtain is raised on a bare, dark stage, and in a scene that anticipates Samuel Beckett, "*the action or content of Scene 1 consists of the curtain's rising, of its absence for one minute and of its falling. Darkness*" (35). The dialogue of the unseen characters follows:

VOICE OF ME: Was that an accident? Or a scene?
VOICE OF HIM: Both I trust.
VOICE OF ME: Did it really mean something?
VOICE OF HIM: It meant nothing, or rather: death.
VOICE OF ME: Oh, I see.
VOICE OF HIM: This is the Other Play.
VOICE OF ME: By Mr. O'Him?
VOICE OF HIM: – The Man in the Mirror.
VOICE OF ME: But tell me, what's this Other Play all about?
VOICE OF HIM: About? It's about anything you like, about nothing and something and everything, about blood and thunder and love and death – in fact, about as much as you can stand.
(35)

A series of scenes in a number of theatrical styles follow. The Doctor from the first scene gives a long monologue as a peddler of patent medicine to cure "cinderella." There is a parody of *The Great God Brown* with two characters named Will and Bill and much play with masks. There is an expressionist scene in which an Englishman in a top hat lugs around a trunk that holds his unconscious. There is a parody of the African American folk play that was having a good deal of popularity in the 1920s, with Dubose and Dorothy Heyward's *Porgy*, produced by the Theatre Guild in 1927 and Paul Green's *In Abraham's Bosom*, a Pulitzer Prize-winner that was produced by the ETI in 1926. There is a parody of the lightly satirical plays in which historical figures behave like contemporary men and women, done by the Provincetown Players in works like John Mosher's *Sauce for the Emperor* (1916) and Harry Kemp's *The Prodigal Son* (1916), and enjoying a vogue in the 1920s with the revival of Shaw's *Caesar and Cleopatra* by the Guild in 1925 and Robert Sherwood's huge hit, *The Road to Rome* (1927). There is a long scene set in a French restaurant with grotesque American tourists. Finally, there is the climactic scene depicting the freak show at a carnival in which the Doctor is the carnie barker and the characters from the previous scenes are the crowd. The scene ends with the three Miss Weirds saying disgustedly and in unison, "It's all done with mirrors" (144). The final scene returns the action to the three-walled room as it first appeared, with Me and Him occupying the same positions as when the room went dark. Me tells Him that she has been thinking about the room, and has discovered it only has three walls. Him looks about in astonishment and starts to count the walls. When he gets to three, he points to the audience through the invisible wall and says, "what do you see there?" Me responds, "People."

HIM: (*Starts*): What sort of people?
ME: Real people. And do you know what they're doing?
HIM: (*Stares at her*): What are they doing?
ME: (*Walking slowly upstage toward the door*): They're pretending that this room and you and I are real. (*At the door, turning, faces the audience*)
HIM: (*Standing in the middle of the room, whispers*): I wish I could believe this.
ME (*Smiles, shaking her head*): You can't.
HIM: (*Staring at the invisible wall*): Why?
ME: Because this is true. (145)

In raising these issues about the theatre itself, cummings was going beyond the presentational aim of most modernist theatre – to break out of the representational conventions of realism and present the audience with a performance that did not claim to be anything but itself. By playing with the tropes of the mirror and the wall, cummings was raising issues about the nature of theatre and of representation. In the end he raises doubts about the very possibility of having theatre that is not representational in some sense. The wildest of expressionist scenes, after all, mirrors the imagination of the playwright, if nothing else. In raising these kinds of questions, cummings lost most of the New York theatre critics, who confessed themselves bewildered, and mostly annoyed, by the play. Alexander Woollcott called it "fatiguing, pretentious and empty." Percy Hammond reported in the New York *Herald Tribune* that "consultation with Mr. [George Jean] Nathan, Mr. [Burns] Mantle, Mr. [Walter] Winchell and other keen clairvoyants of the drama revealed a similar state of bewilderment, though all of them have studied the play with their usual thoroughness."[32] A number of friends of the Provincetown and of cummings came to the play's defense in the newspapers and magazines, however, including Conrad Aiken, Edmund Wilson, and Stark Young in *The New Republic* and writers like John Dos Passos, Waldo Frank, and Genevieve Taggard in the newspapers. The production had been a monumental task for the Provincetown Playhouse. *Him*'s 105 parts were played by 30 actors, who also had to act as stagehands in order to manage the scenery for the play's 21 scenes. The production and the controversy brought a renewed sense of excitement about the experimental theatre to the ETI and a new respect for its director, Jimmy Light, although the momentum was not enough to forestall the closing of the theatre in 1929, just months after the stock market crash that began the Great Depression.

None of these three writers, who received their first professional productions at the Provincetown Playhouse or the Greenwich Village Theater, was to have much of a career as a playwright. Cummings did not have another play produced. Stark Young had his play *The Colonnade* produced by the London Stage Society in 1925 and a translation of Chekhov's *The Seagull* produced by the Theatre Guild in 1938. Wilson had just one more of his plays, *The Little Blue Light*, produced in 1951, although he published two others along with *The Crime in the Whistler Room* in 1937. In other ways, however, each of them played a major role in the cultural development of American modernism. Wilson's widely read critical work, *Axel's Castle* (1931), brought the writing of Proust, Joyce, and Stein into the mainstream of American culture. His and Stark Young's criticism in magazines like *The New Republic*, *Theatre Arts Monthly*, and *The New Yorker* were to interpret modernist literature and theatre for a middle-brow audience for three decades. E. e. cummings, of course, became an enormously popular experimental poet, second only to Robert Frost in readership when he died in 1962. In relation to the Provincetown, their careers are much like those of the playwrights and artists who had preceded them, talented people who formed mutually productive artistic relationships with the Provincetown group for a few years, and then moved on with their careers, enriched by their interaction and collaboration with the other members of the group.

With the exception of O'Neill, the earliest playwrights of the Provincetown Players for the most part went back to their original artistic media, or on to other things. George Cram Cook died in Greece in 1924. Susan Glaspell had two plays produced after she left the Provincetown Players in 1922 to go to Greece with Cook, the Pulitzer Prize-winning *Alison's House* in 1930 and a collaboration with Norman Matson called *The Comic Artist* in 1933. Like Wilbur Steele, she went back to writing fiction, producing eight more novels, including *Ambrose Holt and Family* (1931) and *Judd Rankin's Daughter* (1945), as well as her hagiographic memoir of Cook, *The Road to the Temple* (1927). Like Alfred Kreymborg, Cleon Throckmorton, James Light, Mike Gold, and Eleanor Fitzgerald, however, Glaspell participated in the short-lived Federal Theatre Project, the

United States' only experiment with federally subsidized theatre, acting as Director of the Midwest Play Bureau.

Hutchins Hapgood produced no more plays after he resigned his active membership in the Players in 1917. Neith Boyce wrote a number of plays, several of which were full-length pieces intended for the Broadway theatre. In 1932, Robert Edmond Jones was working with her on a play called *The Faithful Lover*, which they hoped to place with Arthur Hopkins, Jed Harris or Kenneth Macgowan. Jones got as far as doing a set of costume sketches, but nothing came of it.[33] After John Reed and Louise Bryant went to Europe to cover World War I, Reed contributed one experimental play, *The Peace That Passeth Understanding: A Fantasy*, to the Players. Fittingly, Reed's last play was a "cartoon" parody of the Paris Peace Conference exposing the hollowness of Wilson's famous Fourteen Points. According to Edna Kenton, the cast was not listed on the program in order to "avoid possible court trouble."[34] Reed died in Moscow in 1920 and was given a hero's funeral, the only American to be buried next to the Kremlin wall.

Of the artists, Demuth went on to create visual images of the modernist theatre, including his "Study for a Poster Portrait: Eugene O'Neill" (1926) and his "Longhi on Broadway" (1928), both images of his friend O'Neill, in his poster art, some of the best-known images of American modernist painting.[35] After his split with the Players in 1917, Brör Nordfeldt moved to New Mexico, where he developed his neo-impressionist ideas in painting the landscape and images of Indian and Spanish American culture. William Zorach acknowledged the "great education" that he and Marguerite had received from their time with the Provincetown Players, "reading plays, making decisions, influencing people, rehearsing, painting scenery, and planning sets." Noting with pride that he "got to know the theater as well as I got to know painting and sculpture," he wrote that he and Marguerite had designed "some of the first modern and abstract plays ever put on in New York."[36] After their association with the Provincetown, the Zorachs went on to develop as modernist artists. William became a major American sculptor working in forms that were deeply influenced by the primitivism he had shared with the Players. Marguerite worked in several media, becoming famous for the designs in yarn that she called "embroidered tapestries." Her linoleum block carving of the setting for *The Game* (figure 3), used as a logo for the Players for years, is in the Smithsonian American Art Museum.[37] Of the other designers, Robert Edmond Jones became the preeminent modernist stage designer in the American theatre, the primary influence over the younger designers who flourished at mid-century, such as Lee Simonson, who became O'Neill's major designer at the Theatre Guild; Donald Oenslager, who had acted in Jones's production of *Desire Under the Elms* at the Greenwich Village Theater; and Jo Mielziner, Jones's student and assistant in the early 1920s. Jones's book, *The Dramatic Imagination: Reflections and Speculations on the Art of the Theater* (1941), would influence yet another generation of theatre artists who would become the major American designers at mid-century. Cleon Throckmorton went on from his work at the Provincetown to become a prolific designer in the Broadway theatre.

For the most part, the *Others* group continued to work in poetry after their association with the Provincetown and the Other Players. Maxwell Bodenheim wrote several novels as well as poetry, and became a well-known fixture of the Village, even as he descended into alcoholism and poverty. Wallace Stevens went on to become the most important American poet of high modernism. Although he never ventured into the theatre again, his work, as is evident in "The Comedian as the Letter C" and "Of Modern Poetry," is infused with theatrical metaphors that show the theatre's perennial importance to his imagination. Edna Millay quickly became the most famous American woman poet in the early part of the twentieth century. She moved away from the theatre in the 1920s, giving up acting, although she did adapt Ferenc Molnar's *Launzi* for Arthur Hopkins in 1923. Her dialogue poem *Conversation at Midnight* (1937) was produced as a play in 1964. After his performance in *Lima Beans*, William Carlos Williams became fascinated by the theatre. In his *Autobiography*, he confessed,

> I too wanted to have a play on that stage and wrote one calling for an improvised curtain made of newspaper with a flagpole sticking through the center of it over the first seats of the audience. At the start of the play the paper screen was ripped down by the actors and the play was on. A lascivious sort of action of some sort with players designated as Bright Young Men, etc., which Mattie Josephson said reminded him of Dekker or whoever it might be.

Unfortunately, "the whole piece disappeared."[38] Following this presentational work was what he called his "first small playlet in verse," an "important" piece called *The Old Apple Tree*.[39] In his autobiography, Williams accused Kreymborg of losing the manuscript for that play, as well as abandoning the bill they had planned to produce together in favor of putting on Edna Millay's *Aria da Capo*. There is confusion here, since Kreymborg put on *Two Slatterns and a King*, not *Aria da Capo*, but it is clear that something happened between the two in their plans for the theatre, for as Williams put it, "from that time on Kreymborg and I didn't get on so well."[40] Even this did not dampen Dr. Williams's enthusiasm for the theatre and his desire to have his plays produced, however. In his *Autobiography*, he tells of making an outdoor stage in his back yard in Paterson, New Jersey, with the hope of producing the plays he was writing. Discouraged by "an audience of uninvited kids and some grown ruffians egging them on from the driveway next door," Williams reluctantly abandoned the production effort.[41] This did not stop him from writing plays, however. His *Many Loves and Other Plays* (1961) contains five full-length plays that never saw professional production.

Of the *Others* group, it was Alfred Kreymborg who profited most from his work with the Provincetown, both artistically and financially. Having worked out the principles of his puppet theatre using human actors, he found in another Provincetowner, Remo Bufano, a resource for making his puppet theatre literal. Bufano, who played the Burgess in Kreymborg's *Vote the New Moon* and several other parts at the Provincetown, had his own puppet theatre in the Village. Under his tutelage, Kreymborg's wife Dorothy became a skilled puppeteer, and with the gift of a collapsible theatre and a set of puppets, Bufano enabled the Kreymborgs' tour of the Midwest and the West performing Alfred's plays and poems. Kreymborg published three volumes of plays, including his *Puppet Plays* (1923), with a preface by Gordon Craig. Djuna Barnes quickly developed as a modernist playwright to the point where she was ahead of the avant garde in the US. Her play *The Dove* was produced by the Manhattan Theater Club in 1926, but closed after just one performance. She submitted a play to the Triumvirate in 1923, which Eugene O'Neill told Kenneth Macgowan was "one of the finest pieces of work by an American in any line of writing. A real deep original play! It's too wordy maybe and marred by her old fault of the consciously bizarre & ultra-sophisticated in a few spots but as a whole it's corking stuff."[42] Nothing came of this, but she remained interested in the theatre, and wrote a regular column for *Theatre Guild Magazine* from 1929 to 1931. Barnes did her best-known work in fiction, notably the modernist classic *Nightwood* (1936). In many ways, however, her final autobiographical play, *The Antiphon* (1958), in which she at last comes to terms with her family history, may be seen as a culminating work. In 1995, *At the Root of the Stars*, a collection of sixteen of the one-act plays she first published in magazines and newspapers, was published by Sun & Moon Press. It demonstrates clearly the extent of her modernist experimentation with the theatre. It would be foolish to try to catalogue all of the ways in which the interaction of the many talented collaborators in the Provincetown experiment influenced American culture in the twentieth century. But to understand the extent of its impact, it is only necessary to consider the experimental work of a few of these artists.

Notes

1 The founding: myth and history

1. Robert Károly Sarlós, *Jig Cook and the Provincetown Players: Theatre in Ferment* (Amherst: University of Massachusetts Press, 1982) 9.
2. Helen Deutsch and Stella Hanau, *The Provincetown: A Story of the Theatre* (New York: Farrar & Rinehart, 1931) 7.
3. "Many Literary Lights Among the Provincetown Players," *Boston (Sunday) Post* September 10, 1916: 44.
4. Neith Boyce to "her father" 17 July, 1915, quoted in Louis Sheaffer, *O'Neill: Son and Playwright* (Boston: Little, Brown, 1968) 343.
5. Sarlós, *Jig Cook* 1.
6. Ibid. 14.
7. Ibid. 6, 4–5.
8. Sheldon Cheney, *The Art Theatre*. 1917; Rev. Edn. (New York: Alfred A. Knopf, 1925) 43.
9. Sheaffer, *O'Neill: Son and Playwright* 205.
10. Robert A. Rosenstone, *Romantic Revolutionary: A Biography of John Reed* (New York: Knopf, 1975) 84.
11. Susan Glaspell, *The Road to the Temple* (New York: Frederick A. Stokes, 1927) 218.
12. Floyd Dell, *Homecoming, An Autobiography* (New York: Farrar and Rinehart, 1933) 231.
13. "Constitution of the Provincetown Players" in "Minute Book of the Provincetown Players, Inc." From September 4, 1916, to November 8, 1923, 11, Billy Rose Theatre Collection, New York Public Library for the Performing Arts (microfilm).
14. Linda Nochlin, "The Paterson Strike Pageant of 1913," *Art in America* 52 (May–June, 1974): 68.
15. Ibid. 67.
16. Ibid. 68.
17. Martin Green, *New York 1913: The Armory Show and the Paterson Strike Pageant* (New York: Scribner, 1988) 164.
18. Rosenstone 249.
19. Glaspell, *Road to the Temple* 250.
20. "Pageant of the Paterson Strike," *Survey Midmonthly* 30 (June 28, 1913): 428.

21. Mabel Dodge Luhan, *Movers and Shakers* (New York: Harcourt Brace, 1936) 204.
22. Quoted in Nochlin 66.
23. Keith Norton Richwine, "The Liberal Club: Bohemia and the Resurgence in Greenwich Village, 1912–1918." PhD diss. University of Pennsylvania, 1968 xxxii.
24. Dell, *Homecoming* 247–248.
25. Ibid. 250.
26. Steven Watson, *Strange Bedfellows: The First American Avant-Garde* (New York: Abbeville Press, 1991) 153–154.
27. Dell, *Homecoming* 262, 261.
28. Lawrence Langner, *The Magic Curtain* (New York: E. P. Dutton, 1951) 92.
29. Ibid. 99.
30. Ibid. 94.
31. Barbara Ozieblo, *Susan Glaspell: A Critical Biography* (Chapel Hill: University of North Carolina Press, 2000) 67. See Glaspell, *Road to the Temple* 250–251.
32. For details of these negotiations, see Leona Rust Egan, *Provincetown as a Stage: Provincetown, the Provincetown Players, and the Discovery of Eugene O'Neill* (Orleans, MA: Parnassus, 1994) 122.
33. Sarlós, *Jig Cook* 17.
34. Sheaffer, *O'Neill: Son and Playwright* 346. Bryant was living with Jack Reed at the time, but not yet married to him.
35. Glaspell, *Road to the Temple* 254.
36. Eastman wrote in his autobiography: "At the first meeting I was elected to a committee to draft a constitution, but I saw other committees and boards of directors looming behind it. Recalling my boyhood technique of pretending to be impractical, I failed to remember when the committee was to meet. Jack Reed brought the draft to show me, and my contribution consisted of saying, 'I think that's swell!'" (*Enjoyment of Living* [New York: Harper, 1948] 564).
37. "Constitution of the Provincetown Players" 9.
38. "'Resolutions' ordered spread upon the minutes as the sense of the meeting of Thursday, Sept. 5, 1916 (In lieu of by-laws)," "Minute Book of the Provincetown Players, Inc." 11–12.
39. Dell, *Homecoming* 251–252.
40. Langner, *Magic Curtain* 93.
41. Edna Kenton, *The Provincetown Players and the Playwrights' Theatre 1915–1922*, ed. Travis Bogard and Jackson R. Bryer (Jefferson, NC: McFarland, 2004) 43–44. It is unlikely that Glaspell, who took a "sabbatical" in Provincetown during the 1919–1920 season to work on her own writing, read all the plays.
42. Sarlós, *Jig Cook* 71.
43. Alfred Kreymborg, *Troubadour: An Autobiography* (New York: Liveright, 1925) 312.
44. Actor Mary Pyne wrote to Mary Heaton Vorse in September of 1916 about the renovation activities on Macdougal Street: "Jig and Nordfeldt are working like galley slaves – painting, hanging beams, sawing wood." Vorse Papers, Wayne State University, quoted in Egan 221–223.
45. Cheryl Black, *The Women of Provincetown, 1915–1922* (Tuscaloosa: University of Alabama Press, 2002) 37.
46. Ibid. 35.

47. Nina Moise to Edna Kenton, October 16, 1933, Edna Kenton Papers, Fales Library, New York University.
48. Kenton, *Provincetown Players* 54–55.
49. Ozieblo, *Susan Glaspell* 134.
50. Glaspell, *Road to the Temple* 262.
51. Cook wrote to Susan Glaspell on May 24, 1918, complaining that his contribution to the Players had been ignored in Edna Kenton's three-column article in the *Boston Transcript* (George Cram Cook Papers, Berg Collection, New York Public Library).
52. Glaspell, *Road to the Temple* 276–277.
53. Arthur Wertheim, *The New York Little Renaissance: Iconoclasm, Modernism, and Nationalism in American Culture, 1908–1917* (New York University Press, 1976) 243.
54. Allan Antliff, *Anarchist Modernism: Art, Politics, and the First American Avant-Garde* (University of Chicago Press, 2001) 99.
55. Daniel Joseph Singal, "Toward a Definition of American Modernism," *American Quarterly* 39.1 (Spring 1987): 16–17.
56. Henry F. May, *The End of American Innocence: The First Years of Our Own Time, 1912–1917* (New York: Knopf, 1959) 142.
57. Ibid.
58. Rosenstone 85. The article is "Reminiscence," *The American Magazine* 73 (November, 1911): 16.
59. Hutchins Hapgood, *A Victorian in the Modern World* (New York: Harcourt Brace, 1930) 70.
60. Neith Boyce, *The Modern World of Neith Boyce: Autobiography and Diaries*. Ed. Carol DeBoer-Langworthy (Albuquerque: University of New Mexico Press, 2003) 185.
61. Antliff 110.
62. Singal, "Toward a Definition" 17–18.
63. Quoted in Daniel Aaron, *Writers on the Left: Episodes in American Literary Communism* (New York: Harcourt Brace, 1961) 38.
64. Quoted in Wertheim 34.
65. Max Eastman, *Enjoyment of Living* 564.
66. Black, *Women of Provincetown* 12.
67. Hapgood, *Victorian* 313.
68. Black, *Women of Provincetown* 11.
69. May 206.
70. David Weir, *Anarchy & Culture: The Aesthetic Politics of Modernism* (Amherst: University of Massachusetts Press, 1997) 185.
71. Dell, *Homecoming* 197.
72. Ibid. 197–198.
73. Quoted in Aaron 61.
74. Dell, *Homecoming* 150.
75. Glaspell, *Road to the Temple* 182.
76. Ibid. 204.
77. Ibid. 168.
78. Ibid. 271.

79. "The New Psychology and American Drama," in Adele Heller and Lois Rudnick, eds., *1915: The Cultural Moment* (New Brunswick, NJ: Rutgers University Press, 1991) 149.
80. Dell, *Homecoming* 150–151.
81. Glaspell, *Road to the Temple* 138.
82. Ibid. 223–224.
83. Ibid. 386.
84. Ibid. 224.
85. Ibid. 225.
86. Ibid. 252.
87. Ibid. 252–253.
88. Sarlós, *Jig Cook* 36.
89. Ibid.
90. Ibid.
91. Glaspell, *Road to the Temple* 191–192.
92. Ozieblo, *Susan Glaspell* 38.
93. Ibid. 47.
94. Ibid. 173.
95. Edna Kenton to Susan Glaspell, September 8, 1922, Harvard Theatre Collection, Houghton Library, Harvard University.
96. Mark W. Estrin, ed., *Conversations with Eugene O'Neill* (Jackson: University of Mississippi Press, 1990) 81.
97. Eugene O'Neill to Benjamin De Casseres, June 22, 1927 in Travis Bogard and Jackson R. Bryer, eds., *Selected Letters of Eugene O'Neill* (New Haven: Yale University Press, 1988) 246.
98. See Barrett H. Clark, *Eugene O'Neill: The Man and His Plays* (New York: McBride, 1929) 4 and Agnes Boulton, *Part of a Long Story* (London: Peter Davies, 1958) 61.
99. See Patrick Bridgwater, *Nietzsche in Anglosaxony: A Study of Nietzsche's Impact on English and American Literature* (Leicester University Press, 1972); Egil Törnqvist, "Nietzsche and O'Neill: a Study in Affinity," *Orbis Litterarum* 23 (1968): 97–126; Eric M. Levin, "Hidden Perspectivism: a Contemporary Nietzschean Approach to O'Neill's *Days without End*," *Journal of American Drama and Theatre* 10 (Fall 1998): 1–10; Gerhard Hoffman, "Eugene O'Neill: America's Nietzschean Playwright" in Manfred Putz, ed., *Nietzsche in American Literature and Thought* (Columbia, SC: Camden House, 1995) 197–221; Samuel A. Weiss, "O'Neill, Nietzsche, and Cows," *Modern Drama* 34 (December 1991): 494–498.
100. Hapgood, *Victorian* 67.
101. May 257.
102. Dell, *Homecoming* 170.
103. Quoted in Glaspell, *Road to the Temple* 35.
104. Weir 132.
105. Floyd Dell, *Intellectual Vagabondage: An Apology for the Intelligentsia* (New York: 1926) 113–114.
106. William Zorach to Marguerite Thompson [July, 1911] and Marguerite Thompson to William Zorach (July? 1911), Papers of William Zorach, Library of Congress.
107. Dell, *Homecoming* 91–92.

108. Ozieblo, *Susan Glaspell* 31, 44.
109. May 173.
110. Quoted in Glaspell, *Road to the Temple* 191.
111. Dell, *Homecoming* 150.
112. Glaspell, *Road to the Temple* 199.
113. Ibid.
114. May 173.
115. Quoted in Antliff 112.
116. "The American Reception of Psychoanalysis, 1908–1922," in Heller and Rudnick, *1915* 128.
117. Wertheim 71.
118. "Speaking of Psycho-analysis," *Vanity Fair* (December, 1914): 53.
119. See Max Eastman, "Exploring the Soul and Healing the Body," *Everybody's Magazine* 32 (1915): 741–750 and "Mr.–er–er–Oh! What's his Name!" *Everybody's Magazine* 33 (1915): 95–103.
120. Louis Sheaffer, *O'Neill: Son and Artist*. (New York: Paragon House, 1990) 82.
121. Hapgood, *Victorian* 383.
122. Ibid. 382–383.
123. Glaspell, *Road to the Temple* 250.
124. Matthews 149.
125. Dell, *Homecoming* 263.
126. Max Stirner, *The Ego and Its Own*, quoted in Antliff 76.
127. Quoted in Weir 14.
128. Weir 190.
129. Hapgood, *Victorian* 277–278.
130. Antliff 1.
131. Weir 8.
132. Antliff 47.
133. Weir 145–146.
134. Weir 157.
135. See "What Is Anarchism?," *New York Globe* October 14, 1911: 10; "The Insurgents in Art," *New York Globe* October 24, 1911: 6; "Authority in Art," *New York Globe* January 28, 1912: 10; "The Trend of the Time," *New York Globe*, March 12, 1912: 4; "Life at the Armory," *New York Globe*, February 17, 1913.
136. Hapgood, "Life at the Armory."
137. Antliff 34.
138. Quoted in Glaspell, *Road to the Temple* 185.
139. George Cram Cook, "Socialism the Issue in 1912," *The Masses* 4 (July, 1912): 7.
140. Rosenstone 107.
141. Black, *Women of Provincetown* 13.
142. Wertheim 108.
143. Black, *Women of Provincetown* 5.
144. Nancy F. Cott, *The Grounding of Modern Feminism* (New Haven: Yale University Press, 1982) 15.
145. Edna Kenton, "Feminism Will Give – Men More Fun, Women Greater Scope . . . ," *Delineator* 85 (July, 1914): 17.

146. Cott 15.
147. Quoted in Lois Rudnick, "The New Woman," in Heller and Rudnick 77.
148. Black 3.
149. Ibid. 27.
150. Ibid. 31.
151. Wertheim 80.
152. Ibid. 87.
153. Hapgood, *Victorian* 152.
154. Ibid.
155. Ellen Kay Trimberger, *Intimate Warriors: Portraits of a Modern Marriage 1899–1940* (New York: Feminist Press, 1991) 20.
156. Ozieblo, *Susan Glaspell* 173.
157. Trimberger 28.
158. William Zorach, *Art Is My Life: The Autobiography of William Zorach* (Cleveland: World, 1967) 189–190.
159. Gerhard Bach, "Susan Glaspell: Provincetown Playwright," *Great Lakes Review: A Journal of Midwest Culture* 4.2 (1978): 36.
160. Ibid. 35.
161. Ibid.
162. Ibid.
163. Ozieblo, *Susan Glaspell* 108.
164. Hapgood, *Victorian* 394.
165. Glaspell, *Road to the Temple* 248.
166. Wertheim 113.
167. Dell, *Homecoming* 238.
168. Hapgood, *Victorian* 341.
169. "*The Masses* and Modernism" in Heller and Rudnick 207.
170. Antliff 27.
171. *Provincetown Advocate*, September 17, 1914.
172. Mary Heaton Vorse, *Time and the Town: A Provincetown Chronicle* (1942; rpt. ed. Adele Heller; [New Brunswick: Rutgers, 1991]) 204.
173. George Cram Cook, *Change Your Style* in Heller and Rudnick 292.
174. Zorach 45, 47.
175. A. J. Philpott, "The Modernists," Boston *Globe*, August 9, 1915.
176. Marilyn Friedman Hoffman, *Marguerite and William Zorach, the Cubist Years: 1915–18* (Ex. Cat. Manchester, NH: Currier Gallery of Art, 1987) 39.
177. Ibid. 11.
178. Zorach 22.
179. Ibid. 33.
180. Ibid. 65.
181. Ibid. 66.
182. Marilyn Friedman Hoffman 6.
183. Ibid. 15.
184. Ibid. 23.
185. Ibid. 25–26.
186. Ibid. 22.

187. Quoted in Marilyn Friedman Hoffman 19.
188. Quoted in Marilyn Friedman Hoffman 19.
189. Zorach 55.
190. Ibid. 45.
191. Van Deren Coke, *Nordfeldt the Painter* (Albuquerque: University of New Mexico Press, 1972) 49.
192. Ibid. 29.
193. Ibid.
194. Zorach 23.
195. Andrew Carnduff Ritchie, *Charles Demuth* (New York: Museum of Modern Art, 1950) 8.
196. Ibid. 9.
197. Emily Farnham, *Charles Demuth: Behind a Laughing Mask* (Norman: University of Oklahoma Press, 1971) 81.
198. Langner, *Magic Curtain* 71.
199. Quoted in Ritchie 5.
200. Robin Jaffe Frank, *Charles Demuth Poster Portraits: 1923–1929* (New Haven: Yale University Art Gallery, 1994) 83.
201. Hapgood, *Victorian* 426–427.
202. Sheaffer, *O'Neill: Son and Playwright* 410–411; also see accounts in Farnham 107–108 and Boulton 78–83.

2 The first plays

1. Although most of the playlists put out by the Provincetown Players list only twelve plays during the two summer seasons, Robert Sarlós suggests that *Enemies* was also put on in the summer of 1916 before it was produced in New York at the Macdougal Street Playhouse in November (Robert Károly Sarlós, *Jig Cook and the Provincetown Players: Theatre in Ferment* [Amherst: University of Massachusetts Press, 1982] 27–28), and his case is backed up by the memory of Hutchins Hapgood (Hapgood, *A Victorian in the Modern World* [New York: Harcourt Brace, 1930] 395). I am not including the children's theatre project *Mother Carey's Chickens* in this analysis.
2. "The Provincetown Players' Experiments with Realism" in William Demastes, ed. *Realism and the American Dramatic Tradition* (Tuscaloosa: University of Alabama Press, 1996) 61–62.
3. Martin Bucco, *Wilbur Daniel Steele* (New York: Twayne, 1972) 17.
4. Steele was actually a distant cousin of Vorse's husband through his mother.
5. Leona Rust Egan, *Provincetown as a Stage: Provincetown, the Provincetown Players, and the Discovery of Eugene O'Neill* (Orleans, MA: Parnassus, 1994) 195.
6. Bucco 101.
7. Wilbur Daniel Steele, *"Not Smart": A Farce in One Act* in George Cram Cook and Frank Shay, eds., *The Provincetown Plays* (Cincinnati: Stewart Kidd, 1921) 249. Subsequent page references appear in the text.
8. Marius de Zayas, "How, When, and Why Modern Art Came to New York," *Arts Magazine* 54 (April, 1980): 109.

9. John Reed, *The Eternal Quadrangle: A Farce Adapted from the Wiener-Schnitzler*, in Barbara Ozieblo, ed., *The Provincetown Players: A Choice of the Shorter Works* (Sheffield Academic Press, 1994) 105. Subsequent page references appear in the text.
10. Mabel Dodge Luhan, *Movers and Shakers* (New York: Harcourt Brace, 1936) 356.
11. Ellen Kay Trimberger, *Intimate Warriors: Portraits of a Modern Marriage 1899–1940* (New York: Feminist Press, 1991) 22.
12. Barbara Ozieblo notes that an early version of the play was entitled *The Faithful Lover* (Ozieblo, *Provincetown Players* 63).
13. Neith Boyce, *Constancy*, in Ozieblo, *Provincetown Players* 55. Subsequent page references appear in the text.
14. Hapgood, *Victorian* 395.
15. *Enemies: A Play* in Cook and Shay 121. Subsequent page references appear in the text.
16. Hapgood, *Victorian* 395.
17. Susan Glaspell, *The Road to the Temple* (New York: Frederick A. Stokes, 1927) 250.
18. J. Ellen Gainor, *Susan Glaspell in Context: American Theater, Culture, and Politics, 1915–48* (Ann Arbor: University of Michigan Press, 2001) 26.
19. Floyd Dell, "Speaking of Psycho-analysis" Max Eastman, "Exploring the Soul and Healing the Body," *Everybody's Magazine* 32.6 (June, 1915): 741–750. See also, Max Eastman, "Mr.–er–er–Oh! What's His Name?" *Everybody's Magazine* 33.1 (July, 1915): 95–103.
20. Eastman, "Exploring" 750.
21. Ibid.
22. Susan Glaspell and George Cram Cook, *Suppressed Desires* in Ozieblo, *Provincetown Players* 39. Subsequent page references appear in the text.
23. Fred Matthews, "The New Psychology and American Drama" in Adele Heller and Lois Rudnick, eds., *1915: The Cultural Moment* (New Brunswick, NJ: Rutgers University Press, 1991) 151.
24. Gainor 34.
25. Ibid. 36.
26. George Cram Cook, *Change Your Style* in Heller and Rudnick 293. Subsequent page references appear in the text.
27. See "The Church and the Unemployed," *The Masses* 5 (April, 1914): 10–11; Max Eastman, "The Tannenbaum Crime," *The Masses* 5 (May, 1914): 6–8; Mabel Dodge Luhan, *Movers and Shakers* (New York: Harcourt Brace, 1936) 96–116; Arthur Wertheim, *The New York Little Renaissance: Iconoclasm, Modernism, and Nationalism in American Culture, 1908–1917* (New York University Press, 1976) 12; Heller and Rudnick 273.
28. Wilbur Daniel Steele, *Contemporaries: An Episode of the Church Raids* in Ozieblo, *Provincetown Players* 64. Subsequent page references appear in the text.
29. Glaspell, *Road to the Temple* 253–254.
30. Harry Kemp, "Out of Provincetown," *Theatre Magazine* 51 (April, 1930): 22.
31. Hapgood, *Victorian* 396.
32. Louis Sheaffer, *O'Neill: Son and Playwright* (Boston: Little, Brown, 1968) 278.
33. Eugene O'Neill, *Bound East for Cardiff* in *Complete Plays. 1913–1920*, ed. Travis Bogard (New York: Library of America, 1988) 187. Subsequent page references appear in the text.

34. Neith Boyce, *Winter's Night* in Frank Shay, *Fifty More Contemporary One-Act Plays* (New York: D. Appleton, 1932) 41. Subsequent page references appear in the text.
35. For Barlow's insightful analysis of *Winter's Night*, see Judith E. Barlow, "Susan's Sisters: the 'Other' Women Writers of the Provincetown Players" in Linda Ben-Zvi, ed., *Susan Glaspell: Essays on Her Theater and Fiction* (Ann Arbor: University of Michigan Press, 1995) 262–266. For an interesting treatment of the theme of creativity, see Nicholas F. Radel, "Provincetown Plays: Women Writers and O'Neill's American Intertext," *Essays in Theatre* 9 (1990): 31–43.
36. Glaspell, *Road to the Temple* 255.
37. Ibid. 256.
38. See Linda Ben-Zvi, "'Murder She Wrote': the Genesis of Susan Glaspell's *Trifles*" in Ben-Zvi, *Susan Glaspell* 19–48; Gainor, *Susan Glaspell* 37–60; Artem Lozynsky, "The Case of the Missing Canary: a New Look at Glaspell's *Trifles*," *Feminist Studies in English Literature* 7.2 (Winter, 2000): 141–158; Karen Alkalay-Gut, "Murder and Marriage: Another Look at *Trifles*," in Ben-Zvi, *Susan Glaspell* 71–81.
39. Susan Glaspell, *Trifles* in *Plays by Susan Glaspell*, ed. C. W. E. Bigsby (Cambridge University Press, 1987) 36. Subsequent page references appear in the text.
40. The figurative use of the preserves presents interesting interpretive questions in the context of Glaspell's use of metonymy in the play. The exploding preserves with their single intact jar of cherries certainly has sexual implications, much like those of the notorious red pickle dish in Edith Wharton's *Ethan Frome*, published just four years before the play was written. The intact cherries suggest that the Wrights' marriage has never been consummated. Although, considering the Wrights' childlessness, this might be read in a physical way, I would read it as an emotional reference in the context of Glaspell's figurative scheme. Minnie's essential identity has remained intact, not penetrated by the "icy wind" of John Wright's personality, the effect of which has been to freeze her to the point of exploding in the only emotion left to her – rage.
41. Gainor, *Susan Glaspell* 49.
42. Hapgood, *Victorian* 354.
43. Helen Deutsch and Stella Hanau, *The Provincetown: A Story of the Theatre* (New York: Farrar & Rinehart, 1931) 11 and Gerhard Bach, "Susan Glaspell: Provincetown Playwright," *Great Lakes Review: A Journal of Midwest Culture* 4.2 (1978): 35.
44. Sarlós, *Jig Cook* 21.
45. Robert A. Rosenstone, *Romantic Revolutionary: A Biography of John Reed* (New York: Knopf, 1975) 122.
46. Daniel Aaron, *Writers on the Left: Episodes in American Literary Communism* (New York: Harcourt Brace, 1961) 38.
47. *Freedom: A Prison Play* in Ozieblo, *Provincetown Players* 79. Subsequent page references appear in the text.
48. Olivia Coolidge, *Eugene O'Neill* (New York: Scribner, 1966) 108.
49. Eugene O'Neill, *Thirst* in *Complete Plays. 1913–1920*, 44. Subsequent page references appear in the text.
50. See, for example, Crane's well-known story "The Open Boat" and the poem "A Man Adrift on a Slim Spar."

51. Deutsch and Hanau 15.
52. Arthur and Barbara Gelb, *O'Neill: Life with Monte Cristo* (New York: Applause, 2000) 573.
53. Barrett H. Clark, *Eugene O'Neill: The Man and His Plays* (New York: McBride, 1929) 69.
54. Cheryl Black, *The Women of Provincetown, 1915–1922* (Tuscaloosa: University of Alabama Press, 2002) 36.
55. Quoted in Black, *Women of Provincetown* 36.
56. Barbara Gelb, *So Short a Time: A Biography of John Reed and Louise Bryant* (New York: Norton, 1973) 89.
57. William Zorach, *Art Is My Life: The Autobiography of William Zorach* (Cleveland: World, 1967) 45–46.
58. Louise Bryant, *The Game* in Frank Shay, ed., *The Provincetown Plays: First Series* (New York: F. Shay, 1916) 28. Subsequent page references appear in the text.
59. "Russian Ballet Modified," *New York Times*, January 26, 1916: 12.
60. Zorach 46.
61. Sarlós, *Jig Cook* 24–25.
62. Zorach 46.
63. Black, *Women of Provincetown* 123–124.
64. Mary Pyne to Mary Heaton Vorse [September, 1916], Vorse Papers, Wayne State University, quoted in Egan 222.

3 *Others* and the Other Players

1. Alfred Kreymborg, *Troubadour: An Autobiography* (New York: Liveright, 1925) 148.
2. Ibid. 155.
3. Frederick J. Hoffman, Charles Allen, and Carolyn F. Ulrich, *The Little Magazine: A History and a Bibliography* (Princeton University Press, 1946) 44.
4. Arthur Wertheim, *The New York Little Renaissance: Iconoclasm, Modernism, and Nationalism in American Culture, 1908–1917* (New York University Press, 1976) 100.
5. *Others: A Magazine of the New Verse* 5.1 (December, 1918): 1.
6. Kreymborg, *Troubadour* 240.
7. Ibid. 243.
8. William Carlos Williams, *The Autobiography of William Carlos Williams* (New York: Random House, 1951) 135.
9. For a more complete history of *Others*, see Suzanne W. Churchill, "Making Space for Others: a History of a Modernist Little Magazine," *Journal of Modern Literature* 22 (Fall, 1998): 47–68.
10. Kreymborg, *Troubadour* 240.
11. Editor's Note, *Others: A Magazine of the New Verse* 1.4 (October, 1915): 53–54.
12. Kreymborg, *Troubadour* 342.
13. Ibid. 308.
14. Ibid.
15. Williams, *Autobiography* 138.
16. Kreymborg, *Troubadour* 309. See Robert K. Sarlós, *Jig Cook and the Provincetown Players: Theatre in Ferment* (Amherst: University of Massachusetts, 1982) 70.

17. Kreymborg, *Troubadour* 309.
18. Edna Kenton recorded the expense at $13.85. See *The Provincetown Players and the Playwrights' Theatre 1915–1922*, ed. Travis Bogard and Jackson R. Bryer (Jefferson, NC: McFarland, 2004) 46.
19. William Zorach, *Art Is My Life: The Autobiography of William Zorach* (Cleveland: World, 1967) 46.
20. Carolyn Burke, *Becoming Modern: The Life of Mina Loy* (New York: Farrar, Straus, and Giroux, 1996) 221.
21. Kreymborg, *Troubadour* 310.
22. Williams, *Autobiography* 139.
23. Kreymborg, *Troubadour* 310–311.
24. Kenton, *Provincetown Players* 44–46.
25. Alfred Kreymborg, *Lima Beans*, in Barbara Ozieblo, ed., *The Provincetown Players: A Choice of the Shorter Works* (Sheffield Academic Press, 1994) 131. Subsequent page references appear in the text.
26. Marianne Moore's description of the first meal she ate with Kreymborg and his first wife Gertrude in 1915 is interesting in this light: "We had potatoes and lima beans and salsify and carrots I think, beautifully cooked and applesauce and bread [and] jam. They gave me six times more than I could eat." She said the Kreymborgs were on a vegetarian diet because they were recovering from an illness (*The Selected Letters of Marianne Moore*, ed. Bonnie Costello [New York: Knopf, 1997] 106).
27. Kreymborg, *Troubadour* 312.
28. Kenton, *Provincetown Players* 63.
29. Kreymborg, *Troubadour* 312.
30. Ibid. 314–315.
31. Zorach 46.
32. Williams, *Autobiography* 139.
33. Ibid. 140.
34. Kreymborg, *Troubadour* 316.
35. Zorach 46.
36. Kreymborg, *Troubadour* 316.
37. Kathleen Cannell to Robert K. Sarlós, September 6, 1965, quoted in Sarlós, *Jig Cook* 88–89.
38. Kreymborg, *Troubadour* 319.
39. Ibid. 320.
40. New York *Tribune*, March 31, 1918, sec. 4: 4.
41. Zorach 46.
42. Kreymborg, *Troubadour* 299.
43. Alfred Kreymborg, *Manikin and Minikin: A Bisque Play in One Act* (New York: Samuel French, 1925) 1. Subsequent page references appear in the text.
44. Paul Rosenfeld, *Men Seen: Twenty-Four Modern Authors* (New York: The Dial Press, 1925) 141.
45. Alfred Kreymborg, *Jack's House* in *Puppet Plays* (New York: Samuel French, 1926) 61. Subsequent page references appear in the text.
46. Edna St. Vincent Millay, *Two Slatterns and a King*, in *Three Plays* (New York: Harpers, 1926) 5. Subsequent page references appear in the text.

47. Cheryl Black, *The Women of Provincetown, 1915–1922* (Tuscaloosa: University of Alabama Press, 2002) 27.
48. Mary Carolyn Davies, *The Slave With Two Faces: An Allegory* in Ozieblo, *Provincetown Players* 183. Subsequent page references appear in the text.
49. Kreymborg, *Troubadour* 312.
50. Maxwell Bodenheim and William Saphier, *Knotholes* in Selected Scripts, 1917–1934, microfilm, Billy Rose Theatre Collection, New York Public Library for the Performing Arts.
51. Maxwell Bodenheim, *The Gentle Furniture-Shop* in Ozieblo, *Provincetown Players* 179. Subsequent page references appear in the text.
52. Kenton, *Provincetown Players* 63.
53. "Minute Book of the Provincetown Players, Inc." From September 4, 1916, to November 8, 1923, Billy Rose Theatre Collection, New York Public Library for the Performing Arts (microfilm), 45.
54. Sarlós, *Jig Cook* 107.
55. Ibid. 108.
56. Alexander Woollcott, *New York Times*, November 9, 1919: sec. 8, 2.
57. Kenneth Macgowan, "Getting Unmarried," *Smart Set* (April, 1918): 98.
58. Wallace Stevens to Harriet Monroe, May 29, 1916, *Letters of Wallace Stevens*, ed. Holly Stevens (Berkeley: University of California Press, 1966) 194.
59. Wallace Stevens to Ronald Lane Latimer, November 5, 1935, ibid. 291.
60. Wallace Stevens to Harriet Monroe, March 4, 1920, ibid. 216.
61. Robley Evans, "Three Travelers Watch a Sunrise," *The Wallace Stevens Journal* 6.1–2 (Spring, 1982): 28, 29.
62. Ruth M. Harrison, "Wallace Stevens and the Noh Tradition," *The Wallace Stevens Journal* 27.2 (Fall, 2003): 189.
63. Maureen T. Kravec, "*Bowl, Cat and Broomstick*: Sweeping the Stage of Souvenirs," *Twentieth Century Literature* 37.3 (Fall, 1991): 310.
64. Glen MacLeod, *Wallace Stevens and Company: The Harmonium Years, 1913–1923* (Ann Arbor: UMI, 1981) 38–39.
65. The issue of Stevens's racism has been a matter of spirited debate among critics in recent years. Most notably, Jacqueline Vaught Brogan, in *The Violence Within, The Violence Without: Wallace Stevens and the Emergence of a Revolutionary Poetics* (Athens: University of Georgia Press, 2003), argues against charges by Mark Halliday, Adrienne Rich, and Rachel Blau DuPlessis that Stevens "was unwaveringly racist throughout his poetic career" (142). My reading of *Three Travelers* suggests that, at the very least, Stevens was aware of the issue of lynching in 1916, and that the play presents it as a human reality that cannot be ignored, even by an artist who would like to resist the "invasion of humanity" by practicing a purely formalist art.
66. Wallace Stevens, *Three Travelers Watch a Sunrise* in *Opus Posthumous* (New York: Knopf, 1957), 132. Subsequent page references appear in the text.
67. Harriet Monroe, "Mr. Yeats and the Poetic Drama," *Poetry* 16.1 (April, 1920): 37.
68. Ibid.
69. Lawrence Langner, *Pie* in *Five One-Act Comedies* (Cincinnati: Stewart Kidd, 1922) 108–140.

70. Kreymborg, *Troubadour* 259.
71. Ibid. 261.
72. "Convention in a Blaze," *New York Times*, June 15, 1916: 1.
73. Ibid.; see also "Pacifist Slant Dismays Leaders," *New York Times*, June 15, 1916: 1; "Mr. Glynn's Speech," *New York Times*, June 15, 1916: 10.
74. Alfred Kreymborg, *Vote the New Moon: A Toy Play* in *Plays for Merry Andrews* (New York: The Sunwise Turn, 1920) 7. Subsequent page references appear in the text.
75. Quoted in Nancy Milford, *Savage Beauty: The Life of Edna St. Vincent Millay* (New York: Random House, 2001) 178.
76. Mary J. McKee, "Millay's *Aria da Capo*: Form and Meaning," *Modern Drama* 9 (1966): 166.
77. Robert F. Storey, *Pierrot: A Critical History of a Mask* (Princeton University Press, 1978) 97.
78. Quoted in Storey 135–136.
79. Edna St. Vincent Millay, "Suggestions for the Production of 'Aria da Capo,'" in *Aria da Capo: A Play in One Act* (New York: Harper, 1920) 47.
80. Ibid.
81. Edna St. Vincent Millay, *Aria da Capo* in Ozieblo, *Provincetown Players* 220. Subsequent page references appear in the text.
82. See William Carlos Williams, *Autobiography* 138–139. Williams remembered the effect but was confused about the play, which he remembered as *Fog*.
83. Millay, "Suggestions" 45.
84. Ibid. 48.
85. Milford 183.
86. Quoted in Milford 183.
87. Alexander Woollcott, *New York Times*, December 14, 1919: sec. 8: 2.
88. Alexander Woollcott, "Second Thoughts on First Nights," *New York Times* April 4, 1920: sec. 6: 6.
89. Quoted in Phillip Herring. *Djuna: The Life and Work of Djuna Barnes* (New York: Penguin, 1995) 97.
90. For a discussion of this abuse and its effect on her work, see Herring, *Djuna* 52–59; Mary Lynn Broe, "My Art Belongs to Daddy: Incest as Exile, the Textual Economics of Hayford Hall," in Mary Lynn Broe and Angela Ingram, eds., *Women's Writing in Exile* (Chapel Hill: University of North Carolina Press, 1989) 41–86; Anne B. Dalton, "'This Is Obscene': Female Voyeurism, Sexual Abuse, and Maternal Power in *The Dove*," *The Review of Contemporary Fiction* 13.3 (Fall, 1993): 117–140.
91. Djuna Barnes, *Three from the Earth* in *At the Roots of the Stars: The Short Plays*, ed. Douglas Messerli (Los Angeles: Sun and Moon, 1995) 69. Subsequent page references appear in the text.
92. Sarlós, *Jig Cook* 109.
93. *New York Times* November 9, 1919, sec. 8: 2.
94. Djuna Barnes, "The Songs of Synge: the Man Who Shaped His Life as He Shaped His Plays," *New York Morning Telegraph Sunday Magazine*, February 18, 1917: 8.
95. Herring, *Djuna* 59–61.

96. *Kurzy of the Sea* in *At the Roots of the Stars* 83. Subsequent page references appear in the text.
97. Djuna Barnes, *An Irish Triangle*, in Ozieblo, *Provincetown Players* 239. Subsequent page references appear in the text.
98. Sarlós, *Jig Cook* 122.
99. Kenton, *Provincetown Players* 120.
100. Letters from Kenton to George Cram Cook and Susan Glaspell in 1921 and 1922, now in the Harvard Theatre Collection, Houghton Library, Harvard University, make these alliances clear.

4 Glaspell and O'Neill

1. Quoted in Barrett H. Clark, *Eugene O'Neill: The Man and His Plays* (New York: McBride, 1929) 82–83.
2. Susan Glaspell, *The People* in Susan Glaspell, *Plays by Susan Glaspell* (Boston: Small, Maynard, 1920) 48. Subsequent page references appear in the text.
3. Barbara Ozieblo, *Susan Glaspell: A Critical Biography* (Chapel Hill: University of North Carolina Press, 2000) 112–113.
4. Susan Glaspell, *Close the Book* in *Plays by Susan Glaspell* 95.
5. Mabel Dodge Luhan, *Movers and Shakers* (New York: Harcourt Brace, 1936) 403.
6. Quoted in Leona Rust Egan, *Provincetown as a Stage: Provincetown, the Provincetown Players, and the Discovery of Eugene O'Neill* (Orleans, MA: Parnassus, 1994) 142.
7. Ibid. 143.
8. Susan Glaspell, *The Outside* in *Plays by Susan Glaspell*, ed. C. W. E. Bigsby (Cambridge University Press, 1987) 48. Subsequent page references appear in the text.
9. J. Ellen Gainor, *Susan Glaspell in Context: American Theatre, Culture, and Politics, 1915–48* (Ann Arbor: University of Michigan Press, 2001) 76. See also Ann E. Larabee, "'Meeting the Outside Face to Face': Susan Glaspell, Djuna Barnes, and O'Neill's *The Emperor Jones*," in June Schlueter, ed., *Modern American Drama: The Female Canon* (Rutherford, NJ: Fairleigh Dickinson University Press, 1990) 80.
10. Ozieblo, *Susan Glaspell* 114.
11. Gainor, *Susan Glaspell in Context* 81.
12. Ibid. 78.
13. Veronica Makowsky, "Susan Glaspell and Modernism" in Brenda Murphy, ed., *The Cambridge Companion to American Women Playwrights* (Cambridge University Press, 1999) 57–58.
14. Eugene O'Neill, *Ile* in *Complete Plays. 1913–1920*, ed. Travis Bogart (New York: Library of America, 1988) 492. Subsequent page references appear in the text.
15. See Louis Sheaffer, *O'Neill: Son and Playwright* (Boston: Little, Brown, 1968) 374–375 and Arthur and Barbara Gelb, *O'Neill: Life with Monte Cristo* (New York: Applause, 2000) 631–632.
16. In 1920, O'Neill wrote to his wife Agnes about his negotiations with Tyler to produce Glaspell's *Chains of Dew*, writing "her play will be received with gratitude

at the Tyler office and given a quick reading, I'm sure of that," and offering to deliver the script personally if she sent it to him. (Eugene O'Neill to Agnes Boulton O'Neill, January 14, 1920, in Travis Bogart and Jackson R. Bryer, eds., *Selected Letters of Eugene O'Neill* (New Haven: Yale University Press, 1988) 103.

17. Eugene O'Neill to Nina Moise, April 9, 1918, in Bogard and Bryer, 81.
18. Agnes Boulton, *Part of a Long Story* (London: Peter Davies, 1958) 175–176.
19. Quoted in Clark 89.
20. Eugene O'Neill, *Where the Cross Is Made* in *Complete Plays* 698. Subsequent page references appear in the text.
21. Agnes Boulton reported that in the summer of 1918, when O'Neill was writing the play in Provincetown, he was spending so much time with Susan Glaspell that she, as a new wife, felt considerable jealousy. Boulton also recorded that Jamie O'Neill spent the summer with the couple, and that the two brothers had long, drunken, confessional talks. (Boulton, *Part of a Long Story*, 162–164; 134–150.)
22. Quoted in Clark 78.
23. Eugene O'Neill to George C. Tyler, December 9, 1920, in Bogard and Bryer 143.
24. Eugene O'Neill to Nina Moise, August 29, 1920, in Bogard and Bryer 137.
25. Edna Kenton, *The Provincetown Players and the Playwrights' Theatre 1915–1922*, ed. Travis Bogard and Jackson R. Bryer (Jefferson, NC: McFarland, 2004) 82.
26. Quoted in Clark 89.
27. Kenton, *Provincetown Players* 82.
28. Ibid. 83.
29. Eugene O'Neill to Nina Moise, August 29, 1920, in Bogard and Bryer 135.
30. Ibid.
31. Kenton, *Provincetown Players* 126.
32. In August, 1921, Cook wrote from New York to Glaspell in Provincetown that he would not be able to return for his son Harl's birthday party and was too busy to buy him a present because of preparations for the rehearsals for the uptown production of *The Spring* that began on August 29. He also told her that he and Harry Weinberger, a lawyer who handled many legal matters for the Players *pro bono*, had each put $1,000 into the Broadway production and that Jasper Deeter, who was co-director of the play with Cook, had asked the Executive Committee to consider putting Provincetown Players' funds into the production as they had into *The Emperor Jones*, risking loss and sharing in profits. He reported that, at this point, the Provincetown Players' secretary, Eleanor Fitzgerald, had said she didn't think it was a good idea. (*The Spring*'s run at the Provincetown Playhouse had not been financially successful.) Nevertheless, Cook was consulting the rest of the Executive Committee – his wife, Edna Kenton, and Eugene O'Neill. He asked Glaspell to write her opinion on a separate sheet of paper so he could show it to the others, and to write a motion to hire Edna Kenton as publicity agent for *The Spring* and keep her on as Provincetown Players' publicity agent for the rest of the season. Even if the Players did not support the production financially, he wanted the play announced as a Provincetown Players' production (George Cram Cook to Susan Glaspell, August, 1921, George Cram Cook Papers, Berg Collection, New York Public Library). Cook was successful in getting the Provincetown's name on the bill, but not in getting the group to invest in the play. And on September 10, the Executive Committee voted that Edna Kenton would be

engaged as publicity agent as well as "to read all plays promptly – sort out and have returned all impossible plays, holding the possible ones for other readers to pass on." The Executive Committee was also reduced to five: Cook, Glaspell, O'Neill, Kenton, and Fitzgerald, giving the Cook faction a majority vote on the committee ("Minutes of the Executive Committee Meeting," September 10, 1921, "Minute Book of the Provincetown Players, Inc." From September 4, 1916, to November 8, 1923: 52, Billy Rose Theatre Collection, New York Public Library for the Performing Arts).

33. Kenton, *Provincetown Players* 141.
34. Eugene O'Neill, *The Emperor Jones* in *Complete Plays. 1913–1920* 1030. Subsequent page references appear in the text.
35. Robert Károly Sarlós, *Jig Cook and the Provincetown Players: Theatre in Ferment* (Amherst: University of Massachusetts Press, 1982) 124.
36. Travis Bogard, *Contour in Time: The Plays of Eugene O'Neill*, rev. edn. (New York: Oxford University Press, 1988) 141.
37. Although there are estimated to be only eight extant copies of the book, a number of the images have been reproduced in *The Photography of Charles Sheeler: American Modernist*, ed. Theodore E. Stebbins, Jr., Gilles Mora, and Karen E. Haas (Boston: Bulfinch Press, 2002).
38. Marius de Zayas, "How, When, and Why Modern Art Came to New York," *Arts Magazine* 54 (April, 1980): 109.
39. J. Michael Dash, *Haiti and the United States: National Stereotypes and the Literary Imagination*, 2nd edn. (New York: St. Martin's Press, 1997) 36–37.
40. For some other points of view on these issues, see John Cooley, "*The Emperor Jones* and the Harlem Renaissance," *Studies in the Literary Imagination* 7.2 (1974): 73–83 and "In Search of the Primitive: Black Portraits by Eugene O'Neill and Other Village Bohemians," in Victor A. Kramer, *The Harlem Renaissance Re-Examined* (New York: AMS, 1987) 51–64; Gabriele Poole, "'Blarsted Niggers!': *The Emperor Jones* and Modernism's Encounter with Africa," *The Eugene O'Neill Review* 18 (Spring–Fall, 1994): 21–37; Ruby Cohn, "Black Power on Stage: *The Emperor Jones* and King Christophe," *Yale French Studies* 46 (1971): 41–47; Robert Hamner, "Dramatizing the New World's African King: O'Neill, Walcott and Cesaire on Christophe," *Journal of West Indian Literature* 5 (1992): 30–47; and Peter R. Saiz, "The Colonial Story in *The Emperor Jones*," *The Eugene O'Neill Review* 17 (Spring–Fall, 1993): 31–38.
41. Quoted in Doris V. Falk, *Eugene O'Neill and the Tragic Tension: An Interpretive Study of the Plays*, 2nd edn. (New York: Gordian Press, 1982) 66.
42. Falk 66.
43. Ibid. 67.
44. Michael Hinden, "*The Emperor Jones*: O'Neill, Nietzsche, and the American Past," *The Eugene O'Neill Newsletter* 3.3 (1980): 2–3.
45. Ibid. 3.
46. Quoted in Hamilton Basso, "Profiles: the Tragic Sense," *New Yorker* (March 13, 1948); rpt. Mark W. Estrin, ed., *Conversations with Eugene O'Neill* (Jackson: University of Mississippi Press, 1990) 230.
47. Timo Tiusanen, *O'Neill's Scenic Images* (Princeton University Press, 1968) 101. Ronald Wainscott notes that "American expressionism in the 1920s was often

identified as any method that objectified the subjective," but that "more specifically, both American and German expressionism were methods of presenting theatrical event, character, language, and location that objectified and externalized theatrically either what is subjective and internal for the characters in the play or the point of view of the theatrical artists presenting the work. Objectification of the subjective and externalization of the internal were accomplished through scenery, performance, use of space, and interpretation of events. The result on stage was an 'extreme subjectivism' that distorted, abstracted, and fragmented representational event, location, and character, often leading to depictions of destruction, madness, and irrational emotional expression" (Ronald H. Wainscott, *The Emergence of the Modern American Theater 1914–1929* [New Haven: Yale University Press, 1997] 91–92).

48. Tiusanen 101. Wainscott suggests that the technique of *The Emperor Jones* might be called surrealistic, using the term surrealism "to signify a full invasion of the dream or subconscious world of the character into the drama; an intrusion that allows neither the central character nor the audience to discern the difference between what is real and what is dream" (Wainscott 109).

49. Isaac Goldberg, "At the Beginning of a Career," from *The Drama of Transition* (Cincinnati: Stewart Kidd, 1922); rpt. Oscar Cargill, N. Bryllion Fagin, and William J. Fisher, eds., *O'Neill and his Plays: Four Decades of Criticism* (New York University Press, 1961) 240.

50. See Brenda Murphy, "McTeague's Dream and *The Emperor Jones*: O'Neill's Move from Naturalism to Modernism," *Eugene O'Neill Review* 17 (1993): 21–29.

51. Wainscott 96.

52. Kenton, *Provincetown Players* 125.

53. Ibid. 126.

54. Ibid.

55. Heywood Broun, "'The Emperor Jones by O'Neill Gives Chance for Cheers," New York *Tribune*, November 4, 1920, Provincetown Players Scrapbook, Billy Rose Theatre Collection, New York Public Library for the Performing Arts.

56. Kenneth Macgowan, "The New Play," *New York Globe*, November 4, 1920, Provincetown Players Scrapbook, Billy Rose Theatre Collection, New York Public Library for the Performing Arts. *The Jest* and *Richard III* were designed by Robert Edmond Jones for Arthur Hopkins.

57. Alexander Woollcott, "The New O'Neill Play," *New York Times*, November 7, 1920, Provincetown Players Scrapbook, Billy Rose Theatre Collection, New York Public Library for the Performing Arts.

58. Broun, "The Emperor Jones."

59. Woollcott, "The New O'Neill Play."

60. Sarlós, *Jig Cook* 178.

61. For revealing discussions of this technique in Glaspell's work, see Marcia Noe, "Reconfiguring the Subject/Recuperating Realism: Susan Glaspell's Unseen Woman," *American Drama* 4 (Spring, 1995): 36–54; Jackie Czerepinski, "Beyond the Verge: Absent Heroines in the Plays of Susan Glaspell" in Linda Ben-Zvi, ed., *Susan Glaspell: Essays on Her Theater and Fiction* (Ann Arbor: University of Michigan Press, 1995) 145–154; and Susan Kattwinkel, "Absence as a Site for

Debate: Modern Feminism and Victorianism in the Plays of Susan Glaspell," *New England Theatre Journal* 7 (1996): 37–55.
62. Ozieblo, *Susan Glaspell* 136–137.
63. Heywood Broun, *New York Tribune*, 4 March 1918. Quoted in Ozieblo, *Susan Glaspell* 120.
64. Ozieblo, *Susan Glaspell* 119.
65. Susan Glaspell, *Bernice* in *Plays by Susan Glaspell* 169. Subsequent page references appear in the text.
66. Susan Glaspell, *The Verge* in *Plays by Susan Glaspell*, ed. C. W. E. Bigsby 58. Subsequent page references appear in the text.
67. Glaspell felt that she had in a sense betrayed her artistic convictions trying to please a Broadway audience, and also felt some envy toward O'Neill who was finding it easier to make his way in the Broadway theatre because of his father's connections. (Ozieblo, *Susan Glaspell* 144; Bogard and Bryer 115). Ironically, *Chains of Dew* was eventually produced by the Provincetown Players after Glaspell had left for Greece with Cook. This inept production was the last Glaspell would have with the Provincetown Players.
68. Wainscott 114.
69. Margit Sichert, "Claire Archer – a 'Nietzscheana' in Susan Glaspell's *The Verge*," *REAL: The Yearbook of Research in English and American Literature* 13 (1997): 272.
70. Friedrich Nietzsche, *Thus Spake Zarathustra: A Book for All and None*, trans. Thomas Common, rev. Oscar Levy and John L. Beevers (London: Allen & Unwin, 1967) 120.
71. Sichert 273, 274.
72. Ibid. 276.
73. Friedrich Nietzsche, *Daybreak*, ed. Michael Tanner (Cambridge University Press, 1982) [9] 11.
74. Sichert 287.
75. Friedrich Nietzsche, *The Gay Science*, quoted in Sichert 284.
76. Gainor, *Susan Glaspell in Context* 163. Gainor develops this idea with a slightly different emphasis in "A Stage of Her Own: Susan Glaspell's *The Verge* and Women's Dramaturgy," *Journal of American Drama and Theatre* 1 (Spring, 1989): 96.
77. Sichert 295.
78. In the first critical book on Glaspell, Arthur Waterman wrote that "Claire's final actions indicate that the playwright was making her an extreme case for dramatic purposes and was acknowledging the limitations that have to be placed on aspiration, the boundaries beyond which no one may go" (Arthur Waterman, *Susan Glaspell* [New York: Twayne, 1966] 81). Christopher Bigsby concurred that Glaspell "is critical of Claire," asserting that "art is, finally, not an ultimate value in her lexicon ... for the imagination has its own coercive power and the price of locating meaning in aesthetics was finally a surrender of humanity. She had read her Nietzsche but she had not swallowed him whole" (C. W. E. Bigsby, *A Critical Introduction to Twentieth-Century American Drama*. Volume 1: 1900–1940 [Cambridge University Press, 1982] 32). Veronica Makowsky suggests that through Claire, "Glaspell explores the causes and the tragic consequences of the high modernist's alienation from the life around her" (Makowsky, "Susan Glaspell and

Modernism" 62). Marcia Noe contends that *The Verge* is Glaspell's attempt "to show us the futility of attempting to transcend form" (Marcia Noe, "*The Verge: L'Ecriture Féminine* at the Provincetown," in Ben-Zvi, *Susan Glaspell* 140–141. On the other hand, Christine Dymkowsky sees "Claire's madness at the end of the play" as "a personal triumph" (Christine Dymkowski, "On the Edge: the Plays of Susan Glaspell," *Modern Drama* 31 (March, 1988): 91–105), and Barbara Ozieblo contends that Claire "is now her own God and cannot be reached by societal structures and compunctions. She has broken out and is existentially free, alone in the transcendental beyond" (Ozieblo, *Susan Glaspell* 187).

79. Unidentified clipping, Provincetown Scrapbook, Billy Rose Theatre Collection, New York Public Library for the Performing Arts.
80. Kenneth Macgowan, "The New Play." Clipping, Provincetown Players Scrapbook, Billy Rose Theatre Collection, New York Public Library for the Performing Arts.
81. Stephen Rathburn, "Spanish Operetta, Musical Comedy and Two Dramas Arrive Thanksgiving Week." Clipping, Provincetown Players Scrapbook, Billy Rose Theatre Collection, New York Public Library for the Performing Arts.
82. Quoted in Clark 125.
83. Bogard 243.
84. Louis Sheaffer, *O'Neill: Son and Artist* (New York: Paragon House, 1990) 76.
85. *The Hairy Ape* in *Eugene O'Neill: Complete Plays. 1920–1931*, ed. Travis Bogard (New York: Library of America, 1988) 126–27. Subsequent page references appear in the text.
86. Quoted in Mary B. Mullett, "The Extraordinary Story of Eugene O'Neill," *American Magazine* 94 (November, 1922); rpt. Estrin 35.
87. Ibid.
88. Quoted in "Eugene O'Neill Talks of His Own and the Plays of Others," New York *Herald Tribune*, November 16, 1924; rpt. Estrin 62.
89. Quoted in "Eugene O'Neill Talks of His Own and the Plays of Others," 62.
90. Quoted in "Eugene O'Neill Talks of His Own and the Plays of Others," 61.
91. Eugene O'Neill to Kenneth Macgowan, December 24, 1921, in Jackson R. Bryer, ed., *"The Theatre We Worked For": The Letters of Eugene O'Neill to Kenneth Macgowan* (New Haven: Yale University Press, 1982) 31–32.
92. Tiusanen 125.
93. Sheaffer, *O'Neill: Son and Artist* 78.
94. Ibid. 79.
95. See Kenton, *Provincetown Players* 155; Minutes of the Executive Committee Meeting of the Provincetown Players, February 23, 1922, in Minute Book of the Provincetown Players, Inc. From September 4, 1916, to November 8, 1923, Billy Rose Theatre Collection, New York Public Library for the Performing Arts (microfilm).
96. Sarlós, *Jig Cook* 140.
97. Quoted in Cheryl Black, *The Women of Provincetown, 1915–1922* (Tuscaloosa: University of Alabama Press, 2002) 128.
98. Quoted in Sheaffer, *O'Neill: Son and Artist* 79–81.
99. Kenton, *Provincetown Players* 155.
100. Sheaffer, *O'Neill: Son and Artist* 80.

101. Alexander Woollcott, "Second Thoughts on First Nights," *New York Times* in Provincetown Players Scrapbook, Billy Rose Theatre Collection, New York Public Library for the Performing Arts.
102. Walter Prichard Eaton, "The Theatre," *The Freeman*, April 26, 1922, in Provincetown Players Scrapbook, Billy Rose Theatre Collection, New York Public Library for the Performing Arts.
103. Kenton, *Provincetown Players* 146, 155.
104. Kenton's efforts are detailed in her letters to Cook and Glaspell for May and June, 1922, in the Harvard Theatre Collection, Houghton Library, Harvard University.
105. Kenneth Macgowan, *The Theatre of Tomorrow* (New York: Boni and Liveright, 1921) 286.
106. Eugene O'Neill to Kenneth Macgowan, March 18, 1921, in *"The Theatre We Worked For"* 19.
107. Eugene O'Neill to Kenneth Macgowan, January 22, 1922, in *"The Theatre We Worked For"* 32.
108. Eugene O'Neill to Kenneth Macgowan, [Spring, 1923], in *"The Theatre We Worked For"* 35.
109. Harry Weinberger to Eugene O'Neill, September 24, 1923, in *"The Theatre We Worked For"* 41.
110. Eugene O'Neill to Kenneth Macgowan, [late September, 1923], in *"The Theatre We Worked For"* 43–44.
111. Eugene O'Neill to Harry Weinberger, [September, 1923], in *"The Theatre We Worked For"* 48.
112. "Minute Book", 57.
113. Kenneth Macgowan, "Introduction" in Helen Deutsch and Stella Hanau, *The Provincetown: A Story of the Theatre* (New York: Farrar & Rinehart, 1931) x.
114. Eugene O'Neill to Kenneth Macgowan, July 15, [1926], in *"The Theatre We Worked For"* 118.

5 The legacy

1. Eugene O'Neill, *Welded*, in *Complete Plays. 1920–1931*, ed. Travis Bogard (New York: Library of America, 1988) 235. Subsequent page references appear in the text.
2. "There have never been the elm trees of my play," Eugene O'Neill to Kenneth Macgowan, [after August 12, 1926], in *"The Theatre We Worked For": The Letters of Eugene O'Neill to Kenneth Macgowan*, ed. Jackson R. Bryer (New Haven: Yale University Press, 1982) 132.
3. Eugene O'Neill, *Desire Under the Elms* in *Complete Plays. 1920–1931* 318.
4. Kenneth Macgowan, *The Theatre of Tomorrow* (New York: Boni and Liveright, 1921) 233.
5. Eugene O'Neill, *The Fountain* in *Complete Plays. 1920–1931* 224–225.
6. Eugene O'Neill, *All God's Chillun Got Wings* in *Complete Plays. 1920–1931* 279. Subsequent page references appear in the text.

7. Kenneth Macgowan and Herman Rosse, *Masks and Demons* (New York: Harcourt Brace, 1923) vii.
8. Eugene O'Neill, "Second Thoughts," *American Spectator* (December, 1932) in Oscar Cargill, N. Bryllion Fagin, and William J. Fisher, eds., *O'Neill and His Plays: Four Decades of Criticism* (New York University Press, 1961) 119.
9. James Light, "The Mask," in *Provincetown Playbill*, Season 1923–24, no. 3: 1.
10. Eugene O'Neill, "Memoranda on Masks," *American Spectator* (December, 1932), Cargill 117.
11. Eugene O'Neill, *Lazarus Laughed*, in *Complete Plays. 1920–1931* 541. Subsequent page references appear in the text.
12. Eugene O'Neill, "A Dramatist's Notebook," *American Spectator* (January, 1933), Cargill 120.
13. Eugene O'Neill, "Memoranda on Masks," Cargill 116–117.
14. Kenneth Macgowan, "The Mask in Drama," *Greenwich Playbill*, Fourth Bill, January 23, 1926: 1.
15. Ibid. 6.
16. Eugene O'Neill, *The Great God Brown*, in *Complete Plays. 1920–1931* 519. Subsequent page references appear in the text.
17. Eugene O'Neill, "Second Thoughts," Cargill 119.
18. Ibid. 120.
19. Kenneth Macgowan, "'More Tosh,'" *Provincetown Playbill* Season 1924–25, no. 1: 4.
20. Robert Edmond Jones, "A Note on the Theatre," *Provincetown Playbill*, Season 1923–24, no. 3: 4.
21. Eugene O'Neill to Kenneth Macgowan, January 21, [1927], in *"The Theatre We Worked For"* 146.
22. *Pie* was produced by the Provincetown Players in February, 1920.
23. When *The Emperor Jones* proved a hit and was moved to the Selwyn Theater, *Matinata* was replaced by Cook and Glaspell's *Suppressed Desires*.
24. For details of the production, see Brenda Murphy, "Interpreting *Marco Millions*: Two New York Productions," *The Recorder*, special Eugene O'Neill Centennial Issue, 3 (1989): 127–136.
25. Lawrence Langner, *The Magic Curtain* (New York: E. P. Dutton, 1951) 232.
26. Macgowan, *Theatre of Tomorrow* 240.
27. John Schuyler, "The Dream in Drama," *Provincetown Playbill*, Season 1924–25, no. 1: 2, 5.
28. Edmund Wilson, *The Crime in the Whistler Room* in *This Room and This Gin and These Sandwiches, Three Plays by Edmund Wilson* (New York: The New Republic, 1937) 47. Subsequent page references appear in the text.
29. Stark Young, *The Saint: A Play in Four Acts* (New York: Boni and Liveright, 1925) 9. Subsequent page references appear in the text.
30. Program for *Him*, Provincetown Playhouse, [1928]: 1.
31. e. e. cummings, *Him* (New York: Liveright, 1927) 3. Subsequent page references appear in the text.
32. Quoted in *Him and the Critics: A Collection of Opinions on e. e. cummings's Play at the Provincetown Playhouse*. Pamphlet. Provincetown Players Scrapbook. Billy Rose Theatre Collection, New York Public Library for the Performing Arts.

33. See letters from Robert Edmond Jones to Neith Boyce, January 27, 1932, and March 8, 1932, Hapgood Family Papers, Beinecke Rare Book and Manuscript Library, Yale University. The Hapgood Family Papers include manuscript materials for about twenty plays by Boyce.
34. Edna Kenton, *The Provincetown Players and the Playwrights' Theatre 1915–1922*, ed. Travis Bogard and Jackson R. Bryer (Jefferson, NC: 2004) 93.
35. See Robin Jaffe Frank, *Charles Demuth Poster Portraits: 1923–1929* (New Haven: Yale University Art Gallery, 1994).
36. William Zorach, *Art Is My Life: The Autobiography of William Zorach* (Cleveland: World, 1967) 46.
37. Accessible online as "Untitled Blockprint," 1915 by Marguerite Zorach, http://americanart.si.edu/index3.cfm. Smithsonian American Art Museum. 1991.93.15.
38. William Carlos Williams, *The Autobiography of William Carlos Williams* (New York: Random House, 1951) 139.
39. Ibid. 139–140.
40. Ibid. 140.
41. Ibid. 153–154.
42. Eugene O'Neill to Kenneth Macgowan [June? 1923] in Travis Bogard and Jackson R. Bryer, eds., *Selected Letters of Eugene O'Neill* (New Haven: Yale University Press, 1988) 180.

Bibliography

Archives and special collections

Several library collections have been indispensable to this study. A list of the most important includes the following:

New York Public Library

The Billy Rose Theatre Collection, New York Public Library for the Performing Arts includes the Minute Book and Scrapbooks of the Provincetown Players as well as correspondence, scripts, clippings files, photographs and other materials related to the Provincetown productions.

The Berg Collection includes correspondence to and from George Cram Cook and Susan Glaspell.

Beinecke Rare Book and Manuscript Library, Yale University

The Eugene O'Neill Collection includes programs, scripts, correspondence, and photographs related to the Provincetown Players.

The Hapgood Family Papers includes correspondence, manuscripts, pictures, and other materials related to Neith Boyce and Hutchins Hapgood.

Houghton Library, Harvard University

The Harvard Theatre Collection includes correspondence and other materials related to the Provincetown Players, particularly George Cram Cook, Susan Glaspell, and Edna Kenton. The John Reed Collection contains manuscripts and correspondence related to John Reed, Louise Bryant, and the early years of the Provincetown Players.

Fales Library, New York University

Provincetown Players Archive, Special Collections contains manuscripts, correspondence, and clippings related to the Provincetown Players, particularly Edna Kenton.

Thomas R. Dodd Research Center, University of Connecticut Libraries

Contains files of *Others* magazine and other materials related to the Others group.

Charles E. Shain Library, Connecticut College

The Louis Sheaffer Collection contains correspondence, photographs, and other materials related to Eugene O'Neill's participation in the Provincetown Players.

Library of Congress

The William Zorach Papers contain correspondence to and from William Zorach and Marguerite Thompson Zorach.

University of Virginia

The George Cram Cook and Susan Glaspell collections in the Clifton Waller Barrett Library contain correspondence related to the Provincetown Players, chiefly with Edna Kenton, as well as some manuscripts.

University of Maryland, College Park

The Djuna Barnes Papers, Special Collections contains manuscripts, clippings, correspondence, pictures, and other materials.

Works cited and select bibliography

Aaron, Daniel. *Writers on the Left: Episodes in American Literary Communism*. New York: Harcourt Brace, 1961.

Abrahams, Edward. *The Lyrical Left: Randolph Bourne, Alfred Stieglitz, and the Origins of Cultural Radicalism in America*. Charlottesville: University Press of Virginia, 1986.

Ackerman, Alan and Martin Puchner. Eds. *Modernism and Anti-Theatricality*. Special Issue. *Modern Drama* 44 (Fall, 2001): 275–361.

Alkalay-Gut, Karen. "Murder and Marriage: Another Look at *Trifles*," in Ben-Zvi, *Susan Glaspell* 71–81.

Ammons, Elizabeth. *Conflicting Stories: American Women Writers at the Turn Into the Twentieth Century*. New York: Oxford University Press, 1991.
Antliff, Allan. *Anarchist Modernism: Art, Politics, and the First American Avant-Garde*. University of Chicago Press, 2001.
Bach, Gerhard. "Susan Glaspell: Provincetown Playwright." *Great Lakes Review: A Journal of Midwest Culture* 4.2 (1978): 31–43.
Bak, John S. "Eugene O'Neill and John Reed: Recording the Body Politic, 1913–1922." *Eugene O'Neill Review* 20 (Spring–Fall, 1996): 17–35.
Barber, Theodore. "'Wistful Otherworldliness': Symbolist Productions of the Washington Square Players." *Theatre Studies* 33 (Winter, 1988): 29–48.
Barlow, Judith E. "Susan's Sisters: the 'Other' Women Writers of the Provincetown Players." In Ben-Zvi, *Susan Glaspell* 259–300.
Barnes, Djuna. *At the Roots of the Stars: The Short Plays*. Ed. Douglas Messerli. Los Angeles: Sun and Moon, 1995.
   "Days of Jig Cook: Recollections of Ancient Theatre History but Ten Years Old." *Theatre Guild Magazine* 6 (January, 1929): 31–32.
   Special Issue. *The Review of Contemporary Fiction* 13 (Fall, 1993).
   Djuna Barnes's New York. Ed. Alyce Barry. New York: Virago, 1990.
   Greenwich Village as It Is. New York: Phoenix Book Shop, 1978.
   "The Songs of Synge: the Man Who Shaped His Life as He Shaped His Plays." *New York Morning Telegraph Sunday Magazine* February 18, 1917: 8.
Baumrin, Seth. "Jig Cook: Stage Manager for an American Renaissance." *Journal of American Drama and Theatre* 12 (Fall, 2000): 55–74.
Bender, Thomas. *New York Intellect: A History of Intellectual Life in New York City*. New York: Knopf, 1987.
Ben-Zvi, Linda. Ed. *Susan Glaspell: Essays on Her Theater and Fiction*. Ann Arbor: University of Michigan Press, 1995.
   "'Murder She Wrote': the Genesis of Susan Glaspell's *Trifles*." In Ben-Zvi, *Susan Glaspell* 19–48.
   "O'Neill's Cape(d) Compatriot." *The Eugene O'Neill Review* 19 (Spring–Fall, 1995): 129–138.
Bigsby, C. W. E. *A Critical Introduction to Twentieth-Century American Drama*. Volume 1: 1900–1940. Cambridge University Press, 1982.
Black, Cheryl. "Ida Rauh: Power Player at the Provincetown." *Journal of American Drama and Theatre* 6 (Spring–Fall, 1994): 63–80.
   "Pioneering Theatre Managers: Edna Kenton and Eleanor Fitzgerald of the Provincetown Players." *Journal of American Drama and Theatre* 9 (Fall, 1997): 40–58.
   "Technique and Tact: Nina Moise Directs the Provincetown Players." *Theatre Survey* 36 (May, 1995): 55–64.
   The Women of Provincetown, 1915–1922. Tuscaloosa: University of Alabama Press, 2002.
Black, Cheryl and Robert K. Sarlós. "On the Threshold of Sexual Politics in American Theater and Drama: the Provincetown Players." In Barbara Ozieblo and Miriam Lopez-Rodriguez. Eds. *Staging a Cultural Paradigm: The Political and the Personal in American Drama*. Brussels: Presses Interuniversitaires Européennes–Peter Lang, 2002. 133–147.

Bodenheim, Maxwell and William Saphier. *Knotholes* in *Selected Scripts, 1917–1934*. Microfilm, Billy Rose Theatre Collection, New York Public Library for the Performing Arts.
Bogard, Travis. *Contour in Time: The Plays of Eugene O'Neill*. Rev. edn. New York: Oxford University Press, 1988.
Bogard, Travis and Jackson R. Bryer. Eds. *Selected Letters of Eugene O'Neill*. New Haven: Yale University Press, 1988.
Boulton, Agnes. *Part of a Long Story*. London: Peter Davies, 1958.
Boyce, Neith. *The Modern World of Neith Boyce: Autobiography and Diaries*. Ed. Carol DeBoer-Langworthy. Albuquerque: University of New Mexico Press, 2003.
Brazeau, Peter. *Parts of a World: Wallace Stevens Remembered*. New York: Random House, 1983.
Bridgwater, Patrick. *Nietzsche in Anglosaxony: A Study of Nietzsche's Impact on English and American Literature*. Leicester University Press, 1972.
Broe, Mary Lynn. "My Art Belongs to Daddy: Incest as Exile, the Textual Economics of Hayford Hall." In Mary Lynn Broe and Angela Ingram. Eds. *Women's Writing in Exile*. Chapel Hill: University of North Carolina Press, 1989. 41–86.
Brogan, Jacqueline Vaught. *The Violence Within, The Violence Without: Wallace Stevens and the Emergence of a Revolutionary Poetics*. Athens: University of Georgia Press, 2003.
Brown, Milton W. *The Story of the Armory Show*. Rev. edn. New York: Abbeville Press, 1988.
Bryer, Jackson R. Ed. *"The Theatre We Worked for": The Letters of Eugene O'Neill to Kenneth Macgowan*. New Haven: Yale University Press, 1982.
Bucco, Martin. *Wilbur Daniel Steele*. New York: Twayne, 1972.
Burke, Carolyn. *Becoming Modern: The Life of Mina Loy*. New York: Farrar, Straus, and Giroux, 1996.
Burruss, John. "Additions to a Bibliography of Provincetown Players' Dramas." *Papers of the Bibliographical Society of America* 73 (1979) 266.
Cargill, Oscar, N. Bryllion Fagin, and William J. Fisher. Eds. *O'Neill and His Plays: Four Decades of Criticism*. New York University Press, 1961.
Carpenter, Edward. *Love's Coming of Age*. New York: Kennerly, 1911.
Champa, Kermit. "Some Observations on American Art." In *Over Here: Modernism, the First Exile, 1914–1919*. Providence: David Winter Bell Gallery, Brown University, 1989.
Cheney, Anne. *Millay in Greenwich Village*. Tuscaloosa: University of Alabama Press, 1975.
Cheney, Sheldon. *The Art Theater*. 1917; rev. edn. New York: Alfred A. Knopf, 1925.
"The Church and the Unemployed." *The Masses* 5 (April, 1914): 10–11.
Churchill, Suzanne W. "Making Space for Others: a History of a Modernist Little Magazine." *Journal of Modern Literature* 22 (Fall, 1998): 47–68.
Clark, Barrett H. *Eugene O'Neill: The Man and His Plays*. New York: McBride, 1929.
Clayton, Douglas. *Floyd Dell: The Life and Times of an American Rebel*. Chicago: I. R. Dee, 1994.
Cohn, Ruby. "Black Power on Stage: *The Emperor Jones* and King Christophe." *Yale French Studies* 46 (1971): 41–47.

Coke, Van Deren. *Nordfeldt the Painter*. Albuquerque: University of New Mexico Press, 1972.
Connolly, Thomas F. "*The Hairy Ape* in the Context of Early Twentieth-Century American Modernism." *The Eugene O'Neill Review* 25 (Spring–Fall, 2001): 77–79.
Cook, George Cram. *Greek Coins*. New York: George H. Doran, 1925.
  "Socialism the Issue in 1912." *The Masses* 4 (July, 1912): 7.
Cook, George Cram and Frank Shay. Eds. *The Provincetown Plays*. Cincinnati: Stewart Kidd, 1921.
  The Provincetown Plays: Second Series. Great Neck, New York: Core Collection Books, 1976.
Cooley, John R. "*The Emperor Jones* and the Harlem Renaissance." *Studies in the Literary Imagination* 7.2 (1974): 73–83.
  "In Search of the Primitive: Black Portraits by Eugene O'Neill and Other Village Bohemians." In Victor A. Kramer. Ed. *The Harlem Renaissance Re-Examined*. New York: AMS, 1987. 51–64.
Cooley, Winifred Harper. "The Younger Suffragists." *Harper's Weekly* (58 September 27, 1913): 7–8.
Coolidge, Olivia. *Eugene O'Neill*. New York: Scribner, 1966.
Cortissoz, Royal. "The Post-Impressionist Illusion." *Century Magazine* 85 (April, 1913): 805–815.
Cott, Nancy F. *The Grounding of Modern Feminism*. New Haven: Yale University Press, 1987.
Crocker, Bosworth. *Humble Folk, One-Act Plays by Bosworth Crocker*. Cincinnati: Stewart Kidd, 1923.
cummings, e. e. *Him*. New York: Liveright, 1927.
Cunningham, Frank R. "O'Neill's Beginnings and the Birth of Modernism in American Drama." *The Eugene O'Neill Review* 17 (Spring–Fall, 1993): 11–20.
Czerepinski, Jackie. "Beyond the Verge: Absent Heroines in the Plays of Susan Glaspell." In Linda Ben-Zvi, *Susan Glaspell* 145–154.
Dalton, Anne B. "'This Is Obscene': Female Voyeurism, Sexual Abuse, and Maternal Power in *The Dove*." *The Review of Contemporary Fiction* 13.3 (Fall, 1993): 117–140.
Danzer, Ina. "Between Decadence and Surrealism: the Other Modernism of Djuna Barnes." *Arbeiten aus Anglistik und Amerikanistik* 23 (1998): 239–257.
Dash, J. Michael. *Haiti and the United States: National Stereotypes and the Literary Imagination*. 2nd edn. New York: St. Martin's Press, 1997.
Dell, Floyd, *Homecoming, An Autobiography*. New York: Farrar and Rinehart, 1933.
  Intellectual Vagabondage: An Apology for the Intelligentsia. New York: 1926.
  "Speaking of Psycho-analysis," *Vanity Fair* (December, 1914): 53.
Demastes, William. Ed. *Realism and the American Dramatic Tradition*. Tuscaloosa: University of Alabama Press, 1996.
Deutsch, Helen and Stella Hanau. *The Provincetown: A Story of the Theatre*. New York: Farrar & Rinehart, 1931.
de Zayas, Marius. "How, When, and Why Modern Art Came to New York." *Arts Magazine* 54 (April, 1980): 96–126.
Diamond, Elin. "Modern Drama/Modernity's Drama." *Modern Drama* 44.1 (Spring, 2001): 3–15.

Dickinson, Thomas H. *The Insurgent Theatre*. New York: W. B. Huebsch, 1917.
Diggins, John P. *The American Left in the Twentieth Century*. New York: Harcourt Brace Jovanovich, 1973.
Doyle, Charles. Ed. *Wallace Stevens: The Critical Heritage*. London: Routledge and Kegan Paul, 1985.
Dymkowski, Christine. "On the Edge: the Plays of Susan Glaspell." *Modern Drama* 31 (March, 1988): 91–105.
Eastman, Max. *Enjoyment of Living*. New York: Harper, 1948.
  "Exploring the Soul and Healing the Body." *Everybody's Magazine* 32 (1915): 741–750.
  "Mr.–er–er–Oh! What's His Name!" *Everybody's Magazine* 33 (1915): 95–103.
  "The Tannenbaum Crime." *The Masses* 5 (May, 1914): 6–8.
Egan, Leona Rust. *Provincetown as a Stage: Provincetown, the Provincetown Players, and the Discovery of Eugene O'Neill*. Orleans, MA: Parnassus, 1994.
Egbert, Donald D. "The Idea of 'Avant-Garde' in Art and Politics." *American Historical Review* 73.2 (December, 1967): 339–366.
Estrin, Mark W. Ed. *Conversations with Eugene O'Neill*. Jackson: University of Mississippi Press, 1990.
Evans, Robley. "Three Travelers Watch a Sunrise." *Wallace Stevens Journal* 6.1–2 (Spring, 1982): 28–31.
Falk, Doris V. *Eugene O'Neill and the Tragic Tension: An Interpretive Study of the Plays*. 2nd edn. New York: Gordian Press, 1982.
Farnham, Emily. *Charles Demuth: Behind a Laughing Mask*. Norman: University of Oklahoma Press, 1971.
Field, Andrew. *Djuna: The Formidable Miss Barnes*. Austin: University of Texas Press, 1985.
Fishbein, Leslie. *Rebels in Bohemia: The Radicals of The Masses, 1911–1917*. Chapel Hill: University of North Carolina Press, 1982.
Frank, Robin Jaffe. *Charles Demuth Poster Portraits: 1923–1929*. New Haven: Yale University Art Gallery, 1994.
Frank, Steven. "On 'The Verge' of a New Form: *The Cabinet of Dr. Caligari* and Susan Glaspell's Experiments in *The Verge*." In Gewirtz and Kolb, 119–129.
Friedman, Sharon. "Bernice's Strange Deceit: the Avenging Angel in the House." In Ben-Zvi, *Susan Glaspell* 155–163.
Furniss, J. M. "A Stevens Play as Teaching Tool." In John N. Serio and B. J. Leggett. Eds. *Teaching Wallace Stevens*. Knoxville: University of Tennessee Press, 1994. 204–212.
Gainor, J. Ellen. "A Stage of Her Own: Susan Glaspell's *The Verge* and Women's Dramaturgy." *Journal of American Drama and Theatre* 1 (Spring, 1989): 79–99.
  Susan Glaspell in Context: American Theater, Culture, and Politics, 1915–48. Ann Arbor: University of Michigan Press, 2001.
  "The Provincetown Players' Experiments with Realism." In Demastes, 53–70.
Garrison, Dee. *Mary Heaton Vorse: The Life of an American Insurgent*. Philadelphia: Temple University Press, 1989.
Gelb, Arthur and Barbara Gelb. *O'Neill: Life with Monte Cristo*. New York: Applause, 2000.
Gelb, Barbara. *So Short a Time: A Biography of John Reed and Louise Bryant*. New York: Norton, 1973.

Gewirtz, Arthur and James J. Kolb. Eds. *Experimenters, Rebels, and Disparate Voices: The Theatre of the 1920s Celebrates American Diversity*. Westport, CT: Praeger, 2003.
Glaspell, Susan. *Plays by Susan Glaspell*. Boston: Small, Maynard, 1920.
  Plays by Susan Glaspell. Ed. C. W. E. Bigsby. Cambridge University Press, 1987.
  The Road to the Temple. New York: Frederick A. Stokes, 1927.
Goldberg, Isaac. *The Drama of Transition*. Cincinnati: Stewart Kidd, 1922.
Goldman, Arnold. "The Culture of the Provincetown Players." *Journal of American Studies* 12.3 (1978): 291–310.
Green, Martin. *New York 1913: The Armory Show and the Paterson Strike Pageant*. New York: Scribner, 1988.
Hale, Nathan G., Jr. *The Beginnings of Psychoanalysis in the United States, 1876–1917*. New York: Oxford University Press, 1971.
Hamner, Robert. "Dramatizing the New World's African King: O'Neill, Walcott and Cesaire on Christophe." *Journal of West Indian Literature* 5 (1992): 30–47.
Hapgood, Hutchins. "Authority in Art." *New York Globe*, January 28, 1912: 10.
  "The Insurgents in Art." *New York Globe*, October 24, 1911: 6.
  "Life at the Armory." *New York Globe*, February 17, 1913.
  "The Trend of the Time." *New York Globe*, March 12, 1912: 4.
  A Victorian in the Modern World. New York: Harcourt Brace, 1930.
  "What Is Anarchism." *New York Globe*, October 14, 1911: 10.
Harrison, Ruth M. "Wallace Stevens and the Noh Tradition." *The Wallace Stevens Journal* 27.2 (Fall, 2003): 189–204.
Heller, Adele and Lois Rudnick. Eds. *1915: The Cultural Moment*. New Brunswick, NJ: Rutgers University Press, 1991.
Herring, Phillip. *Djuna: The Life and Work of Djuna Barnes*. New York: Penguin, 1995.
  "Djuna Barnes and the Songs of Synge." *Eire–Ireland* 28 (1993): 139–144.
Hinden, Michael. "*The Emperor Jones*: O'Neill, Nietzsche, and the American Past." *The Eugene O'Neill Newsletter* 3.3 (1980): 2–4.
Hoffman, Frederick J., Charles Allen, and Carolyn F. Ulrich. *The Little Magazine: A History and a Bibliography*. Princeton University Press, 1946.
Hoffman, Gerhard. "Eugene O'Neill: America's Nietzschean Playwright." In Manfred Pütz. Ed. *Nietzsche in American Literature and Thought*. Columbia, SC: Camden House, 1995. 197–221.
Hoffman, Marilyn Friedman. *Marguerite and William Zorach, the Cubist Years: 1915–18*. Ex. Cat. Manchester, NH: Currier Gallery of Art, 1987.
Homberger, Eric. *John Reed*. Manchester University Press, 1990.
Innes, Christopher. "Modernism in Drama." In Michael Levenson. Ed. *The Cambridge Companion to Modernism*. Cambridge University Press, 1999. 130–156.
  "Shifting the Frame: Modernism in the Theatre." In Marianne Thormahlen. Ed. *Rethinking Modernism*. Basingstoke: Palgrave Macmillan, 2003. 204–212.
Jones, Robert Edmond. *The Dramatic Imagination: Reflections and Speculations on the Art of the Theatre*. New York: Duell, Sloan, and Pearce, 1941.
  "A Note on the Theatre." *Provincetown Playbill*, Season 1923–24. no. 3: 4.
Kattwinkel, Susan. "Absence as a Site for Debate: Modern Feminism and Victorianism in the Plays of Susan Glaspell." *New England Theatre Journal* 7 (1996): 37–55.
Kellner, Bruce. *Letters of Charles Demuth*. Philadelphia: Temple University Press, 2000.

Kemp, Harry. "Out of Provincetown." *Theatre Magazine* 51 (April, 1930): 22–23, 66.
Kenton, Edna. "Feminism Will Give – Men More Fun, Women Greater Scope..." *Delineator* 85 (July, 1914): 17.
  The Provincetown Players and the Playwrights' Theatre 1915–1922. Ed. Travis Bogard and Jackson R. Bryer. Jefferson, NC: McFarland, 2004.
Krasner, David. "Whose Role Is It Anyway?: Charles Gilpin and the Harlem Renaissance." *African American Review* 29.3 (Fall, 1995): 483–496.
Kravec, Maureen T. "*Bowl, Cat and Broomstick*: Sweeping the Stage of Souvenirs." *Twentieth Century Literature* 37.3 (Fall, 1991): 309–321.
Kreymborg, Alfred. *Manikin and Minikin: A Bisque Play in One Act*. New York: Samuel French, 1925.
  Plays for Merry Andrews. New York: The Sunwise Turn, 1920.
  Puppet Plays. New York: Samuel French, 1926.
  Troubadour: An Autobiography. New York: Liveright, 1925.
Langner, Lawrence. *Five One-Act Comedies*. Cincinnati: Stewart Kidd, 1922.
  The Magic Curtain. New York: E. P. Dutton, 1951.
Larabee, Ann. "The Early Attic Stage of Djuna Barnes." In Mary Lynn Broe. Ed. *Silence and Power: A Reevaluation of Djuna Barnes*. Carbondale: Southern Illinois University Press, 1991. 37–44.
Larabee, Ann E. "'Meeting the Outside Face to Face': Susan Glaspell, Djuna Barnes, and O'Neill's *The Emperor Jones*." In June Schlueter. Ed. *Modern American Drama: The Female Canon*. Rutherford, NJ: Fairleigh Dickinson University Press, 1990.
Lears, T. Jackson. *No Place of Grace: Anti-Modernism and the Transformation of American Culture, 1880–1926*. New York: Pantheon Books, 1981.
Levin, Eric M. "Hidden Perspectivism: a Contemporary Nietzschean Approach to O'Neill's *Days Without End*." *Journal of American Drama and Theatre* 10 (Fall, 1998): 1–10.
Light, James. "The Mask." *Provincetown Playbill*, Season 1923–24, no. 3: 1, 5.
Lippmann, Walter. "Legendary John Reed." *The New Republic* 1 (December 26, 1914): 15–16.
Lozynsky, Artem. "The Case of the Missing Canary: a New Look at Glaspell's *Trifles*." *Feminist Studies in English Literature* 7.2 (Winter, 2000): 141–158.
Luhan, Mabel Dodge. *Movers and Shakers*. New York: Harcourt Brace, 1936.
Lynn, Kenneth. *The Rebels of Greenwich Village. Perspectives in American History*. Volume 8. Cambridge, MA: Harvard University Press, 1974.
Macgowan, Kenneth. "Getting Unmarried." *Smart Set* (April, 1918): 98.
  "The Mask in Drama." *Greenwich Playbill*. Fourth Bill (January 23, 1926): 1, 6.
  "'More Tosh.'" *Provincetown Playbill*, Season 1924–25, no. 1: 3–4.
  The Theatre of Tomorrow. New York: Boni and Liveright, 1921.
Macgowan, Kenneth and Robert Edmond Jones. *Continental Stagecraft*. New York: Harcourt, Brace and Company, 1922.
Macgowan, Kenneth and Herman Rosse. *Masks and Demons*. New York: Harcourt Brace, 1923.
MacLeod, Glen. *Wallace Stevens and Company: The Harmonium Years, 1913–1923*. Ann Arbor: UMI, 1981.

Makowsky, Veronica. "Susan Glaspell and Modernism." In Murphy, *Cambridge Companion to American Women Playwrights* 49–65.
    Susan Glaspell's Century of American Women. New York: Oxford University Press, 1993.
"Many Literary Lights Among the Provincetown Players." *Boston (Sunday) Post* September 10, 1916: 44.
May, Henry F. *The End of American Innocence: The First Years of Our Own Time, 1912–1917*. New York: Knopf, 1959.
McKee, Mary J. "Millay's *Aria da Capo*: Form and Meaning." *Modern Drama* 9 (1966): 165–169.
Milford, Nancy. *Savage Beauty: The Life of Edna St. Vincent Millay*. New York: Random House, 2001.
Millay, Edna St. Vincent. "Suggestions for the Production of 'Aria da Capo.'" In *Aria da Capo: A Play in One Act*. New York: Harper, 1920.
    Three Plays. New York: Harper & Brothers, 1926.
"Minute Book of the Provincetown Players, Inc." From September 4, 1916, to November 8, 1923, Billy Rose Theatre Collection, New York Public Library for the Performing Arts (microfilm).
Moderwell, Hiram. *The Theatre of Today*. New York: John Lane, 1914.
Monroe, Harriet. "Mr. Yeats and the Poetic Drama." *Poetry* 16.1 (April, 1920): 33–35.
Moore, Marianne. *The Selected Letters of Marianne Moore*. Ed. Bonnie Costello. New York: Knopf, 1997.
Morrin, Peter, et al. *The Advent of Modernism: Post-Impressionism and North American Art, 1900–1918*. Ex. Cat. Atlanta: High Museum of Art, 1986.
Mosher, John Chapin. *Sauce for the Emperor*. New York: Frank Shay, 1916.
Murphy, Brenda. *American Realism and American Drama, 1880–1940*. Cambridge and New York: Cambridge University Press, 1987.
    "Interpreting *Marco Millions*: Two New York Productions." *The Recorder*, special Eugene O'Neill Centennial Issue, 3 (1989): 127–136.
    "McTeague's Dream and *The Emperor Jones*: O'Neill's Move from Naturalism to Modernism." *The Eugene O'Neill Review* 17 (1993): 21–29.
Murphy, Brenda. Ed. *The Cambridge Companion to American Women Playwrights*. Cambridge University Press, 1999.
Nietzsche, Friedrich. *Daybreak*. Ed. Michael Tanner. Cambridge University Press, 1982.
    Thus Spake Zarathustra: A Book for All and None. Trans. Thomas Common. Rev. Oscar Levy and John L. Beevers. London: Allen & Unwin, 1967.
Nochlin, Linda. "The Paterson Strike Pageant of 1913." *Art in America* 52 (May–June, 1974): 64–68.
Noe, Marcia. "Intertextuality in the Early Plays of Susan Glaspell and Eugene O'Neill." *American Drama* 11 (Winter, 2002): 1–17.
    "Reconfiguring the Subject/Recuperating Realism: Susan Glaspell's Unseen Woman." *American Drama* 4 (Spring, 1995): 36–54.
    "*The Verge: L'Ecriture Féminine* at the Provincetown." In Ben-Zvi, *Susan Glaspell* 129–142.
Nolan, Patrick J. "*The Emperor Jones*: a Jungian View of the Origin of Fear in the Black Race." *The Eugene O'Neill Newsletter* 4.1–2 (1980): 6–9.

O'Connor, Richard and Dale L. Walker. *The Lost Revolutionary: A Biography of John Reed*. New York: Harcourt Brace, 1967.
O'Neill, Eugene. *Complete Plays. 1913–1920*. Ed. Travis Bogard. New York: Library of America, 1988.
  Complete Plays. 1920–1931. Ed. Travis Bogard. New York: Library of America, 1988.
  "A Dramatist's Notebook." *American Spectator* 2 (January, 1933): 1.
  "Memoranda on Masks." *American Spectator* 1 (December, 1932): 3.
  "Second Thoughts." *American Spectator* 1 (December, 1932): 2.
  Selected Letters of Eugene O'Neill. Ed. Travis Bogard and Jackson R. Bryer. New Haven: Yale University Press, 1988.
  "The Theatre We Worked For": The Letters of Eugene O'Neill to Kenneth Macgowan. Ed. Jackson R. Bryer. New Haven: Yale University Press, 1982.
Oppenheim, James. "A Note on Poetic Drama." *Theatre Arts* 2 (1919): 91–93.
Others: A Magazine of the New Verse. Vols. 1–5. New York: Kraus Reprint Corporation, 1967.
Ozieblo, Barbara. "Avant-Garde and Modernist: Women Dramatists of the Provincetown Players: Bryant, Davies and Millay." *Journal of American Drama and Theatre* 16 (Spring, 2004): 1–16.
  Susan Glaspell: A Critical Biography. Chapel Hill: University of North Carolina Press, 2000.
Ozieblo, Barbara. Ed. *The Provincetown Players: A Choice of the Shorter Works*. Sheffield Academic Press, 1994.
Ozieblo-Rajkowska, Barbara. "The First Lady of the American Drama: Susan Glaspell." *Barcelona English Language and Literature Studies* 1 (1989): 149–159.
"Pageant of the Paterson Strike." *Survey Midmonthly* 30 (June 28, 1913): 428.
Pannekoek, Anton. "Socialism and Anarchism." Trans. Richard Perin. *New Review* 1 (1913); rpt. New York: Greenwood, 1968. 123–127; 147–152.
Parry, Albert. *Garrets and Pretenders: A History of Bohemianism in America, 1885–1915*. 1933; rpt. New York: Dover, 1960.
Pawley, Thomas D. "Eugene O'Neill and American Race Relations." *Journal of American Drama and Theatre* 9 (1997): 66–89.
Peavy, Linda. "Bibliography of Provincetown Players' Dramas, 1915–1922." *Papers of the Bibliographical Society of America* 69 (1975): 569–574.
Peterson, Jane T. "Direction and Design(er): Robert Edmond Jones and the New Provinceotwn Players." In Gewirtz and Kolb, 31–38.
Poole, Gabriele. "'Blarsted Niggers!': *The Emperor Jones* and Modernism's Encounter with Africa." *The Eugene O'Neill Review* 18 (Spring–Fall, 1994): 21–37.
Provincetown Players Scrapbook. Billy Rose Theatre Collection, New York Public Library for the Performing Arts.
Puchner, Martin. *Stage Fright: Modernism, Anti-Theatricality, and Drama*. Baltimore, MD: Johns Hopkins University Press, 2002.
Quinlan, Patrick L. "The Paterson Strike and After." *New Review* 2 (1914); rpt. New York: Greenwood, 1968. 26–33.
Radel, Nicholas F. "Provincetown Plays: Women Writers and O'Neill's American Intertext." *Essays in Theatre* 9 (1990): 31–43.
Reed, John. *The Collected Works of John Reed*. New York: Modern Library, 1995.

The Peace That Passeth Understanding. The Liberator 13 (March, 1919): 25–31.

Retallack, Joan. "One Acts: Early Plays of Djuna Barnes." In Mary Lynn Broe. Ed. *Silence and Power: A Reevaluation of Djuna Barnes.* Carbondale: Southern Illinois University Press, 1991. 46–52.

Richardson, Joan. *Wallace Stevens, a Biography: The Early Years, 1879–1923.* New York: William Morrow, 1986.

Richwine, Keith Norton. "The Liberal Club: Bohemia and the Resurgence in Greenwich Village, 1912–1918." PhD diss. University of Pennsylvania, 1968.

Ritchie, Andrew Carnduff. *Charles Demuth.* New York: Museum of Modern Art, 1950.

Robeson, Paul. "Reflections on O'Neill's Plays." *Opportunity* (December, 1924): 368–370.

Rosenfeld, Paul. *Men Seen: Twenty-Four Modern Authors.* New York: The Dial Press, 1925.

Rosenstone, Robert A. *Romantic Revolutionary: A Biography of John Reed.* New York: Knopf, 1975.

"Russian Ballet Modified." *New York Times,* January 26, 1916: 12.

Saiz, Peter R. "The Colonial Story in *The Emperor Jones.*" *The Eugene O'Neill Review* 17 (Spring–Fall, 1993): 31–38.

Sarlós, Robert K. "Dionysos in 1915: A Pioneer Theatre Collective." *Theatre Research International* 3 (1977): 33–53.

"Eugene O'Neill and the Provincetown Players: Watershed in American Theatre." In Haiping Liu and Lowell Swortzell. Eds. *Eugene O'Neill in China: An International Centenary Celebration.* New York: Greenwood, 1992. 177–181.

"Producing Principles and Practices of the Provincetown Players." *Theatre Research/ Recherches Théâtrales* 10 (1969): 89–102.

"Wharf and Dome: Materials for the History of the Provincetown Players." *Theatre Research/Recherches Théâtrales* 10 (1970): 163–178.

Sarlós, Robert Károly. *Jig Cook and the Provincetown Players: Theatre in Ferment.* Amherst: University of Massachusetts Press, 1982.

"Nina Moise Directs Eugene O'Neill's *The Rope.*" *Eugene O'Neill Newsletter* 6 (Winter, 1982): 9–12.

Schuyler, John. "The Dream in Drama," *Provincetown Playbill,* Season 1924–25, no. 1: 2, 5.

Shay, Frank. *Fifty More Contemporary One-Act Plays.* New York: D. Appleton, 1928.

The Provincetown Plays: First Series. New York: F. Shay, 1916.

Shay, Frank and Pierre Loving. *Fifty Contemporary One-Act Plays.* Cincinnati: Stewart Kidd, 1920.

Sheaffer, Louis. *O'Neill: Son and Artist.* New York: Paragon House, 1990.

O'Neill: Son and Playwright. Boston: Little, Brown, 1968.

Sheeler, Charles. *The Photography of Charles Sheeler: American Modernist.* Ed. Theodore E. Stebbins, Jr., Gilles Mora, and Karen E. Haas. Boston: Bulfinch Press, 2002.

Sichert, Margit. "Claire Archer – A 'Nietzscheana' in Susan Glaspell's *The Verge.*" *REAL: The Yearbook of Research in English and American Literature* 13 (1997): 271–297.

Silvestri, Vito N. "The Washington Square Players: Those Early Off-Broadway Years." *Quarterly Journal of Speech* 51 (1965): 35–44.

Singal, Daniel Joseph. Ed. *Modernist Culture in America.* Belmont, CA: Wadsworth, 1991.

"Toward a Definition of American Modernism." *American Quarterly* 39.1 (Spring, 1987): 7–26.
Stevens, Wallace. *Letters of Wallace Stevens*. Ed. Holly Stevens. Berkeley: University of California Press, 1966.
Opus Posthumous. Ed. Samuel French Mouse. New York: Knopf, 1957.
Storey, Robert F. *Pierrot: A Critical History of a Mask*. Princeton University Press, 1978.
Tancheva, Kornelia. "'I Do Not Participate in Liberations': Female Dramatic and Theatrical Modernism in the 1910s and 1920s." In Elizabeth Jane Harrison and Shirley Peterson. Eds. *Unmanning Modernism: Gendered Re-Readings*. Knoxville, TN: University of Tennessee Press, 1997. 153–167.
Tiusanen, Timo. *O'Neill's Scenic Images*. Princeton University Press, 1968.
Törnqvist, Egil. "Nietzsche and O'Neill: a Study in Affinity." *Orbis Litterarum* 23 (1968): 97–126.
Tridon, Andre. "The Exhibition of the Independents." *New Review* 1 (1913); rpt. New York: Greenwood, 1968. 347–350.
"New Tendencies in Drama and Art." *New Review* 1 (1913); rpt. New York: Greenwood, 1968. 477–480.
"The Truth About the Irish Players." *New Review* 1 (1913); rpt. New York: Greenwood, 1968. 253–255.
Trimberger, Ellen Kay. Ed. *Intimate Warriors: Portraits of a Modern Marriage 1899–1944*. New York: Feminist Press, 1991.
Tucker, Benjamin R. *Instead of a Book by a Man Too Busy to Write One: A Fragmentary Exposition of Philosophical Anarchism*. New York: Benjamin Tucker, 1893; rpt. New York: Arno Press, 1972.
Vorse, Mary Heaton. *Time and the Town: A Provincetown Chronicle*. 1942; rpt. Ed. Adele Heller. New Brunswick: Rutgers University Press, 1991.
Wainscott, Ronald H. *The Emergence of the Modern American Theater 1914–1929*. New Haven: Yale University Press, 1997.
Waldau, Roy S. *Vintage Years of the Theatre Guild 1928–1939*. Cleveland: Case Western Reserve University Press, 1972.
Walker, Julia A. "Bodies, Voices, Words: Modern Drama and the Problem of the Literary." In Jani Scandura and Michael Thurston. Eds. *Modernism, Inc.: Body, Memory, Capital*. New York University Press, 2001. 68–80.
Walling, Anna Strunsky. "Nietzsche." *New Review* 3 (1915); rpt. New York: Greenwood, 1968. 166–167.
Walling, William English. "Pragmatism and Socialism." *New Review* 1 (1913); rpt. New York: Greenwood, 1968. 718–719.
Waterman, Arthur. *Susan Glaspell*. New York: Twayne, 1966.
"Susan Glaspell and the Provincetown." *Modern Drama* 7 (1964): 174–184.
Watson, Steven. *Strange Bedfellows: The First American Avant-Garde*. New York: Abbeville Press, 1991.
Weales, Gerald. "Mike Gold's Theatre." *Journal of American Drama and Theatre* 4 (Winter, 1992): 23–44.
Weir, David. *Anarchy & Culture: The Aesthetic Politics of Modernism*. Amherst: University of Massachusetts Press, 1997.

Weiss, Samuel A. "O'Neill, Nietzsche, and Cows." *Modern Drama* 34 (December, 1991): 494–498.
Wertheim, Arthur. *The New York Little Renaissance: Iconoclasm, Modernism, and Nationalism in American Culture, 1908–1917*. New York University Press, 1976.
Wetzsteon, Ross. *Republic of Dreams: Greenwich Village: The American Bohemia, 1910–1960*. New York: Simon and Schuster, 2002.
Williams, Gary Jay. "Turned Down in Provincetown: O'Neill's Debut Re-Examined." *The Eugene O'Neill Newsletter* 12 (Spring, 1988): 17–27.
Williams, Louise Blakeney. *Modernism and the Ideology of History: Literature, Politics, and the Past*. Cambridge University Press, 2002.
Williams, William Carlos. *The Autobiography of William Carlos Williams*. New York: Random House, 1951.
   Many Loves and Other Plays: The Collected Plays of William Carlos Williams. New York: New Directions, 1961.
   The Selected Letters of William Carlos Williams. Ed. John C. Thirlwall. New York: McDowell, Oblensky, 1957.
Wilson, Edmund. *This Room and This Gin and These Sandwiches, Three Plays by Edmund Wilson*. New York: The New Republic, 1937.
Young, Stark. *The Saint: A Play in Four Acts*. New York: Boni and Liveright, 1925.
Zayas, Marius de. "How, When, and Why Modern Art Came to New York." *Arts Magazine* 54 (April, 1980): 96–126.
Zorach, William. *Art Is My Life: The Autobiography of William Zorach*. Cleveland: World, 1967.
Zurier, Rebecca. *Art for The Masses: A Radical Magazine and Its Graphics, 1911–1917*. Philadelphia: Temple University Press, 1988.

Index

Aaron, Daniel 89
Abbey Players 3–4, 78, 154
"About Six" (Grace Potter) 112
Adams, Henry 228
Aiken, Conrad 104, 232
Aldis, Mary 104
Allegory 95, 96, 97, 100
Anarchism 31–34, 77
   Hutchins Hapgood on 32
   philosophical 32–34
   syndicalist 32
Anderson, Sherwood 8, 29, 57
Andreyev, Leonid 9, 224
Annunzio, Gabriele d' 24
Antliff, Allan 32–33
   on Hutchins Hapgood 19
Arensburg, Walter 102, 103, 131
Armory Show xiii, 34, 35, 43, 44, 52, 61
Art Theatre 3
As a Man Thinks (Augustus Thomas) 42
Ashcan School xvi, 33, 35, 43

Bach, Gerhard 40–41, 89
Baker, George Pierce 5
Bakst, Léon 11, 97, 106
Ballantine, E. J. (Teddy) 7, 12, 213
Ballantine, Stella 7, 11, 95
Barlow, Judith E. 85
Barnes, Djuna xiv, 104, 131, 150–154, 236–237
   Antiphon, The 153, 236
   At the Root of the Stars 237
   Dove, The 236
   Irish Triangle, An 131, 151, 157–159
   Kurzy of the Sea 131, 151, 155–157, 158
   Nightwood 151, 236

   Passion Play, A 151
   Ryder 153
   Three from the Earth 131, 151, 152, 155
   and J. M. Synge 154–155, 157
   marriage to Percy Faulkner 155, 157
Barnes, Wald 153
Barnes, Zadel 153, 155
Basso, Hamilton 184
Beach, Lewis 9
Beckett, Samuel 231
Bel Geddes, Norman 215
Bellows, George xvi, 35, 43, 45
Bennett, Arnold 224
Ben-Zvi, Linda 85
Bergson, Henri 30
Beyond (Walter Hasenclever) 217
Black, Cheryl xiv, 15, 36, 95, 124
   The Women of Provincetown, 1915–1922 xiv, 36
   on Ida Rauh 21
   on women at the Provincetown Players 37
Bly, Nelly 151
Bodenheim, Maxwell xiv, 49, 103, 104, 127, 128, 235
   Gentle Furniture-Shop, The 111, 124, 128–129
   Knotholes 111, 124, 128
Bogard, Travis 180
Boni, Albert and Charles 102
Boyce, Neith xiii, 2, 7, 9, 12, 17, 19, 38, 58, 69, 78, 79, 159, 168, 234
   Autobiography 19, 61
   Constancy 2, 9, 10, 11, 19, 43, 55, 64–66, 85, 163
   Enemies 11, 15, 19, 43, 55, 66–69
   Faithful Lover, The 234
   Winter's Night 10, 43, 55, 78, 82–85, 87–88
   and Mabel Dodge 64–65, 163

274 INDEX

Boyce, Neith (cont.)
  on Hutchins Hapgood 19
  on origin of Provincetown Players 2
Brancusi, Constantin 181
Braque, George 47
Brill, A. A. 69
Broun, Heyward 114, 115, 187, 188, 190
Brown, Alice 9
Browne, Maurice 4
Bruno, Guido 151
Bryant, Louise 10, 11, 12, 13, 14, 15, 17, 46, 51, 55, 161, 163, 234
  Game, The 10–11, 46, 55, 85, 94, 95–100, 106
  and Eugene O'Neill 61, 163
  attitude of the Provincetown Players toward 95
Bucco, Martin 56–57
Bufano, Remo 139, 236
Burt, Frederick 2, 12, 79
Butler, James 139

Cabinet of Dr. Caligari, The 204
Cannell, Kathleen (Rihani) 99, 102, 103, 104, 108, 112, 113, 114, 118
  on static dances 114
Cannell, Skipwith 102, 103, 104
Carb, David 15
Carlin, Terry 79
Carpenter, Edward 29, 37
  Art of Creation, The 29
  Love's Coming of Age 29
Carrus, Paul 28
Cary, Lucian 14, 15
Cézanne, Paul 47, 50, 51, 52
Chapman, John Jay 133
Chase, William Merrit 45
Cheney, Sheldon 3, 4
Chicago Little Theatre 4–5, 7, 50
Clark, Barrett 26, 94, 95
Coke, Van Deren 50–51
Connelly, Marc 224
Cook, Ellen Dodge 162
Cook George Cram xiii, xiv, 2, 3, 4, 5, 7, 10, 12, 13, 14, 15, 16, 17, 18, 22, 25, 27, 28, 34, 38, 39, 40, 41, 46, 50, 51, 73, 75, 94, 112, 159, 160, 162, 171, 179, 187, 189, 211, 213, 215, 233
  Athenian Women, The 112, 190
  Change Your Style 10, 20, 42, 46, 54, 55, 69, 73–75
  Chasm, The 22

"Needle and the North, The" 34
  Spring, The 130, 178, 179, 211
  Suppressed Desires 2, 9–10, 30, 31, 42, 55, 66–69, 85, 160, 190
  Tickless Time 28, 190, 192
  and the end of the Provincetown Players 213–214
  and direction of *The Hairy Ape* 211
  and Freudian psychology 30–31
  and James Light 130, 211
  and Nietzsche 22–25, 161
  and plaster dome 187
  and socialism 35
  as anarchist 31, 34
  as character in *Bernice* 191–192
  assumption of directorship of Provincetown Players 16
  death of 233
  election as president of Provincetown Players 12
  on the *Übermensch* 23
  on *Zarathustra* 23
  sabbatical of 130
  sexual experiences of 38
  trip to Greece of 211
Cooley, Winifred Harper 36
Coolidge, Olivia 91, 92
Corley, Don 13, 15, 187
Cott, Nancy 36
Craig, Edward Gordon 3, 4, 6, 99, 222, 236
Crane, Stephen 93, 94
Crocker, Bosworth 130
  Baby Carriage, The 130
Crothers, Rachel 42, 78
  Man's World, A 42
  Ourselves 42
  Three of Us, The 42
Cubism xvi, 30, 43, 44, 47, 48, 51–52, 59, 119, 145
Cui, César 114
cummings, e. e. 233
  Him 226, 229–233

Damon, S. Foster xv
Darwin, Charles 25
Dash, J. Michael 181
Davies, Mary Carolyn 103, 104, 129, 161
  Slave with Two Faces, The 111–112, 124–127
  "Songs of a Girl" 124

INDEX 275

De Casseres, Benjamin 26
Deeter, Jasper 213
Dell, Floyd xiii, 4, 7, 12, 13, 14, 15, 17, 25, 27, 28, 34–35, 38, 58, 59, 112, 160
  King Arthur's Socks 20, 100
  St. George of the Minute 7
  St. George in Greenwich Village 7, 42
  "Speaking of Psycho-analysis" 69
  Sweet and Twenty 112
  Women as World Builders: Studies in Modern Feminism 37
  and feminism 37–38
  and the Monist Society 28
  and socialism 34–35
  on George Cram Cook 22, 23, 27, 31
  on democracy at *The Masses* 12–13
  on Freudian psychology 29–30, 69
  on Nietzsche 21
  on his plays 8
  on Post-Impressionism 44
  on Transcendentalism 27, 28
Dell Players, The 7–8
De Mille, Agnes xv
Demuth, Charles xiii, 7, 10, 12, 40, 45, 51–54, 73, 102, 130, 234
  Azure Adder, The 54, 102
  "Longhi on Broadway" 234
  "Study for a Poster Portrait: Eugene O'Neill" 234
  friendship with Eugene and Agnes O'Neill 53–54, 234
Deutsch, Helen xiv, 1, 89, 94, 215
  Provincetown: A Story of the Theatre, The xiv
Dewey, John xvi, 18
  influence of 19–20
Diaghilev, Serge 97
  L'après-midi d'un faune 97
Dillon, Kathleen 105
Dodge, Edwin 61, 62
Dodge, Mabel xiii, 17, 45, 53, 57, 61, 62, 73, 163, 165
  Movers and Shakers 64, 163
  and John Reed 61, 62, 64
  on the Paterson Pageant 6, 61
  renovation of Peaked Hill Bars 163–164
Doolittle, Hilda (H. D.) 102, 104
Doolittle, Margaret 56
Dos Passos, John 232
Dove, Arthur 34, 35, 48, 102
Drama, non-representational xvi

Dreiser, Theodore 9
  Hand of the Potter, The 179, 210
Duchamp, Marcel 52, 103
  "Nude Descending a Staircase" 52
Dunbar, William 139

Earl, Louie 113
Eastman, Max xiii, 4, 7, 8, 12, 13, 15, 17, 20, 34, 35, 38, 75, 160, 161
  "Exploring the Soul and Healing the Body" 69–70
  "The Tannenbaum Crime" 75
  and John Dewey 20
  involvement in the Provincetown Players 20
  on Friedrich Nietzsche 22
  on Freudian psychology 29–30, 69
  on pragmatism 20
Eaton, Walter Prichard 212
Eclogues (Virgil) 143
Egan, Leona Rust 57, 164
Eliot, T. S. 144
  "Portrait of a Lady" 104
  Waste Land, The 149
Ell, Louis 107
Ellis, Charles 139, 149, 150, 159, 213
Ellis, Havelock, 30, 37
Emerson, Ralph Waldo 25, 27, 29, 101
  influence of 27–28
Ervine, St. John 224
Euripides 4, 50
Evans, Donald 102
Evans, Robley 132
Evreinov, Nicholas 9
Experimental Theater, Inc. (ETI) xv, 216, 217, 221, 222, 223, 226, 229, 231, 233
  and masks 220–222
  and total theatre 222–223

Falk, Doris 182
Farnham, Emily 53
Fashion, or Life in New York (Anna Cora Mowatt) 217
Faulkner, William 57
Fauve school of art xvi, 43, 44, 47, 48, 50, 51, 52
Federal Theatre Project 233
Feminism xvi, 36–39
Feminist Alliance 36–37
Ferrer Center 27, 45
Ficke, Arthur Davidson 7
Fineschreiber, Rabbi 23

276 INDEX

Fitzgerald, Eleanor 159, 213, 215, 216, 233
Fitzgerald, F. Scott 57, 226
France, Anatole 101, 152, 154
Francis, John 163
Frank, Florence Kiper xv, 104, 130
   Gee–Rusalem 130
Frank, Robin 53
Frank, Waldo xv, 232
Freedman, Julian 112, 114
Freeman, Helene 99
Freud, Sigmund xvi, 29–31, 69
Frost, Robert 128, 233
   "Mending Wall" 128, 147
   North of Boston 147

Gainor, J. Ellen 69, 86, 87
   on community theatre 56
   on *The Outside* 165, 167
   on *Suppressed Desires* 71, 72
   on *The Verge* 202
Galsworthy, John 224
Garland, Hamlin 41, 42
Gauguin, Paul 47, 59
Gelb, Arthur and Barbara 94
George Dandin (Molière) 217
Getting Unmarried (Winthrop Parkhurst) 131
Gifford, Sanford 29
Gilpin, Charles 189
Glaspell, Elmer 190
Glaspell, Susan xii, xiii, xiv, 1, 2, 4, 7, 9, 10, 12, 13, 14, 15, 17, 22, 23, 25–26, 28, 35, 38, 40, 41, 75, 78, 79, 130, 159, 160, 161, 165, 166, 170, 171, 179, 189, 211, 213, 214, 215, 233
   Alison's House 233
   Ambrose Holt and Family 233
   Bernice 189–193, 198
   Chains of Dew 179, 196–197, 198, 214
   Close the Book 160, 162
   Comic Artist, The 233
   Constancy 193
   Glory of the Conquered, The 28
   Inheritors 25, 162, 178, 179
   Judd Rankin's Daughter 233
   Outside, The 161, 162–168, 190, 195, 199
   People, The 160–162
   Road to the Temple, The 25, 27, 69, 79, 85, 233
   Suppressed Desires (see Cook, George Cram)
   Trifles 11, 43, 46, 55, 78, 79, 85–88, 160, 189
   Verge, The 25, 46, 161, 166, 168, 179, 189, 193–203, 224
   and Cook's infidelities 166
   and Freudian psychology 30–31
   and Nietzsche 25–26, 161, 179, 189, 193, 194, 198–202
   and *Tickless Time* 190
   and the Übermensch 25, 202
   as character in *Bernice* 190–191
   on *Bound East for Cardiff* 11
   on the Broadway theatre 41–42
   on George Cram Cook 16, 22, 27, 191–192
   on the Monist Society 25
   on O'Neill 79, 192, 196
   on the Paterson Pageant 6
Glebe, The xiv, 54, 102
Gleizes, Albert 113
Glynn, Martin H. 140–141, 143
Goethe, Johann Wolfgang von 32, 101
Gold, Mike xv, 233
Goldberg, Isaac 185
Goldman, Arnold 71
Goldman, Emma 17, 26
Gourmont, Rémy de 152, 154
Green, Martin 5
Gregory, Lady Augusta 4
Grieg, Edvard 114
Group of Eight, The 43, 44

Haeckel, Ernst 25, 28, 29
   Riddle of the Universe, The 28
   influence of 28
Hammond, Percy 232
Hanau, Stella xiv, 1, 89, 94, 215
   Provincetown: A Story of the Theatre, The (see Deutsch, Helen)
Hapgood, Hutchins xiii, 2, 5, 6, 7, 9, 12, 13, 14, 15, 17, 18, 19, 20, 31, 38, 41, 53, 58, 59, 66–69, 102, 159, 163, 234
   Enemies (see Boyce, Neith)
   Story of a Lover 61
   Victorian in the Modern World, A 19, 61
   and anarchism 31, 32
   and Freudian psychology 30
   on the Armory Show 33–34, 44
   on Charles Demuth 53
   on William James 18, 19, 26
   on discovery of O'Neill 79
   on feminism 38
   on Ida Rauh 20
   on John Reed's plays 88–89
   philosophical anarchism of 19

INDEX

Harlequinade 143, 144
Harris, Jed 234
Harrison, Ruth M. 132
Hart, Lorenz 224
Hartley, Marsden 17, 35, 48, 101
Hauptmann, Gerhart 78
Havel, Hyppolyte 160
Hawthorne, Charles Webster 45, 73
Hawthorne, Nathaniel 57, 101
Hays, Blanche 159, 211
Hecht, Ben 9
Helburn, Theresa 224
Heller, Adele xv
  1915: The Cultural Moment xv
Hemingway, Ernest 57
Henri, Robert xvi, 34, 35, 43, 45
Herne, James A. 78, 82
  Margaret Fleming 41
  Shore Acres 82
Heterodoxy 21, 39, 168
Heywood, William ("Big Bill") 17
Hinden, Michael 183
Hoffman, Gerhard 26
Hoffman, Marilyn 46, 47, 48
Holladay, Louis 53
Hopkins, Arthur 211, 234, 235
Howard, Sidney 224
Howells, William Dean 41, 42, 43, 57, 78
Hueffer, Ford Madox 102
Huffaker, Lucy 12, 13, 190
  as character in *Bernice* 190
Hume, Sam 187
Hunt, Eddy 89
Huston, John xv

Ibsen, Henrik 78, 101, 224
  Hedda Gabler 41, 84
Imagism 30
In Abraham's Bosom (Paul Green) 231
International Workers of the World (IWW) 10, 30, 205, 209
  in the Paterson Pageant 5
Iungerich, Helene 52

James, Henry 57
  Beast in the Jungle, The 52
  Turn of the Screw, The 52
James, William xvi, 18, 19, 26–27, 49, 68
  influence of 19–20
Jefferson, Thomas 32

Jeliffe, Smith 29, 30
Johns, Orrick 49, 103, 104
Jones, Robert Edmond xv, 1, 2, 5, 6, 10, 18, 30, 53, 163, 164, 214, 215, 216, 217, 220, 222, 223, 225, 234–235
  Continental Stagecraft (see Kenneth Macgowan)
  Dramatic Imagination, The 235
  design for *The Hairy Ape* 211–212
  on total theatre 223
  work for Experimental Theatre, Inc. 217
Joyce, James 102, 233
Jung, Carl Gustav 31, 181, 182, 217

Kaiser, Georg 204
  From Morn to Midnight 203, 204, 206, 207, 224
Kaufman, George S. 224
  Beggar on Horseback 224
Keats, John 133
Kemp, Harry 7, 79, 130
  Prodigal Son, The 231
Kennedy, Charles O'Brien 210
Kenton, Edna 4, 13, 14, 15, 16, 25, 108, 130, 159, 178, 186, 187, 211, 212, 213–214, 215, 234
  on Maxell Bodenheim 129–130
  on effect of success 178
  on feminism 36
  on *Lima Beans* 108
  on play selection 13–14
  on *Where the Cross Is Made* 176, 177
Key, Ellen 37
Kipling, Rudyard 24
Kravec, Maureen 132
Kreymborg, Alfred xiv, 7, 14, 49, 54, 96, 101–111, 112, 113, 114, 118, 124, 130, 131, 132, 151, 160, 161, 233, 235, 236
  Jack's House: A Cubic Play 112, 113, 114–115, 118–121, 124
  Lima Beans xiv, 14, 105, 106–111, 118, 146, 235
  Manikin and Minikin 112, 114, 115–118, 134
  Puppet Plays 236
  Troubadour 140
  Vote the New Moon: A Toy Play 131, 132, 139, 140–143, 147, 236
  and *The Glebe* 102, 103
  on aesthetics 102, 105–106
  on Maxwell Bodenheim 127–128

Kreymborg, Alfred (cont.)
  on Kathleen Cannell 104
  on *Manikin and Minikin* 115
  on Edna Millay 112, 114
  on Other Players 115
  on *Others* 103
  on play selection process 14
  on William Zorach's acting 113–114
Kreymborg, Dorothy 118, 236
Kropotkin, Peter 26

Lacey-Baker, Marjory 113, 122
LaFarge, Bancel 132
Langner, Lawrence 8, 9, 223, 224, 225
  Matinata 224
  Pie 139, 224
  on Charles Demuth 52
Lardner, Ring 57
Lee, Arthur 64
Lee, Freddie 64
Lewis, Judith 99
Lewis, Sinclair 57
Lewisohn, Sam 163
Liberal Club, The 7–8, 16, 39, 101
Light, James 130, 131, 159, 187, 191, 192, 211, 213, 214, 216, 217, 220, 233
  on direction of *The Hairy Ape* 211
  on masks 220, 221
Little Renaissance xiii, xiv, 7, 16–17, 40, 43, 75, 100
Little Theatre Movement 3
London, Jack 20, 57
  Call of the Wild, The 95
Love for Love (William Congreve) 217
Lowell, Amy 102, 104
Loy, Mina xiv, 49, 54, 96, 102, 104
  "Love Songs" 104
  in *Lima Beans* 107
Lunt, Alfred 225
Lysistrata (Aristophanes) 190

Macgowan, Kenneth xv, 131, 187, 203, 207, 216, 220, 221, 222, 223, 225, 234, 236
  and Experimental Theatre, Inc. 214–216
  and masks 220, 221–222
  Continental Stagecraft 214
  Masks and Demons 220, 221, 222
  Theatre of Tomorrow, The 214, 225
MacKaye, Percy 5
MacLeod, Glen 133

Maeterlinck, Maurice 9, 79, 92, 132, 161
  Blind, The 132
  Intruder, The 132
Magical City, The (Zoë Akins) 9
Makowsky, Veronica 167
Mamoulian, Rouben 225
Man and the Masses (Ernst Toller) 224
Mantle, Burns 232
Marin, John 17, 35, 48, 52, 102
Markham, Kirah 8
Martyn, Edward 3
Masses, The xiii, 4, 5, 7, 8, 12, 13, 17, 20, 27, 30, 35, 37, 43, 45, 89, 103, 160
  on the Tannenbaum incident 75–76
Masters, Edgar Lee 104
Matisse, Henri 47, 51, 52, 181
Matson, Norman 233
Matthews, Brander 78
Matthews, Fred 22, 31, 71
May, Henry F. 27, 28, 29
  on William James 18
  on Friedrich Nietzsche 21
McKee, Mary J. 144
McTeague (Frank Norris) 185
Metaphor 89, 92, 94, 110, 128
Metonymy 78–79, 82, 86, 88
Mielziner, Jo 235
Milford, Nancy 149
Millay, Edna St. Vincent xiv, 1, 7, 38, 40, 54, 96, 112, 113, 115, 118, 159, 213, 226, 235
  Aria da Capo xiv, 113, 128, 131, 143–150, 224, 236
  Conversation at Midnight 235
  Princess Marries the Page, The 130
  Two Slatterns and a King 112, 113, 122–124, 236
Millay, Edna and Norma 113, 122
Millay, Kathleen 139
Millay, Norma 150, 159
Milne, A. A. 224
Moderwell, Hiram 214
  Theatre of Today, The 214
Moeller, Philip 224, 225
Moise, Nina 15, 171, 176
Molnar, Ferenc 224, 235
  Launzi 235
monism 26–29, 87
Monist Society of Davenport, Iowa 25, 28–29
  "Laws of Monism" 28–29
Monroe, Harriet 131–132
  on *Three Travelers Watch a Sunrise* 139
Moore, George 3

INDEX

Moore, Marianne 49, 103, 124
    "Critics and Connoisseurs" 104
    "Poetry" 104
Moscow Art Theatre 78
Mosher, John 15
    Bored 15
    Sauce for the Emperor 231
Murray, T. C. 4

Nana (Emile Zola) 52
Nathan, George Jean 173, 177, 232
Nazimova, Alla 41
New Stagecraft 6, 11, 99, 187
Nietzsche, Friedrich xvi, 21–26, 30, 31, 35, 38, 57, 101, 203
    Birth of Tragedy, The 24, 26, 183, 221
    Ecce Homo 22
    Thus Spake Zarathustra 23, 25, 26, 198
Nochlin, Linda 5
Nordfeldt, Brör (B. J. O.) xiii, 4, 10, 12, 13, 14–15, 17, 40, 45, 46, 50–51, 52, 54, 56, 73, 75, 159, 234
    Joined Together 15
    design of *The Trojan Women* 4, 50
    resignation from the Provincetown Players 15, 213
Nordfeldt, Margaret 12, 13, 15, 16, 159
Norton, Allen 102
Norton, Louise 102

O. Henry 43, 57, 76
O'Brien, Joseph 2, 10
Oenslager, Donald 235
O'Keeffe, Georgia 46, 48
O'Neill, Agnes Boulton 26, 53, 163, 170, 173
    "The Captain's Walk" 173
O'Neill, Carlotta Monterey 53–54
O'Neill, Eugene xiv, xv, xvi, 1, 5, 9, 11, 12, 13, 15, 17, 18, 31, 39, 40, 41, 45, 53, 54, 55, 61, 78, 94, 95, 96, 130, 146, 159, 163, 168–169, 174, 213, 214, 215, 216, 217, 220, 221, 223, 225, 233, 234, 235
    Abortion 79
    All God's Chillun Got Wings xv, 216, 217, 219–220
    Ancient Mariner, The xv, 216, 217, 220, 221
    Before Breakfast 146
    Beyond the Horizon 170, 171, 177, 178
    Bound East for Cardiff 9, 10–11, 15, 43, 55, 78, 79–82, 85, 100
    Chris Christopherson 170, 171
    Days Without End 171

    Desire Under the Elms xv, 26, 152, 216, 217, 218, 223, 235
    Diff'rent 171, 178, 210
    Dreamy Kid, The 171, 172
    Emperor Jones, The 46, 139, 168, 171, 177–189, 197, 203, 207, 210, 211, 213, 217, 218, 224
    Exorcism 171
    Fog 15, 191, 206
    Fountain, The xv, 26, 214, 216, 217, 218–219
    Gold 173, 177, 178
    Great God Brown, The 26, 171, 216, 217, 220, 221–222, 231
    Hairy Ape, The 179, 203–213, 220, 221, 224
    Ile 111, 128, 168, 173
    In the Zone 160, 176
    Lazarus Laughed 25, 26, 220, 221, 222, 223, 225
    Long Day's Journey Into Night 169, 170, 174
    Marco Millions 225
    Moon of the Caribees, The 160, 210
    Mourning Becomes Electra 26, 222
    Movie Man, The 79
    Rope, The 171, 172–173, 176
    SS *Glencairn* plays 160, 176, 217
    Strange Interlude 26, 218, 222, 225
    Straw, The 170, 178
    Tale of Possessors Self-Dispossessed, A 184
    Thirst 11, 55, 88, 92–94, 95, 191, 206
    Thirst and Other Plays 9
    Welded 217, 218, 228
    Where the Cross Is Made 130, 168, 171, 172, 173–177, 185, 189, 210, 218
    and Louise Bryant 61, 95
    and direction of *The Hairy Ape* 211
    and Experimental Theatre, Inc. 215, 216, 217
    and expressionism 185–186, 203–204, 206–210, 218–220
    and family history 169–170
    and Freudian psychology 30, 181
    and masks 220–222
    as anarchist 31
    bifurcation of 171–172
    influence of Nietzsche on 26
    on the Abbey Players 4
    on Djuna Barnes 236
    on James Light 216
    on *The Moon of the Caribees* 160
    on total theatre 223
O'Neill, James 146, 163, 168, 170, 171, 174, 175, 178
    and *The Count of Monte Cristo* 146, 171, 175
    in *The Wanderer* 170

O'Neill, James, Jr. 173, 174
Other Players 112–115, 124, 235
Others: A Magazine of the New Verse xiv, xvi, 49, 54, 102, 103–105, 106, 111, 113, 115, 118, 124, 131, 151, 160, 235, 236
   Des Imagists, An Anthology 102
Overtones (Alice Gerstenberg) 9
Ozieblo, Barbara xiv, 9, 38, 40–41, 61, 162, 190
   Susan Glaspell: A Critical Biography xiv
   on Glaspell's marriage 166
   on Glaspell's philosophical influences 25
   on *Tickless Time* 190

Pageant movement 5–6
Parker, Robert 130
   50–50 130
Paterson Pageant, The 5, 6, 61
   Survey Midmonthly review of 6
Picabia, Francis 17
Picasso, Pablo 34, 47, 59, 181
Pinski, David 224
   The Dollar 15
Pirandello, Luigi 115
   Six Characters in Search of an Author 115, 134
Poe, Edgar Allan 57, 101
   "Masque of the Red Death, The" 52
Poetry magazine 131, 139, 140
Porgy (Dubose and Dorothy Heyward) 231
Post-Impressionism 43, 44, 48, 50–51, 54, 84, 94–95, 102, 115
Pound, Ezra 102, 104–105, 132
Pragmatism 19
Primitivism 59, 181
Prince of Court Painters, A (Walter Pater) 52
Processional (John Howard Lawson) 224
Proust, Marcel 233
Provincetown Players, the xiii, 50, 53, 55, 79, 130, 223, 231, 233
   accomplishments of xiv
   and the Little Renaissance 17–18
   Constitution of 12
   first performance 9–10
   founding of 1–3
   Glaspell on 192
   "massacre" in 13, 15
   members of xiii
   studies of xiii–xiv
Provincetown Playhouse 54, 232, 233
   plaster dome in 187
Pyne, Mary 99

Rathburn, Stephen 203
Rauh, Ida xiii, 7, 8–9, 12, 13, 14, 15, 20, 34, 126, 130, 131, 159, 166, 190, 213
   and John Dewey 20
   radicalism of 20–21
   relationship with George Cram Cook 20, 38, 166, 190
Ray, Man 54, 102, 103
Realism 55, 130
Reed, John xiii, 2, 4, 5, 6, 7, 11, 12, 13, 14, 15, 17, 18, 20, 34, 40, 49, 50, 51, 57, 61, 62, 79, 89, 94, 95, 99, 106, 114, 160, 163, 214, 234
   Eternal Quadrangle, The 11, 43, 55, 61–64, 85
   Freedom: A Prison Play 9, 10, 15, 40, 55, 85, 88, 88–92
   Moondown 9
   Peace That Passeth Understanding, The 234
   Ten Days that Shook the World xiii, 20
   and Louise Bryant 95
   and Mabel Dodge 64
   and William James 20
   and socialism 35
   direction of the Paterson Pageant 6
   jailing of 89
Reinhardt, Max 99, 186, 187, 215, 222
Rice, Elmer 9, 224
   Adding Machine, The 224
   Subway, The 224
Ridge, Lola 49, 104
Ritchie, Andrew 51–52
Robeson, Paul 217
Rodin, Auguste 34, 44
   "Thinker, The" 204, 205, 208, 209, 210
Rodker, John 105
   "Dutch Dolls" 105
Rodman, Henrietta 7
Rogers, Richard 224
Rogue 102
Rousseau, Henri 59
Rudnick, Lois xv
R. U. R. (Karel Čapek) 224
Ryther-Fuller, Martha 99

Sainsbury, Hester 105
Samuels, Maurice 170
   Wanderer, The 170
Sandburg, Carl 104
Saphier, William 104, 128
   Gentle Furniture-Shop, The (see Maxwell Bodenheim)

INDEX

Sarlós, Robert K. xiv, 1, 3, 89, 98, 114, 154, 159, 180, 187, 211
   on George Cram Cook's vision of theatre 24–25
   on the founding of the Provincetown Players 2–3
   on James Light 130–131
Schnitzler, Arthur 4, 9, 61, 159
   Last Masks 159
Scott, Evelyn xiv, 104
   Love 178
Seagull, The (Anton Chekhov) 233
Season of Youth, The 130
Shakespeare, William 65
Shaw, George Bernard 4, 26, 42, 43, 63, 78, 224
   Caesar and Cleopatra 231
   Mrs. Warren's Profession 41
   Quintessence of Ibsenism, The 42
Shay, Frank 7
Sheaffer, Louis 79–80, 204, 210–211, 212
Sheeler, Charles 180
   African Negro Wood Sculpture 180
Sheffield, Justus 8
Sheldon, Edward 42, 78
   Salvation Nell 42
Sherwood, Robert 231
   The Road to Rome 231
Sichert, Margit 197, 200, 202
Simonson, Lee 224, 225, 235
Singal, Daniel J. 18, 19
Sloan, John xvi, 6, 35, 43, 160
   "Calling the Christian Bluff" 76
socialism 34–36
Sonn, Richard 32
Squealer, The (Mary Barber) 130
Stanislavsky, Konstantin 215
Steele, Margaret Thurston 10, 12, 57
Steele, Wilbur Daniel xiii, 12, 17, 40, 43, 56–58, 59
   Contemporaries 10, 20, 43, 55, 57, 75–78
   Meat 57
   "*Not Smart*" 10, 11, 39, 43, 55, 57–61, 85
Stein, Gertrude 51, 102, 118, 233
Sterne, Maurice 163
   near-drowning of 163–164
Stevens, Wallace xiv, 49, 102, 103, 104, 131, 132, 144, 235
   Carlos Among the Candles 132
   "Comedian as the Letter C" 235
   "Domination of Black" 104
   "Of Modern Poetry" 235

"Peter Quince at the Clavier" 104
"Thirteen Ways of Looking at a Blackbird" 104
Three Travelers Watch a Sunrise 131–139
Stieglitz, Alfred xiii, 7, 48
   Photo-Secession Gallery ("291") xiii, 7, 17, 34, 35, 43, 44, 45, 59, 101–102, 106, 181
Storey, Robert F. 144
Strindberg, August 4, 9, 43, 78, 92, 207, 224
   Spook Sonata, The 217
   Stronger, The 66
Sudermann, Hermann 78
Sutherland, Ann xv
Synge, John Millington 4, 101, 154
   Playboy of the Western World, The 157

Taggard, Genevieve 232
Tannenbaum, Frank 10, 75–76, 78
Tannenbaum, Samuel A. 29
Theatre Guild, The 223–225, 233, 235
   and expressionism 224
Thoreau, Henry David 27, 101
Throckmorton, Cleon 187, 188, 211, 213, 214, 215, 233, 235
Tiusanen, Timo 184–185, 207
Tolstoy, Leo 22, 26, 32, 224
transcendentalism 27–28
Treadwell, Sophie xv, 224
   Machinal 224
Trimberger, Ellen 65
Tucker, Benjamin 26
Tyler, George C. 170, 172, 196

Untermeyer, Louis 20
Upanishads 163

Van Gogh, Vincent 47
Van Vechten, Carl 102
Van Volkenburg, Ellen 4
Verlaine, Paul 144
Vorse, Albert 57
Vorse, Mary Heaton xiii, 2, 7, 10, 12, 17, 45, 57, 84, 95, 99, 130, 160
   and Brör Nordfeldt 50, 56
   on Provincetown artists 45–46

Wagner, Richard 24, 25
Wainscott, Ronald 187, 197
Walter, Eugene 42
   Easiest Way, The 42

Washington Square Players 8, 9, 12, 89, 101, 223
  Aims and Objectives 9
  democracy in 13, 103
Watson, Steven 7
Weber, Max 34, 35, 102
Wedekind, Frank 9, 53
  Erdgeist 53
  Pandora's Box 53
Weinberger, Harry 213, 215
Weir, David 21, 32–33
Wellman, Rita 52
  Funiculi-Funicula 128
  String of the Samisen, The 130
Wertheim, Arthur 36, 44
  on Floyd Dell 37–38
  on Little Renaissance 16
  on Max Eastman 20
Wertheim, Maurice 224
Westley, Helen 8, 224
Wharf Theatre 10, 11, 14, 54, 85
  renovation of 10
Whistler, James McNeill 50
Whitman, Walt 24, 27, 101
Widow's Veil, The (Alice Rostetter) 130
Wilde, Oscar 61, 90
  "Ballad of Reading Gaol" 90
  Importance of Being Earnest, The 63
Williams, John D. 170, 172, 196
Williams, Tennessee 229
Williams, William Carlos xiv, 49, 54, 96, 102, 103, 104, 107, 108, 112–113, 131, 132, 166
  Autobiography 235
  Comic Life of Elia Brobitza, The 113
  Many Loves 113, 236
  Old Apple Tree, The 235
  desire to be a playwright 235–236
  in *Lima Beans* 107, 112, 235
  on *Others* 104
Wilson, Edmund xv, 226, 232, 233
  Axel's Castle 233
  Crime in the Whistler Room, The 226–228, 233
  Little Blue Light, The 233

Wilson, Woodrow 140, 141, 234
Winchell, Walter 232
Winston, Harry 139
Wohlheim, Louis 211
Woollcott, Alexander 131, 150, 154, 188, 232
  on Djuna Barnes 131, 150–151
  on *The Hairy Ape* 212
World War I 97, 128, 141, 147

Yeats, William Butler 3, 4, 79
Young, Arthur 76
Young, Stark 217, 232, 233
  Colonnade, The 233
  Saint, The 217, 226, 228–229

Zayas, Marius de 47, 59, 102, 181
  "African Art: Its Influence on Modern Art" 181
  racism of 181
Zorach, Marguerite Thompson xiii, xiv, 11, 12, 17, 27, 39, 40, 45, 46–49, 51, 59, 95, 98, 102, 104, 106, 108, 113, 114, 131, 234
  art class of 45
  linoleum block print of *The Game* 234
Zorach, William xiii, xiv, 11, 12, 17, 27, 39, 40, 45, 46–49, 51, 59, 94, 95, 98, 99, 102, 104, 106, 107, 108, 113, 114–115, 122, 131, 181, 234
  on feminism 39
  on *The Game* 95–96, 98, 99
  on his influences 47
  on *Jack's House* 112, 114–115
  on *Lima Beans* 107
  on Eugene O'Neill 46, 94
  on the Provincetown Players 234
  on *Two Slatterns and a King* 112, 113
Zorach, William and Marguerite 46, 50, 52, 54, 59, 73, 84, 96, 97, 98, 99, 106, 107, 108, 111, 112, 114, 115, 130
  design for *Jack's House* 118–119
Zurier, Rebecca 45

N.H. TECHNICAL INSTITUTE
LIBRARY
CONCORD, NH 03301